The Rolling Stones in Concert, 1962–1982

# The Rolling Stones in Concert, 1962–1982

*A Show-by-Show History*

IAN M. RUSTEN

McFarland & Company, Inc., Publishers
*Jefferson, North Carolina*

LIBRARY OF CONGRESS CATALOGUING-IN-PUBLICATION DATA

Names: Rusten, Ian, author.
Title: The Rolling Stones in concert, 1962–1982 : a show-by-show history / Ian M. Rusten.
Description: Jefferson, North Carolina : McFarland & Company, 2018 | Includes bibliographical references and index.
Identifiers: LCCN 2018043226 | ISBN 9781476673929 (softcover : acid free paper) ∞
Subjects: LCSH: Rolling Stones—Performances. | Rolling Stones—History—Chronology. | Rock musicians—England—Biography.
Classification: LCC ML421.R64 R9 2018 | DDC 782.42166092/2 [B] —dc23
LC record available at https://lccn.loc.gov/2018043226

BRITISH LIBRARY CATALOGUING DATA ARE AVAILABLE

**ISBN (print) 978-1-4766-7392-9**
**ISBN (ebook) 978-1-4766-3443-2**

© 2018 Ian M. Rusten. All rights reserved

*No part of this book may be reproduced or transmitted in any form or by any means, electronic or mechanical, including photocopying or recording, or by any information storage and retrieval system, without permission in writing from the publisher.*

Front cover: The Rolling Stones (from left, Ronnie Wood, Keith Richards, Charlie Watts, Mick Jagger and Bill Wyman), 1978 (Photofest)

Printed in the United States of America

*McFarland & Company, Inc., Publishers
Box 611, Jefferson, North Carolina 28640
www.mcfarlandpub.com*

To my brilliant,
kind and beautiful wife, Rebekah,
who has helped me more than words can express.
Thank you for your patience and support.

I also dedicate this to my three incredible daughters,
Hannah, Kate and Erin.
I love you all.

# Acknowledgments

I wish to thank Ira Korman for the use of his memorabilia collection and all the university librarians who aided me in this project. I'd also like to thank the Rolling Stones for their music, which is an inspiration to the world. I wish to acknowledge friends that helped me translate foreign articles into English: Katti Wachs, Javier Goldaraz, Michael Rohattyn, Daniel Shabasson and Gabriella Skwara. Special thanks to the Witter and Coleman families for their support and to my wife and children, who always encourage me.

# Table of Contents

*Acknowledgments* vi

*Preface* 1

1. 1962     3
2. 1963     12
3. 1964     47
4. 1965     88
5. 1966     126
6. 1967     147
7. 1968     158
8. 1969     164
9. 1970     179
10. 1971     188
11. 1972     194
12. 1973     206
13. 1974     221
14. 1975     225
15. 1976     238
16. 1977     250
17. 1978     254
18. 1979     266
19. 1980     275
20. 1981     277
21. 1982     294

*Appendix 1.*
*BBC Radio and Radio Luxembourg Appearances,*
*1963–1965* 305

*Appendix 2.*
*Television Appearances,*
*1963–1978* 308

*Bibliography* 323

*Index* 325

# Preface

For more than fifty years the Rolling Stones have been performing concerts and pleasing audiences around the world. From their humble beginnings playing in small clubs in 1962, the Stones developed into the acknowledged "greatest rock 'n' roll band in the world." They have played shows in numerous countries, including multiple tours of the United States, Australia and Europe.

Yet, there is no book that provides a comprehensive overview and discusses all their tours over the years in detail. *The Rolling Stones in Concert, 1962–1982: A Show-by-Show History* rectifies this.

Compiling this book required tremendous research. I visited many libraries and pored through old newspapers and periodicals to obtain long forgotten reviews, advertisements and interviews. I looked through many old magazines, such as *Melody Maker, Datebook* and *Hit Parader,* to find interesting articles. I also read virtually every book that I could find about the Stones to make sure that I covered everything of importance that I could. Finally, I sought out and listened to numerous audiotapes and videos of their concerts.

The book starts with a brief opening chapter that introduces the Stones starting with the original band members, Brian Jones, Mick Jagger, Keith Richards, Bill Wyman and Charlie Watts. The introduction also provides a close look at each of their life stories from their childhoods in World War II Britain to the year 1962, when they met and formed the band. The body of the book contains individual chapters that each focus on a specific year. Chapter 1 begins in 1962 and Chapter 21 ends in 1982. Each chapter is a comprehensive chronicle of all of the shows, with an introductory essay that provides an in-depth look at other events in their career that year, such as record releases and notable moments in their personal lives. Two additional chapters (22 and 23) briefly cover the Stones' radio recordings, some of which were performed before live audiences, and performances on television shows.

As the story progresses, we watch the Stones rise from a club band in 1962 to one of the leading concert attractions in the UK by 1963. The book follows the Stones as they conquer the United States during 1964–65 and ultimately become a global phenomenon. Between 1962 and 1967, the Stones toured extensively across the globe and the book covers all of the shows during this era, including the band's first appearances in New York, Los Angeles, Paris, Stockholm and Sydney.

The year 1967 saw the Stones beset by personal problems, including well-known drug busts and interpersonal conflicts between guitarists Keith Richards and Brian Jones. Following a controversial European tour, which included a famous show behind the Iron

Curtain in Poland, the Stones took a two-year break from the road to rest and record music. Founding member Brian Jones declined in health and involvement in the band during this period and was replaced by blues guitarist Mick Taylor in 1969. Jones tragically died that July and the band dedicated their legendary concert at London's Hyde Park to his memory.

Taylor had joined just as the Stones began touring intently again and took part in their notorious free concert at Altamont Speedway in California that December. This concert is chronicled in the Maysles brothers' film *Gimme Shelter*. Hells Angels, hired to act as security, murdered a concertgoer, an event captured on film. The concert ended the 1960s on a depressing note for the Stones. But they bounced back and toured almost every year in the 1970s, while making a number of classic albums, including *Exile on Main Street* and *Sticky Fingers*. They survived yet another personnel change, when Taylor left in 1974 and Ron Wood took his place. He performed with the Stones on their 1975 tour of the U.S. and all subsequent tours around the world. This book provides previously untold details and information about the concerts throughout the 1970s.

Rolling Stones tours attracted much media attention and were always eventful. The Stones seemed to generate controversy everywhere they went. For example, on the 1975 tour they had a giant inflatable phallus that would rise from the stage when they sang "Star Star." Police in some Southern towns threatened to put the band in jail if they used the device. And who can forget when Mick and Keith were arrested on their way to a concert in Boston in 1972 and the mayor had to use his political skills to bail them out and prevent rioting in town?

There have of course been numerous books about the Rolling Stones. The Stones themselves have written about their lives: guitarist Keith Richards published a memoir (*Life*), bassist Bill Wyman wrote two books on his time with the band (*Stone Alone* and *Rolling with the Stones*) and all the Stones participated in a short biography (*According to the Rolling Stones*). None of these books covers the tours in depth as this book does, and the books seldom discuss individual concerts in detail. The Stones have also attracted biographers, including Philip Norman (*The Stones*) and Victor Bockris (*Keith Richards: The Biography*). These books focus on the lives of individual Stones but spend little time on the Stones' performing careers.

There have also been coffee table books of the Stones by noted photographers like Gered Mankowitz and Mark Hayward. These books are wonderful but are mainly pictorial and have little in common with the present work. The Stones' recording career has been covered in detail by Martin Elliot in his excellent *The Rolling Stones: Complete Recording Sessions, 1962-2012*. His book is similar in concept to this one but focuses on recording sessions, not concerts.

Due to the extensive number of shows that the Stones played over the years and the details provided in *The Rolling Stones in Concert, 1962-1982*, this book covers only the first twenty-one years of the Stones' career.

I hope that you enjoy this book. If you are a fan and attended some of these shows then hopefully it brings back great memories. If you are new to the band, I hope it encourages you to seek out the music discussed. Happy listening.

# Chapter 1

# 1962

The Rolling Stones formed in early 1962 when a number of fellow blues enthusiasts, who felt they were the only people in England who appreciated the music, suddenly realized that there were other people just like them. One such blues enthusiast was Lewis Brian Hopkin-Jones. Brian was born on February 28, 1942, in the genteel town of Cheltenham to parents of Welsh ancestry. He came from a musical family and developed an aptitude for playing at a young age. He became a skilled pianist and played clarinet in the school orchestra. Around 1957, Brian became obsessed with jazz, especially the records of legendary alto saxophonist Charlie Parker and convinced his parents to buy him a sax. By 1958 he'd formed his own jazz band and played at a local club four times a week. In addition to the sax, his parents bought him a guitar and he quickly mastered that as well. Brian was good at school but was a non-conformist and rebelled against the stuffy traditions of 1950s Britain. Blonde and good looking, he had no trouble attracting women and had a string of conquests by the time he was nineteen, as well as numerous illegitimate children. Kicked out by his parents, he got his own flat with a friend. Brian took various odd jobs, but showed little inclination to take up a profession. But, in the fall of 1960, Brian's life took a dramatic turn when he attended a concert by the Chris Barber Band.

Barber and his group played traditional Dixieland jazz, but they also dabbled in country blues, which in England was called skiffle. The Barber band had become nationally known in the UK in 1956 when their guitarist Lonnie Donegan hit the top of the charts with "Rock Island Line." Barber was devoted to spreading interest in authentic American R&B and found a willing convert in Brian Jones. After seeing Barber's band, Brian lost all interest in jazz and became a blues devotee. As he related in the *Rolling Stones Book*, "Fact is that the really great rhythm 'n' blues stars all affected me—made me want to listen to them all the time, even to the extent of not worrying much about any other work." But R&B enthusiasts were sparse in Cheltenham and Brian was eager to meet some kindred souls.

This was not such an easy task at that time. As Bill Wyman recalled on BBC Radio, "It was kind of an underground music. We knew about it because of people that came here and toured, like Big Bill Broonzy and Muddy Waters came with Buddy Guy in that '61–'62 period and Sonny Boy Williamson came a bit later. But there were very few people coming over and there was no availability of those records to anyone in the public, in England anyways." So, in the fall of 1961 when Brian heard that the Chris Barber Band was playing in Cheltenham again, he and his friend, fellow blues enthusiast Dick Hattrell, made sure they were at the gig. By this time, the Barber Band included vocalist "Long" John Baldry, harmonica player Cyril Davies and guitarist Alexis Korner, who'd play an important role in the birth of the Stones. He recalled his first meeting with Brian on BBC Radio. "Brian came up to me with a friend of his and started talking about blues. He said he'd always wanted to know about blues. He just came into the dressing room and we started chatting.... I gave him my phone number and address and said if he ever came up to London (he should look me up)... And about a fortnight later, lo and behold, Brian turned up on the doorstep having decided to come up to London for the weekend."

Brian stayed at Korner's flat, poring over his impressive collection of R&B records. He was so taken with the recordings of guitarist Elmore James that when he arrived back in Cheltenham he bought an electric guitar and began practicing James' unusual open-D tuning. By early 1962 Brian had mastered James' slide guitar style and was raring to play. He sat in with local bands but was eager to get away from Cheltenham. When he learned that Korner and Cyril Davies had formed a band called Blues Incorporated, Brian hitchhiked to London to audition. He attended Blues Incorporated's gig at the Ealing Club in West London on March 17, 1962. It was here that Brian first met drummer Charles Robert Watts (born June 2, 1941), a twenty-year-old jazz enthusiast from Wembley with little knowledge of rock or blues music.

Charlie attended Harrow Art School and worked during the day at an advertising agency. But he'd fallen in love with the drums and he spent all his free time playing with local bands. Charlie impressed Brian immediately and Brian, who sat in with the band the following weekend, impressed Charlie. Slide guitar was almost unknown in England and Brian showed a deft touch. In deference to his musical idol, Brian adopted the nom-de-plume of Elmore Lewis. He was invited to sit in again with Blues Incorporated when they played the Marquee Club on April 7. It was here that he encountered Mick Jagger and Keith Richards.

Michael Philip Jagger (born July 26, 1943) grew up in Dartford, 16 miles southeast of London. The son of a physical education teacher, Mick was a sports fanatic. By the late 1950s he was also a huge follower of rock music. Mick recalled on BBC Radio, "I'd never had heroes except in rock music. So my heroes were Little Richard, Bo Diddley and then later on Muddy Waters and Chuck Berry. Chuck Berry was, I guess, a hero. One imagined his kind of lifestyle." An outgoing, confident young man, Mick acquired a guitar and played in various skiffle combos in the Dartford area. Mick and his mates delved deep

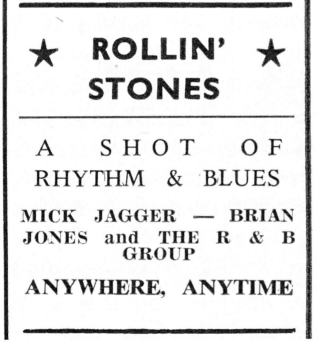

Early advertisement for the Stones (collection of Ira Korman).

into the music and sought out the roots of rock. As Mick's friend Dick Taylor recalled in *Mojo*, "Everyone at school seemed to have some kind of musical passion and Mick, Robert Beckwith and I discovered R&B. I remember Chas McDevitt playing Bo Diddley on his BBC Radio show, *Skiffle Club,* and thinking that was something else. Plus, my sister used to listen to Big Bill Broonzy. Gradually this all came together and we started to hear American R&B records for the first time."

In 1961 Mick graduated from Grammar School and earned a scholarship to the prestigious London School of Economics, but music was his real passion. He occupied his free time jamming with Taylor and other friends and spent the money he earned from temporary jobs on blues records he sent away to America for. Indeed, he had a few records under his arm when he bumped into Keith Richards (the correct spelling of his last name though, at the suggestion of Andrew Oldham, Keith dropped the S during the 1960s) at the Dartford railway station in October 1961.

Keith (born December 18, 1943) was also from Dartford and had known Mick since 1951, when the two attended the same primary school. Like Mick, Keith had acquired a guitar and was obsessed with rock music, especially Chuck Berry. But Keith was shy and seldom played in public until he met Dick Taylor at Sidcup Art College in 1959. Taylor recalled, "Everyone who had a guitar used to gather in the gents cloakroom and play at lunchtime. That's where I got to meet Keith Richards. I kept asking him to come along and meet Mick and the other guys but he said he was too shy." So it was not until the fateful railway encounter in October 1961 that Jagger-Richards reconnected. As Keith recalled in *Rolling Stone* in 1971, "He found out that I could play a little and he could sing a bit…. We'd all go to Dick Taylor's house, in his back room, some other cats would come along and play, and we'd try to lay some of this Little Walter stuff and Chuck Berry stuff. No drummer or anything, just two guitars and a little amplifier." They decided to form a band, Little Boy Blue and the Blue Boys, though Taylor considered it just a lark. "We didn't even consider playing in public. It was just for fun."

The group lacked money for gear but Mick convinced his parents to loan them some. Once properly equipped, they recorded a few rehearsals and a reel-to-reel of one came to light in 1995 (it was sold at Sotheby's and bought by Mick). The tape contained Berry songs like "Beautiful Delilah" and "Around and Around," covers of an early Elvis recording, "You're Right, I'm Left, She's Gone" (which Taylor recalled as a favorite of Keith's) and Ritchie Valens' 1958 hit "La Bamba," and a few blues like "Down the Road Apiece." When Little Boy Blue and the Blues Boys heard that Alexis Korner was playing authentic blues at the Marquee in London, they made sure they attended and were blown away when "Elmore" Lewis played slide guitar.

Dick Taylor recalled on Dutch TV, "Mick and Keith and I sat and watched Brian Jones and our mouths fell open. He played an acoustic guitar with a pickup and he played slide. He was absolutely brilliant." Mick related to Rob Chapman of *Mojo*, "He picked up this Elmore James guitar thing which really knocked me out when I first heard him play it. And it was really good. He really had that down and he was very exciting. The sound was right. The glissandos were all right. There was really a good gut feeling when he played it in the pub." Mick, Keith and Dick were enamored with Brian, who, though he was roughly the same age, seemed more worldly and sophisticated. As Keith recalled in 1971, "He was a good guitar player then. He had the touch and was just peaking. He was already out of school. He'd been kicked out of university and had a variety of jobs. He was already into living on his own and trying to find a pad for his old lady. Whereas

Mick and I were just kicking around in back rooms, still living at home." Brian was far more serious about music than his new friends.

By April 1962 he'd decided to be a professional. He told fellow blues enthusiast Paul Jones, "I'm going to start a band and I'm going to become rich and famous. Do you want to be my singer?" Jones lacked Brian's faith in music as a viable career and turned him down. But Brian was undeterred. After moving to London with his girlfriend Pat Andrews and their young child, Julian, he placed an ad in the May 2, 1962, *Jazz News*. It stated: "Guitarist and vocalist forming R&B band, require Harmonica and/or Tenor Sax, Piano, Bass and Drums. Must be keen to rehearse. Plenty of interesting work available." Brian began auditioning musicians at a local pub. The first person to turn up was a Scottish jazz pianist, who'd grown up in Cheam, Surrey. Ian "Stu" Stewart (born in 1938) was a gifted musician who fell in love with blues and jazz music in his teens. He was greatly respected by his contemporaries. Pianist Ben Waters commented in *Mojo*, "When he was in the band, they really did swing. He made a big difference." Stu recognized that Brian was also gifted, even if the two didn't really get on with each other. Stu decided to throw in his lot with him and they began seeking other musicians. Brian tried to get singer Brian Knight (of the band Blues by Six) to join but he said no. But by that time, another viable singer had emerged.

After seeing Brian perform, Little Boy Blue and the Blue Boys sent their audition tape to Alexis Korner. One night in May, Mick Jagger sang onstage with Blues Incorporated. From the beginning, Mick showed great confidence onstage, dancing while he sang and shaking his hair. Blues enthusiast Paul Jones recalled on BBC Radio, "He had that stuff much more down than anybody else did. I mean when you looked at people like Brian Knight and me, we just kind of stood there with our eyes closed. He used it to his advantage and had half the world imitating him within a matter of months." Brian was impressed and in June he made a fateful decision. Dick Taylor recalled, "Brian actually asked Mick to join his band and Mick said he wouldn't go without Keith. And then … they said why don't you join the band and play bass. So we went out and I bought a bass."

The proto–Stones rehearsed every Wednesday and Friday at the Bricklayers Arms, a pub in Central London. The band quickly gelled around the two-guitar interplay between Brian and Keith, but lacked a steady drummer. They coveted Charlie Watts but as Ian Stewart recalled on BBC Radio, "We didn't really get Charlie with us permanently for a long time because he was playing with another group that was making money and Charlie needed the money. So we must have used eight or nine different drummers." Future Kink Mick Avory rehearsed with them on a few occasions and may have played at their first gig (though the matter remains disputed) on July 12, 1962, at the Marquee Club, a popular jazz venue owned by Chris Barber and Harold Pendleton. They played at the club thanks to Alexis Korner. His All-Stars were asked to make a BBC broadcast and he convinced the owners to let Brian and Mick fill in. The July 7, 1962, *Disc Weekly* announced that Korner's group would not play and explained, "Their place will be taken by a new rhythm and blues group, Mick Jagger and the Rolling Stones, together with another group headed by Long John Baldry." The band name was coined on the spur of the moment by Brian, who cribbed it from a Muddy Waters song. Not everyone loved it. Stu recalled, "I said it was a terrible name. It sounded like the name of an Irish show band or something that ought to be playing at the Savoy."

Dick Taylor recalled on Dutch TV that the crowd's response that first night "was mixed. Some people really liked it. I know one person who didn't really like it was the guy who cleaned the place afterwards. He said, 'They'll never get anywhere.' I think he ate his words." However, the band was far from an overnight success. Taylor told writer Pete Doggett, "Gigs were few and far between. We used to play the Marquee and the Ealing Blues Club, and that was about it." The Stones soon acquired drummer Tony Chapman but nothing much happened that fall to inspire them with confidence. Brian, Keith and Mick eventually moved in together at 102 Edith Grove (SW10) in Chelsea. The slovenliness of the apartment disgusted all who entered. Drummer Carlos Little, a member of Screaming Lord Sutch's band who occasionally filled in with the Stones when Tony Chapman was busy, recalled on radio, "I remember going back to their flat at Edith Grove. What an amazing place! I mean, you can imagine four lads living on their own. There was Keith, Mick and Brian and another guy. They used to spit on the walls and chuck things on the ceiling. You couldn't get much lower. Any lower and I suppose you'd be sleeping in a cardboard box somewhere."

Keith and Brian had a passion for the band and, as both were usually unemployed, spent all their free time practicing their "guitar weaving." Their flat mate, however, was not as committed as his two friends. Mick continued to attend classes at the London School of Economics during the day and was weighing his options. Years later, he told Jann Wenner, "It was a good, fun thing to do, but Keith and Brian were beyond that. They wanted to play all the time." The winter of 1962 was a tough time. Keith and Brian were unemployed and relied on Mick's meager LSE grant to pay the rent. Money for food was tight. Keith recalled in *KRLA Beat*, "Sometimes we'd be invited out to a party. That was a high spot because it meant that we could get a drink or two, or at least a snack. They reckon that a lot of musicians have to starve for their art, but honest—our situation was ridiculous!" There were also constant setbacks. In October Dick Taylor quit the band, leaving the Stones without a bassist. Taylor recalled in *Mojo*, "I was a bit cheesed off at having to play bass because I was really a guitarist. And I was trying to get into the Royal Academy of Music. So one day I decided to leave, and I've never regretted it since." But, Mick, Brian and Keith remained committed. In the Stones' 1964 biography, Brian recalled, "I remember one chat between the three of us…. We wondered if we were doing the right thing by not getting into worthwhile jobs and forgetting all about this mad music bit. So we had to think hard. Suppose we failed. Suppose we went on, not doing much, just soaking up music, for a whole year. That would be about the limit we reckoned…. We'd have tried to the best of our ability and we would have nothing to regret in later life."

Things began to improve when the Stones met Bill Wyman. Born William Perks in October 1936, he was older than the Stones with a wife and a steady job. He had started playing music in his early twenties when a mate got him interested in guitar. In 1960 he formed a group called the Cliftons that played weddings and other social events. He soon made the fateful decision to switch from guitar to bass. Cliftons' drummer Tony Chapman also played with the Stones and told Bill they were looking for a replacement for Dick Taylor. Perks went with Chapman to see Glyn Johns and the Presidents perform at the Red Lion in Sutton on December 2. That night Chapman introduced Bill to Stu, who was sharing a flat with Glyn. He told Bill that he should come to the band's next rehearsal. Perks brought his bass and new Vox amplifier to the Wetherby Arms on December 7. He told *NME*, "We went through loads of tunes and messed about a lot. It wasn't a real audition. They didn't like me, but I had a good amplifier, and they were badly in need of amplifiers at that time." He was in and the Stones soon came to greatly appreciate his playing. But Bill didn't think his last name sounded good on a marquee and took the last name Wyman. As 1962 ended four of the five Stones were in place.

## Concerts

**Thursday, July 12:** Marquee Club, 165 Oxford Street, London, UK, with Long John Baldry's Kansas City Blues Band

The Stones made their first public appearance billed as Mick Jagger and the Rolling Stones. The lineup consisted of Brian, Mick, Keith, Ian Stewart, Dick Taylor and a drummer. An announcement in *Jazz News* noted that Mick Avory would play drums. However, he has stated on numerous occasions that he never played an actual gig with the Stones. Others have contended that it was Tony Chapman but, Bill Wyman's book *Rolling with the Stones* reprinted an ad placed by the proto-Stones in *Melody Maker* on August 18 seeking a drummer. As Tony Chapman answered this ad, it appears he didn't play with the band until September. The matter may never be settled.

The set list was written down by Stu and consisted of: "Kansas City" (Wilbert Harrison), "Honey What's Wrong" (Billy Fury), "Confessin' the Blues" (Chuck Berry), "Bright Lights, Big City" (Jimmy Reed), "Dust My Blues" (Elmore James), "Down the Road Apiece" (Chuck Berry), "I Want to Love You" (Charles Smith), "I'm a Hoochie Coochie Man" (Muddy Waters), "Ride 'Em On Down" (Robert Johnson), "Back in the USA" (Chuck Berry), "I Feel Kind of Lonesome" (Jimmy Reed), "Blues Before Sunrise" (Elmore James), "Big Boss Man" (Jimmy Reed), "Don't Stay Out All Night" (Billy Boy Arnold), "Tell Me You Love Me" (Fats Domino) and "Happy Home" (Elmore James).

**Saturday, July 28:** Ealing Club, 42 A The Broadway, Ealing, West London, UK

The Stones' second professional gig took place at the Ealing Club, again filling in for Alexis Korner. He and Cyril Davies had founded the club in March. It was an intimate venue with a maximum capacity of 200 people.

*Right:* **Listing for the Stones' first appearance at the Marquee Club (collection of Ira Korman).**

---

**CLUBS**

**MARQUEE**

THE LONDON JAZZ CENTRE
165, Oxford Street, W.1.

Wednesday, July 11th
★ DOUG RICHFORD'S JAZZMEN
(Members: 4/-
  Guests: 5/-)

Thursday, July 12th
★ MICK JAGGER and the ROLLING STONES
★ LONG JOHN BALDRY'S KANSAS CITY BLUE BOYS
(Members: 4/-
  Guests: 5/-)

Friday, July 13th
★ FAIRWEATHER — BROWN ALL STARS
(Members: 4/-
  Guests: 5/-)

Saturday, July 14th
★ JOE HARRIOTT QUINTET
★ RONNIE ROSS QUARTET
(Members: 6/-
  Guests: 7/6d)

Sunday, July 15th
★ DANKWORTH NIGHT
(Members: 4/-
  Guests: 5/-)

Monday, July 16th
★ CYRIL PRESTON JAZZ BAND
★ COLIN KINGWELL'S JAZZ BANDITS
(Members: 4/-
  Guests: 5/-)

**Saturday, September 15:** Ealing Club, 42 A The Broadway, Ealing, West London, UK
It's likely that Tony Chapman became the Stones' semi-regular drummer at this time, though they apparently never saw him as much more than a stopgap. Keith recalled that Chapman was a "terrible drummer, always comin' in on the on-beat."

**Saturday, September 22:** Ealing Club, 42 A The Broadway, Ealing, West London, UK
The September 26 *Jazz News* announced that the Stones would be taking over Alexis Korner's residency at the Ealing Club "now that Alex is so busy that he can't do the residency anymore."

**Thursday, September 27:** Marquee Club, 165 Oxford Street, London, UK
The Stones filled in for Korner's group again.

**Saturday, September 29:** Ealing Club, 42 A The Broadway, Ealing, West London, UK
Mick later recalled on BBC Radio: "I remember the Ealing Club…. It was dripping off the roof all the time, wasn't it? It was so wet that sometimes we had to put a thing up over the stage, a sort of horrible sheet which was disgustingly dirty, and we put it up over the bandstand and so the condensation didn't drip directly on you, it just dripped through the sheet on you, instead of directly off the ceiling…. It was very dangerous too, you see, cause all this electricity and all those microphones and that."

**Friday, October 5:** Woodstock Hotel, North Cheam, Surrey, UK
This gig was an utter disaster. Dick Taylor recalled that only two people paid to attend, while four others simply loitered outside.

**Saturday, October 6:** Ealing Club, 42 A The Broadway, Ealing, West London, UK

**Saturday, October 13:** Ealing Club, 42 A The Broadway, Ealing, West London, UK

**Saturday, October 20:** Ealing Club, 42 A The Broadway, Ealing, West London, UK
Probably after this show Dick Taylor quit the group.

**Saturday, October 27:** Ealing Club, 42 A The Broadway, Ealing, West London, UK
Prior to this show, the band recorded a demo at Curly Clayton Sound Studios in North London to send to record companies in hopes of getting a contract. The tracks recorded were: "Soon Forgotten," "Close Together" and "You Can't Judge a Book By Its Cover." An acetate, which once belonged to Tony Chapman, came up for auction in 1988 and was bought by a private collector.

**Tuesday, November 6:** Ealing Club, 42 A The Broadway, Ealing, West London, UK
On this night musician Ricky Fenson played bass.

**Wednesday, November 7:** William Morris Hall, South Oxhey, Hertfordshire, UK

**Tuesday, November 13:** Ealing Club, 42 A The Broadway, Ealing, West London, UK

**Wednesday, November 14:** William Morris Hall, South Oxhey, Hertfordshire, UK

**Sunday, November 18:** Ken Colyer Jazz Club (Studio 51), 10 Great Newport St., London, UK, 8 p.m.
This was the first of many appearances at this small club in the basement of 10 Great Newport Street.

**Tuesday, November 20:** Ealing Club, 42 A The Broadway, Ealing, West London, UK

> **A SHOT OF RHYTHM AND BLUES**
> ★ **THE REAL THING** ★
> # THE ROLLIN' STONES
> EVERY WED. — Wm. MORRIS HALL, Sth. OXHEY
> — 7.30 P.M.    (TUBE TO CARPENDERS PARK)
> AVAILABLE  FOR  BOOKINGS:  GER  6601  or
> MANAGEMENT  —  102  EDITH  GROVE  S.W.10

Advertisement for the Stones' appearance at William Morris Hall (collection of Ira Korman).

**Wednesday, November 21:** William Morris Hall, South Oxhey, Hertfordshire, UK

**Friday, November 23:** Red Lion Pub, Sutton, South London, UK
   Stu secured the Stones a semi-regular residency at this pub near where he lived. His friend Colin Folwell played drums for a fee of £3. The venue was very small and people were usually crowded in, barely able to move.

**Sunday, November 25:** Ken Colyer Jazz Club (Studio 51), 10 Great Newport St., London, UK, 8 p.m.

**Tuesday, November 27:** Ealing Club, 42 A The Broadway, Ealing, West London, UK

**Wednesday, November 28:** William Morris Hall, South Oxhey, Hertfordshire, UK

**Friday, November 30:** Piccadilly Jazz Club, 41 Great Windmill Street, London, UK
   The Stones played this basement club, with Ricky Fenson on bass. While the gig wasn't particularly memorable, Brian became friendly with Giorgio Gomelsky, who ran the club and would play a part in the Stones' rise to prominence.

**Sunday, December 2:** Ken Colyer Jazz Club (Studio 51), 10 Great Newport St., London, UK, 8 p.m.

**Tuesday, December 4:** Ealing Club, 42 A The Broadway, Ealing, West London, UK
   Colin Golding played bass.

**Wednesday, December 5:** William Morris Hall, South Oxhey, Hertfordshire, UK
   Ricky Fenson played bass. Bill Wyman noted in his book *Stone Alone* that the band later informed him that there were more people on stage than in the audience.

**Friday, December 7:** Red Lion Pub, Sutton, South London, UK
   Colin Golding played bass on this night but prior to the gig the band auditioned Bill Wyman at the Wetherby Arms Pub.

**Sunday, December 9:** Ken Colyer Jazz Club (Studio 51), 10 Great Newport Street, London, UK, 8 p.m.
   The band apparently played on this night and the following Tuesday without a bassist.

# 1962

**Tuesday, December 11:** Ealing Club, 42 A The Broadway, Ealing, West London, UK

**Wednesday, December 12:** Sidcup Art College, London Borough of Bexley, UK
The Stones played the college which Keith and Dick Taylor attended. Ricky Fenson may have played bass, though it's been alleged that Dick Taylor returned for the gig.

**Friday, December 14:** Ricky-Tick, Star & Garter Pub, Windsor, Berkshire, UK
Bill Wyman made his debut with the Stones at their first appearance at this club situated above the Star & Garter Pub.

**Saturday, December 15:** Sandover Hall, Richmond, UK
The Stones began playing occasional gigs at this small venue situated on the road behind L'Auberge, the most popular coffee bar in Richmond.

**Tuesday, December 18:** Ealing Club, 42 A The Broadway, Ealing, West London, UK
Bill was busy with work, so the Stones again played without a bassist.

**Wednesday, December 19:** William Morris Hall, South Oxhey, Hertfordshire, UK
Bill was again busy with work and didn't play.

**Friday, December 21:** Red Lion Pub, Sutton, South London, UK
Colin Golding played bass at this gig, as Bill was busy.

**Saturday, December 22:** Sandover Hall, Richmond, UK, 7:30 p.m.

**Wednesday, December 26:** Piccadilly Jazz Club, 41 Great Windmill Street, London, UK, with Dave Hunt's Rhythm and Blues Band
A young Ray Davies sat in with headliner Dave Hunt's band on this night and caught his first glimpse of the Stones (with Ricky Fenson on bass and Carlo Little on drums). He later recalled, "I sat down and I saw them play and I saw energy. I saw Brian Jones—a total star. I saw Keith…. I saw Jagger, not so prominent then. They stood in a line, the three of 'em all in their round button collars and their little shirts. The sound was exciting. Couldn't hear the vocal, but that was great—he was just there, a real trebly, bad PA…. I think that was the best I've ever seen 'em play. Really!"

**Saturday, December 29:** Ealing Club, 42 A The Broadway, Ealing, West London, UK

**Sunday, December 30:** Green Man Pub, Blackheath, London, UK
Ricky Fenson apparently subbed for Wyman.

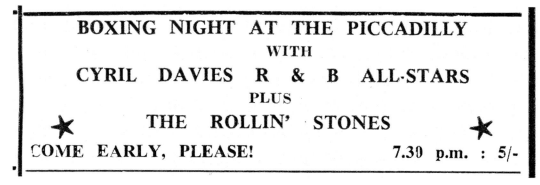

Advertisement for the Stones' December 26, 1962, appearance at Piccadilly Jazz Club (collection of Ira Korman).

# Chapter 2

# 1963

As 1963 began, things started to fall into place. Better paying gigs were still hard to find but, with the addition of Wyman, the Stones became a tighter unit. Long months of rehearsal by Brian and Keith began to pay off. As Stu recalled, "By this time, having lived together and done nothing else but listen to their records and tapes and play together, Brian and Keith had this guitar thing like you wouldn't believe. There was never any suggestion of a lead and rhythm guitar player. They were two guitar players that were like somebody's right and left hand." However, Keith and Brian still felt that something was missing. As Keith's diary attests, the group remained unhappy with drummer Tony Chapman and they were scheming to replace him with Charlie Watts. He had resisted previous requests to join because the Stones weren't a moneymaking proposition. In 1965 he told

A membership card to the Ealing Club (collection of Ira Korman).

*KRLA Beat*, "Honestly, I thought they were mad. I mean they were working a lot of dates without getting paid or even worrying about it. And there was me, earning a pretty comfortable living, which obviously was going to nosedive if I got involved with the Stones.... But.... I liked their spirit and I was getting very involved with rhythm and blues. I figured it would be a bit of an experiment for me and a bit of a challenge too."

With the arrival of Charlie on drums in January, the classic lineup was in place. The Stones recognized that he was the missing piece of the puzzle. The band really swung in concert but they still struggled to obtain gigs. R&B continued to be a hard sell in London clubs. As Bill Wyman recalled on BBC Radio, "There were either modern jazz clubs, like the Flamingo, with Georgie Fame and Graham Bond, all playing like soul jazz, with all the hip kids all saying 'groovy man' and trying to be cool cats and the rest of it was like traditional or modern jazz. It wasn't our scene really.... It was very difficult to get bookings. So we went in and did intervals playing 'authentic' blues music." The Stones, however, remained committed to their goals. Mick wrote a letter to *Melody Maker*, published on January 5, in which he stated his firm belief that blues music would catch on in England but "it has got to move out of London. Only two or three clubs are making any money at the moment and it has got to be spread to live." The Stones saw themselves as the prophets who'd popularize the blues to the masses and decided they needed to make a record.

On March 11 producer/engineer Glyn Johns helped them make demos at IBC Studios. Keith later recalled, "He had the keys so he let us in at night ... he kept worrying about whether the night watchman was going to come round. It was a very surreptitious session." However, Johns was only allowed to record acts that agreed to let IBC have the masters. Acting as "manager" of the group, Brian signed an agreement with IBC giving them a six-month option on the songs recorded. The Stones had recorded five tunes: "Baby What's Wrong" and "Bright Lights, Big City" by Jimmy Reed, Bo Diddley's "Diddley Daddy" and "Roadrunner," and Willie Dixon's "I Want to Be Loved." They had high hopes for the recordings, but every company that IBC offered them to passed (the songs were officially released on the "super deluxe" edition of the Stones' compilation *GRR* in 2012).

It was only when the band hooked up with Giorgio Gomelsky that their luck began to change. He ran a popular jazz club in the back room of a pub in the Station Hotel in Richmond and was known to be a big R&B enthusiast. Brian convinced him to come and see the Stones play on February 6. Gomelsky told writer David Dalton, "I went to see them in Sutton, at the Red Lion. I liked what they were doing. I said, 'Listen, I promised this guy I would give him a job but the first time he goofs, you're in.' And then came that famous day. Dave Hunt had a terrible problem getting everybody together, he just wasn't together, and the next Sunday they didn't turn up.... So Monday I called Ian Stewart: 'tell everybody in the band you guys are on next Sunday.'"

The Stones' early appearances at the club were rather staid affairs. To remedy the situation, Gomelsky encouraged the audience to dance. He later recalled, "That was the beginning of that whole real Stones thing, that Crawdaddy thing was that audience participation, opening that scene between the band and the audience and that's where the audience sort of went, wow." The Stones developed a fervent cult and word spread that something exciting was happening in Richmond. By April, over 300 people were attending their Sunday shows. The band realized their moment had arrived. Mick recalled on BBC Radio, "We were playing at the Station Hotel, Richmond, and it started to become like slightly hysterical. When the audience becomes quite hysterical and over the edge than you realize that it's gone from being this interesting blues band experience." Gomelsky made a verbal contract with the Stones to act as their manager. He recalled in the Stones' first biography, "I worked as hard as I could for the boys for a number of reasons. First, they were doing a great job for my club—really lifting it from the doldrums. Second, they were playing a brand of music that appealed to me personally and had fired me with an ambition to see it better appreciated here in Britain. And third, I was fed up with a lot of the insipid rubbish that was making the Top Twenty."

Gomelsky talked up the Stones wherever he went. In April his hard work began to pay off. Journalist Barry May attended a Stones performance and gave them their first major exposure in the April 13 *Richmond and Twickenham Times*: "A musical magnet is drawing the jazz beatniks … to a new mecca in Richmond…. The deep, earthy sound produced at the hotel on Sunday evenings is typical of the best of rhythm and blues that gives all who hear it an irresistible urge to stand up and move." The night after the article appeared, the Beatles themselves came to see what the fuss was about. They were impressed and developed a friendship with their future rivals. It was Peter Jones of *Record Mirror*, however, who really got the ball rolling for the Stones. He was so impressed by the band that he raved about them to everyone he knew, including Beatles publicist Andrew Loog Oldham.

Oldham (born January 29, 1944) was ambitious to get into record management. He sensed that the Stones might be his ticket to the big time. He saw them perform at the Crawdaddy on April 21 and a week later he brought agent Eric Easton (born in 1927), whom he hoped to interest in co-managing the band. Oldham turned to Easton because he knew he could get the Stones better paying gigs through his contacts and had the financial resources to fund his schemes to break the exciting band. In 1965 Easton recalled the visit in *KRLA Beat*: "It was absolutely jammed with people. But it was also the most exciting atmosphere I've ever experienced in a club or ballroom. And I saw right away that the Rolling Stones were enjoying every minute of it. They were producing this fantastic sound and it was obvious that it was exactly right for the kids in the audience." The Stones sized up their prospective managers and decided that they could do more for them then Gomelsky. Despite the fact that they had a verbal agreement with him, the Stones told Oldham and Easton that they had no current manager. On May 1, Brian signed an agreement on behalf of the Stones giving Oldham and Easton the right to manage the band.

Easton was a middle-aged businessman whose tastes ran to other types of music, but the Stones quickly took a liking to Andrew, who was full of enthusiasm. Charlie recalled in *According to the Rolling Stones*, "We all got on well with him and we all liked what he was saying…. And he could see the possibilities, otherwise we'd have still been schlepping round the clubs playing in Bournemouth for ever and never moving on." Andrew suggested that the Stones could be as big as the Beatles if they took his advice. Mick later recalled to Roy Carr, "It was … very exciting. I mean we really wanted to be very big. You gotta want to be that big, you gotta really want to be a big star." Easton and Oldham were determined to get the Stones signed to a label, so they formed their own independent recording company, which they called Impact Sound. The Stones agreed that Oldham and Easton would receive 25 percent of any earnings they made. However, there was a hiccup. Brian revealed that he'd signed a contract with IBC and that they owned the Stones' demo recordings. The ever-devious Oldham quickly hatched a plan to have Brian inform IBC owner George Clouston that he'd quit the group and needed

# THE ROLLING STONES

**Summer 1963 promotional card. This is probably the earliest mass produced promotional material for the Stones. It shows the Stones (from left, Brian, Charlie, Keith, Mick and Bill) in their early matching uniforms (collection of Ira Korman).**

to break the contract so that he could have a bright future with his new band. Brian performed his acting well. For £90, Clouston, who hadn't attracted any interest in the Stones' demo anyways, agreed to let him out of the contract. As Brian was the only signatory to the deal, all the Stones were thus freed of any obligations to IBC. On May 6 Brian signed a three-year contract on behalf of the Stones with Impact Sound.

Success beckoned but signing with Oldham and Easton soon led to friction within the group. Andrew wanted to make the Stones into pop stars like the Beatles. He felt that the lantern-jawed Ian Stewart did not fit the bill and he was sacked. Stu's friend Glyn Johns recalled "I was in the next room when I heard it—I went ape-shit, told Andrew what an arsehole he was. It didn't make a blind bit of difference of course." Stu was forced to accept Oldham's offer to be road manager (a job he kept until his death in 1985) and pianist (though Stu only played on songs he liked). Brian tried to make Stu feel better by promising him that he'd keep receiving equal pay. But the promise wasn't kept and Stu never forgave Brian for not sticking up for him in the interest of fame. Momentous events for the Stones continued to occur that month.

Dick Rowe of Decca Records was still smarting from his decision not to sign the Beatles the previous year and when George Harrison urged him to check out the Stones he didn't hesitate. According to Bill Wyman, Rowe attended the Stones' May 5 concert at the Crawdaddy. Two days later he met with Oldham and Easton to discuss a recording contract. In a bold move, to speed up the process and prevent Rowe from having second thoughts, Andrew got his friend Maurice Clark of Jewel Music to spread the rumor that EMI was about to sign the band. Rowe took the bait and within a week the Stones were

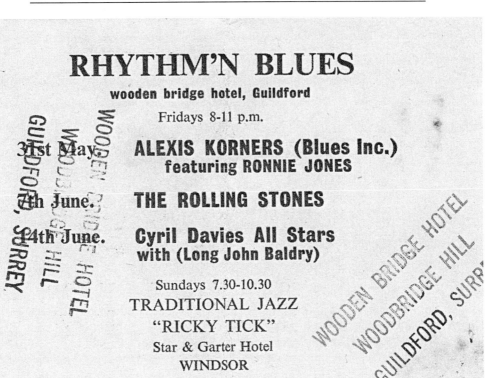

**Handbill for a Stones show at Wooden Bridge Hotel in Guilford (collection of Ira Korman).**

signed to the label, with Impact Sound acting as middlemen (and receiving a 14 percent royalty on records, while the Stones received 6 percent).

On May 10 the Stones were at Olympic Studios in Barnes recording their first single, a fast-paced cover of Chuck Berry's "Come On," with Willie Dixon's bluesy "I Want to Be Loved" on the flipside. Although the Stones weren't entirely happy with the poppy sound of "Come On," it was definitely commercial and sped up the British charts when released on June 7, reaching a respectable #21. A month later the nation got its first glimpse of the Stones when they appeared on the summer edition of the ABC TV show *Thank Your Lucky Stars*. At the insistence of Andrew, the band wore matching checkered suits with black velvet collars. Keith recalled in 1971 "For a month on the first tour, we said, 'All right, we'll do it. You know the game. We'll try it out.' But then the Stones thing started taking over. Charlie would leave his jacket in some dressing room and I'd pull mine out and there'd be whiskey stains all over it or chocolate pudding."

The Stones had outgrown the clubs and that fall they headed out on their first tour of Britain with Bo Diddley and the Everly Brothers. Despite the talent on display, sales were slow and within a week promoter Don Arden had added the outrageous Little Richard to the bill. The Stones were in heaven, playing with their idols from America and traveling around the country. Keith related to Stanley Booth, "This is our first contact with the cats whose music we've been playing. Watching Little Richard and Bo Diddley and the Everly Brothers every night was the way we were drawn into the whole pop thing.... We never had to present ourselves onstage before. We'd just gone out there and played where people danced. But now we were playing for an audience that was sitting. That was when Mick really started coming into his own." So Brian began to lose control of the band he'd formed.

Early in September, Mick and Keith moved out of Edith Grove and into a house on Mapesbury Road with Andrew. For the next few years, the "unholy trio" of Mick, Keith and Andrew was never far from each other. Brian moved in with girlfriend Linda Lawrence's parents in Windsor. He still considered the Stones his band, but Andrew was pushing Mick and Keith to the fore and encouraging them to write together. Brian's leadership role began to be threatened. Nor did he help himself by his behavior. Stu told Stanley Booth, "Brian … used to be very tactless, and say things like, 'As I'm the leader of the group, I'm gonna have an extra five pounds a week.' We used to stay in cheap hotels 'cause we didn't have any money…. So we'd stay in a medium-class hotel, but Brian would say, 'In a few months time, when we're earning more for a gig, I'm gonna stay in the Hilton because I'm the leader, and everybody else will be staying with you somewhere.' So, eventually they got sick to fucking death of him." But even if Brian had lost the admiration of his fellow Stones, he still remained a crucial part of the band.

They now needed a second single. Influenced by the Hollies, the Stones were momentarily tempted to head in a more vocal oriented direction and recorded "Poison Ivy" by the Coasters. But Oldham knew they needed an original song to make a name. He used his connections with former boss Brian Epstein to get the most famous songwriting duo in Britain to lend a hand. On September 10, a band rehearsal was interrupted by the arrival of John Lennon and Paul McCartney. They finished a new song, "I Wanna Be Your Man," in front of the Stones and offered it to them. Mick recalled in *Rolling Stone* in 1968: "They were really hustlers then. I mean the way they used to hustle tunes was great…. So they played it and we thought it sounded pretty commercial, which is what we were looking for, so we did it like Elmore James or something." The song was released in November and made it to number 12 on the charts. It featured a blistering steel solo by Brian that put everyone in the band in awe and sounded like nothing heard on radio in staid Britain before. As 1963 ended the Stones were poised for greater things.

## Concerts

**Thursday, January 3:** Marquee Club, 165 Oxford Street, London, UK, with Cyril Davies All Stars

The Stones got a big break when they were invited by Cyril Davies to be his opening act at his weekly residency at the Marquee. They probably played without a bass player on this date. In his diary, Keith recorded: "Very good set. 'Bo Diddley' received with very good applause. 612 people attended session. 1st set good warm up. 2nd set swung fabulously. Impressed some very big people."

**Friday, January 4:** Red Lion Pub, Sutton, South London, UK

Colin Golding played bass on this night, as Bill was busy. Keith recorded in his diary that the band played "poorly" and that Tony Chapman's drumming was "diabolical." He explained to Robert Greenfield in 1971, "Cat would start a number and end up either four times as fast as he started it or three times as slow, but never stay the same." In his defense, Chapman later noted that he frequently had to play without a bassist to accompany him in holding down the bottom.

**Saturday, January 5:** Sandover Hall, Richmond, UK

Ricky Fenson subbed for Wyman. Keith had problems with his guitar on this night, so Brian loaned him his and played only harmonica. The band received £37 for the night.

**Monday, January 7:** Flamingo Club, 33 Wardour St., London, UK

This was another important booking for the Stones, as the Flamingo was an important hangout for "cool jazz" fans and attracted large crowds, dressed in zoot suits. Unfortunately, the scruffy Stones had to play minus a bassist and with equipment badly in need of replacement. Despite this, they secured a weekly Monday residency.

**Tuesday, January 8:** Ealing Club, 42 A The Broadway, Ealing, West London, UK

Keith recorded in his diary that "band played quite well. 'Bo Diddley' was an absolute knockout. If we can repeat this performance at the Marquee we'll be laughing!"

**Thursday, January 10:** Marquee Club, 165 Oxford Street, London, UK, with Cyril Davies All Stars

This gig was marred by electrical problems in the area, which weakened Keith and Brian's amps throughout the night.

**Friday, January 11:** Ricky-Tick, Star & Garter Pub, Windsor, Berkshire, UK

In *Stone Alone*, Bill Wyman stated that after this gig the band informed drummer Tony Chapman that he was fired. The Stones were worried that Bill, who was friends with Chapman, would also leave, taking his precious amplifier with him. But Wyman made an important decision. He recalled that Chapman "was furious. Pulling me aside, he said 'Come on Bill let's go and start a new band.' I replied that I was quite happy with the Stones. He left us there, red faced and angry."

**Saturday, January 12:** Ealing Club, 42 A The Broadway, Ealing, West London, UK

This momentous show marked Charlie's first appearance as a Stone. However, he missed a few future gigs due to work commitments. The band members received no money, as they'd agreed to forfeit earnings for two weeks to save up for new amps and microphones.

**Monday, January 14:** Flamingo Club, 33 Wardour St., London, UK

Because of other commitments, Bill was absent. Ricky Fenson played bass and Carlo Little played drums. Keith recalled that Fenson was a "lovely player" and that Carlos Little was "a killing drummer, great energy."

**Tuesday, January 15:** Ealing Club, 42 A The Broadway, Ealing, West London, UK

Keith recorded in his diary that the Stones attracted a "poor crowd" at the Ealing Club on this night and that the band was in poor shape as he and Brian were recovering from a flu and Charlie "hasn't got right sound yet."

**Thursday, January 17:** Marquee Club, 165 Oxford Street, London, UK, with Cyril Davies All-Stars and the Velvets

Though the band was enthusiastic about Charlie's joining, there were some initial hiccups. Keith recorded in his diary that "Charlie swings very nicely but can't rock. Fabulous guy though." Watts was given orders to start listening to the rock and blues music the Stones loved, so he could play in a style more suited to this music.

**Friday, January 18:** Red Lion Pub, Sutton, South London, UK

Colin Golding subbed for Bill on bass.

**Saturday, January 19:** Sandover Hall, Richmond, UK
Ricky Fenson and Carlos Little subbed for Bill and Charlie.

**Monday, January 21:** Flamingo Club, 33 Wardour St., London, UK
Ricky Fenson and Carlos Little subbed for Bill and Charlie.

**Tuesday, January 22:** Ealing Club, 42 A The Broadway, Ealing, West London, UK
For unexplained reasons, only two people showed up for this gig and the band went home after a couple of numbers.

**Wednesday, January 23:** Red Lion Pub, Sutton, South London, UK
The Stones did not play their usual Thursday gig at the Marquee on January 24. They learned from Ricky Fenson and Carlos Little that Cyril Davies was "scared" of the applause they were getting.

**Saturday, January 26:** Ealing Club, 42 A The Broadway, Ealing, West London, UK
Ricky Fenson subbed for Bill and Carlos Little for Charlie. The band earned £16.

**Monday, January 28:** Flamingo Club, 33 Wardour St., London, UK, with the Graham Bond Trio
This was the Stones' last gig at the Flamingo. The band was apparently too "rock and roll" for the crowd. But they took some souvenirs to remember the club. Bill recalled, "When we left we stole three old metal stools which we carried around in the van and Brian, Mick and Keith used onstage everywhere we played. I would sit on my wardrobe bass cabinet, laid on its side most nights. We would perform like this, stopping between songs to light up cigarettes and drink beer and chat between ourselves."

**Thursday, January 31:** Marquee Club, 165 Oxford Street, London, UK, with Cyril Davies All Stars
The Stones were pulling in upwards of 600 people to the Marquee, so they asked Cyril Davies for a raise after the show. Much to their surprise, he fired them. Bill later suggested Davies was jealous of the attention they were getting. The band did not play at the Marquee again until 1971.

**Friday, February 1:** Red Lion Pub, Sutton, South London, UK

**Saturday, February 2:** Ealing Club, 42 A The Broadway, Ealing, West London, UK
Keith recorded in his diary that this was a "fabulous evening with big crowd. Sound returned with a bang. Charlie fabulous."

**Tuesday, February 5:** Ealing Club, 42 A The Broadway, Ealing, West London
Bill recalled that due to heavy snow only six people turned out to see the Stones, who played in their winter coats.

**Wednesday, February 6:** Red Lion Pub, Sutton, South London, UK
This was an important gig. Giorgio Gomelsky attended and was impressed.

**Thursday, February 7:** Harringay Jazz Club, Manor House Pub, London, UK, with Blues by Six, 8 p.m.
Having lost their Marquee spot, the Stones managed to get a weekly Thursday gig at this Jazz Club in North London. Bill recalled that they seldom attracted many patrons.

**Friday, February 8:** Ricky-Tick, Star & Garter Pub, Windsor, Berkshire, UK

**Saturday, February 9:** Ealing Club, 42 A The Broadway, Ealing, West London, UK
Keith noted in his diary that the band played to a packed house.

**Tuesday, February 12:** Ealing Club, 42 A The Broadway, Ealing, West London, UK
The day after this gig the band rehearsed new numbers that Brian had decided to add to the act including "Who Do You Love?," "Route 66" and a revamped version of "Hey Crawdaddy" that they often closed gigs with.

**Thursday, February 14:** Harringay Jazz Club, Manor House Pub, London, UK, with Blues by Six, 8 p.m.
A small crowd turned out. Keith noted sarcastically in his diary, "Blues By Six frightened them all away."

**Friday, February 15:** Red Lion Pub, Sutton, South London, UK
The Stones quickly tired of the small venues they played, such as the Red Lion Pub. In his diary, Keith complained that the band "can't get any sound out of this place." However, he expressed enthusiasm over the fact that Gomelsky had offered them a gig at the larger Station Hotel.

**Saturday, February 16:** Ealing Club, 42 A The Broadway, Ealing, West London, UK

**Tuesday, February 19:** Ealing Club, 42 A The Broadway, Ealing, West London, UK

**Wednesday, February 20:** Red Lion Pub, Sutton, UK

**Thursday, February 21:** Harringay Jazz Club, Manor House Pub, London, UK, with Blues by Six, 8 p.m.

**Friday, February 22:** Ricky-Tick, Star & Garter Pub, Windsor, Berkshire, UK

**Saturday, February 23:** Ealing Club, 42 A The Broadway, Ealing, West London, UK

**Sunday, February 24:** Station Hotel, Richmond, 8:15 p.m.
The Stones made their first appearance at the now legendary Crawdaddy Club, though it wasn't named that yet. They played in the back room of a hotel situated opposite Richmond Station. The Stones played two forty-five-minute sets, with an intermission. Giorgio Gomelsky agreed to pay the six piece band £1 each to play every Sunday. About thirty people attended the first night.

**Thursday, February 28:** Harringay Jazz Club, Manor House Pub, London, UK, with Blues by Six, 8 p.m.

**Saturday, March 2:** Ealing Club, 42 A The Broadway, Ealing, West London, UK
Bill recalled in *Stone Alone* that by this time the band had outgrown the Ealing Club and grumbled about playing there because they never made any money. After this show they did not play there again.

**Sunday, March 3:** Ken Colyer Jazz Club (Studio 51), 10 Great Newport St., London, 4 p.m., and Station Hotel, Richmond, UK
The Stones began appearing on Sundays at Ken Colyer's Soho Jazz Club in the late afternoon. Shirley Arnold, who eventually ran the Stones' fan club, recalled "Mick and Keith went down to Ken Colyer's jazz club one afternoon and said, 'Look, can we play when Ken has his break, can we go in and play for nothing?' So they said, 'Yeah, you can do it.' No one was really interested, it wasn't that packed, and I could see them, and I just

fell in love with them." The Stones than went to Richmond. The set for their appearance at the Station Hotel consisted of: "Route 66" (Chuck Berry), "Little Egypt" (Coasters), "Poison Ivy" (Coasters), "I'm Alright" (Bo Diddley), "I'm a King Bee" (Slim Harpo), "You Better Move On" (Arthur Alexander), "Nadine" (Chuck Berry), "You Can't Judge a Book" (Bo Diddley), "Honest I Do" (Jimmy Reed), "I Want to Be Loved" (Willie Dixon), "Beautiful Delilah" (Chuck Berry), "Memphis Tennessee" (Chuck Berry) "Walking the Dog" (Rufus Thomas) "Pretty Thing" (Bo Diddley) and "Hey Crawdaddy" (Bo Diddley).

**Wednesday, March 6:** Red Lion Pub, Sutton, South London, UK

**Thursday, March 7:** Harringay Jazz Club, Manor House Pub, London, UK, with Blues by Six, 8 p.m.

**Friday, March 8:** Ricky-Tick, Star & Garter Pub, Windsor, Berkshire, UK

**Saturday, March 9:** Wooden Bridge Hotel, Guildford, Surrey, UK

The Stones began playing occasional gigs at this venue southwest of central London.

**Sunday, March 10:** Ken Colyer Jazz Club (Studio 51), 10 Great Newport St., London, 4 p.m., and Station Hotel, Richmond, UK

**Thursday, March 14:** Harringay Jazz Club, Manor House Pub, London, UK, with Blues by Six, 8 p.m.

**Sunday, March 17:** Ken Colyer Jazz Club (Studio 51), 10 Great Newport St., London, 4 p.m., and Station Hotel, Richmond, UK

**Wednesday, March 20:** Red Lion Pub, Sutton, South London, UK

**Friday, March 22:** Ricky-Tick, Star & Garter Pub, Windsor, Berkshire, UK

**Sunday, March 24:** Ken Colyer Jazz Club (Studio 51), 10 Great Newport St., London, 4 p.m., and Station Hotel, Richmond, UK

**Friday, March 29:** Ricky-Tick, Star & Garter Pub, Windsor, Berkshire, UK

**Saturday, March 30:** Wooden Bridge Hotel, Guildford, Surrey, UK

**Sunday, March 31:** Ken Colyer Jazz Club (Studio 51), 10 Great Newport St., London, 4 p.m., and Station Hotel, Richmond, UK

**Wednesday, April 3:** Red Lion Pub, Sutton, South London, UK

**Sunday, April 7:** Ken Colyer Jazz Club (Studio 51), 10 Great Newport St., London, 4 p.m., and Crawdaddy Club, Station Hotel, Richmond, UK

The Richmond show attendance was 320 people, the highest attendance up to that point. The Stones usually ended gigs with a long improvisational version of "Hey Crawdaddy," which generated incredible enthusiasm. It was so popular that Gomelsky began calling his club the Crawdaddy.

**Sunday, April 14:** Ken Colyer Jazz Club (Studio 51), 10 Great Newport St., London, 4 p.m., and Crawdaddy Club, Station Hotel, Richmond, UK

Gomelsky did his best to help make the Stones a success. He visited the ITV studios in Teddington, where the Beatles were filming *Thank Your Lucky Stars,* and convinced them to come to Richmond and have a look. They duly attended the Stones' second set at the Crawdaddy. George Harrison later recalled, "It was a real rave. The audience shouted and screamed and danced on tables…. The beat the Stones laid down was solid; it shook off the walls, and seemed to move right inside your head. A great sound." After the gig, the Beatles came backstage and ended up hanging out with the Stones at Edith Grove. Brian, Mick and Keith returned the favor by attending the Beatles' show at the Royal Albert Hall in London on April 18.

**Friday, April 19:** Wooden Bridge Hotel, Guildford, Surrey, UK

**Sunday, April 21:** Crawdaddy Club, Station Hotel, Richmond, UK
　Giorgio Gomelsky thought the Stones had star potential and decided to make a self-financed movie of them. Filming took place on this day but has never surfaced. The appearance was more memorable because Andrew Oldham was in the audience to see them perform. In his memoir *Rolling Stoned*, he recalled the powerful effect that the band had on him, "It reached out and went inside me—totally. It satisfied me. I was in love…. I heard what I always wanted to hear." Oldham set his sights on managing the band and arranged to bring agent Eric Easton back with him to see them the following week.

**Wednesday, April 24:** Hotel Dancehall, Eel Pie Island, Twickenham, UK
　The Stones began making regular appearances at the Hotel Dancehall, a longstanding jazz venue on an island in the Thames. The day before this show, the Stones auditioned for the BBC at Maida Vale Studios. Charlie and Bill still had day jobs so Carlo Little and Ricky Fenson stood in. The BBC passed on the Stones.

**Friday, April 26:** Ricky-Tick, Star & Garter Pub, Windsor, Berkshire, UK

**Sunday, April 28:** Ken Colyer Jazz Club (Studio 51), 10 Great Newport St., London, 4 p.m., and Crawdaddy Club, Station Hotel, Richmond, UK
　It was on this night that Andrew brought Eric Easton to see the Stones at the Crawdaddy. They made an agreement with Brian to manage the band on May 1.

**Wednesday, May 1:** Hotel Dancehall, Eel Pie Island, Twickenham, UK

**Friday, May 3:** Ricky-Tick, Star & Garter Pub, Windsor, Berkshire, UK

**Saturday, May 4:** Battersea Funfair, Battersea Park, London, UK
　This was the first gig that Oldham and Easton booked for the Stones, an appearance at an outdoor charity concert organized by *News of the World*.

**Sunday, May 5:** Ken Colyer Jazz Club (Studio 51), 10 Great Newport St., London, 4 p.m., and Crawdaddy Club, Station Hotel, Richmond, UK

**Wednesday, May 8:** Hotel Dancehall, Eel Pie Island, Twickenham, UK
　Two days after this gig the Stones held their first recording session for Impact Sound and recorded "Come On."

**Sunday, May 12:** Ken Colyer Jazz Club (Studio 51), 10 Great Newport St., London, 4 p.m., and Crawdaddy Club, Station Hotel, Richmond, UK
　On Saturday the band received a very important mention in the national music magazine *Record Mirror*. Writer Norman Jopling declared, "The Rolling Stones are probably destined to be the biggest group in the R&B scene if it continues to flourish…. The fact is that unlike all the other R&B groups worthy of the name, the Rolling Stones have

a definite visual appeal.... They sing and play in a way one would expect more from a colored U.S. R&B team than a bunch of wild, exciting white boys who have the fans screaming—and listening—to them."

**Wednesday, May 15:** Hotel Dancehall, Eel Pie Island, Twickenham, UK
The day after this show, the Stones held another recording session to finish "Come On."

**Friday, May 17:** Wooden Bridge Hotel, Guildford, Surrey, UK
According to a memo from Giorgio Gomelsky, who'd booked this gig before he was replaced by Oldham and Easton, the Stones were paid £22 for this show.

**Sunday, May 19:** Ken Colyer Jazz Club (Studio 51), 10 Great Newport St., London, 4 p.m., and Crawdaddy Club, Station Hotel, Richmond, UK

**Wednesday, May 22:** Hotel Dancehall, Eel Pie Island, Twickenham, UK

**Friday, May 24:** Ricky-Tick, Star & Garter Pub, Windsor, Berkshire, UK

**Sunday, May 26:** Ken Colyer Jazz Club (Studio 51), 10 Great Newport St., London, 4 p.m., and Crawdaddy Club, Station Hotel, Richmond, UK

**Wednesday, May 29:** Hotel Dancehall, Eel Pie Island, Twickenham, UK

**Friday, May 31:** Ricky-Tick, Star & Garter Pub, Windsor, Berkshire, UK

**Sunday, June 2:** Ken Colyer Jazz Club (Studio 51), 10 Great Newport St., London, with John Mayall, 4 p.m., and Crawdaddy Club, Station Hotel, Richmond, UK
According to Wyman's diary the Stones' set at the Crawdaddy included "Bye Bye Johnny," "Down the Road Apiece," "Route 66," "Diddley Daddy," and "Pretty Thing."

**Monday, June 3:** Ken Colyer Jazz Club (Studio 51), 10 Great Newport St., London, UK, 8 p.m.

**Wednesday, June 5:** Hotel Dancehall, Eel Pie Island, Twickenham, UK

**Friday, June 7:** Wooden Bridge Hotel, Guildford, Surrey, UK
This was a momentous day for the Stones. Decca released their first single, "Come On." On June 8 Norman Jopling reviewed the disc in *Record Mirror* and interviewed the Stones.

**Sunday, June 9:** Ken Colyer Jazz Club (Studio 51), 10 Great Newport St., London, 4 p.m., and Crawdaddy Club, Station Hotel, Richmond, UK
By this time the Stones had developed a fanatical following at the Crawdaddy. Patrick Doncaster of *The Daily Mirror* described a typical scene: "The guitars and the drums started to twang and bang.... Shoulder to shoulder on the floor stood 500 youngsters, some in black leather, some in sweaters. You could have boiled an egg in the atmosphere.... Their feet stamped in tribal style. If they could, the dedicated occasionally put their hands above their heads and clapped in rhythm.... In its fervor it was like a revivalist meeting in America's deep south."

**Monday, June 10:** Ken Colyer Jazz Club (Studio 51), 10 Great Newport St., London, UK, 8 p.m.

**Wednesday, June 12:** Hotel Dancehall, Eel Pie Island, Twickenham, UK

During this period, Mick's new girlfriend, Chrissie Shrimpton, brought a young Rod Stewart to see "her boyfriend's band" at Eel Pie Island. Rod recalled in a documentary that the Stones inspired him to start his own singing career. "The night we saw Mick with The Rolling Stones, they all sat on stools, wearing cardigans, singing blues numbers. The singer could hold the room's attention and I remember thinking that the band was great. But I had the nagging feeling that I could do that."

**Friday, June 14:** Ricky-Tick, Star & Garter Pub, Windsor, Berkshire, UK

**Saturday, June 15:** Ken Colyer Jazz Club (Studio 51), 10 Great Newport St., London, UK

**Sunday, June 16:** Ken Colyer Jazz Club (Studio 51), 10 Great Newport St., London, 4 p.m., and Crawdaddy Club, Station Hotel, Richmond, UK

**Wednesday, June 19:** Hotel Dancehall, Eel Pie Island, Twickenham, UK

**Thursday, June 20:** Scene Club, Ham Yard, London, UK

The Scene Club was a popular jazz club that became a mod hangout in this period.

**Saturday, June 22:** Wooden Bridge Hotel, Guildford, Surrey, UK

**Sunday, June 23, and Monday, June 24:** Ken Colyer Jazz Club (Studio 51), 10 Great Newport St., London, UK

**Wednesday, June 26:** Hotel Dancehall, Eel Pie Island, Twickenham, UK

**Thursday, June 27:** Scene Club, Ham Yard, London, UK

The Stones had quickly grown tired of "Come On," which they believed was too much of a pop record. They stopped playing it in their shows. According to Bill Wyman, Andrew read them the riot act for being unprofessional and not playing their hit. The band grudgingly returned it to their act.

**Friday, June 28:** Ricky-Tick, Star & Garter Pub, Windsor, Berkshire, UK

The Stones received their first feature in the music weekly *New Musical Express* on June 29. Discussing the sudden surge of "Beat" groups in England, Mick commented: "Some groups are jumping on the bandwagon. The ones who are styled on R&B as we know it start their music where we leave off. They're more familiar with the Coasters, the Shirelles and Chuck Berry than with Jimmy Reed or Muddy Waters. But we'll play the stuff we like as long as people come to hear it."

**Sunday, June 30:** Crawdaddy Club, Athletic Grounds, Richmond, UK

To accommodate the large crowds turning out to see the Stones, the Crawdaddy Club moved to the Richmond Athletic Grounds, which could hold 1,200 people (500 turned out on this night). It remained, however, a no-frills affair. The stage was built of beer cases with planks over them.

**Monday, July 1:** Ken Colyer Jazz Club (Studio 51), 10 Great Newport St., London, UK, 8 p.m.

By this time the Stones were receiving 50 percent of the gate and a minimum of £35 for their appearances at Studio 51.

**Wednesday, July 3:** Hotel Dancehall, Eel Pie Island, Twickenham, UK

**Thursday, July 4:** Scene Club, Ham Yard, London, UK

The Beatles again attended a Stones show. Charlie commented in *NME*: "I don't suppose they come down just to see us. They can't like our faces. They must like the music."

**Friday, July 5:** Ricky-Tick, Star & Garter Pub, Windsor, Berkshire, UK

Two days after this gig the Stones were in Birmingham to tape their first national TV appearance on the ABC series *Lucky Stars Summer Spin*. They mimed to "Come On" in matching uniforms.

**Monday, July 8:** Ken Colyer Jazz Club (Studio 51), 10 Great Newport St., London, UK, 8 p.m.

On Tuesday the Stones recorded "Fortune Teller" at Decca Studios.

**Wednesday, July 10:** Hotel Dancehall, Eel Pie Island, Twickenham, UK

**Thursday, July 11:** Scene Club, Ham Yard, London, UK

In Richard Houghton's book *You Had to Be There*, a fan recalled that "there was hardly anybody there. The place was empty."

**Friday, July 12:** Twickenham Design College Dance, Eel Pie Island, Twickenham, UK

With a single on the charts, the Stones were able to charge higher fees for gigs. They received the prodigious sum of £73 for this show.

**Saturday, July 13:** Outlook Club, Middlesbrough, Yorkshire, UK, with the Hollies, 7:30 p.m.

With a national TV appearance under their belts, the Stones began touring outside London. This was the farthest north they'd yet played. The Outlook Club was a small basement venue that served only soft drinks. The Stones, dressed in their checked suits, opened for the Hollies, the famed Manchester band featuring Graham Nash and Allan Clarke. The polished group amazed the Stones. Brian was especially awed by their three-part harmony. A disgusted Stu recalled that after the gig "Brian immediately said, 'Right, everybody's got to sing.' Andrew and them (briefly) changed the group right around, and the emphasis became on 'Poison Ivy' and 'Fortune Teller,' numbers like that."

**Sunday, July 14:** Ken Colyer Jazz Club (Studio 51), 10 Great Newport St., London, 4 p.m., and Crawdaddy Club, Athletic Grounds, Richmond, UK

**Monday, July 15:** Ken Colyer Jazz Club (Studio 51), 10 Great Newport St., London, UK, 8 p.m.

On Tuesday, the Stones held a Decca session for "Poison Ivy."

**Wednesday, July 17:** Hotel Dancehall, Eel Pie Island, Twickenham, UK

**Friday, July 19:** Debutante Ball, Hastings, East Sussex, UK

A gig at the Wooden Bridge Hotel in Guildford was canceled when Brian got sick. In his book, Keith Richards alleged that the Stones instead played an otherwise unattested gig at the subterranean caves in Hastings. According to Keith, "We'd played a debutante's ball at Hastings Caves, for somebody called Lady Lampson, all via Andrew Oldham, an awfully super-duper, upper crusty affair doing a lowlife bash in Hastings caves, which are quite big."

Handbill for a canceled show on July 19, 1963 (collection of Ira Korman).

**Saturday, July 20:** Corn Exchange, Wisbech, Cambridgeshire, UK
This was one of the band's first ballroom gigs, for which they were paid £18. Bill recalled that the gig "was exciting for the sight of pictures and posters of ourselves outside as we arrived, but apart from a few enthusiastic girls at the front, the audience was dull."

**Sunday, July 21:** Ken Colyer Jazz Club (Studio 51), 10 Great Newport St., London, 4 p.m., and Crawdaddy Club, Athletic Grounds, Richmond, UK

**Monday, July 22:** Ken Colyer Jazz Club (Studio 51), 10 Great Newport St., London, UK, 8 p.m.

**Wednesday, July 24:** Hotel Dancehall, Eel Pie Island, Twickenham, UK

**Friday, July 26:** Ricky-Tick, Star & Garter Pub, Windsor, Berkshire, UK

**Saturday, July 27:** California Ballroom, Dunstable, Bedfordshire, UK, with the Mavericks and Russ Sainty and the Nu-Notes

This venue had two rooms for performances. The Stones played in the smaller secondary room and attracted only a tiny crowd at first but by their second set many people had left the larger ballroom to see what was happening in the back room. The set for this show allegedly included "The Jaguar and the Thunderbird," "I'm Movin' On," "Come On," "Walking the Dog," "High Heeled Sneakers," "Can I Get a Witness" and "You Better Move On."

**Sunday, July 28:** Ken Colyer Jazz Club (Studio 51), 10 Great Newport St., London, 4 p.m., and Crawdaddy Club, Athletic Grounds, Richmond, UK

**Monday, July 29:** Ken Colyer Jazz Club (Studio 51), 10 Great Newport St., London, UK, 8 p.m.

**Tuesday, July 30:** Ricky-Tick, Star & Garter Pub, Windsor, Berkshire, UK

This was the Stones' last appearance at the Star & Garter before the venue moved to the larger Thames Hotel. Tony Russell, future music journalist, was a young blues fanatic at the time and recalled in *Mojo* that "what struck me more than their performance was their material, which I was pleased to find was mostly covers: Chuck Berry and Bo Diddley, Slim Harpo's 'I'm a King Bee,' that sort of thing. I was greatly impressed that they not only name checked the original artist, but, at least once, the original record label. I doubt if they did that for much longer."

**Wednesday, July 31:** Hotel Dancehall, Eel Pie Island, Twickenham, UK

**Friday, August 2:** Wooden Bridge Hotel, Guildford, Surrey, UK

This was the Stones' last appearance at this venue, though not by choice. Ian Stewart recalled in *Datebook*, "We used to meet at the Wooden Bridge Hotel on the Guildford bypass, where the Stones would play on a low stage at the end of a long room with a timbered ceiling. There had been rows with the landlord because we would never turn down our amplifiers. This night we decided to get a better sound by slinging them from the beams. The landlord objected as well and we had another row. Then just by a stroke of bad luck, that very same evening a fight broke out. Like all pub fights, it grew until people were slinging punches in all directions. Naturally he blamed us and we were banned."

**Saturday, August 3:** St. Leonard's Hall, Horsham, Sussex, UK, with Peter & the Hustlers

The Stones were paid £50 for this appearance.

**Sunday, August 4:** Ken Colyer Jazz Club (Studio 51), 10 Great Newport St., London and Crawdaddy Club, Athletic Grounds, Richmond, UK

**Monday, August 5:** Botwell House, Hayes, Middlesex, UK

This venue was a popular dancehall attached to a local church.

**Tuesday, August 6:** Ricky-Tick, Thames Hotel, Windsor, Berkshire, UK

This was the Stones' first appearance at the new venue for the Ricky-Tick in the garden of the Thames Hotel. The band played on a small wooden stage a foot off the ground that could barely contain them and their equipment and gave Mick little room to maneuver. In Richard Houghton's book *You Had to Be There* a fan recalled that Mick "had to be content with his strange jigging and clapping semi-static dance."

**Wednesday, August 7:** Hotel Dancehall, Eel Pie Island, Twickenham, UK

The day after this show, the Stones recorded "Bye, Bye Johnny," "Money" and "You Better Move On" at Decca Studios. These songs eventually appeared on their first EP. The band also allegedly recorded the unreleased Coasters song "I'm a Hog for You."

**Friday, August 9:** California Ballroom, Dunstable, Bedfordshire, UK, with Russ Sainty and the Nu-Notes

**Saturday, August 10:** Plaza Dance and Social Club, Handsworth, Birmingham, and First Birthday Party Dance, Plaza Ballroom, Old Hill, Staffordshire, UK

The Stones began playing more ballrooms, which necessitated changes to the act. Bill recalled in the Go-Set, "When we went into the Ballrooms … we soon found out that you couldn't play such things as those slow Jimmy Reed blues–type numbers. You were expected to play music for them to dance to, but they stood there in front of you and gaped. So at that time, we started concentrating on much more up-tempo songs … fast rhythm things … hard rockers which seemed to work out quite well."

**Sunday, August 11:** Ken Colyer Jazz Club (Studio 51), 10 Great Newport St., London, 4 p.m., and Athletic Association Ground, 3rd National Jazz Festival, Richmond, UK, with Long John Baldry, Cyril Davies All Stars, the Velvettes, Acker Bilk, Terry Lightfoot's Jazzmen, the Freddy Randall Band and the Blue Note Jazz Band, 6:30 p.m.

Giorgio Gomelsky convinced skeptical promoters to allow the Stones to play at the prestigious Richmond Jazz Festival, though they were bottom of the bill and only received £30. But organizer Harold Pendleton later recalled,

Advertisement for the Third National Richmond Jazz Festival, at which the Stones appeared in August 1963 (collection of Ira Korman).

"The Stones were an absolute sensation and the Jazz Festival was turned upside down by this, which stunned everyone. From then on it was called the Jazz and Blues Festival."

**Monday, August 12:** Ken Colyer Jazz Club (Studio 51), 10 Great Newport St., London, UK, 8 p.m.

**Tuesday, August 13:** Town Hall, High Wycombe, Buckinghamshire, UK

**Wednesday, August 14:** Hotel Dancehall, Eel Pie Island, Twickenham, UK

**Thursday, August 15:** Dreamland Ballroom, Margate, Kent, UK, with the Barron Knights
   Playing at ballrooms meant dealing with larger crowds, not all of whom were fans of the band or their looks. Brian commented, "We were rather worried about playing these halls. We had suspicions that some of the hard cases would start taking the ... er, rise, out of our haircuts. They do a little for the first number sometimes."

**Friday, August 16:** Winter Gardens, Banbury, Oxfordshire, UK, with the Astranaughts
   Ethel Usher, proprietor of the Winter Gardens, insisted that all performers be dressed sharply. When she saw the scruffy Stones, she ordered them to go buy some new clothes. They reluctantly purchased some lilac colored shirts at a local store, but tossed them in the trash afterwards. According to a fan, as a request the Stones performed Bill Haley's "Shake, Rattle and Roll" as their last number.

**Saturday, August 17:** Memorial Hall, Chester Way, Northwich, Cheshire, UK, with Lee Curtis
   Lee Curtis may have been one of the few acts to upstage the Stones by taking a cue from James Brown. Keith recalled that Curtis "pulled an incredible scene to steal the show, where he'd do Conway Twitty's 'Only Make Believe,' and he'd faint onstage. Guys came and carried him off, singing 'Only Make Believe.' Then they'd carry him half on again.'"

**Sunday, August 18:** Ken Colyer Jazz Club (Studio 51), 10 Great Newport St., London, 4 p.m., and Crawdaddy Club, Athletic Grounds, Richmond, UK
   It's believed that the Crawdaddy show on this day, attended by a crowd of 800, is the one recorded in incomplete form on two reel-to-reel tapes sold at auction in 2004. The set list consisted of: "Route 66," "Come On," "Talkin' 'bout You," "Love Potion No. 9," "Roll Over Beethoven," "Pretty Thing," "Jaguar and the Thunderbird," "Don't Lie to Me," "Our Little Rendezvous," "Baby What You Want Me to Do," "Brown Eyed Handsome Man," "Diddley Daddy" and "Money."

**Monday, August 19:** Atlanta Ballroom, Woking, Surrey, UK

**Tuesday, August 20:** Ricky-Tick, Thames Hotel, Windsor, Berkshire, UK

**Wednesday, August 21:** Hotel Dancehall, Eel Pie Island, Twickenham, UK

**Saturday, August 24:** Il Rondo Ballroom, Leicester, UK

**Sunday, August 25:** Ken Colyer Jazz Club (Studio 51), 10 Great Newport St., London, 4 p.m., and Crawdaddy Club, Athletic Grounds, Richmond, UK

**Monday, August 26:** Ken Colyer Jazz Club (Studio 51), 10 Great Newport St., London, UK, 8 p.m.

**Tuesday, August 27:** Ricky-Tick, Thames Hotel, Windsor, Berkshire, UK

Despite Brian's absence due to illness, the band played their Tuesday spot at the Ricky-Tick anyway.

**Wednesday, August 28:** Hotel Dancehall, Eel Pie Island, Twickenham, UK

Brian again missed this show. But he was with them the next day in Manchester to tape an appearance on Granada TV's *Scene at 6:30*.

**Friday, August 30:** Oasis Club, Manchester, UK, with the Crestas

The Stones were originally scheduled to appear at the New Brighton Tower in Preston and posters advertising the gig were printed, but a fire at the venue led to the cancelation of the show. Instead, they played this club.

**Saturday, August 31:** Royal Lido Ballroom, Prestatyn, Wales, UK

The Stones played their first show outside England at this Welsh venue also played by the Beatles.

**Sunday, September 1:** Ken Colyer Jazz Club (Studio 51), 10 Great Newport St., London, 4 p.m., and Crawdaddy Club, Athletic Grounds, Richmond, UK

**Monday, September 2:** Ken Colyer Jazz Club (Studio 51), 10 Great Newport Street, London, UK, 8 p.m.

Illustrating their increasing prosperity, Bill Wyman at last traded in the homemade bass he'd been playing at gigs since he joined the band for a red Framus Star Bass Guitar.

**Tuesday, September 3:** Ricky-Tick, Thames Hotel, Windsor, Berkshire, UK

**Wednesday, September 4:** Hotel Dancehall, Eel Pie Island, Twickenham, UK

Brian had a bad reaction to prescription medicine and again became ill. He left this show in the middle and missed the next three gigs.

**Thursday, September 5:** Strand Palais, Walmer, Kent, UK, with the Paramounts, 8 p.m.

Bill disparaged the Strand Palais in *Stone Alone* as "a dump" and recalled, "The audience comprised about 350 thugs. We were paid 55 pounds and were glad to get away without any trouble—the promoter had failed to get a drinking license, which probably saved us." The Ghost Riders were advertised as openers but were replaced by the Paramounts, a band that included keyboardist Gary Brooker of future Procol Harum fame.

**Friday, September 6:** Grand Hotel Ballroom, Lowestoft, Suffolk, UK, with the Felines, 8 p.m.

Brian again missed this show, for which the Stones received £20. This was his loss, according to Bill, as the Stones received their first taste of Beatles-style hysteria from screaming girls.

**Saturday, September 7:** King's Hall, Aberystwyth, Wales, UK, with Jimmy Leach and his Organolean Quartet, 8:30 p.m.

The Stones made a tedious van journey to play their second gig in Wales. Brian remained sick in bed and the other Stones arrived late, forcing opener Jimmy Leach to play for an extra half-hour while they got ready. There was little rhyme or reason to their bookings at this time. Immediately after the low-paying gig in Wales, the Stones drove all night to get to Birmingham in time to tape an appearance on the ABC TV *Lucky Stars Summer Spin* the next day, where they were rejoined by Brian.

Poster for a canceled show on August 30, 1963 (collection of Ira Korman).

**Monday, September 9:** Ken Colyer Jazz Club (Studio 51), 10 Great Newport St., London, UK, 8 p.m.

**Tuesday, September 10:** Ricky-Tick, Thames Hotel, Windsor, Berkshire, UK

**Wednesday, September 11:** Hotel Dancehall, Eel Pie Island, Twickenham, UK

**Thursday, September 12:** Cellar Club, Kingston upon Thames, UK

This gig was memorable due to the ruthless behavior of the promoter. When the show ended and the crowd left, he told the Stones that they had five minutes to get their stuff and get out. It soon became clear that he wasn't joking and as they got into their cars he came out holding a gun.

**Friday, September 13:** Ritz Ballroom, Kings Heath, Birmingham and Plaza Ballroom, Old Hill, Staffordshire, UK, with the Eagles Group and the Atlantics

Stones fan James Hurst had become friendly with the band, after meeting them at a taping of *Thank Your Lucky Stars* in July. He attended this show and recalled in *The Birmingham Mail*, "They were probably the best covers band there was. They only stole the best. They stole covers of Chess and Stax records—Muddy Waters, Chuck Berry and some of the New Orleans stuff. There was no screaming at the Ritz—you didn't tend to get that at dance halls."

**Saturday, September 14:** California Ballroom, Dunstable, Bedfordshire, UK, with Mike and the Crestas and Roy Powell and the Offbeaters, 8 p.m.

This gig is listed on some websites as occurring on Friday, but an advertisement in the newspaper lists it as on Saturday.

**Sunday, September 15:** Great Pop Prom, Royal Albert Hall, London, UK, with the Beatles, the Brook Brothers, Billie Davis, Shane Fenton and the Fentones, Clinton Ford, the Lorne Gisbon Trio, Arthur Greenslade and the Gee-Men, Kenny Lynch, the Vernon Girls, the Viscounts and Susan Maugham, 2:15 p.m., and Crawdaddy Club, Athletic Grounds, Richmond, UK

The Stones played for the largest crowd they'd encountered up to this time at the Great Pop Prom. Three years later, Mick commented in *Flip Magazine* that performing at this concert was the biggest thrill he could recall. The Stones shared the bill with the Beatles, for the first of only two occasions. They were greatly impressed by the wild reception the Fab Four got. The 6,000 people in the audience screamed and yelled and repeatedly tried to rush the stage to touch the Beatles, who sped off in a car right after they finished their act. The Stones, however, were also well received. Bob Bedford of *Record Mirror* reported, "The Rolling Stones started off-not the easiest thing in the word to do-but after their good renderings of R&B numbers like 'Talkin' 'bout You,' 'Love Potion No. 9,' and 'Pretty Thing,' the audience went mad for the group, especially during their hit, 'Come On.' Bigger things are in store for these boys—the audience reaction was enough to show they'll soon be one of Britain's biggest vocal groups."

**Monday, September 16:** Ken Colyer Jazz Club (Studio 51), 10 Great Newport St., London, UK ☒(8 p.m. Show)

**Tuesday, September 17:** British Legion Hall, Harrow on the Hill, London, UK, with the Men of Mystery

**Wednesday, September 18:** Hotel Dancehall, Eel Pie Island, Twickenham, UK

**Thursday, September 19:** St. John's Hall, Watford, Hertfordshire, UK

**Friday, September 20:** Savoy Ballroom, Southsea, Hampshire, UK, with Rod Watts and the Rivals

The Stones received £75 for their appearance at this now-demolished seaside venue.

**Saturday, September 21:** Corn Exchange, Peterborough, Northamptonshire, UK, with the Dynatones, 8 p.m.

Beginning their long rivalry with the Beatles, the Stones were billed as "The South's Answer to Liverpool."

**Sunday, September 22:** Ken Colyer Jazz Club (Studio 51), 10 Great Newport St., London, 4 p.m., and Crawdaddy Club, Athletic Ground, Richmond, UK

This was the Stones' last gig at the Crawdaddy. So many fans turned up to see them that bouncers had to turn many away. It was the end of an era.

**Monday, September 23:** Ken Colyer Jazz Club (Studio 51), 10 Great Newport St., London, UK, 8 p.m.

Prior to the show at Studio 51, the Stones taped an appearance for the BBC show *Saturday Club* at Maida Vale. Bo Diddley was also at Maida Vale that day and the Stones backed him up on his performances of "Road Runner," "Pretty Thing" and "Hey, Bo Diddley."

**Tuesday, September 24:** Ricky-Tick, Thames Hotel, Windsor, Berkshire, UK

This was the Stones' last appearance at this venue, which they'd outgrown.

**Wednesday, September 25:** Hotel Dancehall, Eel Pie Island, Twickenham, UK

**Friday, September 27:** Teen-Beat Night '63, Floral Hall Ballroom, Morecambe, Lancashire, UK, with the Merseybeats, Dave Berry & the Cruisers and the Doodle Bugs, 8 p.m.

Aspiring promoter Mike Wilcock booked the Stones, whom he'd never heard of, for £95. To his surprise, he sold 2,000 tickets. But, though they attracted a crowd, it was not a memorable concert. Wilcock told *The Visitor*, "(the audience) were exceptionally quiet. People were just getting their own pints from the bar and not even looking at them. People weren't used to dancing to their kind of music, the American blues. As far as we were concerned they were just Cockneys coming up to the Northwest. It was the first and only time they played here though. Very soon the price went right up!"

Banner poster for the Stones concert at Floral Hall Ballroom in Morecambe on September 27, 1963 (collection of Ira Korman).

**Saturday, September 28:** Assembly Hall, Walthamstow, East London, UK, with the Skyways, 7:30 p.m.

With the growing workload, the Stones hired John "Spike" Palmer to aid Stu in the driving and setting up at gigs. This show was a fund-raiser for the Contemporary Youth Club, which the Stones agreed to play for £150, half of what they were now commanding. Unfortunately for the Youth Club, the money they saved on the Stones' fee was offset by costs to the dressing room. Fans broke all the windows in an effort to reach their idols.

**Sunday, September 29:** New Victoria Theatre, London, UK, with the Everly Brothers, Bo Diddley, Julie Grant, Mickie Most and the Flintstones, 6 and 8:30 p.m.

These two shows were the opening date of the Stones' first UK package tour promoted by Don Arden, with future Led Zeppelin impresario Peter Grant acting as stage manager. The band was paid £1,275 for 60 shows, two gigs per night. Thus each member of the Stones received about £4 per show. This was hardly a princely sum, but the experience of touring larger venues for the first time was priceless. The Stones got to meet and hang out with people they'd idolized since they were kids. Topping the bill were the legendary Everly Brothers. Their record sales had declined in the States but they remained extremely popular in the UK and had recently hit the top forty with the singles "It's Been Nice (Goodnight)" and "The Girl Sang the Blues." The Stones were even more excited about sharing a bill with co-headliner Bo Diddley, whose Checker LP *Bo Diddley* had reached number 11 on the UK charts the previous year. Among the non-headliners on the bill were Julie Grant, a UK pop singer with a version of the Drifters' "Up On the Roof" on the charts, and Mickie Most, who'd become more famous as a producer but had a minor hit with "Mister Porter." The Stones' ten-minute set consisted of: "Poison Ivy," "Fortune Teller," "Come On," and "Money." Chris Hutchins reviewed the tour opener for *New Musical Express* but dismissed the Stones. He noted "they won great appreciation ... but not from me." However, Tony Noakes of *Disc* commented, "The Rolling Stones really moved the audience with 'Poison Ivy' and 'Come On.'"

**Monday, September 30:** Rex Ballroom, Cambridge, UK, 8 p.m.

This was a solo show and not part of the tour. The contract has come to light. Brian signed it on behalf of the group on September 20. The band agreed to play for £150.

**Tuesday, October 1:** Odeon Theatre, Streatham, South London, UK, with the Everly Brothers, Bo Diddley, Julie Grant, Mickie Most and the Flintstones, 7 and 9:10 p.m.

Mick commented in *Record Mirror* that the group "after the first few nervous nights have now settled down to the different surroundings of the theatre tour quicker than I thought we would. Everybody has been very friendly and great to work with. The audiences have been great too, though sometimes a little too exuberant for the theatre management. I can quite understand their displeasure at our dressing room windows being broken by a flurry of autograph books, stones, sweets and cigarettes."

**Wednesday, October 2:** Regal Theatre, Edmonton, North London, UK, with the Everly Brothers, Bo Diddley, Julie Grant, Mickie Most and the Flintstones, 6:45 and 9 p.m.

Keith later commented on *Friday Night Videos*: "It was the most terrifying moment of my life really. Six weeks around England with Bo Diddley, the Everly Brothers were top of the bill and Little Richard. I mean we probably learnt more in those six weeks from Richard. We did our bit and then slowly got used to the size of the stage, the expansion and the audience. We didn't really look forward to playing on that stage, because

Handbill for the opening show of the Stones' first UK package tour. Headliners the Everly Brothers and Bo Diddley are pictured (collection of Ira Korman).

we figured that we were a club band. What we really looked forward to was getting our bit out of the way and watching those guys work. We'd be hanging from rafters and find the little places where you could get a good viewpoint of how they did. We'd watch everything."

**Thursday, October 3:** Odeon Theatre, Southend, Essex, UK, with the Everly Brothers, Bo Diddley, the Rattles, Julie Grant, Mickie Most and the Flintstones, 6:45 and 9 p.m.

These shows were enlivened by the presence of Ringo Starr in the audience. He came backstage to meet the performers afterwards. *The Southend Standard* reported, "We couldn't really give a verdict on the Stones, the up and coming young group with the caveman hairstyles, because we hardly understood a word they sang but the teenage girls screamed and they are the ones who put such groups on the recording map."

**Friday, October 4:** Odeon Theatre, Guildford, Surrey, UK, with the Everly Brothers, Bo Diddley, the Rattles, Julie Grant, Mickie Most and the Flintstones, 6:45 and 9 p.m.

The Stones jammed backstage prior to this gig with their idol Bo Diddley. Stu later recalled, "I'll never forget Bo's face when Brian played some of those Elmore James things."

**Saturday, October 5:** Gaumont Theatre, Watford, Hertfordshire, UK, with the Everly Brothers, Bo Diddley, the Rattles, Little Richard, Julie Grant, Mickie Most and the Flintstones, 6:15 and 8:45 p.m.

To boost ticket sales, Little Richard joined the tour. He'd only returned to rock music in 1962, after five years of recording mostly gospel material, and had recently completed a tour with the Beatles. The Stones were greatly impressed by his performing skills. Mick commented in *Record Mirror*, "I had never seen him before on the stage and I heard so much about the audience reaction that I thought there must be some slight exaggeration-but not so…! There is no single phrase to describe Richard's hold on the audience. To some it may excite, to others it may terrify. At times it reminds one of the Rock and Roll riots of early '57 and '58 with the whole theatre jumping as the audience, mainly boys, jumped up on stage and jived in the aisles."

**Sunday, October 6:** Capital Theatre, Cardiff, Wales, UK, with the Everly Brothers, Bo Diddley, the Rattles, Little Richard, Julie Grant, Mickie Most and the Flintstones, 5:45 and 8 p.m.

On their way to this gig, the Stones had a scare when their brand new Volkswagen van careened off a bridge. Luckily it landed upright. Little Richard stole the shows that night, and most nights on the tour. Mick commented, "At Cardiff on Sunday, night, we played to two packed house and Richard drove the whole audience into a complete frenzy." As a result the reviewer for the *Cardiff and Suburban News* had little to say about anyone else on the bill, but still found time to comment, "Of the groups—the Rolling Stones were five young men in need of a haircut and considerably more stage experience, while the Rattles from Germany were almost as good as the Beatles." There was no show the next day but the group recorded their next single, "I Wanna Be Your Man"/"Stoned" at De Lane Lea Studios.

**Tuesday, October 8:** Odeon Theatre, Cheltenham, Gloucestershire, UK, with the Everly Brothers, the Rattles, Bo Diddley, Little Richard, Julie Grant, Mickie Most and the Flintstones, 7 and 9:10 p.m.

The tour played in Brian's hometown for the first time, giving him the chance to shine. Bill Wyman told *Record Mirror* "almost every fan that met us wanted only to see Brian."

**Wednesday, October 9:** Gaumont Cinema, Worcester, UK, with the Everly Brothers, Bo Diddley, the Rattles, Little Richard, Julie Grant, Mickie Most and the Flintstones, 6:45 and 9 p.m.

The Stones often traveled in their own van, driven by Stu. However, they couldn't resist soaking up as much time as they could with the headliners and sometimes traveled on the bus with the rest of the acts. Mick told *Record Mirror*, "We get on like a house on fire with the Bo Diddley threesome and traveling on the coach with Bo and Jerome makes the otherwise tedious journey great fun, as they are the life and soul of the party."

**Thursday, October 10:** Gaumont Cinema, Wolverhampton, UK, with the Everly Brothers, Bo Diddley, Little Richard, Julie Grant, the Rattles, Mickie Most and the Flintstones, 6:30 and 8:45 p.m.

Robert Plant, who'd later achieve fame as lead singer of Led Zeppelin, attended this show but he recalled that he was more impressed by seeing Bo Diddley then the largely unknown Rolling Stones.

**Friday, October 11:** Gaumont Theatre, Derby, UK, with the Everly Brothers, Bo Diddley, Little Richard, the Rattles, Julie Grant, Mickie Most and the Flintstones, 6:30 and 8:45 p.m.

**Saturday, October 12:** Gaumont Theatre, Doncaster, Yorkshire, UK, with the Everly Brothers, Bo Diddley, the Rattles, Little Richard, Julie Grant, Mickie Most and the Flintstones, 6:15 and 8:30 p.m.

At the hotel after these shows, Brian wrote a letter to manager Eric Easton. He told him that he'd played an acetate copy of "I Wanna Be Your Man" to everyone on the tour and "people very impressed—many forecasts for a No. 1! … Little Richard, his manager, Bo Diddley and the Everly Brothers and entourage all say we would go really big in the States—worth thinking about."

**Sunday, October 13:** Odeon Theatre, Liverpool, UK, with the Everly Brothers, Bo Diddley, the Rattles, Little Richard, Julie Grant, Mickie Most and the Flintstones, 5:40 and 8 p.m.

**Tuesday, October 15:** City Hall, Hull, Yorkshire, UK, with Johnny Kidd and the Pirates, Heinz, Saints, Plus Four and Sammy King and the Voltairs, 6 and 8:40 p.m.

This was an extra gig and not part of the tour. Brian wrote a letter to girlfriend Linda Lawrence the next day and commented, "The girls were mad—the screaming nearly split my eardrums—we stole the show!"

**Wednesday, October 16:** Odeon Theatre, Manchester, UK, with the Everly Brothers, Bo Diddley, Little Richard, the Rattles, Julie Grant, Mickie Most and the Flintstones, 6:20 and 8:45 p.m.

Following these shows, the group traveled to Liverpool to see the Big Three perform at the legendary Cavern Club. They were excited by the enthusiastic reception they got in the Beatles' stronghold. Mick told *NME*: "We were really chuffed. We only went there to relax, but as soon as the word got around that we were there, we were swamped with requests for autographs. You know you hear some talk about the animosity which some Liverpool musicians and fans feel towards London groups, but it just isn't true."

**Thursday, October 17:** Odeon Theatre, Glasgow, Scotland, UK, with the Everly Brothers, Bo Diddley, Little Richard, the Rattles, Julie Grant, Mickie Most and the Flintstones, 6:45 and 9 p.m.

Keith told *Record Mirror* that he was excited to visit Scotland. He also commented that he'd "picked up as many hints on guitar playing as I can from Don Peake, who is the Everly Brothers' guitarist. He really is a fantastic guitarist and the great thing about him is that he is always ready to show me a few tricks."

**Friday, October 18:** Odeon Theatre, Newcastle, UK, with the Everly Brothers, Bo Diddley, Little Richard, the Rattles, Julie Grant, Mickie Most and the Flintstones, 7 and 9:30 p.m.

The Stones were only an opening act and most people paid their money to see the Everly Brothers. Reaction to the Stones in the tough city of Newcastle was mixed. One audience member recalled in *The Journal*, "Of course they were a long way from their peak. We had Mick Jagger, with his tambourine; long hair, dancing about the stage, looking very effeminate and soon the audience had had enough. The Geordies couldn't take this and booed their efforts."

**Saturday, October 19:** Gaumont Theatre, Bradford, Yorkshire, UK, with the Everly Brothers, Bo Diddley, Little Richard, the Rattles, Julie Grant, Mickie Most and the Flintstones, 6:20 and 8:45 p.m.

**Sunday, October 20:** Gaumont Theatre, Hanley, Staffordshire, UK, with the Everly Brothers, Bo Diddley, Little Richard, Julie Grant, the Rattles, Mickie Most and the Rattles, 6:15 and 8:30 p.m.

**Tuesday, October 22:** Gaumont Theatre, Sheffield, UK, with the Everly Brothers, Bo Diddley, Little Richard, the Rattles, Julie Grant, Mickie Most and the Flintstones, 6:30 and 8:45 p.m.

**Wednesday, October 23:** Odeon Theatre, Nottingham, UK, with the Everly Brothers, Bo Diddley, Little Richard, the Rattles, Julie Grant, Mickie Most and the Flintstones, 6:15 and 8:30 p.m.

According to a fan who attended the show, "The Rolling Stones wore matching dogtooth jackets and performed on a small riser which was wheeled on and off with their equipment and all of them clinging onto it."

*The Evening Post* reviewer showed little interest in the Stones, dismissing their set as "almost inaudible behind the barrage of electronic sound." But the Stones still enjoyed their stop in Nottingham, attending a party at a fan's house in Beeston after the gig. Joan West recalled in *The Nottingham Post*, "At one point they all fetched their guitars from the tour bus, sat in a circle in my lounge and began singing. I wish I had had a recorder. But no one got drunk, there wasn't enough beer!"

**Thursday, October 24:** Odeon Theatre, Birmingham, UK, with the Everly Brothers, Bo Diddley, Little Richard, the Rattles, Julie Grant, Mickie Most and the Flintstones, 6:45 and 9 p.m.

While in Birmingham, a joint birthday party was held for Bo Diddley's sister "The Duchess" and Bill Wyman. The entire touring cast attended the late night party.

**Friday, October 25:** Gaumont Theatre, Taunton, Somerset, UK, with the Everly Brothers, Bo Diddley, Little Richard, the Rattles, Julie Grant, Mickie Most and the Flintstones, 7 and 9:20 p.m.

The reviewer from the *Taunton Courier* reported, "I watched as the lesser-known performers came and went with not so much as a peep from the audience. Things livened up with the arrival of the Rolling Stones, a quintet of beatniks, who appeared bored with the orgiastic transports their music brought about."

**Saturday, October 26:** Gaumont Theatre, Bournemouth, UK, with the Everly Brothers, Bo Diddley, Little Richard, the Rattles, Julie Grant, Mickie Most and the Flintstones, 6:15 and 8:30 p.m.

**Sunday, October 27:** Gaumont Theatre, Salisbury, Wiltshire, UK, with the Everly Brothers, Bo Diddley, Little Richard, the Rattles, Julie Grant, Mickie Most and the Flintstones, 6:15 and 8:30 p.m.

Julie Grant later recalled that by this point in the tour everyone knew who the Stones were. "I would be announced and I would hear people chanting, 'We want the Stones.' And nobody wanted poor Mickie Most who was on first. They wanted the Stones."

**Tuesday, October 29:** Gaumont Theatre, Southampton, Hampshire, UK, with the Everly Brothers, Bo Diddley, Little Richard, Julie Grant, the Rattles, Mickie Most and the Flintstones, 7 and 9:30 p.m.

By this time, reviewers felt obliged to mention the Stones in their articles about the tour. The *Herts Advertiser* reported, "The Stones whipped up a storm with top rate versions of 'Memphis Tennessee' and 'Come On.'"

**Wednesday, October 30:** Odeon Theatre, St. Albans, Hertfordshire, UK, with the Everly Brothers, Bo Diddley, Little Richard, Julie Grant, the Rattles, Mickie Most and the Flintstones, 6:45 and 9 p.m.

This was the first chance for many people who had purchased the Stones first single to see them live. A new fan who attended this show recalled in the *Herts Advertiser*, "We were just intrigued to see them really and to see what they looked like, rather than what they sounded like. I remember being shocked, as they were the first people that we saw visibly with long hair."

**Thursday, October 31:** Odeon Theatre, Lewisham, London, UK, with the Everly Brothers, Bo Diddley, Little Richard, Julie Grant, the Rattles, Mickie Most and the Flintstones, 6:30 and 8:45 p.m.

Beatle George Harrison attended this show and hung out afterwards with the Stones. Due to their similar role in each other's group, he gravitated to Brian. This was the last night on the tour for the German band the Rattles.

**Friday, November 1:** Odeon Cinema, Rochester, Kent, UK, with the Everly Brothers, Bo Diddley, Little Richard, Julie Grant, Mickie Most and the Flintstones, 6:45 and 9 p.m.

The Stones' second single "I Wanna Be Your Man" was released on this day and began moving up the charts, eventually peaking at number 12.

**Saturday, November 2:** Gaumont Theatre, Ipswich, Suffolk, UK, with the Everly Brothers, Bo Diddley, Little Richard, Julie Grant, Mickie Most and the Flintstones, 6:45 and 8:55 p.m.

As the tour drew to a close, Charlie Watts told the *Record Mirror*, "This, of course, has been our first major trek around the country and our first opportunity of meeting all the people who have bought our record 'Come On' and have since written to me asking when they were going to see us. We have been knocked out by the reception we have met everywhere and can't wait to get back on the road again."

**Sunday, November 3:** Hammersmith Odeon, London, UK, with the Everly Brothers, Bo Diddley, Little Richard, Julie Grant, Mickie Most and the Flintstones, 6:30 and 8:45 p.m.

This was the last date of the Stones' first major tour. A certain J. Worley attended the show and wrote in to the *New Musical Express* to complain, "Having seen the Stones at the Odeon, Hammersmith, I can only say that their so-called R&B sounds as anemic as they look and it is deplorable that they should dare to perform with artists of the caliber of Bo Diddley and Little Richard."

**Monday, November 4:** Top Rank Ballroom, Preston, Lancashire, UK

This was the first of two shows the Stones played for NEMS Enterprises, Brian Epstein's Liverpool company. They received £145 for appearances in Preston and Liverpool. Having ditched the checked jackets, the Stones' image began to take shape. *The Preston News* reported, "While the noise they make is tremendous, the appearance is stupefying. Onstage they wear high-heel boots, tight pants, black leather waistcoats and even ties, except for Mick, who wears his shirt with collar detached. Offstage they wear a jumbled assortment of jeans, silk cardigans, camel jackets or sloppy sweaters."

**Tuesday, November 5:** Cavern Club, Liverpool, UK, with the Mastersounds

The Stones made their only concert appearance (though they'd visited it as guests on a previous trip) at the legendary club that the Beatles made famous. They were rapturously

```
         ODEON HAMMERSMITH
    6-30 | SUNDAY, NOVEMBER 3, 1963 | 8-45
              ON THE STAGE
          DON ARDEN ENTERPRISES LTD. present
                 THE DYNAMIC
              LITTLE RICHARD
                 THE FABULOUS
              EVERLY BROS.
              BO DIDDLEY
          "WITH THE DUCHESS AND JEROME"
            ROLLING STONES
                  "COME ON"
            PLUS AN ALL STAR BILL
```

**Handbill for the closing show of the Stones' first UK package tour (collection of Ira Korman).**

received. Keith, however, was unimpressed. He told Stanley Booth, "It was like playing a Turkish bath, all stone, had a terrible sound. You can't imagine what a myth was built around it."

**Wednesday, November 6:** Queen's Hall, Leeds, UK

**Friday, November 8:** Club A Go-Go, Newcastle-upon-Tyne, UK

The Stones performed at this small club, made famous as the stomping grounds of Eric Burdon and the Animals.

**Saturday, November 9:** Club A Go-Go, Whitley Bay, North Tyneside, UK

**Sunday, November 10:** Sunday Star Club, Town Tall, Crewe, Cheshire, UK, with Frankenstein and the Monsters and the Crestas, 7:30 p.m.

The Stones were paid £210 for their appearance by promoter John Edgley. Asked about this show many years later by a fan, Bill commented, "We arrived pretty late. I blew my bass amp again and also broke a string. We never had spare amps or guitars then so I played the rest of the set with three strings! We had a terrible show and a bad audience."

**Monday, November 11:** Pavilion Ballroom, Bath, Somerset, UK, with the Colin Anthony Combo

**Tuesday, November 12:** Town Hall, High Wycombe, Buckinghamshire, UK

**Wednesday, November 13:** City Hall, Sheffield, UK, with the Big Three, Wayne Fontana and the Mindbenders, Karen Young, the Sheffields, Johnny Tempest and the Cadillacs, Vance Arnold and the Avengers, the 4 Plus 1, and the Vantennas

Also on the bill at this show were Vance Arnold and the Avengers. Vance was in fact Joe Cocker, who'd go on to a successful singing career. Following the show, the band returned to London. On November 14 they held a session at De Lane Lea Studios to record "Money," "Poison Ivy" and "Talkin' 'Bout You."

**Friday, November 15:** Co-Op Ballroom, Nuneaton, Warwickshire, UK, with the Liverbirds, two shows

The afternoon show was a "junior session" and attracted a large number of children, who threw cream cakes at the band. Charlie, rooted to his kit, was covered in cake by the end of the gig.

**Saturday, November 16:** Matrix Ballroom, Coventry, Warwickshire, UK

On November 17 the Stones were in Birmingham to mime to "I Wanna Be Your Man" on the ABC TV show *Thank Your Lucky Stars*.

**Tuesday, November 19:** Gaumont Ballroom, Kilburn, London, UK

A near-riot broke out after this gig and the Stones raced towards their dressing room to avoid being mobbed. Charlie was caught up in the crowd and pulled to the ground. By the time bouncers freed him, he'd lost his vest and shirt. *The Gaumont Times* commented, "The Stones drew even a bigger crowd than the Beatles here. Is this an omen that they are soon to be crushed by the Stones?"

**Wednesday, November 20:** Chiswick Polytechnic Dance, Athletic Club, Richmond, UK

**Thursday, November 21:** McIlroys Ballroom, Swindon, Wiltshire, UK, with Frankie Roy and the Soundcasters

This venue was a department store that hosted gigs on the second floor. Only a few hundred people turned out to see the Stones, most of them students from the nearby college. *The Evening Advertiser* was chiefly impressed by Brian, who showed up late for the gig: "His command of the style is authoritative, and he managed to achieve a mellow, amplified sound where most West Country 'rock' groups only muster a harsh twang."

**Friday, November 22:** Greenwich Town Hall, London, UK

Prior to this show the band performed "I Wanna Be Your Man" on *Ready Steady Go!* at Kingsway TV Studios. While having a drink at the bar they learned that President Kennedy had been killed. Nevertheless, the show went on. Chris Welch of *The Bexleyheath & Welling Observer* noted that at one point during the concert "somebody shouted during a brilliant display of originality: 'Git yer 'air cut.' Replied Mick Jagger (harmonica, vocals): 'What? And look like you?'" It appears that David Jones (the future David Bowie) was in the audience as he recalled this exact incident during an interview on the BBC TV show *Parkinson* in 2004. He commented that when he heard Jagger's reply he knew that he wanted to be a rock star.

**Saturday, November 23:** Swimming Baths, Leyton, East London, UK, with the Skyways and Chez Don Club, Dalston, London, UK

The gig in Leyton took place on a temporary stage placed on top of a swimming pool. A fan recalled in *The Enfield Independent,* "Because it was a full size swimming pool they would lay a temporary wooden floor over the top, which would bounce up and down as the kids performed their moves… (The Stones) performed all the songs from their first album and I remember being amazed how good they were—and how loud. It was incredible."

**Sunday, November 24:** Ken Colyer Jazz Club (Studio 51), 10 Great Newport St., London and Majestic Ballroom, Luton, Bedfordshire, UK

The band continued to play weekly sessions at the Jazz Club but the legions of screaming girls following them around made it clear that their club days were numbered. Brian commented to *Record Mirror*, "It's all very nice to know you're appreciated. But it's also rather frightening. And sometimes we worry quite a lot about this sort of thing—of course when any girls faint in our audience we see them after to make sure everything is ok with them."

**Monday, November 25:** Parr Hall, Warrington, Cheshire, UK

The Stones sold out this 1,100-capacity venue.

**Tuesday, November 26:** Stamford Hall, Altrincham, Cheshire, UK

**Wednesday, November 27:** Empress Ballroom, Wigan, Greater Manchester, UK, with the Fabulous Beat Boys and the Cheetahs, 7:30 p.m.

A fan who attended this show recalled, on Lankybeat.com, the moment the Stones took the stage: "Five bobbing heads of long hair was the first thing I saw. Then it was a new style of rock 'n' roll mayhem for the next hour, which became the Stones classic trademark performance. I came away exhilarated, mesmerized and totally exhausted."

**Thursday, November 28:** Memorial Hall, Northwich, Cheshire, UK

**Friday, November 29:** The Baths, Urmston, Lancashire, UK, with Herman's Hermits

The Stones played to a very small but appreciative crowd.

**Saturday, November 30:** King's Hall, Stoke-on-Trent, Staffordshire, UK

**Sunday, December 1:** Oasis Club, Manchester, UK, with the Ko-dels

The Stones made their second appearance at this popular coffee house/dance club. Ed Parkinson of opening band the Ko-dels recalled that when the Stones started playing "the atmosphere was fantastic. Several girls were in a state of hysteria and fainted, they were taken to our dressing room to recover. After the show, when all the artists were clearing up, Jagger came over and asked if we wanted his autograph. We felt a bit confused and said 'no, not really' because at the time we though we were going to be bigger than the Stones!"

**Monday, December 2:** Assembly Rooms, Tamworth, Staffordshire, UK, with the Three Spirits

The *Tamworth Herald* reported that when the Stones took the stage, "The Assembly Rooms erupted to a crescendo of female screams. Five lads with a pulsating beat streaming from their amps. Lads with more hair hanging over their ears and over their shoulders than the Beatles ever had, produced the biggest audience appeal that there has ever been here. When you consider the talent that has stepped onto this stage, the Beatles, the Big Three … you have an idea of the impact made by the Stones."

**Tuesday, December 3:** Floral Hall, Southport, Lancashire, UK, with the Teenbeats

**Wednesday, December 4:** The Baths, Doncaster, Yorkshire, UK

**Thursday, December 5:** Gaumont Theatre, Worcester, UK, with Gerry & the Pacemakers, the Original Checkmates, Peter Jay and the Jaywalkers and Pete McClaine and the Clan, two shows

The Stones began a short tour with Liverpool band Gerry and the Pacemakers, who had a number one hit with "You'll Never Walk Alone."

**Friday, December 6:** Odeon Theatre, Romford, Essex, UK, with Gerry and the Pacemakers, the Overlanders, the Original Checkmates and Pete McClaine and the Clan, 6:15 and 8:45 p.m.

**Saturday, December 7:** Fairfield Hall, Croydon, South London, UK, with Gerry and the Pacemakers, Peter Jay and the Jaywalkers, the Original Checkmates and Pete McClaine and the Clan, 6:15 and 8:45 p.m.

Such was the popularity of the Stones in Croydon that they were forced to perform an unscheduled two-song encore to appease the crowd. Gerry and the Pacemakers came onstage after intermission to find a half-empty hall, as Stones fans exited without seeing the Liverpool band.

**Sunday, December 8:** Olympia Ballroom, Reading, Berkshire, UK, 3 p.m., and Gaumont Theatre, Watford, Hertfordshire, UK, with Gerry and the Pacemakers, the Searchers, the Original Checkmates and Pete McClaine and the Clan, two shows

**Wednesday, December 11:** King's And Queen's Hall, Bradford, Yorkshire, UK, with Mike Sagar and the Tornados and the Art Tilburn All-Stars, 8 p.m.

**Thursday, December 12:** Locarno Ballroom, Liverpool, UK

**Friday, December 13:** Hillside Ballroom, Hereford, UK, with the Valiants, 9 p.m.

Amongst the audience at this gig was Stan Tippins, who later sang with Mott the Hoople. He recalled on the BBC, "It was only half full, most people didn't know who they were. (But) they were fantastic. They were unbelievable. The movements of Jagger astonished me. He was such a great mover onstage."

**Saturday, December 14:** Baths Hall, Epsom, Surrey, UK, with the Presidents, 8 p.m.

Promoter Brian Howard booked the group to play some months before this show

Handbill for the Stones concert with Gerry and the Pacemakers in Romford (collection of Ira Korman).

and was therefore able to get the Stones for only £60, far less than they could by then command.

**Sunday, December 15:** Civic Hall, Guildford, Surrey, UK, with Georgie Fame and the Blue Flames, the Yardbirds, Graham Bond Quartet and Carter Lewis and the Southerners, 8 p.m.

The Stones shared the bill with a number of up and coming bands, including Giorgio Gomelsky's new discovery, the Yardbirds, featuring Eric Clapton. Coincidentally, Clapton's future partners in Cream, Jack Bruce and Ginger Baker, were members of the Graham Bond Quartet, also on the bill.

**Tuesday, December 17:** Town Hall, High Wycombe, Buckinghamshire, UK, with the Soundtrekkers, 7:30 p.m.

This show was advertised as a Tuesday Club Christmas Dance and promised ticket buyers the chance to take part in "the selection of Miss High Wycombe."

**Wednesday, December 18:** St. Nicholas Market Corn Exchange, Bristol, UK

**Thursday, December 19:** St. Michael's Hall, Sydenham, Greater London, UK, with Rolf Harris and Dusty Springfield

This was not a proper gig. The Stones were hired by BBC TV to act as a band for a dramatic show called *Cops And Robbers* hosted by Rolf Harris. The pilot never aired and the footage is apparently lost, but the Stones received £52 for their services.

**Friday, December 20:** Lido Ballroom, Winchester, Hampshire, UK, with the Strangers, 8 p.m.

About 3,000 people attended this show, for which the Stones received £200. According to Bill Wyman, "It was a wild crowd and we had a really great show." However, the band's elation was deflated when they were refused service at the ballroom bar for having long hair.

**Saturday, December 21:** Kayser Bondor Ballroom, Baldock, Hertfordshire, UK

**Sunday, December 22:** St. Mary's Hall, Putney, SW London, UK, with the Detours

The opening band was the Detours, who'd soon be rechristened the Who. Guitarist Pete Townshend was a big Stones fan. He even volunteered to induct them into the Rock and Roll Hall of Fame in 1989. In his speech that night he noted that Brian had been very important to him. He'd befriended him at this early point in his career and gave him encouragement.

**Tuesday, December 24:** X-mas Eve Dance, Town Hall, Leek, Staffordshire, UK, with the Escorts

Mick and Andrew were two hours late arriving at this gig because of heavy snow and the band played only one of their two scheduled sets.

**Thursday, December 26:** Selby's Restaurant, Hanover Street, London

**Friday, December 27:** Town Hall, Reading, Berkshire, UK

The Stones were paid £200 by promoter Tito Burns, minus his 5 percent commission for booking the gig. Prior to their evening show the Stones mimed to "I Wanna Be Your Man" on *Ready Steady Go!*

**Saturday, December 28:** All Night Rave, Club Noreik, Tottenham, London, UK, midnight

**Monday, December 30:** Ken Colyer Jazz Club, Studio 51, 10 Great Newport St., London, UK, with Jimmy Powell and the Five Dimensions

This was the Stones' final appearance at this venue. The opening band featured a young Rod Stewart on vocals.

**Tuesday, December 31:** Drill Hall, Lincoln, UK

Following this New Year's Eve gig, Bill retired early to his room. Mick, Keith and Brian decided to play a prank on him and dressed up Brian in a sheet to make him look like a ghost. They turned out the hall lights and knocked on his door but the imperturbable bassist took one look and simply said, "Go to bed Brian and stop messing about!" A crestfallen Brian said, "You bastard! It's taken us an hour to get this together."

# Chapter 3

# 1964

The Rolling Stones became stars in 1964. They were true revolutionaries. They looked and sounded like no other group in Britain. There was something rebellious and dangerous about them, which captured the essence of rock 'n' roll. The year began with the release of the Stones' first EP, which consisted of a fabulous version of Chuck Berry's "Bye Bye Johnny," the Coasters' "Poison Ivy" (the Stones' second attempt at this number), Arthur Alexander's ballad "You Better Move On" and Barret Strong's "Money." It was a testament to the Stones growing popularity in Britain that the EP raced to the top of the charts. The group were elated by their success but had little time to soak it in.

Coinciding with the EP's release, the Stones hit the road for their first headlining tour of Britain, which lasted from January 6 to 27. Also on the bill were the Ronettes, who'd become huge stars in America, with songs like "Be My Baby." The Stones enjoyed being on tour with the girl group. Mick commented to *NME*, "They just stopped us in our tracks! We were just knocked out-by their looks, their sense of humor, everything." Keith was also impressed: "They couldn't help but draw big audiences. They do such a tremendous act. It's not just singing—they twist around and shake like mad."

When the tour ended in February, the Stones released their third UK single, a cover of Buddy Holly's "Not Fade Away." The song, recorded earlier in the month at Regent Sound, featured help from special guests. Keith explained to *NME*, "We had been working on the number for about five minutes when two of the Hollies turned up, then Gene Pitney arrived. Phil Spector was already there, so everything came to a halt while everyone started talking. When we got around to recording again, Phil had grabbed hold of Mick's maracas and was shaking the daylights out of them. He really had a ball and it's him you hear on the disc." The song, propelled along by Brian's manic harmonica playing and Keith's inspired guitar riffs, became the band's biggest hit so far, reaching number 3 on the UK charts.

By this time, Andrew had hit upon the brilliant idea of positioning the Stones as the "Anti-Beatles." As he commented to reporter Keith Altham, "There is always one black sheep in the pop world, someone that the Establishment can knock. In Cliff Richard's day it was Billy Fury. It's the Stones who now fill this gap." He encouraged the band to grow their hair longer than other acts and act in a loutish way towards the establishment. He also planted stories in the press to aid the bad boy image. An article in the March 7, 1964, *Melody Maker* had Mick pondering the question "Why do parents hate us?" while the March 14 issue featured a story by Ray Coleman with the famous title (dreamed up by Andrew) "Would You Let Your Sister Go with a Rolling Stone?" The

SIDE 1
1. ROUTE 66
2. I JUST WANNA MAKE LOVE TO YOU
3. HONEST I DO
4. MONA
5. NOW I'VE GOT A WITNESS
6. LITTLE BY LITTLE

SIDE 2
1. KING BEE
2. CAROL
3. TELL ME
4. CAN I GET A WITNESS
5. YOU CAN MAKE IT IF YOU TRY
6. WALKIN' THE DOG

**A BOMBSHELL FOR THE L.P. CHARTS!**

DECCA — LK 4605 (MONO ONLY)

Advertisement for the Stones' first UK album in April 1964 (collection of Ira Korman).

group went along with the charade, though Brian, especially, came to resent accusations that the Stones were unclean and didn't wash their hair. The "bad" publicity certainly didn't hurt the band.

In April the Stones released their first LP, *The Rolling Stones*, which made it to number one on the UK charts. It contained many of the covers the band had been playing live, including Rufus Thomas' "Walking the Dog," Bo Diddley's "Mona" (with Brian's great guitar work), Slim Harpo's "I'm a King Bee" and Muddy Waters "I Just Want to Make Love to You." It was a thrilling debut that illustrated why the Stones attracted such a fervent following in the clubs. It also showcased their musicianship on cuts like "Now I've Got a Witness" and "Little by Little" and hinted at the more pop oriented direction the band would soon take with a cover of Marvin Gaye's soul classic "Can I Get a Witness." Ten years later, Keith commented to Nick Kent, "I still listen to that album, y'know. The enthusiasm there.... We had all those numbers we'd been playing for ages and at that point they were just ready to be got down in the studio. A first album can be incredible. All that energy ... unbelievable! It's almost sad in a way, because you know it can only be a once ever experience."

The album was also notable for including the dramatic ballad "Tell Me," the first Jagger-Richards original released by the Stones. Andrew had been pushing Mick and Keith to try writing songs since late 1963. Their first efforts were awful (many can be heard on the 1975 Decca revenge compilation *Metamorphosis*), but Andrew forced them to keep at it. Keith later commented, "One thing I can never thank Andrew Oldham enough for ... was that he turned Mick and me into songwriters. It would never have occurred to me to try unless he had forced it on us, brutally speaking. He'd say 'Look at the other boys, they're writing their own songs.'"

But, the Jagger/Richard partnership shifted power in the band away from Brian Jones. Although he wrote some music, Brian lacked encouragement to develop them into songs. As Keith recalled on BBC Radio, "There's a lot of musicians in the same position/situation as Brian. They're very good musicians and they can write, but it's a personality thing. They never get over that barrier of one actually putting their ideas together into one song and presenting it to everybody else to play. Saying, 'Right, it goes like this.' They'll write a piece of music, than they'll write another little bit, than they'll write another. They're all great little bits but they never actually put them together. And on top of that Brian was always in a way shyer of presenting any of his creations to us." Oldham made no secret of his lack of chemistry with Brian and pushed Mick and Keith to the fore. As a result, Brian became more peripheral to the band's creative success and increasingly frustrated as time went on. However, in 1964 this problem was just developing.

The Stones were still on an upward climb. By May they'd conquered Britain and were ready to head to America, where a British music invasion, spearheaded by the Beatles, was under way. Unfortunately, the Stones' first tour was hastily arranged and poorly planned by Eric Easton, who was increasingly out of his depth as their fame grew. The band did not have a hit record in the States and were virtually unknown outside of major cities on the East and West Coasts. The June tour saw them playing to large and excited crowds in New York and California but to half-empty halls in Nebraska and Texas. The Stones also faced criticism and hostility from members of the older generation for their "unkempt" appearance. Middle America didn't know what to make of them. A Texan whom Mick encountered told him that if his son looked like him, he'd hide him in a

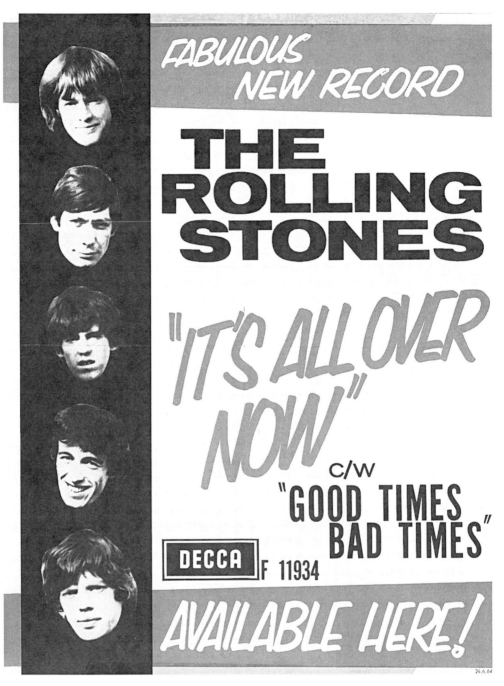

**Advertisement for the Stones' UK single "It's All Over Now," released on June 26, 1964 (collection of Ira Korman).**

cellar. The band would long remember singer Dean Martin's derisive remarks about them when they appeared on the ABC TV show *Hollywood Palace* to sing "I Just Want to Make Love to You." After they left the stage, Martin looked at the camera and said sarcastically "The Rolling Stones, aren't they great?" while rolling his eyes.

The highlight of the trip for the Stones was undoubtedly recording at Chess Studios in Chicago, where musical idols like Chuck Berry had made their famous records. To add to the excitement, Jack Hutton reported in *Melody Maker* that songwriter Willie Dixon stopped by to say hello and "Muddy Waters arrived in time to help the boys carry their guitars upstairs." (Keith has repeatedly described the group walking in to Chess to see Muddy Waters ignominiously painting the ceiling, an anecdote denied by others present.) Hutton also noted that Chuck Berry dropped by while the band was recording one of his tunes and commented "Swing on, gentlemen, you are sounding well, if I may say so." Mick later commented to writer Roy Carr, "It was the first studio we felt really at ease in. Everything was good about Chess, especially the engineer Ron Malo." One song the band recorded at Chess was "It's All Over Now," a minor hit by the Valentinos that disc jockey Murry the K had played for them. The song was released in Britain on June 26 and gave the Stones their first UK number one on the *Discs Weekly* chart.

The States took longer to succumb, but things had definitely changed by the time of the Stones second visit in October. Though the Stones were still not household names, their popularity had increased tremendously. As Mick commented to Ray Coleman of *Melody Maker*, "The first time we went, it was really like being a new group trying to break through. This time, it was like having the popularity we had when our first EP came out [in England]." On their second visit, the Stones benefited from a strong single, "Time Is on My Side," on the U.S. charts (it reached number 6) and better pre-tour planning. Oldham and Easton secured the Stones a spot on the influential CBS TV show *Ed Sullivan Show*, which had already catapulted Elvis and the Beatles to national fame. They also booked them at major venues across the country. By the time the Stones left for England in November, America had been conquered.

The Stones ended the year with one more UK number one, a cover of Howlin' Wolf's "Little Red Rooster." A straight-ahead blues with fantastic slide guitar from Brian, it was in some sense a goodbye to all that. The Stones had begun as a blues band but by late 1964 their music had embraced pop and soul to form a new exciting sound all their own. After a year of honing their songwriting craft, Jagger and Richards were increasingly confident in their abilities and 1965 would see the Stones focus more on original material. Indeed, they would not release a cover song as a single again until the 1980s.

## Concerts

**Friday, January 3:** Glenlyn Ballroom, Forest Hill, London, UK, with the Detours

On New Year's Day, the Stones had taped an appearance on *Top of the Pops* in Manchester. They spent part of this day and the next at Regent Sound recording songs for their first album, including "Carol," "Mona," "Route 66," "Walking the Dog," and "You Can Make It If You Try."

**Saturday, January 4:** Town Hall, Oxford, UK, with the Vibratones

**Sunday, January 5:** Olympia Ballroom, Reading, Berkshire, UK, 3 p.m.

**Monday, January 6:** Granada Theatre, Harrow, London, UK, with the Ronettes, Marty Wilde and the Wildcats, Swinging Blue Jeans, the Cheynes, Dave Berry and the Cruisers and Bern Elliot and the Fenmen, two shows

This was the first date of "Group Scene 1964," a three-week tour with the Ronettes promoted by the George Cooper Organization. For the first time, the Stones were top of the bill, receiving £125 a night. Other acts included Marty Wilde, a major British rocker in the late '50s; the Swinging Blue Jeans, a Liverpool band that had hits with "It's Too Late Now" and "Hippy, Hippy Shake"; and Dave Berry and the Cruisers, who were on the charts with a cover of Chuck Berry's "Memphis." Andy Gray of *NME* reported that the Stones, "tore into their act with 'Girls' and followed with 'Come On'.... Lead singer Mick Jagger whips out a harmonica occasionally and brews up more excitement, while the three guitars and drums throb away at the back. 'Hey Mona' was another R&B compeller before a quieter 'You Better Move On,' very appealingly sung by Brian. Back to the torrid stuff for the last two numbers—'Roll Over Beethoven' and 'I Wanna Be Your Man' taking the act to encore applause."

**Tuesday, January 7:** Adelphi Theatre, Slough, Berkshire, UK, with the Ronettes, Marty Wilde and the Wildcats, Swinging Blue Jeans, the Cheynes, Dave Berry and the Cruisers and Bern Elliot and the Fenmen, two shows

Philip Norman reported in his biography of Mick that the Stones ended up eating at Heathrow Airport after this show, because it was the only restaurant still open. Some rowdy Americans allegedly insulted the group and when Mick confronted them he received a punch in the face.

**Wednesday, January 8:** Granada Theatre, Maidstone, Kent, UK, with the Ronettes, Marty Wilde and the Wildcats, Swinging Blue Jeans, the Cheynes, Dave Berry and the Cruisers and Bern Elliot and the Fenmen, two shows

**Thursday, January 9:** Granada Theatre, Kettering, Northamptonshire, UK, with the Ronettes, Marty Wilde and the Wildcats, Swinging Blue Jeans, the Cheynes, Dave Berry and the Cruisers and Bern Elliot and the Fenmen, two shows

**Friday, January 10:** Granada Theatre, Walthamstow, London, UK, with the Ronettes, Marty Wilde and the Wildcats, Swinging Blue Jeans, the Cheynes, Dave Berry and the Cruisers and Bern Elliot and the Fenmen, 7 and 9 p.m.

Prior to these gigs the Stones recorded three songs at Regent Sound: "Honest I Do," "I'm a King Bee" and an early version of "Not Fade Away."

**Saturday, January 11:** The Baths, Epsom, Surrey, with Patrick Dane and the Quiet Five

This was an extra gig and not part of the tour. The Stones played on temporary maple flooring installed over the 100-foot-long swimming pool.

**Sunday, January 12:** Granada Theatre, Tooting, London, UK, with the Ronettes, Marty Wilde and the Wildcats, Swinging Blue Jeans, the Cheynes, Dave Berry and the Cruisers, Johnny Kidd and the Pirates and Bern Elliot and the Fenmen, 6 and 8:30 p.m.

**Monday, January 13:** Barrowlands Ballroom, Glasgow, Scotland, UK

The Stones traveled to Scotland for a one-off gig. Brian told *NME*, "It was a fantastic scene. They all went raving mad, there were several hundred people chanting all the time. We played about three numbers and had to be taken off. It was terrific."

**Tuesday, January 14:** Granada Theatre, Mansfield, Nottinghamshire, UK, with the Ronettes, Marty Wilde and the Wildcats, Swinging Blue Jeans, the Cheynes, Dave Berry and the Cruisers and Bern Elliot and the Fenmen, two shows

A fan who attended this show reported that the Stones' set consisted of: "Come On," "Mona," "You Better Move On," "Roll Over Beethoven" and "I Wanna Be Your Man."

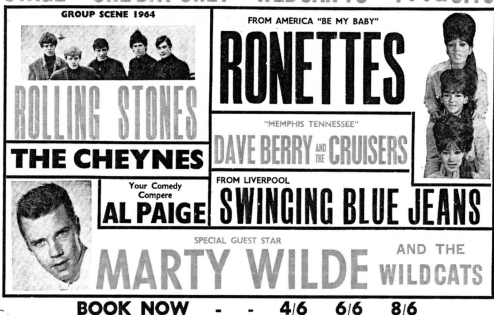

Handbill for the Stones' second UK package tour, on which they were billed with the Ronettes (collection of Ira Korman).

**Wednesday, January 15:** Granada Theatre, Bedford, UK, with the Ronettes, Marty Wilde and the Wildcats, Swinging Blue Jeans, the Cheynes, Dave Berry and the Cruisers and Bern Elliot and the Fenmen, 7 and 9:10 p.m.

**Thursday, January 16:** McIlroys Ballroom, Swindon, Wiltshire, UK, with the Hummelflugs, 8 p.m.

This was another extra gig. *The Swindon Echo* reported, "It was the biggest night in teenage entertainment of the winter—the visit of London rhythm-and-blues stars The Rolling Stones…. Dancing was forgotten when the longhaired Stones filed out on stage. A false start, a change of equipment and the group were off to a galaxy of screams. Their chief assets—a driving rhythm and the extraordinary haircuts that make The Beatles' look like short-back-and-sides."

**Friday, January 17:** City Hall, Salisbury, Wiltshire, UK, with Johnny Carr and the Cadillacs

This was another extra gig. The set: "Come On," "I Wanna Be Your Man," "Talkin' 'bout You," "Poison Ivy," "Fortune Teller," "Pretty Thing," "Love Potion No. 9," "Route 66," "Roll Over Beethoven," "Road Runner," and "Memphis."

**Saturday, January 18:** Happy Ballroom, Hastings Pier, Hastings, Sussex, UK, with the Four Aces
   This gig was not part of the tour.

**Sunday, January 19:** Coventry Theatre, Coventry, Warwickshire, UK, with the Ronettes, Patrick Dane and the Quiet Five, Freddy and the Dreamers and the Barron Knights, two shows

**Monday, January 20:** Granada Theatre, Woolwich, SE London, UK, with the Ronettes, Marty Wilde and the Wildcats, Swinging Blue Jeans, the Cheynes, Dave Berry and the Cruisers, Johnny Kidd and the Pirates and Bern Elliot and the Fenmen, two shows

**Tuesday, January 21:** Granada Theatre, Aylesbury, Buckinghamshire, UK, with the Ronettes, Marty Wilde and the Wildcats, Swinging Blue Jeans, the Cheynes, Dave Berry and the Cruisers, Heinz, and Bern Elliot and the Fenmen, two shows
   These shows were played without Brian. Keith Altham reported in *Fabulous Magazine* that the roads were shrouded in fog and Brian, driving in his own car, lost his way. The Ronettes nearly missed the first show as well, arriving five minutes before the end of the concert.

**Wednesday, January 22:** Granada Theatre, Shrewsbury, Shropshire, UK, with the Ronettes, Marty Wilde and the Wildcats, Swinging Blue Jeans, the Cheynes, Dave Berry and the Cruisers, 6:15 and 8:30 p.m.

**Thursday, January 23:** South Pier, Lowestoft, Suffolk, UK, with Johnny and the Blue Rockets, 8 p.m.
   The appearance in Lowestoft was another non-tour gig.

**Friday, January 24:** Wimbledon Palais, London, UK
   Over 3,000 fans attended this gig. Earlier in the day the Stones taped an appearance on the BBC Radio show *Go Man Go* at Maida Vale.

**Saturday, January 25:** California Ballroom, Dunstable, Bedfordshire, UK
   This was another extracurricular gig.

**Sunday, January 26:** De Montfort Hall, Leicester, UK, with the Ronettes, Marty Wilde and the Wildcats, Swinging Blue Jeans, the Cheynes, Dave Berry and the Cruisers and Bern Elliot and the Fenmen, two shows

**Monday, January 27:** Colston Hall, Bristol, UK, with the Ronettes, Marty Wilde and the Wildcats, Swinging Blue Jeans, the Cheynes, Dave Berry and the Cruisers and Bern Elliot and the Fenmen, two shows
   This was the last date of the tour. On January 28 and 29 the Stones recorded their next single "Not Fade Away" at Regent Sound. On January 29 they also taped *Top of the Pops* in Manchester.

**Friday, January 31:** Public Hall, Preston, Lancashire, UK

**Saturday, February 1:** "A Night with the Stars," Royal Albert Hall, London, UK, with Brian Poole and the Tremeloes, Dusty Springfield, the Heartbeats, the Jet Blacks, the Original Checkmates, the Seekers, the Swinging Blue Jeans, Terry Judge and the Barristers

**Sunday, February 2:** Haverstock Hill Country Club, Hampstead, UK

On February 3 the Stones taped an appearance for BBC Radio show *Saturday Club* at the Playhouse Theatre. On February 4 they recorded at Regent Sound with Phil Spector and Gene Pitney. Songs recorded included "Can I Get a Witness," "Little by Little," and "Now I've Got a Witness."

**Wednesday, February 5:** Baths, Willenhall, Staffordshire, UK, with Keith Powell and the Valets (7:30 p.m.)

The day after this show, the Stones recorded a jingle for Kellogg's Rice Krispies at Pye Studios. It aired on ITV in early 1964. On February 7 they were at Elstree Studios to tape an appearance on the ATV *Arthur Haynes Show*.

**Saturday, February 8:** Regal Theatre, Edmonton, North London, UK, with John Leyton, Mike Berry & The Innocents, Swinging Blue Jeans, Mike Sarne, Jet Harris, Billie Davis, Don Spencer, Billy Boyle, the Dowlands, and the Le Roys, two shows, and Club Noreik, Tottenham, London, midnight

The Stones began their third British package tour, dubbed "All Stars 64," for which they were paid £142 a show. Top of the bill was John Leyton, who'd scored a UK number one in 1961 with "Johnny Remember Me." The bill also included Mike Berry, who had chart success with "Tribute to Buddy Holly" and "Don't You Think It's Time," and Jet Harris, who had scored a number one the previous year with "Diamonds." The Stones' increasing popularity was in evidence on the first date in Edmonton. Graeme Andrews reported in *NME*: "Welcomed by a tremendous barrage from boys and girls alike, the Stones opened with 'Talking 'bout You' but it was almost lost in the noise from the fans, who quieted down for Mick Jagger's harmonica break in 'Road Runner,' which followed. The screams did not let up for the slower 'You Better Move On,' or 'I Wanna Be Your Man,' with which the caveman-like quintet ended."

**Sunday, February 9:** De Montfort Hall, Leicester, UK, with John Leyton, Mike Berry & the Innocents, Swinging Blue Jeans, Mike Sarne, Jet Harris, Billie Davis, Don Spencer, Billy Boyle and the Le Roy

The set: "Talkin' 'bout You," "Road Runner," "Come On," "Roll Over Beethoven," "Walking the Dog," "You Better Move On," and "I Wanna Be Your Man."

**Monday, February 10:** Odeon Theatre, Cheltenham, Gloucestershire, UK, with John Leyton, Mike Berry & the Innocents, Swinging Blue Jeans, Mike Sarne, Jet Harris, Billie Davis, Don Spencer, Billy Boyle and the Le Roys, 6:30 and 8:45 p.m.

**Tuesday, February 11:** Granada Theatre, Rugby, Warwickshire, UK, with John Leyton, Mike Berry & the Innocents, Swinging Blue Jeans, Mike Sarne, Jet Harris, Billie Davis, Don Spencer, Billy Boyle and the Le Roys, 6:20 and 8:30 p.m.

**Wednesday, February 12:** Odeon Theatre, Guildford, Surrey, UK, with John Leyton and the Le Roys, Mike Berry & the Innocents, Swinging Blue Jeans, Mike Sarne, Jet Harris, Billie Davis, Don Spencer, Billy Boyle and the Le Roys, 6 and 8:15 p.m.

Talking to Ray Coleman of *Melody Maker* about the tour, Mick commented: "One thing I find hard about touring the country is that it's hard to find somewhere to eat. Last night, someone suggested we went to a nightclub and that was all right, but usually we wind up having Chinese chop suey—not because we like Chinese food but because the English stuff is so bad."

**Thursday, February 13:** Granada Theatre, Kingston upon Thames, UK, with John Leyton, Mike Berry & the Innocents, Swinging Blue Jeans, Mike Sarne, Jet Harris, Billie Davis, Don Spencer, Billy Boyle, and the Le Roys, 7 and 9:10 p.m.

Prior to this gig, the band recorded the early Jagger-Richards compositions "Some Things Just Stick in Your Mind" and "Try a Little Harder" at Regent Sound.

**Friday, February 14:** Gaumont Theatre, Watford, Hertfordshire, UK, with John Leyton, Mike Berry & the Innocents, Swinging Blue Jeans, Mike Sarne, Jet Harris, Billie Davis, Don Spencer, Billy Boyle, and the Le Roys, 6:15 and 9 p.m.

Prior to these shows, the Stones taped *Ready Steady Go!*

**Saturday, February 15:** Odeon Cinema, Rochester, Kent, UK, with John Leyton, Mike Berry & the Innocents, Swinging Blue Jeans, Mike Sarne, Jet Harris, Billie Davis, Don Spencer, Billy Boyle, the Dowlands, and the Le Roys, two shows

**Sunday, February 16:** The Guildhall, Portsmouth, UK, with John Leyton, Mike Berry & the Innocents, Swinging Blue Jeans, Mike Sarne, Jet Harris, Billie Davis, Don Spencer, Billy Boyle, and The Le Roys, 5:40 and 8 p.m.

**Monday, February 17:** Granada Theatre, Greenford, West London, UK, with John Leyton, Mike Berry & the Innocents, Swinging Blue Jeans, Mike Sarne, Jet Harris, Billie Davis, Don Spencer, Billy Boyle, and the Le Roys, two shows

**Tuesday, February 18:** Rank Theatre, Colchester, Essex, UK, with John Leyton, Mike Berry & the Innocents, Swinging Blue Jeans, Mike Sarne, Jet Harris, Billie Davis, Don Spencer, Billy Boyle, and the Le Roys, two shows

One fan recalled in *The Guardian* that the audience at these shows had mostly come to see headliner John Leyton and were taken aback "when a load of screaming teenagers erupted in the middle of the theatre as soon as the Stones came on stage. They were wonderful, but the thing I remember most apart from the music is Mick Jagger's amazing green trousers, totally unlike anything men in Essex were wearing!"

**Wednesday, February 19:** Rank Theatre, Stockton-on-Tees, UK, with John Leyton, Mike Berry & the Innocents, Swinging Blue Jeans, Mike Sarne, Jet Harris, Billie Davis, Don Spencer, Billy Boyle, and the Le Roys, two shows

Bill recalled in *Tiger Beat* that at this show, "One girl threw her shoe on stage. Mick made a mistake of picking it up and singing to it. Next minute we're dodging the stilettoes. We've got more shoes than Dolcis. It's a wonder we weren't killed. I'm glad that craze only lasted two or three nights!"

**Thursday, February 20:** Rank Theatre, Sunderland, Tyne and Wear, UK, with John Leyton, Mike Berry & the Innocents, Swinging Blue Jeans, Mike Sarne, Jet Harris, Billie Davis, Don Spencer, Billy Boyle, and the Le Roys, two shows

**Friday, February 21:** Gaumont Theatre, Hanley, Staffordshire, UK, with John Leyton, Mike Berry & the Innocents, Swinging Blue Jeans, Mike Sarne, Jet Harris, Billie Davis, Don Spencer, Billy Boyle, the Dowlands, and the Le Roys, two shows

**Saturday, February 22:** Winter Gardens, Bournemouth, UK, with John Leyton, Mike Berry & the Innocents, Swinging Blue Jeans, Mike Sarne, Jet Harris, Billie Davis, Don Spencer, The Paramounts, Billy Boyle, and the Le Roys, two shows

During the day, the BBC filmed the Stones on a beach to sync with "Not Fade Away." It aired on *Top of the Pops*.

**Sunday, February 23:** Hippodrome Theatre, Birmingham, UK, with John Leyton, Mike Berry & the Innocents, Swinging Blue Jeans, Mike Sarne, Jet Harris, Billie Davis, Don Spencer, Billy Boyle, and the Le Roys, two shows

While in Birmingham, the Stones taped an appearance on the ABC TV show *Thank Your Lucky Stars*.

**Monday, February 24:** Odeon Theatre, Southend, Essex, UK, with John Leyton, Mike Berry & the Innocents, Swinging Blue Jeans, Mike Sarne, Jet Harris, Billie Davis, Don Spencer, Billy Boyle, and the Le Roys, two shows

**Tuesday, February 25:** Odeon Theatre, Romford, Essex, UK, with John Leyton, Mike Berry & the Innocents, Swinging Blue Jeans, Mike Sarne, Jet Harris, Billie Davis, Don Spencer, Billy Boyle, and the Le Roys, two shows

**Wednesday, February 26:** Rialto Theatre, York, UK, with John Leyton, Mike Berry & the Innocents, Swinging Blue Jeans, Mike Sarne, Jet Harris, Billie Davis, Don Spencer, Billy Boyle, and the Le Roys, two shows

**Thursday, February 27:** City Hall, Sheffield, UK, with John Leyton, Mike Berry & the Innocents, Swinging Blue Jeans, Mike Sarne, Jet Harris, Billie Davis, Don Spencer, Billy Boyle, and the Le Roys, two shows

**Friday, February 28:** Sophia Gardens, Cardiff, Wales, UK, with John Leyton, Mike Berry & the Innocents, Swinging Blue Jeans, Mike Sarne, Jet Harris, Billie Davis, Don Spencer, Billy Boyle, and the Le Roys, two shows

Future *NME* journalist Nick Kent caught his first glimpse of the Stones. He later recalled, "Everyone else on the bill wore dark suits and sang through thin chapped lips forever shaped into a forced show business smile of the entertainer whose 15 minutes of fame had just been all used up. The Stones, by contrast, were all scowls and yobbish menace and their short set was an invitation to its spectators to explode into complete and utter mayhem.... I became an instant conscript to the cause of Stones-dom."

**Saturday, February 29:** Hippodrome, Brighton, UK, with John Leyton, Mike Berry & the Innocents, Swinging Blue Jeans, Mike Sarne, Jet Harris, Billie Davis, Don Spencer, Billy Boyle, the Dowlands, and the Le Roys, two shows

**Sunday, March 1:** Empire Theatre, Liverpool, UK, with John Leyton, Mike Berry & the Innocents, Swinging Blue Jeans, Mike Sarne, Jet Harris, Billie Davis, Don Spencer, Billy Boyle, and the Le Roys, two shows

**Monday, March 2:** Albert Hall, Nottingham, UK, with John Leyton, Mike Berry & the Innocents, Swinging Blue Jeans, Mike Sarne, Jet Harris, the Paramounts, Billie Davis, Don Spencer, Billy Boyle, and the Le Roys, two shows

Future music journalist Richard Williams, who was picked to be an usher, attended these shows. He recalled in *The Guardian*, "I have little memory of what the Stones played that night, or how they played it. What I do remember is that they performed their new single, a version of the Crickets' 'Not Fade Away' set to a storming Bo Diddley beat, and that they were the loudest thing I'd ever heard—even though each guitarist had only one small amplifier on stage, while the vocal amplification was consigned to a pair of primitive column PA speakers."

**Tuesday, March 3:** Opera House, Blackpool, UK, with Eden Kane, Bern Elliot and the Fenmen, Mike Sarne, Jet Harris, the Paramounts, Mike Berry & the Innocents, the Hollies, Billie Davis, Don Spencer and Billy Boyle, two shows

**Wednesday, March 4:** Gaumont Theatre, Bradford, Yorkshire, UK, with Eden Kane, Bern Elliot and the Fenmen, Mike Sarne, Jet Harris, Mike Berry & the Innocents, the Hollies, Billie Davis, Don Spencer and Billy Boyle, two shows

Prior to the Bradford shows, the Stones taped appearances on the BBC TV show *Top of the Pops* and Granada TV's *Scene at 6:30* in Manchester.

**Thursday, March 5:** Odeon Theatre, Blackburn, Lancashire, UK, with Eden Kane, Bern Elliot and the Fenmen, Mike Sarne, Jet Harris, Mike Berry & the Innocents, the Hollies, the Paramounts, Billie Davis, Don Spencer and Billy Boyle, two shows

The audience at these shows was highly enthusiastic and there were numerous stage invasions.

**Friday, March 6:** Gaumont Theatre, Wolverhampton, UK, with Eden Kane, Bern Elliot and the Fenmen, Mike Sarne, Jet Harris, Mike Berry & the Innocents, the Hollies, Billie Davis, Don Spencer and Billy Boyle, two shows

Backstage, the Stones gave an interview to *Melody Maker* reporter Ray Coleman. Asked if they were upset that the older generation dismissed them, Keith replied, "We don't care … if they like us, good; if they don't, hard luck. We don't mind." Asked if recent chart success had changed them, Mick commented "Not much. We're just happy, that's all. I don't think we'd change—why should we? We're not an overnight group. You know, we've been going for years."

**Saturday, March 7:** Winter Gardens, Morecambe, Lancashire, UK, with Eden Kane, Bern Elliot and the Fenmen, Mike Sarne, Jet Harris, Mike Berry & the Innocents, the Hollies, Billie Davis, Don Spencer and Billy Boyle, two shows

This was the last show of the tour, and after this the Stones took an eight-day break. During the time, Keith and Mick recorded demos at De Lane Lea Studios.

**Sunday, March 15:** Invicta Ballroom, Chatham, Kent, UK

Charlie and his wife were on holiday in Gibraltar and Micky Waller substituted on drums. Bill recalled the show "as a night of sheer madness. Girls jammed themselves twenty deep all around the stage and stewards struggled throughout the show to prevent them from pulling us down onto the dance floor."

**Tuesday, March 17:** Assembly Hall, Tunbridge Wells, Kent, UK, 7:30 p.m.

Although this was the Stones' first gig in Tunbridge Wells, Mick had been there before. At the age of fifteen he'd made a brief appearance on a TV show called *Seeing Sport* filmed there.

**Wednesday, March 18:** City Hall, Salisbury, Wiltshire, UK, with the Outlaws

The set: "Talkin' 'bout You," "Poison Ivy," "Walking the Dog," "Pretty Thing," "Cops and Robbers," "Jaguar and the Thunderbird," "Don't Lie to Me," "I Wanna Be Your Man," "Roll Over Beethoven," "You Better Move On," "Roadrunner," "Route 66" and "Bye Bye Johnny." On March 19 the Stones taped an appearance for BBC Radio show *Blues in Rhythm* at the Camden Theatre in London.

**Saturday, March 21:** Whitehall, East Grinstead, Sussex, UK

**Sunday, March 22:** Esplanade Pavilion, Ryde, Isle of Wight, UK, with the Cherokees and the Shamrocks, 4 and 7 p.m.

**Monday, March 23:** Guildhall, Southampton, Hampshire, UK, two shows

**Wednesday, March 25:** Town Hall, Birmingham, UK, 6:30 and 8:45 p.m.

**Thursday, March 26:** Town Hall, Kidderminster, Worcestershire, UK, 7:30 p.m.

**Friday, March 27:** Ex-Serviceman's Club, Windsor, Berkshire, UK, with Alex Harvey & His Soul Band

**Saturday, March 28:** Wilton Hall, Bletchley, Tottenham, London, UK, with the Druids, and Club Noreik, Tottenham, London, UK (midnight)

On Sunday, Brian performed with the Yardbirds at the Crawdaddy Club when singer Keith Reif became ill.

**Monday, March 30:** Ricky-Tick, Plaza Ballroom, Guildford, Surrey, UK, with Chris Farlowe, 3 p.m., and Ricky-Tick, Olympia Ballroom, Reading, Berkshire, UK, with Chris Farlowe, 8 p.m.

The Stones arrived late at the Ricky-Tick and were mobbed as they attempted to wade through the crowd to get on stage. Keith was pulled into the crowd and he had to be disentangled by bouncers. *Jackie Magazine* reported, "The Stones blew up a storm. 'Walking the Dog' brought the place down. 'Cops and Robbers,' a talking blues, knocked everybody out. In no time at all, Mick introduced the last number while Brian, Keith and Bill signed autograph books, cigarette packets and photographs thrust up from the crowd. 'We're gonna finish with 'Bye Bye Johnny' drawled Mick. 'I want you to all join in the Bye, Bye chorus and wave your arms.' They started the chorus and nobody joined in. The Stones stopped. 'Listen' said Mick 'If you don't join us we walk off.' Next time around, everyone joined in."

**Tuesday, March 31:** West Cliff Hall, Ramsgate, Kent, UK, 7:30 p.m.

*The Thanet Times* reviewer stated, "The effect they had on the young audience was astounding. At one point during the evening, first aid personnel were kept busy dealing with relays of young girls overcome with emotion."

**Wednesday, April 1:** All Fools Charity Beat Ball, Locarno Ballroom, Stevenage, Hertfordshire, UK, with Big Dee Irwin, the Diamonds, the League of Gentlemen, Terry Judge and the Barristers and the Deltics

A crowd of 2,500 attended this charity event, for which the Stones were paid £500.

**Friday, April 3:** Wimbledon Palais, London, UK, with the Demons

The Stones made their second appearance at the now demolished Wimbledon ballroom. Prior to the concert, they taped an appearance for the ARTV show *Ready Steady Go!*

**Saturday, April 4:** Leas Cliff Hall, Folkestone, Kent, UK

The Stones were paid £1,200 for their appearance at this venue situated on a dramatic clifftop.

**Sunday, April 5:** Gaumont Theatre, Ipswich, Suffolk, UK, with the Bachelors, 5:30 and 8 p.m.

Program for the Stones' show in Birmingham (collection of Ira Korman).

**Monday, April 6:** Royal Hotel Ballroom, Lowestoft, Suffolk, UK

**Wednesday, April 8:** Ready Steady Go Mod Ball, Empire Pool, Wembley, UK, with Billy J Kramer & the Dakotas, the Fourmost, the Merseybeats, Sounds Incorporated, the Searchers, Cilla Black, Freddie & the Dreamers, Kenny Lynch and Manfred Mann, 7:30 p.m.

The Stones performed "Not Fade Away," "Walking the Dog," "Hi-Heel Sneakers" and "I'm Alright" (a Bo Diddley number that became part of their act for the next three years) at this riotous show. *Ready Steady Go!* filmed the event, though, regrettably, the footage was erased. Jack Good, British producer of U.S. TV show *Shindig*, recalled, "When I first saw the Stones I was stunned. It was at the Mod Ball at Wembley. They went on stage to give one of the most devastating performances I have ever seen. With their vibrant personalities they will go far."

The Stones made the mistake of agreeing to perform in the round. Fans repeatedly overran the stage and band members were pulled into the audience a number of times. Brian commented in *The Crazy World of England's Rolling Stones*, "There was Keith falling, well actually he was pulled off the rostrum twice. All because we seated Charlie at the drums and then tried to wander in, like wandering minstrels, whatever they may be. Only it didn't quite go that way. Actually the fans ended up trying to kidnap us: rostrum and all. Dodgy! But you know me, I found it a bit of a giggle."

**Thursday, April 9:** McIlroys Ballroom, Swindon, Wiltshire, UK

This was the Stones' last appearance at this venue. A fan who attended recalled on the BBC, "The group were fantastic and the venue was packed out with people at the back standing on tables and chairs. In fact the promoter had to request them to get down as the windows were open and we were on the second floor."

**Friday, April 10:** The Baths, Leyton, East London, UK

Prior to this show the Stones taped an appearance on *The Joe Loss Pop Show* for BBC Radio.

**Saturday, April 11:** Happy Ballroom, Hastings Pier, Hastings, Sussex, UK, with the Falcons, 8 p.m.

An enthusiastic crowd turned out for this show. *The Hastings Observer* reported, "Only a performance by the Beatles, one imagines, could have produced more enthusiastic scenes than those at Hastings Pier on Saturday. It was the day the Rolling Stones came to town. The unappreciated heroes of the day were the Pier attendants, who stood on each side of the stage as the Stones did their best to make themselves heard above the shrill screams. It was their unenviable task to haul a number of overexcited girls-in various states of collapse-from the front row of the audience and carry them bodily off the stage for a breath of reviving sea air. And they were kept hard at it, such was the effect of the five long haired rhythm and blues specialists."

**Sunday, April 12:** Fairfield Halls, Croydon, South London, UK, with Dave Dee and the Bostons, the Barracudas, the Overlanders, the Worryin' Kind and the Rattles, 6 and 8:30 p.m.

Dave Dee (later to achieve UK fame in Dave Dee, Dozy, Beaky, Mick and Tich) opened for the Stones and recalled on BBC Radio, "I'd never heard any audience scream as loud as this. I didn't know about the worship that all these pop stars had ... and I was totally deaf when this band walked on stage, and of course they were the Rolling Stones." The day after this concert, the Stones taped an appearance on BBC Radio's *Saturday Club*.

**Thursday, April 16:** Cubi Klub, Rochdale, Greater Manchester, UK, with the St. Louis Checks and David John and the Mood, 7:30 p.m., and Locarno Ballroom, Coventry, Warwickshire, UK, with the Mighty Avengers

The Stones only played one gig on this night but were booked for two. The Rochdale show was halted before they took the stage when the crowd rioted. A fan who was present recalled online, "The Stones were definitely there but never played as the place was in absolute chaos.... All the Stones snuck out and left through a fire exit at the back of the club."

**Saturday, April 18:** Royalty Theatre, Chester, Cheshire, UK

Bill later referred to this show as "one of the most bizarre shows we ever did." The theater hired some strange opening acts, including a group of singing sailors.

**Monday, April 20:** Golden Rose International TV Festival, Casino, Montreux, Switzerland, with Petula Clark, Adamo, Les Surfs and Les Missiles

The Stones flew to Geneva on Sunday (B&W footage of them at the airport exists) and then took a boat to Montreaux. *Fabulous 208* reported, "The Lake was covered in mist and the five-hour journey seemed an eternity. Keith and Mick tried to work out a new song. Brian charmed a drink out of the captain and nursed it triumphantly. Charlie and Bill went to sleep.... We landed about seven in the evening, very hungry, very tired. The Stones booked in at their hotel. The staff had never seen anything like them and said so rather rudely in French." According to *Rave Magazine*, the hotel informed them "You are very unusual guests and we just can't cope with you." Brian replied, "We're leaving anyway." They were there to be filmed by *Ready Steady Go!* at the Montreux

Festival. It was the Stones' first appearance outside the UK and promoter Claude Nobs has trouble giving away free tickets. No one in Switzerland had heard of them.

**Wednesday, April 22:** Carlton Ballroom, Slough, Berkshire, UK, 8 p.m.

**Friday, April 24:** Gaumont Theatre, Norwich, Norfolk, UK, with Jet Harris, Heinz, Mike Berry, Billie Davis, the Innocents and the Le Roys, 6:30 and 8:45 p.m.

The Stones provoked wild enthusiasm in Norwich. *The Norwich Times* reported, "On a decibel rating there could have been no doubt at all that the Rolling Stones' appearances at the Gaumont Theatre Norwich last night were an unqualified success…. It was virtually impossible to say what numbers were being played but this didn't matter. It was the Stones themselves that counted. The high point in their act seemed to come when one of them picked up a set of maracas and another bounded forward with a tambourine."

**Saturday, April 25:** Odeon Theatre, Luton, Bedfordshire, UK, two shows

**Sunday, April 26:** NME Poll-Winner's Concert, Empire Pool, Wembley, UK, with the Beatles, the Hollies, the Searchers, the Merseybeats, the Swinging Blue Jeans, the Dave Clark Five, Cliff Richard and the Shadows, Gerry and the Pacemakers, Billy J. Kramer and the Dakotas, the Joe Loss orchestra, Brian Poole and the Tremeloes, Manfred Mann, Jet Harris with Sounds Incorporated, Kathy Kirby, Big Dee Irwin, Joe Brown and the Bruvvers, 2:30 and 8 p.m.

The Stones made the first of four appearances at this star-studded annual event sponsored by *New Musical Express*, which handed out listener-voted awards to top groups. Years later, Charlie recalled in *According to the Rolling Stones,* "They had created an R&B Award because they didn't know what category to put us in. We turned up early and saw the Beatles' van. It was covered in lipstick and we all thought, 'Blimey, that's what our van should be like'! We had exactly the same van but no lipstick." The Stones were filmed performing "Not Fade Away," "I Just Want to Make Love to You" and "I'm Alright." The footage aired on the UK ABC TV show *Big Beat 64* on May 3 and 10. By this time, the Stones were achieving some buzz in the States and New York radio personality Murry the K broadcast the performance on his show.

**Monday, April 27:** Top Beat Pop Prom, Royal Albert Hall, London, UK, with Kenny Ball and his Jazzmen, Freddie and the Dreamers, Billy J. Kramer and the Dakotas and Brian Poole and the Tremeloes, two shows

BBC TV filmed the Stones performing "Not Fade Away," "Hi-Heel Sneakers" and "I'm Alright" at one of these shows. Unfortunately, the footage was erased. A Japanese 7" single of "Tell Me/Time Is on My Side" released in 1968 features a color photo of the Stones at this event.

**Tuesday, April 28:** Wallington Public Hall, Wallington, Surrey, UK

The day after this show, the Stones performed "I Just Want to Make Love to You" on BBC TV show *Top of the Pops* in Manchester.

**Thursday, April 30:** Majestic Ballroom, Birkenhead, Cheshire, UK

The Stones' appearance set off a riot. Over 500 fans invaded the stage, bringing an abrupt end to the show. The Stones hid backstage while Stu attempted to prevent their equipment from disappearing.

**Friday, May 1:** Imperial Ballroom, Nelson, Lancashire, UK, with the Dynamic Elders and Ken Reece and the Swinging Sounds, 8 p.m.

**Saturday, May 2:** Spa Royal Hall, Bridlington, Yorkshire, UK, with the Mighty Avengers, two shows

**Sunday, May 3:** Palace Theatre, Manchester, UK, with Pete McClain and the Four Just Men, the Sunliners, the Overlanders, the McKinleys, the Swinging Hi-Four and Julie Grant, 6 and 8:15 p.m.

The day after these shows the Stones appeared on the Granada TV show *Scene at 6.30*. On May 6 they performed "Not Fade Away" on the ITV show *Two Go Round* in Southampton.

**Thursday, May 7:** Savoy Ballroom, Southsea, Hampshire, UK, with the J. Crow Combo

**Friday, May 8:** Town Hall, Hove, Sussex, UK

**Saturday, May 9:** Savoy Ballroom, Catford, London, UK, with Bobby King and the Sabres

During the day, the Stones taped an appearance on the BBC2 TV show *Open House* at London's Riverside Studios. Afterwards, members of the band attended Chuck Berry's show at Finsbury Park, causing them to be late for their own concert. They had considerable trouble getting into the venue, which was surrounded by fans, eager to get a piece of them.

**Sunday, May 10:** Colston Hall, Bristol, UK, with Gene Vincent & the Shouts, Johnny Carr and the Cadillacs, Mike Tobin and the Magnettes, Millie Small and the No Names, the Avon Cities, Christine Marlowe and the Ray Bush Rhythm and Blues Band, 5:30 and 7:45 p.m.

The Stones' visit to Bristol started off badly, as they were refused service at the prestigious Grand's Restaurant because of their scruffy appearance. When informed he'd have to put on a jacket and tie to eat, Mick replied: "I'm not going to dress up in their clothes. We dress like this and that's that." The Stones instead headed to the Bali Restaurant where they dined on curried prawns. The Stones headlined a bill that included legendary American rocker Gene Vincent of "Be Bop-a-Lula" fame. A *Bristol Post* reporter attended the second show and noted, "Shrieking teenagers bobbed up and down in their seats as the Stones earthy rhythm and blues music rose to fever pitch. One girl leapt on the stage and flung her arms around lead singer Mick Jagger before being dragged from the hall by two attendants. Two more jumped from down from the seats behind the stage as the last number, 'I Wanna Be Your Man,' finished. They hurled themselves at drummer Charlie Watts, only to be rugby tackled by officials."

**Monday, May 11:** Winter Gardens, Bournemouth, UK, with Cliff Bennett & the Rebel Rousers, Peter Jay & the Jaywalkers, Julie Grant and Keith Powell & the Valets, two shows

The day after the Bournemouth show the Stones held a session at Regent Sound, where they taped "Congratulations," "Don't Lie to Me" and "Susie Q."

**Wednesday, May 13:** City Hall, Newcastle, UK, with Cliff Bennett & the Rebel Rousers, Peter Jay & the Jaywalkers, Julie Grant and the Gamblers, 6:15 and 8:45 p.m.

Other acts on the bill included Cliff Bennett & the Rebel Rousers, a British band that had been recording since 1957 with only middling success (they later signed with Brian Epstein and achieved greater fame), and Peter Jay and the Jaywalkers, an instrumental band that had scored a hit in 1962 with "Can Can '62."

**Thursday, May 14:** St. George's Hall, Bradford, Yorkshire, UK, with Cliff Bennett & the Rebel Rousers, Peter Jay & the Jaywalkers, Julie Grant and Keith Powell & the Valets, two shows

**COLSTON HALL — BRISTOL**

Entertainments Manager: F. K. COWLEY

**SUNDAY, MAY 10th, 1964**

at 5.30 and 7.45 p.m.

WESTERN SCENE presents by arrangement with Malcolm A. Rose

# The Rolling Stones

| JOHNNY CARR & THE CADILLACS | MIKE TOBIN & THE MAGNETTES |

## MILLIE & The No Names

| The Avon Cities | Christine Marlowe |
| The Ray Bush R&B Group | The Echoes |

## Gene Vincent & The Shouts

Compere — Brian K. Jones

Tickets: 12/6, 10/6, 7/6, 5/-
FROM COLSTON HALL BOOKING OFFICE — Tel. 21768

WESTERN SCENE — The West of England's Original Beat Paper

Handbill for the Stones' appearance with rock legend Gene Vincent (collection of Ira Korman).

*The Telegraph & Argus* reported, "A screaming mob of teenage girls literally tore the clothes off the back of (one of) the Rolling Stones pop group last night after the group's first-house performance at St George's Hall. The victim of 'Stones-mania' was 19-year-old Brian Jones, the group's … harmonica player." Stu later recalled that, in between shows, the Stones decided to run across the road to the hotel they were staying at. "They all made it except Brian, who chickened out before he got to the hotel entrance because there were people running after him. He eventually turned around and ran the other way. So all these people are chasing Brian through the streets in Bradford, tearing clothes off him. The police finally brought him back without a jacket, without a shirt, and he'd lost a shoe and a handful of hair."

**Friday, May 15:** Trentham Gardens, Stoke-on-Trent, UK, with Peter Jay & the Jaywalkers, Julie Grant, the Sunliners and Pat Wayne and the Beachcombers, two shows

**Saturday, May 16:** Regal Theatre, Edmonton, North London, UK, two shows

**Sunday, May 17:** Odeon Cinema, Folkestone, Kent, UK, with Jet Harris, Billie Davis and Mike Berry & the Innocents, two shows

The Stones attracted an extremely enthusiastic crowd. Brian told a reporter, "The audience were just great!" Indeed, *The Folkestone Herald* reported, "Intoxicated by the rhythm and atmosphere, they shouted, jumped, raved, and threw sweets and ice cream cartons on the stage while the solemn faced Stones belted out their music."

**Monday, May 18:** Chantinghall Hotel, Hamilton, Scotland, UK, with Freddie and the Dreamers, Peter and Gordon, Mark Peters and the Silhouettes, Millie and the Five Embers, Dave Berry and the Cruisers

Promoter Ronnie Kirkwood completely underestimated the Stones' popularity when he booked them into this tiny venue near Glasgow with Liverpool band Freddie and the Dreamers (of "I'm Telling You Now" fame) and Peter and Gordon. Instead of the 2,000 fans he expected, 4,000 showed up and rioted when they were refused entry. To make matters worse, it turned out that scalpers had given away forged tickets and many with actual tickets were stuck outside. Kirkwood decided to let everyone with a ticket in, which resulted in a crush of people with no room to move. Hundreds fainted in the hot atmosphere and had to be dragged out to fresh air. The *Hamilton Advertiser* reported, "Their 50-minute appearance was a howling success. As the crowd went wild watching the frantic jerking of the long-haired youths and listening to their equally frantic rhythm and blues music, five bouncers had a full-time job keeping over-eager, screaming fans from scaling the steel barrier. They even resorted to throwing buckets and jugs of water."

**Tuesday, May 19:** Capitol Cinema, Aberdeen, Scotland, UK, with Freddie and the Dreamers, Peter and Gordon, Mark Peters and the Silhouettes, Millie and the Five Embers, Dave Berry and the Cruisers, 6:30 and 8:50 p.m.

**Wednesday, May 20:** Caird Hall, Dundee, Scotland, UK, with Freddie and the Dreamers, Peter and Gordon, Millie and the Five Embers, Dave Berry and the Cruisers, 6:15 and 8:50 p.m.

Promoter Andy Lothian booked this show over six months before, when the Stones were relatively unknown and Freddie and the Dreamers were already big stars. But, by the time the show took place things had changed. Lothian recalled in Lorraine Wilson's book *Take It to the Bridge*, "The crowd went nuts at the Rolling Stones and when Freddie came on, there was nothing he could do to win them back—even dropping his trousers didn't work." Before the curtains opened for the second show, Freddie and the Dreamers agreed to switch places with the Stones and open for them.

**Thursday, May 21:** Regal Theatre, Edinburgh, Scotland, UK, with Freddie and the Dreamers, Peter and Gordon, Millie and the Five Embers, Dave Berry and the Cruisers, two shows

**Saturday, May 23:** Leicester University, Leicester, UK, 8 p.m.

**Sunday, May 24:** Coventry Theatre, Coventry, Warwickshire, UK, with the Overlanders, Duke D'Mond and the Barron Knights, Julie Grant, David John and the Mood and the Caravelles, two shows

The female duo the Caravelles, who'd had a hit the previous year with "You Don't Have to Be a Baby to Cry," replaced Peter and Gordon for these concerts. Prior to the evening shows in Coventry, the Stones were at Alpha Studios in Birmingham taping an appearance on the ABC TV show *Thank Your Lucky Stars*, which aired on May 30.

**Monday, May 25:** Granada Theatre, East Ham, London, UK, with Peter & Gordon, the Overlanders, Duke D'Mond and the Barron Knights, Julie Grant, David John and the Mood and the Cyclones, two shows

Over fifty police officers were called to the Granada when fans rioted. Richard Green of *NME* reported, "The Stones were at their best and, when they could be heard, they were churning out a great sound. Mick's dancing was grade one and served to incite fresh attacks of frenzy from the fans.... After 'Not Fade Away,' Mick called Charlie to the front to announce the next number. It was almost two minutes before the drummer could say 'I Wanna Be Your Man' and it was over ten minutes after the act finished with that song before the fans stopped chanting 'We want the Stones!'" Prior to the shows, the band taped an appearance on the BBC Radio show *Saturday Club*.

**Tuesday, May 26:** Town Hall, Birmingham, UK, with Peter & Gordon, the Overlanders, Duke D'Mond and the Barron Knights, Julie Grant, David John and the Mood and the Cyclones, two shows

Keith and Bill were big fans of support act Duke D'Mond and the Barron Knights, who had a UK hit in 1964 with the parody record "Call Up the Groups." Keith told *Pop Pics Magazine*: "They're so great! It's a sin they haven't been more widely recognized."

**Wednesday, May 27:** Danilo Theatre, Cannock, Staffordshire, UK, with Peter & Gordon, the Overlanders, Duke D'Mond and the Barron Knights, Julie Grant, David John and the Mood and the Cyclones, 6:20 and 8:30 p.m.

*The Cannock Advertiser* reported, "The Rolling Stones rolled into Cannock's Danilo Theatre on Wednesday for a one-night stand, much to the delight of their hundreds of fans. Not much of the group's actual singing was heard, but the fans did not worry about that. They had come to see the country's most unconventional five pop music idols."

**Thursday, May 28:** Essoldo Theatre, Stockport, Greater Manchester, UK, with Peter & Gordon, the Overlanders, Duke D'Mond and the Barron Knights, Julie Grant, David John and the Mood and the Cyclones, 6:20 and 8:30 p.m.

**Friday, May 29:** City Hall, Sheffield, UK, with Peter & Gordon, the Overlanders, Duke D'Mond and the Barron Knights, Julie Grant, David John and the Mood and the Cyclones, 6:20 and 8:50 p.m.

**Saturday, May 30:** Adelphi Theatre, Slough, Berkshire, UK, with Peter & Gordon, The Overlanders, Duke D'Mond and the Barron Knights, Julie Grant, David John and the Mood and the Cyclones, two shows

**Sunday, May 31:** "The Pop Hit Parade," Empire Pool, Wembley, UK, with Adam Faith, Wayne Fontana and the Mindbenders, Freddie and the Dreamers, Julie Grant, the Hollies, Eden Kane and the Downbeats, Duke D'Mond and the Barron Knights, the Merseybeats, the McKinleys, the Roulettes, Kevin Scott and the Kinsmen, the Swinging Blue Jeans and the Undertakers, 2:30 and 7 p.m.

**Friday, June 5:** Swing Auditorium, San Bernardino, CA, with the Cascades, 8 p.m.

This was the opening date of the Stones' first North American tour. The group, accompanied by Andrew, Eric Easton and Stu, landed at JFK Airport in New York City on Monday, June 1. Only 500 screaming fans awaited them on the tarmac, a far cry from the thousands who greeted the Beatles on their visit in February. But thousands of other Stones fans were prevented from entering the airport by police. The Stones held a filmed press conference at the airport, presided over by WINS Radio DJ Murry "The K" Kaufman (who took charge of showing them around the city, including a visit to the Peppermint Lounge). Following the conference, each Stone jumped into a separate limo, so individual reporters could interview them on the way to the Astor Hotel. Mick shared his cramped limo with six reporters and a large English sheepdog brought along for corny publicity photos.

New York police underestimated the popularity of the band and only assigned four cops to guard them when they arrived at their hotel. *Song Hits Magazine* reported: "(Fans) swarmed over the cars and started pulling the boys out (of their limos). A policeman shouted, 'Run, it's every man for himself!' In three seconds the dignified hotel became an insane asylum…. In ran the boys, followed by the dog, followed by 70 or more screaming hysterical girls with the police close behind! Bellboys dropped their bundles, guests ran screaming for cover and all hell broke loose." Eventually the band made it to their rooms, but found it difficult to leave without attracting a crowd. The group made a live late night appearance on WABC TV's *Les Crane Show* (the footage is lost), on which the Stones were interviewed by the host and took call-in questions from viewers. Bill Wyman later recalled "It all got a bit bitchy after a while with Les Crane trying to take the mickey out of us: we rose above it and were back at the hotel by 3 a.m." On June 3 they flew to Los Angeles to tape an appearance on the ABC TV variety show *Hollywood Palace*.

The tour proper began on June 5. American Bob Bonis was hired to act as tour manager. The Stones were not well known and generally played secondary markets. Keith Richards had fond memories of the concert in San Bernardino, played before an audience of 3,500. He told Robert Greenfield in 1971 that the show "was a straight gas, man. They all knew the songs and they were all hopping. It was like being back home. 'Ah, love these American gigs' and 'Route 66' mentioned San Bernardino, so everybody was into it." Jack Hutton of *Melody Maker* had flown over with the group and reported, "Girls … hoisted banners saying 'We love the Stones' and than started invading the stage like divebombers, one at a time…. One grabbed singer Mick Jagger round the waist and dragged him 15 feet across the stage. Three 6 ft. policemen ripped her off. Guitarist Keith Richard kept on playing with a girl around his neck. Brian Jones nearly had his harmonica pushed down his throat. The boys beamed happily as they tumbled off the stage."

**Saturday, June 6, and Sunday, June 7:** Teen Fair of Texas, Joe Freeman Coliseum, San Antonio, TX, with Bobby Vee, Diane Renay, George Jones, the Marquis Chimps, Amandis Troupe and the Fire Twirling Lounsbury Sisters, 2 and 8 p.m. each day

After the excitement of New York and California, the Stones were brought back to earth by a lukewarm reception in Texas. Tony Delano of the *Daily Mirror* reported that at the show he attended only 3,000 of 20,000 seats were sold. He commented, "Local singers were cheered wildly. A tumbling act and a trained monkey were called to the stage for encores. But the long-haired Rolling Stones ... were booed." The group was not greatly impressed with San Antonio either, though they did visit the Alamo. Mick was particularly bothered by the segregation he encountered. He told Jack Hutton of *Melody Maker* that "the colored people have a ropey time here. You know they wouldn't take us through the colored section of San Antonio. I kept asking them to let me see it, but they'd never let me through."

**Friday, June 12:** Big Reggie's Danceland, Excelsior Park, MN, with Mike Waggoner and the Bops and Danny's Reasons, 8 p.m.

The Stones headed to Chicago, where they appeared live on WMAQ radio's *Jack Eigen Show*. The band hoped to visit some R&B clubs, but their American handlers nixed the idea. The Stones were told that because of race problems the South Side of Chicago was too dangerous to visit. In any event, on June 10 and 11 the band was able to fulfill a longtime dream by recording at Chess Studios. To drum up publicity, Andrew decided to stage an impromptu traffic-blocking press conference in the middle of Michigan Avenue. Police quickly descended and the Stones were hustled away. But, Andrew achieved his goal, as the story appeared in many newspapers.

The concert in Minnesota was a hastily arranged gig at a tiny venue on Lake Minnetonka, where the Beach Boys had played. Owner Ray Colihan chose not to advertise, because he feared too many kids might show up and he'd lose his license. Only 283 people attended. Bill Wyman recalled in *Hit Parader*, "Nobody had heard of us. I think the reaction was the same as we experienced in England a year ago—complete disbelief and curiosity. There weren't many people there because the tickets were three dollars but by the end they seemed to know what was going on."

**Saturday, June 13:** Civic Auditorium Music Hall, Omaha, NE, 7:30 p.m.

The Stones' first appearance in Nebraska was a disaster. They appeared on the local TV show *Dancestand* to promote the gig but still failed to attract much of a crowd. Keith recalled in 1971, "Nobody in Omaha had ever heard of us. We thought, 'Wow we've made it. We must be heavy.' And we get to the Auditorium and there are 600 people there in a 15,000 seat-hall." In actuality, 651 people attended, mostly teenage girls. The Stones, however, did not seem fazed by the tiny crowd. Bill told a reporter from the *Omaha World Herald* "We know we're not established stars here. We came to promote our records." Mick was already planning the next visit, telling the same reporter "We might be back before the end of the year."

**Sunday, June 14:** Olympia Stadium, Detroit, MI, 6 p.m.

The Stones headed to the Motor City, where they experienced one perk of fame. Ian Stewart recalled in *Fabulous 208*, "In Detroit they turned Bill, Charlie and I loose in a

Advertisement for the Stones' concert in Nebraska on their first U.S. tour (collection of Ira Korman).

record store and told us to help ourselves. It was like a dream come true. I came back with over 50 fabulous LPs." That night, however, the Stones again played to a tiny crowd. Only 500 fans turned out at the 13,000-seat stadium. Bill Wyman told the *Detroit Free Press*, "People didn't know we were coming to Detroit. In the past three days we've sold 8,000 albums in this city—but fewer then 1,000 heard us Sunday." An unimpressed A. L. McClain reported in *The Detroit News*, "Occasionally the Beatles will sing a ballad for their young listeners in a change of pace that is good showmanship. But the Rolling Stones never slow up. 'I Wanna Be Your Man,' 'Put Your Best Dress on Baby,' and 'I'm Alright' were all sung with the same beat. Their hair is longer than the young girls are wearing on Washington Boulevard but a hairdo is not stage presence. Their movements are not synchronized, while one or two are jumping around, the other three usually stood stiffly aside."

While only a small audience attended the concert, many were fanatical fans. They found out where the band was staying and patrolled the halls looking for their idols. Mick reported, "When I got into my room last night there were 25 girls. In England the police don't permit that, you know. If a girl manages to sneak in it's a real achievement." The Holiday Inn wasn't able to get rid of them until 5 in the morning. As a result the Stones secretly departed early on Monday for another hotel. While in Detroit, the Stones had planned on visiting Windsor, Ontario, just across the bay, but Keith had lost his passport and the Stones were advised that they'd have trouble reentering the States if they left before he got a replacement. They didn't visit Canada until 1965.

**Wednesday, June 17:** West View Park Danceland, Pittsburgh, PA, with Bobby Goldsboro, the Chiffons, the Pixies Three and Bobby Comstock, 8 p.m.

Radio station KQV heavily promoted this show but only 400 people attended. The band was scheduled to appear in New Haven the next day (and some concert handbills were created) but the show was canceled because of poor ticket sales and they instead spent the day in Cleveland taping an appearance on KYW TV's *Mike Douglas Show*.

**June 19:** Farm Show Arena, Harrisburg, PA, with Bobby Goldsboro, Patty & the Emblems and Bobby Comstock & the Counts, 8:15 p.m.

Promoters Norman Rosen and Buzz E. Long booked this show and paid General Artists Corp. a total of $4,000 for all the acts that played. Though Harrisburg was only 15 miles from the Stones' hotel in Hershey, PA, they flew there so that they could attend a big airport reception that had been planned for weeks. The Stones then went to a record signing at Caplan's in downtown Harrisburg, but hardly anyone turned up. The audience that night was also small. America was both exciting and confounding for the Stones. Mick later remarked to the British press, "I enjoyed the trip but I couldn't live there. Their outlook was outdated. The funny thing was, the kids had never heard of Muddy Waters. They've got the greatest blues singer living among them and they don't even know."

**Saturday, June 20:** Carnegie Hall, New York, NY, with Cathy Carr, the Counts, Bobby Goldsboro, and Jay and the Americans, 2:30 and 7:30 p.m.

The Stones returned to New York to appear on WPIX TV's *Clay Cole Saturday Show*. They then concluded their U.S. tour with two shows at the prestigious Carnegie Hall emceed by Murry the K. Chris Hutchins reported in *NME*, "There were riots during their first house at Carnegie Hall, which resulted in police insisting that the group should close the first half on the second house and be whipped away before the audience poured out." The Stones made a big impression on those in attendance. Jackie Kallen of *Teenbeat* commented, "The Stones are different in every respect from their predecessors. They are wilder, shaggier in appearance, more casual in dress. A rebellion against society, authority, convention and parenthood, they have overwhelmed the American teenagers with their image, catching newspapers and magazines with empty biographical files. They turned Carnegie Hall into a teenville heaven."

Despite some setbacks, the Stones had a great experience on the first tour, but regretted not having more time to see the States (especially New York). Hilda Skarfe of *Song Hits* reported, "They resented the fact that they couldn't get to their following and just talk with them. They loved America, but wished they could have gone sight seeing and at least talk to Americans, other than press people. They were terribly lonely, as even their closest friends couldn't get through the police lines to see them."

**Monday, June 22:** "Commemoration Ball," Magdalen College, Oxford, UK, with Falling Leaves, Sadler, Arnold and Gould, Freddie and the Dreamers, John Lee Hooker and the Tubby Hayes Band

The Stones arrived home from New York early on Monday. The British press was at the airport to greet them and asked if the stories were true that they'd "bombed" in America. Mick commented, "Sure, we bombed in some places but so have all the other British groups, with the exception of the Beatles." Keith proudly showed off his souvenir from America, a gun. "You can buy them as easily as you can buy candy floss." The Stones intended to spend more time in the States, but had been contracted to appear at Magdalen College and the school refused to move the date. To add insult to injury, the gig had been booked a year earlier and the band only received £100. By this time they seldom played for less than £500.

**Friday, June 26:** "All Night Rave," Alexandra Palace, London, UK, with Millie & the Five Embers, John Lee Hooker, John Mayall's Blues Breakers, Duke D'Mond and the Barron Knights, Jimmy Powell and the Five Dimensions, the Downliners Sect, Alexis Korner and Tony Colton & the Crawdaddies, 9 p.m.

The Stones were the headliners at this event to welcome them home. The crowd was extremely enthusiastic and Brian was chased from the stage by a large group of fans at one point. Backstage he told *Disc*: "America was terrific. I know we didn't go down well everywhere we appeared but that was because we played a lot of the smaller places where nobody had ever heard of us anyway. I liked the States though. I'd love to live there. It's just the place for me—particularly New York!"

The Stones made numerous TV appearances at this time. Prior to this concert, the band taped an appearance on *Ready Steady Go!* On June 27 they appeared on the BBC TV shows *Juke Box Jury* and *Top of the Pops* and on July 6 Brian was a panelist on the ITV show *Ready Steady, Win*.

**Saturday, July 11:** Spa Royal Hall, Bridlington, Yorkshire, UK

During the day the band appeared on the ITV show *Day by Day*. At the show that night, Brian debuted his custom made Vox six-string guitar. The instrument's body was in the shape of a teardrop and became his trademark for the next few years. The concert was filmed. Clips of "Hi-Heel Sneakers" and "Not Fade Away" were broadcast on the Granada TV show *World in Action* on September 21.

**Sunday, July 12:** Queens Hall, Leeds, UK, with Lulu and the Luvers, Ray Anton and the Peppermint Men and the Ryles Brothers with Dallas, 5:45 and 8:15 p.m.

The band played on a revolving stage in the center of the theatre. When the show ended they had no choice but to make a run through the crowd to the exit. Brian was dawdling with his equipment and got trapped by the mob. His clothes were torn to pieces. On July 15 the band appeared on *Top of the Pops*. Two days later they taped more radio shows for the BBC (*The Joe Loss Pop Show* and an episode of *Top Gear*).

**Saturday, July 18:** Beat City Club, 79 Oxford St., London, UK, with Tom Jones and the Squires

The show was advertised as "The Stones only London club date!"

**Sunday, July 19:** Hippodrome, Brighton, UK, with the Echoes, Julie Grant, Kenny Lynch, Marty Wilde and the Wildcats and Kevin Scott & the Kinsmen, 6 and 8:30 p.m.

Fans smuggled in packets of Rice Krispies to throw at the Stones, as their infamous jingle for the cereal aired that summer. Mick had to watch his step when dancing to avoid them. Illustrating their enthusiasm for R&B music, Bill, Keith and Charlie attended the taping of Ray Charles' ARTV special *The Man They Call Genius* in Croydon the next night. They are visible in the audience. On July 23 the Stones again appeared on the *Ready Steady Go!* TV show.

**Friday, July 24:** Empress Ballroom, Blackpool, UK, with the Executives, 7 p.m.

The Stones were nearly killed at one of the most terrifying concerts in their career. This was the gig Keith had in mind when he told Robert Greenfield in 1971 that "there was one ballroom number in Blackpool, during Scots week when all the Scots came down and get really drunk and let it rip. A whole gang of 'em came to this ballroom and they didn't like us and they punched their way to the front, right through the whole 7,000 people, straight to the stage and started spitting at us. This guy in front spitting, his head was just football size, just right. In those days for me, I had a temper, and 'you spit on me?' and I kicked his face in."

According to *UPI*, Keith swung his guitar at teens in the crowd and threatened to "bash someone" if they didn't stop spitting. The angry crowd responded by swarming "all over the stage, routing Richard and four other Rolling Stones and demolishing an estimated $5,600 worth of amplifiers and drums." The Stones frantically fled the melee they'd created and escaped by climbing on the roof. Brian, who was hit in the face with a bottle during the riot, told the press, "It was terrifying. At one time I counted ten fights going on in front of us. I saw one fellow smash two girls in the face."

**Saturday, July 25:** Imperial Ballroom, Nelson, Lancashire, UK, with the Silhouettes and the Thunderbeats, 7:30 p.m.

**Sunday, July 26:** De Montfort Hall, Leicester, UK, with the Barron Knights, two shows

The Stones enjoyed a few days off after these shows. On July 28 they were in Teddington to appear on the ABC TV show *Lucky Stars Summer Spin*.

**Friday, July 31:** Ulster Hall, Belfast, Northern Ireland, UK, and Flamingo Ballroom, Ballymena, Northern Ireland, UK, with the Cossacks, 9 p.m. to 2 a.m.

The Stones made their first visit to Ireland. They traveled to the BBC Studios in Belfast to be interviewed for the TV show *6.10*. The concert at Ulster Hall was canceled after twelve minutes when fans stormed the stage. Silent footage exists.

**Saturday, August 1:** Happy Ballroom, Hastings Pier, Hastings, Sussex, UK, with the Sabres and the Worrying Kind, 8 p.m.

The Stones had outgrown the ballrooms they'd played the previous year. Such large crowds surrounded this venue that the group had to be smuggled in and out in an ambulance.

**Sunday, August 2:** "3rd Pop Festival," Longleat House, Wiltshire, UK, with Tony Rivers and the Castaways and Danny Clarke and the Jaguars

This unusual concert took place on the grounds of the mansion of the 58-year-old Marquis of Bath, who paid the Stones £1,000. Over 25,000 fans turned out and riots broke out when many stormed the barricades separating them from the stage. Police threatened to stop the show, but the Marquis intervened. A short silent film of the gig exists. On August 5 the Stones taped an appearance for the American CBS TV show *Red Skelton Hour* at the London Palladium.

# 1964

**Friday, August 7:** 4th National Jazz And Blues Festival, Richmond Athletic Grounds, London, UK, with the T-Bones, the Authentics and the Grebbels, 7:30 p.m.

Prior to the show, the Stones taped an appearance on *Ready Steady Go!* Following the taping, they raced off to Richmond. But fans got wind of what car they were in and ripped the door off. The car drove off, minus a door and Brian, who was accidently left behind. He was hustled into a taxi and told to lie on the floor for the ride to Richmond. The concert was partly filmed on 8mm in color and a small portion is seen in the documentary *25×5*. Richard Green of *NME* reported, "'Walking the Dog,' 'Hi-Heel Sneakers,' 'It's All Over Now' and 'It's Alright' came across like a Sabre jet. The Stones were on top of the world and the fans let them know it!"

**Saturday, August 8:** Kurhaus, Scheveningen, Netherlands

Poster for the Stones' concert in Ballymena, Ireland (collection of Ira Korman).

The Stones' first Dutch concert was halted after only eight minutes when the audience rioted and destroyed the venue. Stu later recalled to Stanley Booth, "The police formed a chain like firefighters and when a teenager came forward, he was passed along, thumped and thrown out of the door and down some steps, where there were more waiting to help him on his way. I have never seen policemen so vicious as they were that night in Holland." The show was partly filmed and brief excerpts of the rioting were seen on Dutch news outlets. Footage of the Stones playing "Carol" in the video documentary *25×5* comes from this gig.

**Sunday, August 9:** New Elizabethan Ballroom, Belle Vue, Manchester, UK, 8 p.m.

The Stones flew to London from Holland and then took a connecting flight to Manchester. But Stu's van stalled and when it became clear that he wasn't going to make it, the band was forced to play with borrowed instruments. *The Daily Express* reported, "A crowd of 2,000 teenagers, kept waiting for half an hour last night by the Rolling Stones pop group, went wild when they finally appeared—and more than 100 girls fainted during the Stones' 40-minute act. Forty police with linked arms blocking the way to the stage at Belle Vue's New Elizabethan ballroom, Manchester, were forced to their knees by the stampede." Former Stone Dick Taylor's group the Pretty Things were also playing in Manchester and later that night Mick and Keith attended their show at the Oasis Club, and Mick sang a few numbers.

**Monday, August 10:** Tower Ballroom, New Brighton, Merseyside, UK, with Bobby and the Bachelors, Rik-E-Darne and the Defenders, the Downbeats, the Hustlers, Jay-El and the Executives, the Markfour, the Johnny Taylor Five, the Tokens, the Topspots, the Trakkers, the Wyverns and Dale Young and the Seminoles, 7:30 p.m.

The Stones were scheduled to play in Blackpool on August 11, but the promoter canceled the gig after the riots in July. The concert in New Brighton (which featured a battle of the bands as 12 opening acts competed for a recording test) also had its share of drama. Merrick Winn reported in *The Daily Express*, "The Rolling Stones are on a high stage and below on the low stage are 34 burly bouncers facing a wooden barricade and 4,000 scream-agers…. The bouncers work swiftly, ruthlessly, and non-stop dealing with girls in fits and girls in faints…. Girls come spinning, reeling off the low stage, laughing, crying, coming round slowly it seems from some anesthetic. Young faces in front contorted in the ecstasy and agony the rest of us would save up for the Day of Judgment."

**Thursday, August 13:** Palace Ballroom, Douglas, Isle of Man, UK

**Friday, August 14:** Wimbledon Palais, London, UK, with the Demons
On August 17 Mick appeared as a panelist on the ITV show *Ready Steady, Win*.

**Tuesday, August 18, to Thursday, August 20:** New Theatre Ballroom, St. Peter Port, Guernsey, UK
The Stones visit to the Channel Islands started on a sour note. Stu related in *Datebook*: "We were climbing up the steps to our plane, when the air hostess said in a stage whisper 'Well boys have you washed today?' This is the sort of comment that really annoys the Stones. But, though she could see that they were all angry, she didn't let it rest at that. Instead, she added 'when did you last have your haircut?' That was it! The boys tore into her quite mercilessly, asking for drinks, coffee and cigarettes, so that she was running up and down the plane while they criticized her slightest fault, christening her Hilary Hedgehopper. By the time the plane reached Guernsey the hostess was in tears…. We were told that we could never fly BUA again. Not that it worried us. As Brian said afterwards, we should have bought the airline to teach them a lesson!"

**Friday, August 21, and Saturday, August 22:** Springfield Ballroom, St. Helier, Jersey, UK
The concerts in the Channel Islands witnessed more riotous behavior. *The Daily Mirror* reported, "During the last set a peach and four tomatoes hit Mick Jagger. On the balcony a scuffle broke out while a running fight raged on the floor of the ballroom among 4,000 teenagers at the concert last night."

**Sunday, August 23:** Gaumont Theatre, Bournemouth, UK, with Duke D'Mond and the Barron Knights, the Overlanders, the Worrying Kind, the Paramounts and Julie Grant, 6:15 and 8:30 p.m.

**Monday, August 24:** Gaumont Theatre, Weymouth, Dorset, UK, with Duke D'Mond and the Barron Knights, the Overlanders, the Worrying Kind and Millie and the Five Embers, 6:30 and 8:45 p.m.

**Tuesday, August 25:** Odeon Theatre, Weston-super-Mare, UK, with Duke D'Mond and the Barron Knights, the Overlanders, the Worrying Kind and Millie and the Five Embers, 6 and 8:30 p.m.

Prior to the concerts, the Stones performed "It's All Over Now" on the TWW TV show *Here Today*.

**Wednesday, August 26:** Odeon Theatre, Exeter, Devon, UK, with Duke D'Mond and the Barron Knights, the Overlanders, the Worrying Kind and Millie and the Five Embers, two shows

The appearance in Exeter was relatively sedate. *The Express & Echo* reported, "Ambulance men and police were on duty, but only one girl was reported to have fainted. But a coat hanger and hat were taken from a van belonging to the Barron Knights, another group in the show. The items were found on two girls by a police constable and were smeared with lipstick."

**Thursday, August 27:** ABC Theatre, Plymouth, Devon, UK, with Duke D'Mond and the Barron Knights, the Overlanders, the Worrying Kind and Millie and the Five Embers, 6:15 and 8:30 p.m.

**Friday, August 28:** Gaumont Theatre, Taunton, Somerset, UK, with Duke D'Mond and the Barron Knights, the Overlanders, the Worrying Kind and Millie and the Five Embers, two shows

While the Stones were on tour, fans learned Mick and Keith's address and raided their flat, stealing clothes as souvenirs. Keith told *Disc*: "It's getting ridiculous. We can't keep moving. It's not the value of the clothes or anything it's just the inconvenience of the whole thing." Fans also continually vandalized the Stones' cars, so Eric Easton bought them a big station wagon to travel around in when they were touring the UK. But Keith complained, "It's just not big enough so this week we're changing it for a huge Pontiac!"

**Saturday, August 29:** Town Hall, Torquay, Devon, UK, with Duke D'Mond and the Barron Knights, the Overlanders, the Worrying Kind and Millie and the Five Embers, two shows

A blogger on the *Torquay Herald Express* website who attended this show reported, "Anything we, or the Town Hall, had witnessed before ... was tame by comparison. This was a raw, high energy, high octane mix of rock and rhythm and blues from a band destined to fulfill the prophecies of greatness." Following the show, the Stones returned to their rooms at the Gran Torquay, where they held a jam session until 4 a.m. Ian Stewart recalled in *Datebook*, "The manager came down in his silk pajamas and carpet slippers and started to shout. He sacked the night porter who had opened the drink cupboard and then raved at us, 'and you'll be out in the morning!'" The Stones were banned from the hotel for life.

**Sunday, August 30:** Gaumont Theatre, Bournemouth, UK, with Duke D'Mond and the Barron Knights, the Overlanders, the Worrying Kind and Long John Baldry, 6:15 and 8:30 p.m.

A new face, Mike Dorsey, joined the Stones at the behest of Eric Easton. He remained with them for the next year as Easton's representative, with the title of production manager. His baptism of fire came early. The authorities in Bournemouth were informed that some girls had run away from home, leaving a note that they were going to meet the

| AN ABC THEATRE |
| **ABC** — PLYMOUTH |
| Manager: T. B. PURDIE    Phone: 63300 |
| **6-15**   THURSDAY, 27th AUGUST   **8-30** |
| TWO PERFORMANCES ONLY |

**FOR ONE DAY ONLY**   **ON THE STAGE**   **FOR ONE DAY ONLY**
(INSTEAD OF THE USUAL FILM PROGRAMME)

JOHN SMITH presents

# THE ROLLING STONES

# THE BARRON KNIGHTS
featuring DUKE D'MOND

| THE WORRYIN' KIND | THE OVERLANDERS | GERRY CLEMENTS |

# MILLIE
AND THE
# FIVE EMBERS

PRICES: STALLS 12/6  10/-  7/6    CIRCLE 12/6  10/-  7/6

BOX OFFICE            POSTAL BOOKING FORM
ABC THEATRE           Thursday, 27th August, 1964
PLYMOUTH              The Rolling Stones & Co.   Date..........................

Please forward .........STALLS: 12/6  10/-  7/6  .........CIRCLE: 12/6  10/-  7/6
for the EVENING 6.15 / 8.30 performance on ...................................................
I enclose stamped addressed envelope and P.O. / Cheque value £     :    s.    d.
(Please delete words not applicable)
NAME ............................................................................................... (Block letters)
ADDRESS ...............................................................................................................
Use this form if inconvenient to call. The best available seats will be allotted to you.

Printed by Electric (Modern) Printing Co. Ltd., Manchester 8.

Stones. Ian Stewart recalled in *Datebook* that the police "followed us wherever we went and even went back to our hotel after the show. Brian invited the police to join us in the lounge for coffee. While we were sitting there—it was two o'clock by this time—the chief inspector himself arrived.... And then in through the door walked one of the girls on the arm of our other road manager! All hell let loose! But the police soon realized that she hadn't been in any danger and just whisked her back home to her parents."

Following these shows, the Stones spent five days in the studio recording various tracks, including "Little Red Rooster," "Off the Hook," "Under the Boardwalk," and "Sleepy City." They also taped an appearance on *Top of the Pops* on September 2.

**Saturday, September 5:** Astoria Theatre, Finsbury Park, London, UK, with Inez and Charlie Foxx, Mike Berry and the Innocents, the Mojos, Simon Scott and the Le Roys, 6:30 and 9 p.m.

This was the opening date of the Stones' fourth British package tour, which lasted until October 11. Robert Stigwood promoted the tour. The Stones were apparently promised 40 percent of the profits in exchange for accepting £50 per week. They later claimed that Stigwood reneged on his promises and sued him in 1965 to get their money. Other acts on the bill included Inez and Charlie Foxx, a soul duo from North Carolina that achieved fame in America with "Mockingbird" and had a hit in the UK with "Hurt by Love," and the Mojos, a Liverpool group that scored with "Everything's Alright." The Stones' set: "Not Fade Away," "I Just Want to Make Love to You," "Walking the Dog," "If You Need Me," "Around and Around," "I'm a King Bee," "I'm Alright," and "It's All Over Now." Much of their act, however, was drowned out by audience screams, which reached a crescendo during "I'm Alright." Richard Green of *NME* reported, "Brian was scream-provoker in chief as he dashed backwards and forwards bashing a tambourine. He was aided by Keith, who can't stand still for more than two notes and Mick, who kept creeping dangerously near to the edge of the stage. In contrast, Charlie and Bill were very calm."

**Sunday, September 6:** Odeon Theatre, Leicester, UK, with Inez and Charlie Foxx, Mike Berry and the Innocents, the Mojos, Simon Scott and the Le Roys, 5:30 and 8 p.m.

**Tuesday, September 8:** Odeon Theatre, Colchester, Essex, UK, with Inez and Charlie Foxx, Mike Berry and the Innocents, the Mojos, Simon Scott and the Le Roys, two shows

**Wednesday, September 9:** Odeon Theatre, Luton, Bedfordshire, UK, with Inez and Charlie Foxx, Mike Berry and the Innocents, the Mojos, Simon Scott and the Le Roys, 6:30 and 8:50 p.m.

**Thursday, September 10:** Odeon Theatre, Cheltenham, Gloucestershire, UK, with Inez and Charlie Foxx, Mike Berry and the Innocents, the Mojos, Simon Scott and the Le Roys, two shows

The Stones played in Brian's hometown. *The Gloucestershire Echo* reported, "Police officers, security men, commissionaires and first aid men linked arms last night to prevent screaming fans from rushing the stage at both performances by the Rolling Stones at the Odeon Cinema. One girl managed to clamber onto the platform, but was quickly hauled down. During their lively act the Stones were pelted with sweets and other objects as tokens of affection.... After the show crowds of fans waited outside in front of the cinema,

*Opposite:* **Handbill for a Stones concert in Plymouth, 1964 (collection of Ira Korman).**

but the Rolling Stones slipped out the back way with a police escort and went off in their own car."

**Friday, September 11:** Capitol Theatre, Cardiff, Wales, UK, with Inez and Charlie Foxx, Mike Berry and the Innocents, the Mojos, Simon Scott and the Le Roys, 6 and 8:50 p.m.

**Sunday, September 13:** Empire Theatre, Liverpool, UK, with Inez and Charlie Foxx, Mike Berry and the Innocents, the Mojos, Simon Scott and the Le Roys, 5:40 and 8 p.m.

Following their Empire show, the Stones attended a birthday party for Inez Foxx.

**Monday, September 14:** ABC Theatre, Chester, Cheshire, UK, with Inez and Charlie Foxx, Mike Berry and the Innocents, the Mojos, Simon Scott and the Le Roys, two shows

Keith recalled this show in an interview on BBC 6: "One time in Chester we had the Chief Constable of Cheshire with us in full regalia with the ribbons and the medals and the swagger stick. (He tells us) Show's finished earlier than he expects. The whole theatre is surrounded. Mayhem. Maniac teenage girls, bless their hearts. 'Right,' he says. 'The only way out, up the stairs, over the rooftops, I know the way!' ... So we get up on the Chester rooftops and it's raining. The first thing that happens is the Chief Constable almost slides off the roof.... We're standing in the middle of this rooftop saying 'I'm not too familiar with this area. Where do we go?' ... They manage to get us down through a skylight and out of a laundry chute, or something. That was what happened every day and you took it as normal."

**Tuesday, September 15:** Odeon Theatre, Manchester, UK, with Inez and Charlie Foxx, Mike Berry and the Innocents, the Mojos, Simon Scott and the Le Roys, two shows, and Blue Angel Club, Liverpool, 2 a.m.

While in Manchester, the Stones appeared on the Granada TV show *Scene at 6.30*. They were staying in Liverpool that night and headed to the popular Blue Angel Club to hear a local band called the Pawns. Numerous Liverpool luminaries were present including Rory Storm of the Hurricanes and the Remo Four. When the Pawns finished playing, the Stones decided to take the stage and treated those in the club to an impromptu hour-long set. Charlie Watts arrived late so Brian Low, of Scottish band Blues System, sat in. However, when Charlie arrived he took over on drums. Inez and Charlie Foxx then jumped onstage to perform "Can I Get a Witness" and their hit "Mockingbird" with the Stones. Mick and Inez then dueted on "The Sky Is Crying."

**Wednesday, September 16:** ABC Theatre, Wigan, Greater Manchester, UK, with Inez and Charlie Foxx, Mike Berry and the Innocents, the Mojos, Simon Scott and the Le Roys, two shows

Extra police and ambulances were present at the Stones' two shows, but the local paper reported, "Apart from nearly bringing the roof in with their screaming, the Wigan teenagers were satisfied just to stand and wave. Only three young girls tried to dash to the front during the night, but they were turned back by dress-suited attendants and police on duty inside the theatre."

**Thursday, September 17:** ABC Theatre, Carlisle, Cumbria, with Inez and Charlie Foxx, Mike Berry and the Innocents, the Mojos, Simon Scott and the Le Roys, 6:15 and 8:30 p.m.

The Stones' shows in Carlisle were riotous affairs. Keith related in *Disc*, "About six girls got onto the stage with something like 20 attendants chasing them! This was in the middle of our set and at one time there were only Bill and Charlie playing because of all the commotion. But we carried on regardless. We don't really mind these things happening, providing that no harm is done. And we have been lucky so far in that respect."

**Friday, September 18:** Odeon Theatre, Newcastle, UK, with Inez and Charlie Foxx, Mike Berry and the Innocents, the Mojos, Simon Scott and the Le Roys, two shows

**Saturday, September 19:** Usher Hall, Edinburgh, Scotland, UK, with Inez and Charlie Foxx, Mike Berry and the Innocents, the Mojos, Simon Scott and the Le Roys, two shows

While staying in Edinburgh, Keith talked to *Disc* about the current tour: "The other people on the show are a really wonderful crowd and we spend most of our time between performances wandering around the dressing rooms talking to them. Charlie and Inez Foxx are going over fantastically, which pleases us because we asked for them to be included on the bill.... On several occasions we have played extra time because when we get in the mood just anything goes and no one can stop us!"

**Sunday, September 20:** ABC Theatre, Stockton-on-Tees, UK, with Inez and Charlie Foxx, Mike Berry and the Innocents, the Mojos, Simon Scott and the Le Roys, 5:30 and 8 p.m.

**Monday, September 21:** ABC Theatre, Hull, Yorkshire, UK, with Inez and Charlie Foxx, Mike Berry and the Innocents, the Mojos, Simon Scott and the Le Roys, 6:15 and 8:30 p.m.

Pathé News filmed the Stones backstage and onstage, for a color newsreel, *The Rolling Stones Gather No Moss,* that was shown in British cinemas. The Stones were seen performing "Around and Around." Video was also filmed of them on the side of the road trying to hitchhike.

**Tuesday, September 22:** ABC Theatre, Lincoln, UK, with Inez and Charlie Foxx, Mike Berry and the Innocents, the Mojos, Simon Scott and the Le Roys, 6:15 and 8:30 p.m.

**Thursday, September 24:** Gaumont Theatre, Doncaster, Yorkshire, UK, with Inez and Charlie Foxx, Mike Berry and the Innocents, the Mojos, Simon Scott and the Le Roys, 6:15 and 8:30 p.m.

**Friday, September 25:** Gaumont Theatre, Hanley, Staffordshire, UK, with Inez and Charlie Foxx, Mike Berry and the Innocents, the Mojos, Simon Scott and the Le Roys, 6:45 and 8:50 p.m.

**Saturday, September 26:** Gaumont Theatre, Bradford, Yorkshire, UK, with Inez and Charlie Foxx, Mike Berry and the Innocents, the Mojos, Simon Scott and the Le Roys, 6:15 and 8:40 p.m.

The Stones returned to Bradford, where Brian had his clothes ripped off by fans months earlier. To avoid a repeat, the Stones were picked up by a police van outside town and smuggled into the venue. But fans inside tried their best to reach the group. *The Telegraph & Argus* reported, "As the Stones went into their first number the air became thick with flying objects as adoring fans showered the stage with autograph books, scarves, sweets—everything.... Girls jumped up and down on the seats. Girls just wept. And the screams went on. Little could be heard of the group through the noise. Had it not been for the thud of the drums and the almost eerie vibration from the amplified guitars, the group could have been practicing a mime."

**Sunday, September 27:** Hippodrome Theatre, Birmingham, UK, with Inez and Charlie Foxx, Mike Berry and the Innocents, the Mojos, Simon Scott and the Le Roys, two shows

**Monday, September 28:** Odeon Theatre, Romford, Essex, UK, with Inez and Charlie Foxx, Mike Berry and the Innocents, the Mojos, Simon Scott and the Le Roys, 6:30 and 8:45 p.m.

Recalling these shows in *Datebook*, Ian Stewart commented, "One night in Romford when (Mick) was in the middle of a number, this hysterical teenager rushed at him from the wings, sobbing, with her arms outstretched. Mick ducked quickly, caught her in a fireman's lift and then danced her over his shoulders back to the wings, where she was taken away by an attendant. Mick then carried on as if nothing had happened!" On September 28 and 29 the Stones spent the day at Regent Sound recording tracks, including "Grown Up Wrong" and "Surprise, Surprise." Keith also attended a Marianne Faithfull session on September 30.

**Thursday, October 1:** Colston Hall, Bristol, UK, with Inez and Charlie Foxx, Mike Berry and the Innocents, the Mojos, Simon Scott and the Le Roys, two shows

**Friday, October 2:** Odeon Theatre, Exeter, Devon, UK, with Inez and Charlie Foxx, Mike Berry and the Innocents, the Mojos, Simon Scott and the Le Roys, 6:30 and 8:45 p.m.

The usual wild scenes occurred in Exeter. *The Express & Echo* reported, "The fans howled and screamed, surrounded the building, tried to enter the dressing-rooms and were kept at bay by a strong police contingent, plus 20 strong-arm men who lined the front of the stage as 'The Stones' went into their act."

**Saturday, October 3:** Regal Theatre, Edmonton, North London, UK, with Inez and Charlie Foxx, Mike Berry and the Innocents, the Mojos, Simon Scott and the Le Roys, two shows

**Sunday, October 4:** Gaumont Theatre, Southampton, Hampshire, UK, with Inez and Charlie Foxx, Mike Berry and the Innocents, The Mojos, Simon Scott and the Le Roys, two shows

**Monday, October 5:** Gaumont Theatre, Wolverhampton, with Inez and Charlie Foxx, Mike Berry and the Innocents, the Mojos, Simon Scott and the Le Roys, two shows

**Tuesday, October 6:** Gaumont Theatre, Watford, Hertfordshire, UK, with Inez and Charlie Foxx, Mike Berry and the Innocents, the Mojos, Simon Scott and the Le Roys, two shows

**Thursday, October 8:** Odeon Theatre, Lewisham, South London, with Inez and Charlie Foxx, Mike Berry and the Innocents, the Mojos, Simon Scott and the Le Roys, 6:45 and 9 p.m.

Prior to these shows, the Stones appeared on the BBC Radio show *Rhythm and Blues* hosted by Alexis Korner.

**Friday, October 9:** Gaumont Theatre, Ipswich, Suffolk, UK, with Inez and Charlie Foxx, Mike Berry and the Innocents, the Mojos, Simon Scott and the Le Roys, 6:35 and 8:45 p.m.

**Saturday, October 10:** Odeon Theatre, Southend, Essex, UK, with Inez and Charlie Foxx, Mike Berry and the Innocents, the Mojos, Simon Scott and the Le Roys, 6:30 and 8:45 p.m.

**Sunday, October 11:** Hippodrome, Brighton, UK, with Inez and Charlie Foxx, Marty Wilde and the Wildcats, the Echoes, Simon Scott and the Le Roys, 6 and 8:30 p.m.

**Tuesday, October 20:** Olympia Theatre, Paris, France, with Vince Taylor, Les Haricots Rouge, Jean-Paul Sevre, Rocky Roberts et les Airbales, Bobby Solo, Ron et Mel, Conrad Pringle, Pierre Perret and Jean-Marie Proslier

The Stones made a quick visit to Belgium and France. The Belgium trip almost didn't happen as the minister of the interior had banned the group after hearing about riots they'd provoked in the Netherlands. The TV producer who had invited the Stones convinced the minister to change his mind. Over 5,000 fans turned out to greet the group on Sunday when they landed in Brussels. They played no concerts, but taped the TV show *Tienerklanken* at the Amerikaans Theatre, which was overrun with enthusiastic fans. They than headed to Paris, where they appeared on the TV show *Quoi De Neuf?* on October 19. The next day 2,000 fans attended the Stones' concert. The set: "Around and Around," "Carol," "Bye Bye Johnny," "It's All Over Now," "Time Is on My Side," "Not Fade Away," "Walking the Dog," "If You Need Me," "I'm Alright," "Confessin' the Blues" and "Tell Me."

Fifty bouncers were on hand to make sure the crowd did not get out of hand. But, the *Daily Mirror* reported, "Hundreds of stampeding teenagers smashed seats and broke windows … at the end of a show given by Britain's Rolling Stones beat group." The Stones were hustled out of the venue after the show and into a waiting armored police van, which drove around town until the crowds had died down. Mick told Brian Harvey of *Record Mirror*, "It was all right I suppose but when I noticed a rack of sten guns above our head I began to wonder what sort of trouble they were expecting." He eventually got so bored that when the van stopped in traffic he got out and fled into a crowd, irritating police.

**Saturday, October 24:** Academy of Music, New York, 2 and 7 p.m.

The Stones arrived in New York on October 23 to begin their second North American tour. Stu, Andrew Oldham, Eric Easton and road manager Mike Dorsey accompanied them. The Stones' popularity had grown in the States and a press conference at the Astor Hotel was far better covered, though the questions were just as inane. Asked if it was true he was getting married, Brian replied, "It was just a rumor." When the clueless reporter followed up with "So you're not going out with any girls?" Brian broke up the room with his reply: "Oh, many girls!" When the laughter subsided he added "Actually, no girls to speak of." Mick was asked if the bad publicity the Stones got bothered him and replied, "First of all we're not dirty. We're not. They have to make up something like that to get readers, I suppose. It's all right as long as they talk about us." Asked why they didn't dress alike, Mick commented, "We're musicians, we're not an act. How we sound is more important than how we look."

After settling in at the hotel, the Stones began rehearsals for their appearance on CBS TV's *Ed Sullivan Show* and taped interviews for *The Ed Rudy Radio Show*, which later appeared on a specially pressed LP. Rudy asked Mick why the Stones recorded many covers of American artists and he explained, "You know we find that these American songs are better for ourselves. The songs that Keith and I write we give to other people because they're mostly ballads and things like that." Asked how they got along, Mick commented: "It goes along very well. We have our arguments, every group has arguments, about what records we're going to do and things like that, but on the whole we get along fine."

On October 24 the Stones taped a morning interview with Murry the K at WINS Radio. Fans surrounded the studio. Bill recalled, "When the show ended we couldn't get out. The cops finally arrived and decided that the only method was muscle. A whole gang of them forced their way to our two limousines." Bill somehow got separated from his protectors and had to flee back to the radio station to avoid being torn limb from limb. A special police escort helped him to join the Stones at WPIX TV studios to film the *Clay Cole Show*. That night the Stones opened their tour at the Academy of Music, a now demolished venue on Fourteenth Street and Third Avenue. Over 7,000 fans attended the shows. *Record Mirror* reported, "Despite the presence of cops onstage, several girls fought their way to the stage. One managed to clamber up and kiss Keith Richard before she was dragged down by cops."

**Monday, October 26:** Memorial Auditorium, Sacramento, CA, with the Righteous Brothers, Keith Allison and the Goodnighters and Jody Miller, 8 p.m.

Following their Sunday appearance on the *Ed Sullivan Show*, the Stones flew to California to appear in Sacramento. Greg Huff of *The Sacramento Union* devoted most of his review to the crowd's response, noting, "During the last few songs, the kids began dumping over chairs, gathering in the aisles and pressing closer to the stage. When the houselights came on and it was obvious that the show was over, a dozen girls broke for the stage, throwing themselves at the edge, trying to clamber over the footlights. Just as quickly, the police caught the girls, flinging them back to the floor."

**Tuesday, October 27, to Thursday, October 29:** Teen Age Music International (TAMI) Awards, Civic Auditorium, Santa Monica, CA, with Jan and Dean, Chuck Berry, Gerry and the Pacemakers, Smokey Robinson and the Miracles, Marvin Gaye, Lesley Gore, Billy J. Kramer and the Dakotas, the Supremes, the Barbarians, James Brown and the Beach Boys (one show on Wednesday, two shows on Thursday)

Bill Sargent organized the Teenage Music International (TAMI) Show. The plan was to film a multi-act rock concert and release it in theaters. The event was filmed in Electronovision, a process with higher resolution than regular TV cameras. Steve Binder directed the film and Jack Nietzsche acted as music arranger. Members of Phil Spector's "Wrecking Crew," served as the house backup band. Mick later recalled, "What was interesting about the TAMI show was that there was a huge list of acts, not only all the black acts—Chuck Berry, Marvin Gaye, the Supremes—but a lot of white acts too—the Beach Boys and Jan and Dean—everybody who was popular in LA at the time, basically." The producers had that the performers play three shows (two concerts in front of a live audience each night and one additional show with no audience on Thursday afternoon) so they'd have multiple performances to select from.

The Stones closed the concerts and were understandably nervous, as they had to follow James Brown, who put on an incendiary show. Keith later recalled, "That did make me a little tight. Thank God the audience was mostly white. However, everybody else was just as nervous." Mick told Guy Stevens of *Record Mirror*, "We tried for two days to get it changed around, but it was no good. I mean, you can't follow an act like that. Luckily when we actually did the film there was a ten minute break, which gave the audience time to cool down." Despite their trepidation, the Stones put on a very exciting performance. They played "Around and Around," "Off the Hook," "Time Is on My Side," "It's All Over Now" and "I'm Alright." They also took part in the big closing number "Get Together," for which all the acts, black and white, crowded onto the stage together and

Handbill for the Stones' concert in Sacramento, October 1964 (collection of Ira Korman).

danced, which was revolutionary in its own way. The film was released nationally on December 29. It was highly successful and remained in theaters through the first half of 1965. A restored DVD was released in 2012.

**Saturday, October 31:** Swing Auditorium, San Bernardino, CA, 8:30 p.m.

The Stones had no shows on October 30 and spent the day trying on clothes at the posh store Beau Gentry in Hollywood. That night they attended a party at singer Phil Everly's home. On Saturday they returned to San Bernardino, where they'd received such a good reception on their previous visit. Rather than send its own reviewer to cover the show, the *San Bernardino County Sun* gave two high school students the honor. They reported, "We thought the way they started off their show with 'Not Fade Away' was terrific. The audience reaction to 'Route 66,' one of their better numbers, was highlighted by the fact that San Bernardino is mentioned in it. Our favor song was 'Mona,' which received the most reaction from 'the mob.' Closing with 'It's All Over Now' was clever."

**Sunday, November 1:** Civic Auditorium, Long Beach, CA, with Don and the Deacons, the Vibrants, the Spats, Jimmy Clanton, the Soul Brothers and Dick and Dee-Dee, 2 p.m., and Balboa Park Bowl, San Diego, CA, with the Accents, the Pyramids, the Misfits, Rosie and the Originals, Josephine, Joel Hill and the Invaders and Joey Page, 6:30 p.m.

The afternoon show in Long Beach was a wild affair. One fan told *The Press Telegram*, "Everyone stood on their seats and girls were even on the backs of their chairs, clinging onto the balcony above for balance and they had to stop the show to warn the audience to behave." Following the show, the Stones flew to San Diego to play Balboa Park Bowl. Although only 2,000 fans attended, promoters hired over 70 private patrolmen to prevent riots. Jim Box of the *San Diego Union* reported that the crowds remained calm, but "young girls pelted the Stones with candy, gum and combs" throughout.

The Stones then flew to Los Angeles. On November 2 they went to RCA to work on their next album with engineer Dave Hassinger. Arranger Jack Nitzsche also took part in the sessions, which produced "Down Home Girl," two versions of "Everybody Needs Somebody to Love," "Heart of Stone," "Hitch Hike," "Oh Baby" and "Pain in My Heart." Keith later remarked, "The atmosphere and studio, plus the fact that we knew we had good material, made the session a good one. We didn't think it would work out at first, as the studio is so gigantic we were terrified to use it. Then Andrew hit on the idea of putting us in one corner, shutting off the main lights and just using a spotlight, to make it more cozy. The control room was also in darkness. A bit mad, but it did the trick."

**Tuesday, November 3:** Public Hall, Cleveland, OH, 7:30 p.m.

The Stones' first concert in Cleveland was attended by less than 1,000 people. Promoters blamed Mayor Ralph Locher's decision to ban future rock concerts. Locher argued the shows led to violence. As a result, many parents refused to let their children attend. Mick commented to *Rolling Stones Monthly*, "We noticed several empty seats—obviously some of the kids had been prevented from seeing the show, but everyone that did come had a rave." Within 45 seconds of the Stones taking the stage riots began breaking out, as screaming girls struggled to break through the police cordon and get on stage. Colin Leinster of *The Plain Dealer* reported, "Girls who surged forward were shoved back. So were girls who looked as though they were about to do something they shouldn't."

**Wednesday, November 4:** Loews Theater, Providence, RI, with Georgie Porgie & the Cry Babies, 8 p.m.

The Providence concert was a typically riotous affair. Mick recalled in *The Rolling Stones Monthly*, "They'd covered the orchestra pit with a thin plywood top. Lots of girls rushed down the aisles, jumped on to the plywood, which promptly gave way, and down they went into the pit! Incredible sight!" Police stopped the show after 20 minutes. Bradford Swan of *The Providence Journal* reported, "The Stones had them standing (not rolling) in the aisles, and on the arms and seats of their chairs. The Rolling Stones ... are at least as distinctive, as are the Beatles. The Stones, however, are a little nearer to jazz than most of the current crop of rock 'n' rollers. They are also more musically inclined than the Beach Boys."

The group took a train to New York after the gig. They had a week off to do whatever they wanted. While Charlie hit the jazz clubs, Mick, Keith and Andrew attended James Brown's show at the Apollo Theater. Brian and Bill spent their time exploring Greenwich Village, hanging out with blues singer John Hammond, Jr. On Sunday, November 8, the Stones returned to Chess Studios in Chicago to record with engineer Ron Malo. Mick commented in *Melody Maker*, "We wrote several originals, including a thing called 'What a Shame.' It wasn't quite the same atmosphere this time, because it was a Sunday, and nobody was about. Sunday in Chicago is like Sunday in Scotland—dead."

**Wednesday, November 11:** Auditorium, Milwaukee, WI, with Alan Black, 7:30 p.m.

On Monday, the Stones drove from Chicago to promote their upcoming Milwaukee concert. They gave a press conference at the Coach House Motor Inn. The band had grown tired of these daily affairs, where they were asked the same inane questions, and they responded with sarcasm. Asked how he got that biting sound from his harmonica, Brian replied, "Bite it." Asked what he wanted to be, Charlie replied, "Happy." Following the conference, they headed back to Chicago. Brian had complained of feeling lousy. It turned out he had bronchitis and was admitted to a hospital on November 10. He missed the gigs in Milwaukee, Fort Wayne, Dayton and Louisville. On top of Brian's illness, the Stones had to deal with fallout from the mayor of Milwaukee's decision to condemn the Stones' concert as immoral, which caused parents to keep kids from attending. The *Milwaukee Journal* reported, "The Rolling Stones serenaded 1,274 customers and 4,992 empty seats in the Auditorium Wednesday night. Perhaps these shaggiest of the British intruders have proved that even nonconformity has its limits…. Screams from a thousand throats drowned out all but the most insistent electronic cacophony and the two fisted smashes of drummer Charlie Watts."

**Thursday, November 12:** Allen County Memorial Coliseum, Fort Wayne, IN, with the Green Men and the Shangri-Las

2,029 people turned out for this concert. On taking the stage, Mick commented, "I just want to say we won't sound like we usually do. There are only four of us now." But the *Journal Gazette* reported that it didn't really matter as they could hardly be heard: "Never did so few people make such a racket for so little cause as did those in the Allen County Memorial Coliseum Thursday night at the sight of four scrawny, mussed up, pasty-faced, dirty looking creatures (the Rolling Stones)… Perhaps in some areas of the Coliseum, the microphones picked up the music sung by Jagger, who sometimes managed a faint smile, and Keith Richard, who looked a bit jollier, Bill Wyman on the bass, who never smiled by, and the drummer Charlie Watts, who shut his eyes as if he wished he wasn't there."

**Friday, November 13:** Wampler's Hara Arena, Dayton, OH, with Ivan and the Sabers

Less than 1,000 people turned out to see the Stones at the 6,000-seat arena. But reporter Gee Mitchell of *The Dayton Daily News* noted, "What the Stones' audience lacked in numbers it strove valiantly to make up in lungpower. But most of the enthusiasm had to be triggered by the loose-lipped antics of Mick Jagger, the group's lead vocalist. And the Stones didn't really give their faithful much opportunity. They were on stage less than

Handbill for the Stones' appearance in Croydon, December 1964 (collection of Ira Korman).

20 minutes, (and) did eight numbers-or whatever designation is given the component parts of their brand of noise."

During this tour, the Stones continued to be attacked by the press for their "dirty" appearance. Though they professed not to mind, the Stones were upset by the continual criticism. Brian told *16 Magazine*, "How can anyone dislike anyone because of their haircut? I read things that people have supposedly said about us and I really get sad. I guess I should be sad for them though. If they don't like our music, good-let them bypass our performances. But if they hate us because of the way we look and dress, then they are not really very bright, penetrating or thoughtful people and we really don't need them." Keith added, "We're not deliberately untidy. If being a rebel is bad-then America should still be an English colony. I think a lot of this rebel thing has been brought up by people who enjoy exaggerating it."

**Saturday, November 14:** Memorial Auditorium, Louisville, KY, 5 and 8 p.m.

Only 1,700 fans turned out to see the Stones, possibly because James Brown was playing the same night (Mick and Bill visited him backstage). Nevertheless, those in attendance made up for their small numbers by the intensity of their adoration. Rod Larmee of *The Courier Journal* reported, "During the 34 minutes that they were onstage during two performances at Memorial Auditorium, the Stones caused the teenage audience to shriek, pull its hair and lose most of its inhibitions…. The place resembled a Hollywood premiere, with flashbulbs going off constantly. When one of the Stones gave a twitch or wave of the wrist, all the bulbs seemed to go off at once and the volume of screams increased."

**Sunday, November 15:** Arie Crown Theatre, Chicago, IL

5,500 attended the final night of the tour and saw all five Stones (Brian having rejoined) perform. The band flew back to New York on Monday to be photographed for *Billboard* and then on to England on Tuesday.

**Friday, November 20:** Glad Rag Ball, Empire Pool, Wembley, UK, with the Animals, Long John Baldry, Ginger Johnson and his African Drummers and Humphrey Lyttelton, 9 p.m.

The Stones taped an afternoon appearance on *Ready Steady Go* and then appeared at the Glad Rag Ball with the Newcastle band the Animals, fronted by Eric Burdon. The Stones performed "Off the Hook," "Little Red Rooster" and "Around and Around." This appearance was filmed and televised on ARTV, but is unfortunately lost. The Stones then took a break from performing. They were booked by Eric Easton to tape a radio show on November 23 but the band were growing tired of such appearances and opted to skip it, angering the BBC. The Stones did, however, travel to Birmingham on November 29 to tape a special edition of *Thank Your Lucky Stars*.

**Friday, December 4:** Fairfield Hall, Croydon, South London, UK, with Cliff Bennett and the Rebel Rousers, Twinkle and the Quiet Five, 6:45 and 9 p.m.

This was the Stones' last show of a very busy year. Mick and Brian then took a brief holiday together in Paris. However, the Stones didn't entirely relax. On December 15 they were at Shepperton to film videos for the U.S. TV show *Shindig*. On December 31 they taped an appearance for *Ready Steady Go!'s* special New Year's Eve episode.

## Chapter 4

# 1965

The Stones released their second UK LP, *The Rolling Stones No. 2*, on January 15. Like their first album, it consisted mainly of songs from their stage act, including Don Raye's "Down the Road Apiece," Irma Thomas's "Time Is on My Side," and Allen Toussaint's "Pain in My Heart." However, there were also three Jagger-Richards numbers, including "Off the Hook," and "Grown Up Wrong." Like its predecessor, the LP shot up the British charts and spent 15 weeks at number one. In an interview with Keith Altham, Brian remarked that his favorite number on it was Muddy Waters' "I Can't Be Satisfied," because "I play bottle-neck guitar on it. It has one of the best guitar solos I've ever managed." Keith predictably picked the Chuck Berry cover "You Can't Catch Me" as "It has a fantastic heavy beat which builds up like a locomotive coming up behind you." More important for the future of the band was their February 1965 single release, "The Last Time." The song was the first Jagger-Richards tune the band released as a single (though it was loosely based on "Maybe the Last Time" by the Staples Singers) and its smashing success (number one in the UK and number 9 in the U.S.) gave them confidence to stay the course. Mick told *NME*, "I like it a lot. It's far more commercial than 'Little Red Rooster,' but then that wasn't supposed to be commercial. Yes we're all satisfied with it."

The song featured excellent lead guitar from Brian, though by all accounts he felt increasingly alienated from the band he'd created. Mick and Keith now controlled the destiny of the Stones and Brian was relegated to a lesser role, which he found hard to deal with. Indeed, on the April-May North American tour Brian openly expressed his frustration to friends. New York DJ Scott Ross commented in *Stone Alone* that when Brian was in Toronto he called him to say, "He was not going to go to the recording session in Chicago.... I tried to talk him out of it, or at least to realize that it was a pretty big decision and it had implications if he didn't show up, but he didn't care. He just said he couldn't do it. ... He talked about it a lot. He felt like he was being cut out."

Brian also questioned the direction Andrew was urging the group in. As Bill pointed out, "Andrew wanted us to do some much more pop-oriented material. He was always pushing to get us to do Motown things like 'Can I Get a Witness.' And he was more right than we were. And, of course, when Mick and Keith got into writing, the songs came out more like he was looking for." Brian was very proud of the bluesy "Little Red Rooster" but expressed ambivalence about the more poppy "It's All Over Now." The group no longer fulfilled his ambitions. As he tellingly remarked in *Charlie Is My Darling*, the film Peter Whitehead made of the Stones' September 1965 Irish tour, "My ultimate aim in life was never to be a pop star. I enjoy it with reservations but I'm not really satisfied artistically or personally."

Nineteen sixty-five German advertisement for the Stones (collection of Ira Korman).

But Brian was a paradox. While he expressed disdain for pop stardom, he embraced the perks that came with it—especially sex and drugs. Indeed, Brian was the first of the Stones to try LSD. He took it after a Long Beach show and again in New York. His drug use exacerbated his already volatile mood swings. And there was never any shortage of people ready to supply drugs to the most glamorous of Stones. As Keith recalled in 1971, "People were always laying stuff on him because he was a Stone. And he'd try it. He'd take anything. Any other sort of trip too, head-trips. He never had time to work it out 'cause we were on the road all the time, always on the plane the next day."

1965 was indeed a very busy year, with endless touring, punctuated by occasional breaks for recording. The difference, however, was that by now the world had succumbed to Stones-mania. Mick commented in *NME* that September, "In the middle of the performance we used to be able to amble out and have a drink in the pub across the road, than amble back. Nobody disturbed us. After a couple of hits it got a lot tougher, especially in the ballrooms. They're the worst, because often you have to go in at the front because there's no other way." Everywhere they went there were screams and riots. Brian occasionally played "Popeye the Sailor" instead of the tune they were supposed to perform, just to prove that no one was paying any attention. As Keith remarked, the only thing the band rehearsed anymore was the getaway from the venue, because they knew they'd have to run for their lives.

It was while they were on their third tour of the States in May that the band recorded their most famous song at Chess Studios in Chicago and RCA in Hollywood. In 1968 Mick recalled the basic genesis of "(I Can't Get No) Satisfaction" for reporter Jonathan Cott: "It was Keith really. I mean it was his initial idea. It sounded like a folk song when we first started working on it and Keith didn't like it much, he didn't want it to be a single, he didn't think it would do very well." In a 1971 interview, Keith commented: "I wanted to cut it again. It sounded all right but I didn't really like that fuzz guitar. I wanted to make that thing different. But I don't think we could have done, you needed either horns or something that could really knock that riff out." Luckily, Keith was outvoted by his fellow Stones. The song was an instant classic and rocketed to the top of the U.S. charts when released in June (Decca was slow to release it in the UK, but eventually put it out in late August. It went to number one in September).

It was during the summer that the Stones began a business relationship with Allen Klein, who'd previously managed Sam Cooke. Klein was known as a ferocious and single-minded negotiator and he convinced Andrew that he could help the Stones, whose contract with Decca was up, secure a better deal. He was appointed business manager of the group and Eric Easton soon departed. Keith told NME, "We decided on an American as our new business manager because, let's face it, when you are handling worldwide transactions America is the only place to work from, and we do so much business there it's very useful to have a man on the spot." Mick and Keith later had cause to regret entering into business with Klein, but he did secure a better deal with Decca and all the Stones received large checks that summer.

In the midst of all this success, the Stones released their third British LP, *Out of Our Heads*, on September 24. The album showcased the improved songwriting of Jagger-Richards on the exciting opener "She Said Yeah," the moody ballad "Heart of Stone" and the statement of purpose "I'm Free." It also featured the usual solid covers, including Don Covay's "Mercy, Mercy," Otis Redding's "That's How Strong My Love Is" and Marvin Gaye's "Hitch Hike." Many fans argue that the U.S. version released in July had the edge as it included the singles "(I Can't Get No) Satisfaction," "The Last Time" and "Play with Fire." The group followed up the LP with their next single, another Jagger-Richards composition, "Get Off of My Cloud." The fast paced song featured Brian on lead guitar and Ian Stewart on piano. Although Keith was unhappy with the production, fans disagreed. It was highly successful, landing on the top of the UK and U.S. charts and ending 1965 on a high note.

## Concerts

**Wednesday, January 6:** ABC Theatre, Belfast, Northern Ireland, UK, with the Banshees, the Checkmates, Twinkle and the Gonks, two shows

The Stones made a visit to Ireland, accompanied, by Andrew, Stu and Mike Dorsey. Stu's roommate, engineer Glyn Johns, also joined them. The Stones played on a bill with teenage sensation Twinkle, who had a hit with the dramatic ballad "Terry." While in Belfast the UTV show *Six Five* filmed the Stones rehearsing "Little Red Rooster" and interviewed them. Dawn James of *Rave* attended one of the shows and reported: "Brian, Mick, Keith, Bill and Charlie had played and sung their way into the hearts of the Irish audience. Screams had even swamped the Stones' noise and the purple lights had lost their color to eyes dimmed by tears of ecstasy. An ashtray missed Bill's face by inches. An iron bolt hit Mick on the thigh. A mod patent shoe swirled towards Brian. He smiled, and ducked elegantly. A program hissed past Charlie's ear, but he didn't even notice. These strange tokens of a strange love were hurled from the turbulent sea beyond the footlights."

**Thursday, January 7:** Adelphi Cinema, Dublin, Ireland, with the Banshees, the Checkmates, Twinkle and the Gonks, two shows

The Stones performed two sold-out shows. The *Irish Times* reported, "The reception for them by the teenagers was deafening. At the end of the shows there were the inevitable attempts to rushing the stage: the aisles were jammed and those at the back had to stand on their seats to see the stage."

**Friday, January 8:** Savoy Cinema, Cork, Ireland, with the Banshees, the Checkmates, Twinkle and the Gonks, two shows

The short Irish tour had its share of amusing moments. Keith recalled in *NME*, "We stopped outside a fabulous old shop one morning to buy some gear. It was kind of an old Army surplus store right out in the sticks. There was an old fella, behind the counter, who screamed that we had been sent by Oliver Cromwell. He chased us out of the shop and jumped on the hood of the car. Then he proceeded to try and boot the windshield to pieces. He must have been at least eighty!"

**Sunday, January 10:** ABC Commodore Theatre, Hammersmith, London, UK, with the Quiet Five, Julie Grant, Zoot Money's Big Roll Band, Tony Jackson and the Vibrations, the Checkmates and Marianne Faithfull, 5:45 and 8:15 p.m.

These were the Stones' last shows before departing for an Australasian tour. Prior to leaving, they taped appearances on *Thank Your Lucy Stars* on January 13 and *Ready Steady Go!* on January 15. On Sunday, January 17, the Stones flew to Los Angeles to relax. While in LA, Brian, Keith and Andrew went to a club to see Little Anthony and the Imperials.

**Friday, January 22, and Saturday, January 23:** Manufacturer's Auditorium Showgrounds, Sydney, NSW, Australia, with the Torquays, Ray Columbus and the Invaders, the Newbeats and Roy Orbison, two shows on Friday and three shows on Saturday

The Stones began their first tour of Australia and New Zealand on a bill with the legendary Roy Orbison, who'd recently scored a number one with "Pretty Woman," the New Zealand band Ray Columbus and the Invaders and the American band the Newbeats, who'd scored the previous year with "Bread and Butter." The Stones were not huge stars in Australia, though they'd had a hit with the single "Under the Boardwalk." Promoter Harry M. Miller of Pan-Pacific Productions, worried about losing money, insisted that they not bring their own equipment to cut down on freight costs. The group flew to Australia on January 19, crossing the international dateline and losing January 20 in the process. They landed in Sydney on Thursday and immediately were faced with a riot. Three hundred fans got past a fence and raced towards the aircraft as the Stones came down the steps. Police went into action and prevented them from reaching the group. The Stones spent the rest of the day doing promotion, including interviews for the Australian TV show *Bandstand*.

The Stones played five shows in two days in Sydney. They performed nine songs at each show to wildly enthusiastic audiences. A portion of "Not Fade Away" from the first show on January 22 was filmed for a short feature to be shown in theatres called "Stones Roll Down Under." The *Sydney Herald* reported, "From the moment the Stones launched into 'Not Fade Away,' with Brian Jones blowing a wailing harmonica and that distinctive, fuzzy-edged guitar sound coming from somewhere amid the massed amplifiers, it was clear that here was the group which had been listening hard to Muddy Waters, Little Walter and the rest of

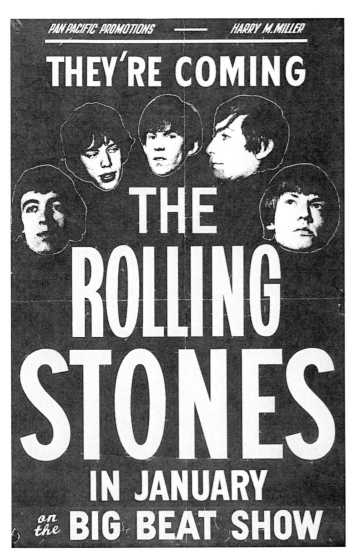

Poster for the Stones' forthcoming 1965 Australian tour with Roy Orbison (collection of Ira Korman).

the U.S. rhythm and blues artists and had managed to capture much of their excitement." One amusing moment happened in the last show on January 23, when a fan threw an egg at Mick. He pointed his finger into the crowd and yelled, "If you want to throw an egg at me don't do it now … try afterwards when I might have an egg of my own."

**Monday, January 25, and Tuesday, January 26:** City Hall, Brisbane, Queensland, Australia, with Ray Columbus and the Invaders, the Newbeats and Roy Orbison, 6 and 8:45 p.m. both days

The Stones flew to Brisbane on January 24, after being smuggled to the airport in a bus. They arrived at Eagle Farm Airport at 11:20 a.m. It was something of a British invasion, as the Kinks, Manfred Mann and the Honeycombs were playing there at the same time. Two thousand fans attended each of the shows on Monday night and crowds of a similar size saw the Stones on Tuesday. The first concert on Monday went off without a hitch, but the second show was almost halted when riots broke out. *The Courier Mail* reported, "Eight frantic teenage girls pierced the wall of police and attacked the group. Three girls grabbed vocalist and leader Mick Jagger and tried to pull him off the stage but were removed by police. Another grabbed guitarist Brian Jones and several others were tackled football style before they could reach the singers." In a separate review, the same newspaper commented, "The Rolling Stones seem to be able to whip a teenage mob into a screaming frenzy.… They play wild music and dress accordingly. Technically, the guitar work of Brian Jones on lead guitar in the song 'Little Red Rooster' is a masterpiece. Singer Mick Jagger has the right voice for R&B. He really 'reached' the primitive instinct in the audience in songs like 'It's All Over Now,' 'Around and Around' and 'Walking the Dog.'"

**Wednesday, January 27:** Manufacturer's Auditorium Showgrounds, Sydney, NSW, Australia, with Ray Columbus and the Invaders, the Newbeats and Roy Orbison, 6 and 8:45 p.m.

The Stones/Orbison show was in such high demand in Sydney that the tour returned for one more night. Brian told *Melody Maker*, "Australia is a gas. We didn't think it would be anything like this. We're doing marvelously out here. This is more like a holiday with work, rather than a tour with a few days off."

**Thursday, January 28, to Saturday, January 30:** Palais Theatre, St. Kilda, Victoria, Australia, with Ray Columbus and the Invaders, the Flies, the Newbeats and Roy Orbison, 6:45 and 8:45 p.m. on January 28 and 29 and 2:30 p.m. on January 30

The Stones flew to Melbourne on January 28 and held a filmed press conference at the airport. Asked about their hair, Brian replied, "We get sick of being just asked about our hair. After all, it's our music which has made us, not our hair." The band played five shows. A reporter from the *Sydney Herald*, clearly from a previous generation commented; "With the Rolling Stones noise hits you from all angles. From the stage singer Mick Jagger slurps and shrieks into the microphone. From the audience teenage girls scream, jump and cry. And there oblivious to it all stand guitar-men Wyman, Richard and Jones nonchalantly delivering whatever tune or beat there happens to be, while drummer Charlie Watts does something nobody seems to hear." While in the area, the Stones appeared on the AVTO TV show *Big Beat 65*, hosted by Roy Orbison. Fans surrounded the venue. The Stones had to be hustled in through a back door to avoid a mob.

**Monday, February 1:** Theatre Royal, Christchurch, South Island, New Zealand, with the Detours, Ray Columbus and the Invaders, the Newbeats and Roy Orbison, two shows

The nine-day trip through New Zealand was hard slogging, as few people were familiar with the Stones. Nevertheless, they made fans wherever they played. *The Christchurch Press* reported, "Little Red Rooster was nearly the downfall of the Theatre Royal last night. Hundreds of whistling, clapping teenagers screamed and stamped until the building vibrated as the visiting British pop group, the Rolling Stones, magnetized their audience with this number, one of their most popular releases…. Their dress is as outrageous as everything else that has been written about them, but you cannot get away from it: for sheer entertainment in the pop field, they are fantastically good."

**Tuesday, February 2:** Civic Theatre, Invercargill, South Island, New Zealand, with the Ecophones, Ray Columbus and the Invaders, the Newbeats and Roy Orbison, two shows

The Stones were pelted with tomatoes during these concerts. Anthony Hollows, who worked for promoter Harry Miller, later told the *Otago Daily Times*, "The Invercargill concerts didn't go very well for the Stones, because most people were there to see Roy Orbison. The audience was dead and there was no yelling or screaming, as there usually was at the end of the Stones' songs. So, Jagger did a slow hand-clap." Mick was unimpressed with Invercargill. He described it as the end of the earth in a conversation with *NME* reporter Chris Hutchins. He complained, "There are 28 rooms in this hotel and only two baths between everybody. The last meal you can get is supper and that finishes at 7 p.m."

**Wednesday, February 3:** Town Hall, Dunedin, South Island, New Zealand, with Ray Columbus and the Invaders, the Newbeats and Roy Orbison, 6 and 8:30 p.m.

*The Otago Daily Times* reported, "On the face of it, they appear the least kempt and longest-haired of the great multitude of groups to visit us so far. Mick Jagger, the vocalist, works hard, but I confess to finding their appearance just a little too anthropoid. Elsewhere, they have been hailed as successors to the Beatles. My verdict: Neither their music nor their personalities compare." Commenting on New Zealand audiences, Bill told *The New Zealand Herald*, "The strange part is that here the average age of the audience is higher than anywhere else we have played. There were forty year olds scattered throughout the audience in Invercargill but they still went wild. They listen to us at home on their records and come to the shows to scream."

**Saturday, February 6:** Town Hall, Auckland, North Island, New Zealand, with Ray Columbus and the Invaders, the Newbeats and Roy Orbison, 2:15, 6 and 8:30 p.m.

The Stones landed at Whenuapai Airport on Thursday. Their arrival was such a closely guarded secret that there was only one fan to greet them and they took the transport bus to the hotel like ordinary tourists. The group relaxed on Friday before playing three sold-out shows Saturday. *The New Zealand Herald* reported, "The shaggy haired Londoners, straight faced except for the odd scared smile, plucked, stomped and yelled their way to triumph. Few words pierced the din but as usual this did not matter. A stomp of the foot, a twist of the torso or a toss of a mopped head were enough to bring squeals of delight." The set consisted of: "Not Fade Away," "Walking the Dog," "Under the Boardwalk," "Little Red Rooster," "Around and Around," "Heart of Stone," "It's Alright," "Time Is on My Side" and "It's All Over Now."

**Monday, February 8:** Town Hall, Wellington, North Island, New Zealand, with Ray Columbus and the Invaders, the Newbeats and Roy Orbison, two shows

**Wednesday, February 10:** Palais Theatre, St. Kilda, Victoria, Australia, with Ray Columbus and the Invaders, the Newbeats and Roy Orbison, two shows

**Thursday, February 11:** Centennial Hall, Adelaide, South Australia, with Ray Columbus and the Invaders, the Clefs, the Newbeats and Roy Orbison, 6 and 8:45 p.m.

**Saturday, February 13:** Capitol Theatre, Perth, West Australia, with Ray Columbus and the Invaders, the Newbeats and Roy Orbison, three shows

**Tuesday, February 16:** Badminton Hall, Singapore, with Sylvia Desayles and the Castaways, 6:45 and 8:45 p.m.

The Stones arrived in Singapore on the night of February 15. The 1,000 fans at the airport were kept at bay by military police that escorted the Stones to their hotel, where they held an obligatory press conference. The Stones were tired and Brian fielded most questions. Asked if they'd soon take over from the Beatles as number one pop group in Britain, he replied, "We don't think we actually will take over. Our music is of a different type. The build-up in the American magazines that we are beating the Beatles is a myth. Anyway, there's room for both groups." Another reporter inquired if, as critics charged, the Stones were sloppy dressers. Brian, looked down at his dark suit and sweater and glanced at the other Stones before answering, "I don't think we are. You know we have just got off the aircraft and haven't had time to wash up and change. We wear what we please at all times. We don't have any set clothes even when we perform. It depends on our mood when we get out of bed in the morning. Some people think we are filthy but we can assure them our laundry bills are fantastic."

The concerts that night were marred by the sounds of fireworks being set off nearby by people celebrating the last night of the Singaporean New Year. The *Straits Times*

Ticket for the Stones' concert in Singapore on February 16, 1965 (collection of Ira Korman).

reported, "Inside the hall a third force competed with the Rolling Stones and the crackers. This was the non-stop banshee screams from the throats of rowdy boys and hysterical girls-the majority the children of British servicemen-who screeched and sobbed. What little could be heard sounded like old style rock 'n' roll except that Mick, Brian Jones, Keith Richard, Bill Wyman and Charlie Watts stamped louder on the stage and strummed harder on their electric guitars."

The Stones then flew to Hong Kong at the request of promoter Freddie Yu. According to Andrew Oldham's memoir *Rolling Stoned*, the Stones were "whisked from a military airstrip, escorted by machine gun-clad jeeps to a circus tent in the middle of an eerie nowhere" where they played an impromptu show for British servicemen in the middle of the night. This concert is undocumented elsewhere and the veracity of the account must remain suspect. In any event, the Stones left for Tokyo on February 17, where they were interviewed for various radio and television programs. They flew to LA on February 18 and Mick and Keith spent some time re-recording vocals for "The Last Time" before heading back to England. The single was released in the UK on February 26. To promote it the Stones made numerous TV appearances including *Ready Steady Go!* (February 26), *The Eamonn Andrews Show* (February 27) and *Top of the Pops* (March 4). They also appeared on the BBC Radio show *Top Gear* on March 1.

**Friday, March 5:** Regal Theatre, Edmonton, North London, UK, with the Hollies, Dave Berry and the Cruisers, Goldie and the Gingerbreads, the Checkmates and the Konrads, 6:30 and 9 p.m.

The Stones began a two-week UK tour with the Hollies, who had a top ten hit with "Yes I Will." Also on the bill were Dave Berry and the Cruisers, a Sheffield band who'd had hits in Europe and the UK with "Crying Game" and "Little Things," and Goldie and the Gingerbreads, an all girl group from New York that scored a hit in the UK with "Can't You Hear My Heart Beat." Stu, Andrew and Mike Dorsey accompanied the Stones. Glyn Johns was present to record the first three nights (London, Liverpool and Manchester) on three-track tape for the UK EP *Got Live If You Want It*. The songs that appeared on it were "Everybody Needs Somebody to Love," "Pain in My Heart," "I'm Moving On," "Route 66" and "I'm Alright." A CD titled *Live in England 1965* was released in conjunction with the DVD of *Charlie Is My Darling* in 2012. The CD contains an entire concert culled from these tapes.

The Stones led off their eight-song set with "Everybody Needs Somebody to Love," then performed "Pain in My Heart," followed by "Down the Road Apiece" and "Time Is on My Side." *Record Mirror* reported "A crescendo of screams greeted every number; a wail of enthusiasm finished each one. 'I'm Alright' was next on the agenda, followed by the hugely successful 'Little Red Rooster.' 'Route 66' was building well to the finale.... 'The Last Time.' The roars and the yells went on and on until the boys tackled a fuller length version of 'Everybody Needs Somebody.' The Stones could have gone on all night and looked fully prepared to do so until the curtain was finally drawn down."

**Saturday, March 6:** Empire Theatre, Liverpool, UK, with the Hollies, Dave Berry and the Cruisers, Goldie and the Gingerbreads, the Checkmates and the Konrads, 6 and 8:30 p.m.

**Sunday, March 7:** Palace Theatre, Manchester, UK, with the Hollies, Dave Berry and the Cruisers, Goldie and the Gingerbreads, the Checkmates and the Konrads, 6 and 8:15 p.m.

The Stones attracted a wild crowd in Manchester. Ron Boyle of *The Daily Express* reported, "The Stones, in their best mood after an all-night party, were swinging crazily and raising a storm. Mick was up front astride the footlights stabbing a finger into the purple bedlam.... 'I Need You. You. You. You.' It was too much. Without warning, one hysterical girlie came soaring out of the circle and crunch into the stalls fifteen feet below. The stretcher gang moved in. Exit one way-out space-walking chick. But five minutes later she was back, minus three teeth."

**Monday, March 8:** Futurist Theatre, Scarborough, Yorkshire, UK, with the Hollies, Dave Berry and the Cruisers, Goldie and the Gingerbreads, the Checkmates and the Konrads, 6:15 and 8:40 p.m.

**Tuesday, March 9:** Odeon Theatre, Sunderland, Tyne and Wear, UK, with the Hollies, Dave Berry and the Cruisers, Goldie and the Gingerbreads, the Checkmates and the Konrads, two shows

The Stones were ordered to leave their hotel in Sunderland by an irate manager, who told the press "They left their rooms in a terrible state." The receptionist also complained, "It was disgusting. They used foul language and were very rude to the staff."

**Wednesday, March 10:** ABC Theatre, Huddersfield, Yorkshire, UK, with the Hollies, Dave Berry and the Cruisers, Goldie and the Gingerbreads, the Checkmates and the Konrads, 6 and 8:30 p.m.

**Thursday, March 11:** City Hall, Sheffield, UK, with the Hollies, Dave Berry and the Cruisers, Goldie and the Gingerbreads, the Checkmates and the Konrads, 6:20 and 8:50 p.m.

Prior to the concerts, the Stones taped an appearance on Granada TV's *Scene at 6.30* in Manchester.

**Friday, March 12:** Trocadero Theatre, Leicester, UK, with the Hollies, Dave Berry and the Cruisers, Goldie and the Gingerbreads, the Checkmates and the Konrads, two shows

**Saturday, March 13:** Granada Theatre, Rugby, UK, with the Hollies, Dave Berry and the Cruisers, Goldie and the Gingerbreads, the Checkmates and the Konrads, 6 and 8:30 p.m.

**Sunday, March 14:** Odeon Theatre, Rochester, Kent, UK, with the Hollies, Dave Berry and the Cruisers, Goldie and the Gingerbreads, the Checkmates and the Konrads, two shows

To prevent the usual chaos, the promoter arranged to let the Stones into the back of the theatre at a prearranged signal, but unfortunately the man at the door didn't recognize them. Stu told *Rolling Stones Monthly*, "He didn't believe we were in the show. After arguing with this stubborn bloke for several minutes, some of the crowd was catching on. They spotted the boys and a gang was rushing towards us. With that Keith lost his temper and pushed him flat on his back so we could get in."

**Monday, March 15:** Odeon Theatre, Guildford, UK, with the Hollies, Dave Berry and the Cruisers, Goldie and the Gingerbreads, the Checkmates and the Konrads, two shows

**Tuesday, March 16:** Granada Theatre, Greenford, West London, UK, with the Hollies, Dave Berry and the Cruisers, Goldie and the Gingerbreads, the Checkmates and the Konrads, two shows

**Wednesday, March 17:** Odeon Theatre, Southend, Essex, UK, with the Hollies, Dave Berry and the Cruisers, Goldie and the Gingerbreads, the Checkmates and the Konrads, 6:30 and 8:45 p.m.

**Thursday, March 18:** ABC Theatre, Romford, Essex, UK, with the Hollies, Dave Berry and the Cruisers, Goldie and the Gingerbreads, the Checkmates and the Konrads, 6:45 and 9 p.m.

It was after this show that a now legendary incident took place at a gas station. As Keith recalled in 1971, "Bill Wyman, who had this prodigious bladder, decided he wanted to have a pee. So we told the driver to stop.... So we leap out and we had chosen a gas station that looked closed but wasn't. There they are up against a wall spraying away. And suddenly this guy steps out. And a cop flashes his torch on Bill's cock and says, 'All right. What you up to then?' ... The next day it was in all the papers. Bill was accused and Brian was accused of insulting language. Because what they did them for was not peeing but for trespassing." Bill, Brian and Mick (who was also charged) appeared in court on July 22. They were found guilty of using "insulting language in which a breach of the peace may have occurred" and fined £5 each.

**Friday, March 26:** Fyens Forum, Odense, Denmark, with the Daisy, the Space Makers, the Teen Beats and the Defenders, 7 and 9:15 p.m.

On March 21 the Stones taped an appearance on *Thank Your Lucky Stars*. They flew to Copenhagen on March 25 to launch a short Scandinavian tour with Andrew, Stu and Mike Dorsey. While there, they gave a TV interview. Asked what they thought of all the screaming at their shows, Mick replied, "It's an accepted form of appreciation. Instead of clapping they scream and they scream everywhere. We think ... well they like us." Brian chimed in, "I think the most important thing to us when we go on stage is that we succeed in communicating with an audience. The only way we can do this is by producing an exciting atmosphere. Therefore, if the kids scream we love it. We react to their reaction."

The first show in Odense was notable for a scary incident. As Bill explained to *NME*, "At a rehearsal, I tried my bass and amplifier out while Mick was testing the microphone. There was no earth on the amplifiers, and suddenly Mick and I became the earth. I got an electric shock and I fainted. I was out for a few minutes. When I regained consciousness I was wet all over with perspiration. Horrible." Brian told a Swedish reporter that it was the worst moment he could recall on a tour: "He fell down. The rest of us thought he was dead. The ambulance arrived. It was horribly nasty."

**Sunday, March 28, and Tuesday, March 30:** Tivoli Konsertsal, Copenhagen, Denmark, with the Lions, the Defenders, the Joe E. Carter Group and Peter Belli & Les Rivals, two shows each night

*The Berlingske Tidende* reported, "No one, not even those who sat glued to the speakers in the Tivoli Concert Hall last night, heard much of the Rolling Stones.... For the whole half hour they were on stage the audience noise drowned out the five on stage.... Every time (Mick Jagger) made one of his well-chosen and challenging movements, the volume of screams from the audience increased another notch.... It must be admitted that here we have a real entertainer.... He can dance and move in an electrifying way, not so far from a brilliant artist like Sammy Davis. He knows his own appeal and uses it every second. When the Rolling Stones disband in a few months or years, Mick Jagger will be a great star. He is bold, modern and in his own way pleasing to the eye."

**Wednesday, March 31:** Masshallen, Gothenburg, Sweden, with the Hitmakers, the Defenders, the Merrymen and the Tages, 6:30 and 9 p.m.

The Stones landed at Gothenburg at 10:35 a.m. and immediately headed to their hotel, disappointing fans eager to get a glimpse of the group. Hundreds camped outside the hotel and screamed their names whenever they approached the windows. Asked how it felt to be so popular, Brian replied "Wonderful. I love the Rolling Stones fans and I like to meet them. But not too many of them at once." A few hours later, the Stones met the Swedish press and were asked the usual silly questions, to which they gave suitably sarcastic responses. (Question: "Are you happy?" Answer: "Are you happy?"). The Stones played two concerts. The set list consisted of "Everybody Needs Somebody to Love," "Tell Me," "Around and Around," "Time Is on My Side," "It's All Over Now," "Little Red Rooster," "Route 66," and "The Last Time."

*Topp Magazine* described the scene as show time approached: "Brian walks around backstage…. 'How's the audience?' he asks. 'It's a nice atmosphere,' responds road manager Ian Stewart. 'Be prepared! Five minutes left.' The last exercise chords on guitars and so…. NOW THE ROLLING STONES! Whistles and screams. Riot already at the back of the room. Mick takes the stage, throws back his head. The hair flutters. He grabs the microphone and spins around, dancing. The rhythm is intense and captivating. 'I want You, You, You.' Mick Jagger is undoubtedly one of the most talented performers. He's learned a lot from the blues singer James Brown, but much is his own, too. In seconds, he has the audience completely in his hands. Collaboration between Mick and the Microphone is completely perfect…. He has personality, charisma. The audience noise is deafening… 'It's All Over Now.' It's earthy music cheeky, fresh and sexy. Filled with youthful joy. Sure, they have borrowed heavily from the American folk music–Big City Blues–like, but they have put their very own stamp on it."

**Thursday, April 1, and Friday, April 2:** Kungliga Tennishallen, Stockholm, Sweden, with the Hitmakers, the Defenders, the Merrymen and the Tages, 6:15 and 9 p.m.

Fans at Bromma Airport were disappointed when only three Stones disembarked from the plane. Keith and Brian opted to drive from Gothenburg. Over 9,000 fans attended the shows that night. Ludvig Rasmusson of *Svenska Dagbladet* commented, "Some critics who heard the Rolling Stones in Gothenburg and Denmark claimed they sounded much worse in person than on disc. I cannot agree with them. In any case, they made an excellent impression from my nice critics' perch in the stalls at the Tennis Hall in Stockholm…. Some of what they did wasn't heard so well, of course, as the girls screamed so much. But what I could hear made me confident that the Rolling Stones are not only a product of smart managers and producers. Above all, they are talented and personable musician who jointly created a unique style. Their sense of what they are playing and singing, and the confidence they do it with is impressive."

Prior to the last show on Friday, the group taped an appearance on the Swedish TV show *Popside*. Brian also granted a radio interview where he expounded on a number of topics. Asked his opinion of Elvis he answered, "He's got a whole thing going but I'm not very interested in Elvis Presley. I think he made some very good records earlier on when he was still interested in his profession. But you know he lost interest in his career a long time ago. It's a very impersonal sort of thing. I mean Presley's records are very impersonal and he has no feeling behind them. I don't bother to listen to Elvis Presley these days. I just wouldn't bother. As far as I'm concerned he's of no importance in the pop music

Program for the Stones' appearance in Stockholm, 1965 (collection of Ira Korman).

world whatever." Asked why he played harmonica less recently, he replied "Well we get a bigger sound with two guitars. But … we might, it's nothing set. It used to mean a lot of changing about. Put a guitar down, pick a harmonica up and you don't have such a big sound with one guitar as you do with two. When I'm playing guitar and Keith's playing guitar we're a much bigger, more powerful sound."

**Sunday, April 11:** NME Poll Winners Concert, Empire Pool, Wembley, UK, with the Moody Blues, Freddie and the Dreamers, Georgie Fame and the Blue Flames, Twinkle, the Seekers, Herman's Hermits, the Ivy League, Sounds Incorporated, the Bachelors, Wayne Fontana and the Mindbenders, the Rockin' Berries, Cilla Black, Donovan, Them (with Van Morrison), Tom Jones, the Searchers, Dusty Springfield, the Animals, the Beatles and the Kinks, 2 p.m.,

The group returned to London and on April 9 they filmed *Ready Steady Goes Live!* at Wembley. Two days later they were back at Wembley to appear on one of the greatest concert bills of all time. The group closed the first half of the show, performing "Everybody Needs Somebody to Love," "Pain in My Heart," "Around and Around," "The Last Time" and a final encore of "Everybody Needs Somebody to Love." Keith Altham reported, "The Stones showed how important it is not only to give the audience something to listen to, but also to watch and Mick's facial dramatics during 'The Last Time' are an education. They rounded off a wild performance with 'Everybody Needs Somebody to Love' as an encore." The whole show was filmed and the Stones' performances of "Pain in My Heart" and "The Last Time" are included as a bonus feature on the 2012 DVD *Crossfire Hurricane*.

**Friday, April 16, to Sunday, April 18:** L'Olympia, Paris, France, with les Jets, Vince Taylor and Evy and Rocky Roberts

The Stones' Paris concert on April 18 was recorded by Musicorama and broadcast on radio. Fans covet the tape because the concert included a rare five-minute version of "Hey Crawdaddy," the Bo Diddley number the Stones used to play in Richmond. The full set consisted of "Everybody Needs Somebody to Love," "Around and Around," "Off the Hook," "Time Is on My Side," "Carol," "It's All Over Now," "Little Red Rooster," "Route 66," "Everybody Needs Somebody to Love," "The Last Time," "I'm Alright," and "Hey Crawdaddy."

**Friday, April 23:** Maurice Richard Arena, Montreal, Canada, with the Kangaroos, Jennie Rock and the Esquires, 8:30 p.m.

The Stones landed in Montreal on April 22 to begin their third North American tour. Andrew, Stu and Mike Dorsey accompanied them. American Bob Bonis also joined them for the tour. Once settled in at their hotel, Jim McKenna interviewed the Stones for the Canadian TV show *Like Young*. Brian was asked what American cities impressed them and responded, "New York and Los Angeles are about the only ones that impressed and they did impress us very much. We like them. I think Chicago's all right and a little place in Texas called San Antonio, which we had a good time in. I like the States with reservations." On Friday the Stones played their first Canadian show. The Montreal media ignored the event, but Bill Wyman informed *NME* readers that the group played "to an audience of 6,500. It was just like home—they went mad and a few made the stage, even though police coverage was excellent."

**Saturday, April 24:** YMCA Auditorium, Ottawa, Canada, with the Esquires, Nev Wells, Sandy Crawley and J.B. and the Playboys, 8:30 p.m.

The Stones drove to Ottawa in time to tape an interview for the CBC TV show *Saturday Date*. They found their hotel surrounded by 200 fans. Police smuggled them inside, but they remained trapped until show time. The *Ottawa Citizen* reported the usual chaotic scene as fans "surged 25 deep against the front of the stage at the Auditorium, clutching, jumping and frantically waving.... It was a situation that prompted master of ceremonies John Pozer three times to threaten to stop the show unless members of the youthful audience returned to their seats." *The Journal* added that, following the show, "the Rolling Stones made a dash for the exits with the girls in hot pursuit.... Four of the performers made it off stage successfully, but the fifth, long-hair flying, was grabbed by a couple of policemen who mistook him for one of the frantic females."

**Sunday, April 25:** Maple Leaf Gardens, Toronto, Canada, with David Clayton Thomas and the Shays, 7 p.m.

Ralph Thomas of *The Toronto Star* expressed little enthusiasm for the Stones. He commented, "In all they were on stage a mere 25 minutes, during which time they mixed obscene gestures with inaudible singing.... That they weren't heard much last night wasn't really their fault. The crowd drowned them out with shrill screams. Some two dozen girls shrieked themselves into hysteria and had to be treated by the St. John ambulance staff."

**Monday, April 26:** Treasure Island Gardens, London, Canada, with JB & the Playboys, the Fortune Tellers, the Runarounds and the Nottingham Three, 8:30 p.m.

The Stones played for 3,500 people. Many fans had made the trip from nearby Michigan, as the Stones weren't playing there. Fearful of anarchy, police placed a 5-foot fence between fans and the stage. Bill described the chaotic scene that followed for *NME*: "At least a dozen (fans) made the stage in the first three songs although there were 50 police in attendance. Then they put the house lights on and half way through 'Off the Hook,' with no warning, the police chief switched the electric power and left Charlie drumming like mad on his own and Mick singing! They wouldn't put it on again, so we continued for a few minutes with Mick on maracas, Brian on tambourine, and Keith and I clapping, but in the end we had to stop and leave the stage." Angry fans rioted and wrecked havoc on the venue. The media lambasted the police for closing down the show for no reason.

**Thursday, April 29:** Palace Theatre, Albany, New York, 6:45 and 8:45 p.m.

The Stones arrived in New York on April 27 and rehearsed for their Sunday return appearance on *The Ed Sullivan Show* on Wednesday. While in the city, Brian, Mick and Keith attended Wilson Pickett's show at the Apollo. On Thursday they headed upstate to play in Albany. *The Albany Times Union* reported, "They performed such apparent favorites as 'The Last Time,' 'I Wanna Be Your Man' and 'Not Fade Away.' They didn't exercise their pelvises as much as Elvis does, nor did they appear as content as the Beatles do. They strolled and shuffled about, twanging mightily, keeping up the same basic beat in almost every number, and grinning freely." The reporter was clearly careless. The Stones did not play "I Wanna Be Your Man," which had disappeared from the set over a year before this show.

**Friday, April 30:** Memorial Auditorium, Worcester, MA, with Joanna Jay and others, 8 p.m.

Over 3,000 teenagers turned out to see the Stones. They were paid $3,500 for their 23-minute set. Backstage Jack Tubert of *The Worcester Telegram* captured the scene: "Mrs.

Handbill for the Stones' 1965 concert in Albany, New York (collection of Ira Korman).

Shirley Watts was with them. The British bride of six months appeared pleased with a giant cake someone sent backstage to her husband. They sat together, waiting to go on stage, weaving gum-wrappers into a rope like string. Equally pleasant was the Stones old piano player, Ian Stewart. He was with them before the balloon went up. Now he's their road manager ... 'I wouldn't be the part of a star for all the tea in China,' said Ian, wheeling the other lads' electrical equipment out of a station wagon. 'I've still got record royalties, and I can still walk along the street without being torn apart.'"

**Saturday, May 1:** Academy of Music, New York, NY, with London Lee, 1 p.m., and Convention Hall, Philadelphia, PA, with Herman's Hermits, Bobby Vee, Freddie Cannon, Round Robin, the Detergents, Bobby Freeman, Reparata and the Delrons, Brenda Holloway and the Hondells, 8 p.m.

The Stones played a matinee in New York and then headed to Philadelphia for an all-star benefit for the March of Dimes attended by 13,000 people. Ronnie Oberman of *The Washington Star* caught up with them backstage. Mick noted that all his favorite artists were Americans: Bo Diddley, James Brown, Chuck Berry, Solomon Burke and Otis Redding. But he pointed out that the record scene in the U.S. "is completely stagnant. In Los Angeles they play the same records today as they did two months ago." Brian admitted liking the Four Seasons and Otis Redding, but added, "We're not a copy of American groups. We get all our inspiration from American rhythm and blues groups, though, and we're proud of it."

Geoffrey James of *The Evening Bulletin* attended the evening show and noted, "The Stones were greeted with an ovation that bodes well for Anglo-American solidarity. There was a forest of Union Jacks in the hall, and the girls threw belts, combs, ballpoint pens, empty cartons and purses. One adorer hurled a high-heeled shoe, then regretted it. She asked a policeman to bring it back." Despite the warm welcome, the concert was something of a debacle for the Stones. Herman's Hermits had a number one record in America with "Mrs. Brown You've Got a Lovely Daughter," but the Stones had little respect for the band and insisted on closing the show. But, they didn't realize that the city had a curfew. Peter Noone of Herman's Hermits intentionally played longer so the Stones would have less time. Mick was quite annoyed when fans started being hustled out of the venue during their fifth number. The Stones then made their second appearance on *The Ed Sullivan Show* on May 2. On May 3 they taped another appearance on the WPIX TV show *Clay Cole Show*.

**Tuesday, May 4:** Hanner Gym, Southern College, Statesboro, GA, with the Apollos, the Bushmen and the Roemans, 8 p.m.

The Stones had a stressful time getting to this show. They flew from New York to Atlanta in the morning, but their luggage got lost in transit and Bob Bonis and Mike Dorsey had to stay behind to locate it. When the Stones' plane was landing in Atlanta, the hydraulic brakes failed and there was a scary moment for everyone on board as the landing gear smoked. Once they recovered, the Stones caught a connecting flight to Savannah and drove fifty miles to Statesboro. The audience was fairly subdued, having little familiarity with the group. While staying at their hotel, the Stones had a funny incident. Someone called the police to complain about "topless women" at a hotel pool. Brian later told a reporter from the Canadian Broadcasting Company "We were in the swimming pool of a motel which happened to be by the roadside and some cops came up and apparently some typical Georgia idiot, and Georgia is full of idiots, said some girls were prancing around."

**Thursday, May 6:** Jack Russell Stadium, Clearwater, FL, with the Roemans, the Intruders, Pam Hall and the Catalinas and the Canadian Legends, 7 p.m.

The Stones flew to Jacksonville on Wednesday and drove to Clearwater, where they spent the night. Three thousand fans attended the show at the outdoor stadium near Tampa. *The Tampa Times* reported that the Stones took the stage ten minutes after the Roemans finished. "Acknowledging the screams, they swung into 'Around and Around,' a bluesy beat number which was accentuated by Mick walking and swaying across the stage. Charlie pounded out the background rhythm, dressed in a brown coat and slacks. Keith, on lead guitar, grinned happily to the girls and began the tune for the next song 'Little Red Rooster.' As the Stones played various people had slipped down from the stands. Soon a small crowd of boys was gathered on the side of the stadium. This signaled a wave of cheers and a gate on the right of the stage was pushed open." Fans stormed the stage, causing the overzealous police to halt the show. The authorities declared that they'd never host another rock concert.

While in Clearwater, Brian allegedly took out some frustrations by beating up a girl he'd taken home for the night. A disgusted Mike Dorsey confronted him and a melee ensued. Brian ended up with two cracked ribs and had to wear bandages the rest of the tour. However, Andrew Oldham, no fan of Brian's, disliked Dorsey even more and in his book *Stoned* he threw some doubt about the veracity of Dorsey's account of the incident, though Andrew was not with the band for this leg of the tour.

**Friday, May 7:** Legion Field, Birmingham, Alabama, with the Beach Boys, the Righteous Brothers, Marty Robbins, Sonny James, Cannibal and the Headhunters, Skeeter Davis, Archie Campbell and Del Reeves, 7 p.m.

Other than the TAMI Show, this was the only time the Stones shared a stage with the Beach Boys. Also on the bill were country stars Marty Robbins of "El Paso" fame and Sonny James, most famous for the 1950s crossover hit "Young Love," as well as the Righteous Brothers, on top of the charts with "You've Lost That Lovin' Feeling." There was little time to socialize, however, as the Stones left straight after the gig for Florida.

**Saturday, May 8:** Jacksonville Coliseum, Jacksonville, FL, with the Righteous Brothers, the Sir Douglas Quintet, Bobbi Martin and the New Beats, 8 p.m.

**Sunday, May 9:** Arie Crown Theater, Chicago, IL, 8 p.m.

The Stones flew into Chicago on Sunday afternoon and were greeted by a sizable crowd at the airport. They had little time to relax, as the concert promoter quickly hustled them off to attend an autograph party for 600 fans at a nearby hotel. Fan Jeri Holloway was in attendance for the party and the show that night. She had a huge crush on Brian and took a bus all the way from California to see him in concert. She reported in *Hit Parader*: "They sang 'Everybody Needs Somebody to Love,' 'Pain in My Heart,' 'Route 66,' 'Time Is on My Side,' 'Off the Hook,' 'I'm Alright,' 'Around and Around,' 'The Last Time' and one or two others. For 'Little Red Rooster,' Charlie came to the mike and announced it, but there was trouble with Brian's guitar so they had to go on to the next number. They worked pretty much the same as last fall, only better. Mick still walked dangerously close to the edge of the stage.... Brian concentrated mostly on his work at hand."

On Monday, the Stones returned to Chess for an all-night session to record songs for their third UK LP *Out of Our Heads*, including "Mercy Mercy," "That's How Strong My Love Is" (left off the album and instead used, with overdubbed screams, to pad out the U.S. LP *Got Live If You Want It* in 1966), "The Under Assistant West Coast Promotion Man" and an early mix of "Satisfaction" (featuring a Brian harmonica part that was later excised).

**Friday, May 14:** Civic Auditorium, San Francisco, CA, with the Byrds, the Beau Brummels, Paul Revere and the Raiders and the Vejtables, 8:30 p.m.

The Stones flew to LA on May 11 to relax for a few days. On Wednesday they held a session at RCA with engineer Dave Hassinger. They overdubbed the Chess recordings (Keith added the now famous fuzz-box guitar on "Satisfaction") and taped more tracks for *Out of Our Heads* including "One More Try," "My Girl," "Good Times" and "The Spider and the Fly." Influential critic Ralph J. Gleason attended the show in San Francisco for *The Chronicle* and reported, "Mick Jagger, who backstage had been full of humor, twisted and wiggled in his dance, clutching the microphone like James Brown.... Just before they got offstage a girl launched herself under road manager Bob Bonis' legs and grabbed a handful of the thick, blonde hair of guitarist Brian Jones. Mick Jagger artfully sidestepped a trio of girls. Charlie Watts dodged a few more struggling in the cops' arms and followed by Keith Richard and Bill Wyman, left the stage."

**Saturday, May 15:** Swing Auditorium, San Bernardino, CA, with the Byrds, the Bushmen, the Driftwoods and the Torquays, 8:30 p.m.

Prior to the gig in San Bernardino, the band taped an appearance on the ABC TV show *Hollywood A Go-Go* in Los Angeles. The Stones returned to San Bernardino for the third time in a year. Backstage, the group admitted they had a soft spot for the city. Mick commented, "It's just like England." They took the stage at 10:15 p.m., with the audience chanting "We want the Stones." Ron Plotkin of *The San Bernardino County Sun* reported, "When they finally appeared on stage, pandemonium broke loose. From that moment until after their last number at 10:45 the huge hall echoed with an almost continual roar-three thousand youngsters screaming themselves hoarse. Three girls tried to break onto the stage and were carried out of the hall by police. Many literally sobbed with joy throughout the performance. Others threw personal items like brushes and combs onto the stage as offerings to the Stones." *KRLA Beat* recorded one scary moment after the gig. "As the car pulled away, a bump was felt. The Stones were sure an innocent fan (one of thousands jammed around the car in San Bernardino) was caught underneath. It proved to be nothing more than a huge boulder placed in the roadway by a quick-thinking but not too thoughtful fan."

**Sunday, May 16:** Long Beach Municipal Arena, Long Beach, CA, with Don and the Deacons, the Vibrants, Jerry Naylor, the Dartells, the Crickets, the Byrds and Paul Revere and the Raiders, 4 p.m.

The concert at Long Beach was a wild affair. The group performed nine songs, including "Time Is on My Side," "Off the Hook," "Little Red Rooster" and "The Last Time." Louise Criscione of *KRLA Beat* reported, "Bedlam broke loose and pandemonium reigned. The Stones got pelted with jellybeans, flashbulbs, lipstick and anything else the audience could lay its hands on." After the show they raced to a black station wagon to head back to the hotel but things didn't go according to plan. "After proceeding halfway around the Arena, the car could not get out, was spotted by throngs of screaming fans and was forced to turn around and begin backtracking. Once outside, the car was engulfed in a mass of surging bodies. The Stones were trapped inside the station wagon behind locked doors and rolled up windows. Policemen and officials did their best to untangle the crowd and get the Stones safely out of the parking lot. It was a tough assignment but about fifteen minutes later they had succeeded and the Stones were gone." The Stones returned to LA to appear on the short-lived ABC TV show *Shivaree,* hosted by KFWB DJ Gene Weed.

**Monday, May 17:** Community Concourse Arena, San Diego, CA, with the Byrds, the Accents and Sandy, 8 p.m.

The band was 30 minutes late getting to this gig and the Byrds were forced to play longer. As a joke, they played Stones songs. Although there were no riots like in Long Beach, over 200 fans did try to gain access to the stage and dozens of girls were carried out on stretchers after fainting from hysteria. The day after the show, the Stones taped new backing tracks for "Little Red Rooster," "The Last Time" and "Play with Fire" at RCA, so Mick could sing live vocals over them when the band appeared on the ABC TV show *Shindig* in LA on May 20.

**Friday, May 21:** Civic Auditorium, San Jose, CA, 8:30 p.m.

**Saturday, May 22:** Ratcliffe Stadium, Fresno, CA, with the Byrds, the Montlairs, the Mann, the Ladybirds, the Roadrunners and the Cindermen, 10 a.m., and Municipal Auditorium, Sacramento, CA, with the Byrds and the Fugitives, 8 p.m.

The Stones took the stage in Fresno at 11:30 in the morning and launched into "Everybody Needs Somebody to Love." They got through most of the set, but *The Fresno Bee* reported, "Jagger announced, 'our last number 'The Last Time.' They never got to finish it. At 12:03 the first of about 25 youngsters jumped the rail and charged towards the bandstand. Helmeted policemen ... crouched and picked off the glassy eyed attackers." The police stopped the show and hustled the Stones out of the venue. Silent color footage exists. In addition, a fan filmed the Stones lounging at a Holiday Inn and signing autographs at the airport. The show that night in Sacramento was equally wild. Indeed, the performance was stopped temporarily midway through the first number so police could restore order.

**Saturday, May 29:** Academy of Music, New York, NY, with the Denims and the Uniques, 1 p.m.

The Stones were back in New York by Friday, May 28. That night Mick and girlfriend Chrissie Shrimpton met up with Eric Burdon and the Animals, who were playing at the Paramount Theatre. Burdon informed Mick that his group wanted to record a live album at the famed R&B mecca the Apollo Theater. Mick commented that he wouldn't want to appear before such a critical audience. Three weeks after playing a sold-out matinee there, the Stones returned to the Academy of Music. A writer from *Hit Parader* reported, "Girls tried to throw themselves onstage, but there was a huge open pit filled with sweating, nervous guards separating them from their hairy heroes. Then from somewhere in the squirming, shouting, stomping crowd came a sweaty hand flinging an article of female underwear through the air. No sooner had it plopped onto the stage than the curtains were closed.... Someone tried to calm the audience. 'We'll have to end the concert if you don't behave.' ... Finally the curtain opened and the Stones went thru their paces anew. The audience seemed to be reacting with more caution than before until some wild girl rushed out from the side of the stage right towards Mick. The guards grabbed her and carted her off. When the Stones finished the number they were doing, the curtain closed. That was it." The Stones returned to England to appear on *Ready Steady Goes Live!* at Wembley on June 4. On June 6 they appeared on

Poster for the Stones' concert at the New York Academy of Music, May 1965 (collection of Ira Korman).

*Thank Your Lucky Stars* in Birmingham. They also taped *Top of the Pops* on June 10 in Manchester.

**Tuesday, June 15:** Odeon Theatre, Glasgow, Scotland, UK, with the Hollies, the Checkmates, Doris Troy, the Cannon Brothers and the Shades, 6:15 and 9 p.m.

The Stones began a short tour with the Hollies. There was the usual riotous behavior, with 150 fans treated by nurses for hysteria and 100 people arrested for "breach of the peace." *The Glasgow Herald* reported, "Pandemonium prevailed during their performance and for much of the time the group were inaudible. For some of the audience they were invisible too, as screaming admirers stood on seats and blocked the aisles. However, everybody seemed happy. Noise was apparently what they wanted and they got plenty of it." The set consisted of: "Route 66," "Pain in My Heart," "Little Red Rooster," "Not Fade Away," "It's All Over Now," "The Last Time," "Play with Fire," "Come On" and "Off the Hook."

**Wednesday, June 16:** Usher Hall, Edinburgh, Scotland, UK, with the Hollies, the Checkmates, Doris Troy, the Cannon Brothers and Mike and the Shades, two shows

Backstage between shows, Mick gave an interview to *Melody Maker*. Asked about the Queen's decision to award the MBE to the Beatles, he commented, "Isn't it funny to think of the Beatles meeting the Queen and having a medal pinned on them? … I think the funniest thing is these stupid old geezers sending their medals back (as a protest)." Asked about the Scottish tour, he replied, "They went a bit potty in Glasgow. Mounted police everywhere and the crowds couldn't get within 250 yards of the theatre. Oh fab gear! It's funny in Scotland, I mean, they're all a bit uncivilized up here."

**Thursday, June 17:** Capitol Theatre, Aberdeen, Scotland, UK, with the Hollies, the Checkmates, Doris Troy, the Cannon Brothers, the Drumbeats, Mike and the Shades, two shows

There were more riots in Aberdeen but Mick defended the fans in *NME*: "The fans don't mean to break the seats, they just stand on them to see better and in some of the older theatres, the seats can't take it. Sure you get a couple of fellows who come along to throw tomatoes but nobody turns up with the idea of wrecking the joint!"

**Friday, June 18:** Caird Hall, Dundee, Scotland, UK, with the Hollies, Doris Troy, the West Five, the Modells, Mike and the Shades, two shows

About 3,500 excited fans attended the shows in Dundee. *The Evening Times* reported, "Forty girls were carried from the Hall hysterical and fainting and were laid out on blankets on the floor."

**Thursday, June 24:** Messehallen, Oslo, Norway, 6:30 and 9 p.m.

The Stones flew to Oslo to begin a short Scandinavian tour. Black and white footage of the arrival at Fornebu Airport on June 23 exists. Norway was somewhat behind the times and the arrival of the Stones was a cultural shock. Many people didn't know what to make of the band. Nor were the Stones particularly impressed with Oslo. Their hotel didn't have bathrooms in the rooms and Keith hated the food. He showed his contempt by dumping it on the floor. Journalist Solvi Bryde commented in *Aftenposten*: "There was just so much contempt in their behavior, scorn for their audience, their fans, for decency. They were irritable and quarreled. Mick provoked Keith, who then attacked an entire tray of open-faced sandwiches, and spread mayonnaise all over the mirrors and benches in the dressing room." The two shows on Thursday, of which silent footage exists, took place in front of a brick wall with Decca spelled out in giant letters. The nine-song set consisted of "Everybody Needs Somebody to Love," "Pain in My Heart," "I'm Moving On," "I'm Alright," "The Last Time," "Little Red Rooster," "Time Is on My Side," "Around and Around," and "Route 66."

**Friday, June 25:** Yyteri Beach, Pori, Finland, with Dario Campeotto, Kari Kuuva, Lenne and the Lee Kings, the Lions, the Diamonds, the Wiremen, Tauno Suojasen, Juhannus Juhlille and Olle Nordstrom

A silent color film of this show exists (Brian stands out the most with a bright red jacket, white pants and teardrop shaped white guitar). Mick commented in *Disc*, "In Finland we played one open air concert to 15,000 people. It was only dark between about 12:30 a.m. and 2 a.m. The concert was held on a beach and the nearest road was several miles away. We had to get to the beach by driving over the sand dunes in a jeep. What a ride! All the people who came slept on the beach in tents. What a scene!"

**Saturday, June 26:** Falkoner Centret, Frederiksberg, Denmark, with the Pussycats, the Someones and Peter Belli and the Rivals, 6 and 9 p.m.

The Stones returned to Denmark for the second time. *The Berlingske Tidende* reported, "The Rolling Stones were given a lavish reception in Falkoner Centret last night.... The spotlight was always directed at Mick Jagger, who from the moment he stepped onto the stage had full control over the crowd. A small wink from Jagger, and the girls went wild. When he suddenly started walking with the microphone on the edge

Poster advertising the Stones' appearance at Yteri Beach in Finland, June 1965 (collection of Ira Korman).

of the orchestra pit, the excitement took the girls out of their seats and into the passageways. The inspectors had to stop Jagger and chase him back onto the stage."

**Tuesday, June 29:** Baltiska Hallen, Malmo, Sweden, two shows

The Stones took a boat to Malmo on June 27 and visited Radio Syd, a floating pirate station. They spent Monday seeing the sights. Keith was particularly impressed, commenting to a Swedish reporter that Malmo was "A truly beautiful and friendly city, not nearly as boring and ordinary as big cities like Paris, Rome, New York and Copenhagen. They are so similar that one gets tired of them." Thousands of fans turned out for the two shows on Tuesday. Among those in the audience were members of two popular bands, the Namelosers and the Gonks. They mentioned to the Stones that they were playing at a local club later that night, and much to the surprise of the small crowd, Keith, Brian and Mick made a surprise appearance and jammed with the bands, before heading to an all-night party at someone's home. The Stones returned to England the next day, with the exception of Brian, who took off on vacation to Copenhagen, where he stayed with photographer Bent Rej and his family.

**Friday, July 16:** Odeon Theatre, Exeter, Essex, UK, with the Walker Brothers, Steampacket, Tommy Quickly and the Remo 4, Elkie Brooks and Thee, 6:15 and 8:30 p.m.

The Stones began a five-day tour with the Walker Brothers, an American group that scored a top twenty hit in June with "Love Her." Amongst the other acts on the bill were Steampacket, which consisted of Rod Stewart, Long John Baldry, Brian Auger and Julie Driscoll, and Tommy Quickly and the Remo 4, a Liverpool band managed by Brian Epstein that had a hit with "Wild Side of Life."

**Saturday, July 17:** Guildhall, Portsmouth, UK, with the Walker Brothers, Steampacket, Tommy Quickly and the Remo 4, Elkie Brooks and Thee, 6:30 and 8:50 p.m.

**Sunday, July 18:** Gaumont Theatre, Bournemouth, UK, with Steampacket, Tommy Quickly and the Remo 4, John Mayall's Bluesbreakers, the Paramounts and Twinkle, 6:30 and 8:45 p.m.

**Sunday, July 25:** ABC Theatre, Great Yarmouth, Norfolk, UK, with the Walker Brothers, Steampacket, Tommy Quickly and the Remo 4, Elkie Brooks and Thee, two shows

**Monday, July 26:** ABC Hall, Leicester, UK, with the Walker Brothers, Steampacket, Tommy Quickly and the Remo 4, Elkie Brooks and Thee, two shows

Prior to these concerts the Stones mimed to "(I Can't Get No) Satisfaction" for ABC TV's *Thank Your Lucky Stars*. On July 28 they taped promo films for use on the U.S. TV show *Shindig*.

**Sunday, August 1:** London Palladium, London, UK, with Sugar Pie Desanto, the Fourmost, Steampacket, Julie Grant, the Quiet Five and the Moody Blues, 5:30 and 8 p.m.

The Stones made their first live appearance at the famed Palladium, though they'd previously filmed there for *The Red Skelton Show*. Charlie was unimpressed and commented, "Well, it's just like any other stage isn't it?" Keith Altham reported in *NME*: "The only thing that marred the show was the strong-armed methods employed by police and ushers to repel stage 'rushers.' Teenage girls trying to get near the stage were roughly manhandled in the gangways by officials using Gestapo-like methods."

Following these shows the Stones took a three-week break. However, they weren't entirely idle. On August 11 they filmed promo films of "Down the Road Apiece" and "Oh

Baby" to be shown on *Shindig*. On August 19 they mimed to "(I Can't Get No) Satisfaction" on *Top of the Pops* and on August 20 they taped two BBC Radio shows, *Yeh! Yeh!* and *Saturday Club*.

**Sunday, August 22:** Futurist Theatre, Scarborough, Yorkshire, UK, with Lulu and the Luvvers, two shows

The day after these shows, the Stones appeared on the Granada TV show *Scene at 6:30*. On August 27 the Stones appeared on *Ready Steady Go! Live* and on August 29 they appeared on *Lucky Stars Summer Spin*. They also taped a special edition of *Ready Steady Go!* on September 2.

**Friday, September 3:** Adelphi Theatre, Dublin, Ireland, two shows

The Stones encountered wild crowds in Ireland. Speaking about this show to *Datebook*, Ian Stewart commented, "Fans rushed the stage. Brian was thrown to the ground and Charlie was toppled over on to his back, his drum kit on top of him. Mick vanished smartly! He is very clever at dealing with situations like this." Brian told Alan Walsh of *Melody Maker*, "I could see it building up in the audience. It seemed to me to be just high spirits even when they rushed the stage. It was after they were on stage that the flare up began. The part I didn't like was the two lads who jumped up and tried to kiss me. Ughh. Horrible!"

Director Peter Whitehead accompanied the Stones to film the documentary *Charlie Is My Darling*. At one of these shows his small crew filmed them performing "The Last Time," "Time Is on My Side" and "I'm Alright." In addition, on this day or the next, Whitehead filmed interviews with Charlie, Bill and Brian.

**Saturday, September 4:** ABC Theatre, Belfast, Northern Ireland, UK, 6:45 and 9 p.m.

Peter Whitehead filmed the Stones traveling to Belfast by train. He captured Andrew, Brian, Mick and Keith singing various old British tunes, like "Maybe It's Because I'm a Londoner." He also filmed one of the shows, including "Everybody Needs Somebody to Love/Pain in My Heart," "Around and Around" and "(I Can't Get No) Satisfaction." In addition cameras captured Mick, Keith and Andrew fooling around at a piano, singing parodies of Elvis and Beatles tunes. Following the tour, the Stones flew to Hollywood to continue recording their next album at RCA. Work was done on a number of tracks, including "Get Off of My Cloud," "The Singer Not the Song," "Blue Turns to Grey," "I'm Free" and "Gotta Get Away."

**Wednesday, September 8:** Palace Ballroom, Douglas, Isle of Man, UK

The Stones rushed back from Hollywood to play this concert, their last ever dancehall appearance, and prepare for an upcoming German tour. The show attracted a wild crowd that surrounded the venue. Mick arrived late and was forced to sneak in through a bathroom window.

**Saturday, September 11:** Halle Münsterland, Münster, West Germany, with the Rivets, the Rackets and Didi and the ABC Boys, 5 and 8:50 p.m.

The Stones' first visit to Germany, sponsored by the magazine *Bravo*, set off pandemonium. Keith Altham reported, "When the group flew into Dusseldorf there were thousands of teenagers awaiting their arrival. They pushed down fences surrounding the public enclosure and police had to drench them with high-pressure jets. Driven back into the airport building the fans went wild, smashed windows and wrenched telephones out of the wall. None of the leading German hotels would accept the Rolling Stones for fear of the damage the fans might cause." A B&W film of the first Munster concert exists, with footage of the Stones performing "Around and Around," "(I Can't Get No) Satisfaction" and "I'm Alright." The latter two songs were included as a bonus on the 2012 DVD *Crossfire Hurricane*.

**Sunday, September 12:** Grugahalle, Essen, West Germany, with the Rivets, the Rackets and Didi and the ABC Boys, 4 and 7 p.m.

About 8,000 excited teenagers attended this show. To prevent riots, the police erected steel crash barriers around the stage and stationed twenty armed men in front of them. There were also mounted police nearby. The precautions proved necessary. *The Daily Mail* reported, "They stood on seats, stamped their feet, shook their bodies and howled. They threw toilet rolls across the hall and unbolted the tubular chairs to wave in the air. At one point they lost all self control and chanting, hand clapping and stamping, surged towards the stage…. These were the wildest audiences the band had played to outside America." Bill commented in *NME*: "One policeman we spoke to said that there had been nothing like it since the old Nazi rallies. The kids were standing on their seats and yelling 'Heil Stones' which is funny if you think about it."

**Monday, September 13:** Ernst-Merck-Halle, Hamburg, West Germany, with the Rivets, the Rackets and Didi and the ABC Boys, 5:30 and 9 p.m.

The Stones arrived in Hamburg at 11 a.m. and were greeted by 2,000 fans at the airport. The band played an afternoon show for teens and an evening concert attended by older fans. About 14,000 people attended the concerts, but demand was even higher. Fans who'd failed to secure tickets rioted outside the gigs and police on horseback charged at them with batons, while the Stones watched in disgust from their dressing room window. The reviewer from the *Hamburger Abendblatt* described the atmosphere: "Girls moan rapturously, sob, are forced back to their seats by the security guards, continue crying…. The hall begins to boil during 'Satisfaction.' There are small altercations with the security guards during the second concert. MJ, the sorcerer with the mike in his hand, suddenly throttles the noise apparatus, pulls back on the noise and the intensity, pauses at a phrase until the commotion has settled, and turns it back up. He does this in an incredibly skilled manner. He has the 6,000 in the hall firmly in his hands."

**Tuesday, September 14:** Circus Krone, Munich, West Germany, with the Rivets, the Rackets and Didi and the ABC Boys, 6 and 9 p.m.

Hundreds of young people waited in the rain for the arrival of the Stones from Hamburg on Tuesday afternoon. Seeing the large crowd, the Stones were reluctant to get off the plane and only came down the gangway after many assurances of their safety. But the 150 police at the airport weren't needed and the Stones drove to the headquarters of *Bravo Magazine,* where they held a press conference and got their first taste of Bavarian beer. The shows that night were memorable for Brian, as he met future girlfriend Anita Pallenberg (born in Italy in 1943) backstage. The two would be inseparable for the next two years, before she moved on to Keith (who she remained linked with until the end of the 1970s). Reporter Sharon Held of *KRLA Beat* was also present and spoke with Mick and Keith backstage. Asked what struck them about German audiences, Keith replied "The Boys." Mick added "Yeah the boys. I'd say that from 60 to 70 percent of the people are boys…. The audiences are made up of kids mainly 12 to 20 and girls just aren't allowed to go out at night like they are in America."

Poster from the Stones' 1965 German tour (collection of Ira Korman).

**Wednesday, September 15:** Waldbühne, Berlin, West Germany, with the Team Beats Berlin, the Rivets, the Rackets and Didi and the ABC Boys, 8 p.m.

The Stones landed in Berlin at 4 p.m. on Wednesday. Over 1,000 fans were there to greet them at Tegelhof Airport. Many figured out where the band was staying and besieged the place. The Stones had booked the hotel under assumed names and the management was not amused. The group were asked to leave and had to scramble to find new accommodations. The Stones' concert that night was a wild affair. It took place outdoors at the evocative Waldbühne, where Nazi rallies once took place. The band walked through old underground bunkers to get to the venue. The large crowd of 21,000 screaming fans was excited. The show was one of the first big concerts in Berlin and gave German youth a chance to let out some pent up aggression. Things quickly got out of control. Marianne Koch of *Bild Zeitung* described the scene: "Now I know what hell is like. My job has taught me to be brave but in the Waldbühne I learned what fear is like. It is a mob out of control, stampeding at the entrances. I was almost crushed. The air was filled with the yelling of the crowd and the hammering beat of the band. It was like a witch's cauldron and the whole place glowed with the atmosphere."

The concert had to be halted after a few minutes when a mob invaded the stage. The Stones were hustled off to a bunker to wait. The show began again twenty minutes later when order was restored. The full set consisted of "Everybody Needs Somebody to Love," "Pain in My Heart," "Around and Around," "Time Is on My Side," "I'm Moving On," "The Last Time," "(I Can't Get No) Satisfaction" and "I'm Alright." Unfortunately, when the Stones split after their performance, outnumbered police panicked and began pushing the crowd out of the venue in a heavy-handed fashion. Many fans became irate and resisted. A full-scale riot ensued. Fans wrecked the venue, tearing out seats and smashing them. The riots spread to the streets and over forty car windows were smashed and train cars overturned. The Stones could hear the noise from their hotel and Brian got a taxi to drive him around to see what was going on, occasionally rolling down the window to give a facetious Nazi salute. Police arrested over 300 people that night. Berlin authorities blamed the band and rock music in general. Beat concerts were banned in Berlin for a year and the Stones didn't return until 1970.

**Friday, September 17:** Stadthalle, Vienna, Austria, with the Rivets, the Rackets and Didi and the ABC Boys, 8 p.m.

As a result of the riots in Berlin, Vienna police were out in force for the concert in the Stadthalle. The 12,500 fans who attended remained calm, but the *Arbeiter Zeitung* reported, "The vortex of sound that erupted from the audience of 12,000 young people was so bad that one could hardly hear any of the music." The next day the Stones returned to the UK. On September 23 they appeared on *Top of the Pops*. That same day, *Rolling Stones Monthly* reported that the Stones took a nostalgic trip back to Ken Colyer's Club on Newport Street, where they'd last played in December 1963, to rehearse for their upcoming tour.

**Friday, September 24:** Astoria Theatre, Finsbury Park, London, UK, with the Checkmates, the Spencer Davis Group, Charles Dickens and the Habits, the End and Unit Four + 2, 6:40 and 9:10 p.m.

The Stones, accompanied by new road manager Tom Keylock, opened a 23-day tour with the Spencer Davis Group (which included singer Steve Winwood). Also on the bill were Unit Four + 2, a Decca band that had a number one with "Concrete and Clay," and Charles Dickens and the Habits, who had a hit record with "Hey Little Girl." Dickens was actually fashion photographer David Anthony. The Stones seemed happy to be back touring Britain. Norrie Drummond of *NME* reported, "The group appeared on a darkened stage and opened with 'She Said Yeah,' accompanied of course by a mighty barrage of screams. They then went on to play four numbers from their new album *Out of Our Heads*: 'Mercy Mercy,' 'Cry to Me,' 'That's How Strong My Love Is' and 'Oh Baby (We Got a Good Thing Going).' They also included 'I'm Moving On' and 'The Last Time,' before closing with 'Satisfaction.'"

**Saturday, September 25:** Gaumont Theatre, Southampton, Hampshire, UK, with the Checkmates, the Spencer Davis Group, Charles Dickens and the Habits, the End and Unit Four + 2, 6:15 and 8:40 p.m.

While in Southampton, the Stones were interviewed by a reporter from *The Daily Echo*. Keith told him, "The screaming fans don't really worry us. After all, they pay to see us and if they want to scream, I think they are entitled to. Of course, when fans start rioting like they did in Germany recently it can be dangerous for everyone."

**Sunday, September 26:** Colston Hall, Bristol, UK, with the Checkmates, the Spencer Davis Group, Charles Dickens and the Habits, the End and Unit Four + 2, 5:30 and 7:45 p.m.

During "(I Can't Get No) Satisfaction" two girls reached the stage and launched themselves on Charlie, who was briefly knocked off his drum stool.

**Monday, September 27:** Odeon Theatre, Cheltenham, Gloucestershire, UK, with the Checkmates, the Spencer Davis Group, Charles Dickens and the Habits, the End and Unit Four + 2, 6:15 and 8:45 p.m.

**Tuesday, September 28:** Capitol Theatre, Cardiff, Wales, UK, with the Checkmates, the Spencer Davis Group, Charles Dickens and the Habits, the End and Unit Four + 2, 6 and 8:30 p.m.

It may have been this show that Ian Stewart referred to when he told *Datebook*, "One night at Cardiff Capitol, I heard a yelp of pain from Charlie and turned to see him clutching his face, where a wound was welling with blood. He had been hit by an air-gun pellet!"

**Wednesday, September 29:** Granada Theatre, Shrewsbury, Shropshire, UK, with the Checkmates, the Spencer Davis Group, Charles Dickens and the Habits, the End and Unit Four + 2, 6:15 and 8:30 p.m.

**Thursday, September 30:** Gaumont Theatre, Hanley, Worcestershire, UK, with the Checkmates, the Spencer Davis Group, Charles Dickens and the Habits, the End and the Moody Blues, 6:30 and 9 p.m.

**Friday, October 1:** ABC Theatre, Chester, Cheshire, UK, with the Checkmates, the Spencer Davis Group, Charles Dickens and the Habits, the End and the Moody Blues, 6:15 and 8:30 p.m.

**Saturday, October 2:** ABC Theatre, Wigan, Greater Manchester, UK, with the Checkmates, the Spencer Davis Group, Charles Dickens and the Habits, the End and the Moody Blues, 6:20 and 8:35 p.m.

**Sunday, October 3:** Odeon Theatre, Manchester, UK, with the Checkmates, the Spencer Davis Group, Charles Dickens and the Habits, the End and Unit Four + 2, 5:15 and 8 p.m.

The Stones attracted a wild crowd in Manchester. During the second show, a flying bottle knocked Keith unconscious for five minutes and Charlie had to defend his drum kit from stage invaders who wanted to take it as a souvenir.

**Monday, October 4:** Gaumont Theatre, Bradford, Yorkshire, UK, with the Checkmates, the Spencer Davis Group, Charles Dickens and the Habits, the End and Unit Four + 2, 6:15 and 8:40 p.m.

The Stones returned to Bradford, where fans had ripped Brian's clothes off his back the year before. But, the *Telegraph & Argus* reported, "This time the cinema was only half-full for the first house and three-quarters full for the second. This means that there were well over 2,000 empty seats. It's doubtful whether so many girls have fainted at a Bradford show before, however. 'There were literally dozens,' said Mr. Peter Davis, the Gaumont manager. A more than 30-strong St Ambulance Brigade unit dealt with the fainting–setting up headquarters in an exit way during the first house and in the orchestra pit during the second. Several seats were broken and some pierced by high heels."

**Tuesday, October 5:** ABC Theatre, Carlisle, UK, with the Checkmates, the Spencer Davis Group, Charles Dickens and the Habits, the End and Unit Four + 2, 6:15 and 8:30 p.m.

**Wednesday, October 6:** Odeon Theatre, Glasgow, Scotland, UK, with the Checkmates, the Spencer Davis Group, Charles Dickens and the Habits, the End and Unit Four + 2, 6:15 and 9 p.m.

Joan Baez was on tour in the UK and came backstage to meet the Stones.

**Thursday, October 7:** City Hall, Newcastle, UK, with the Checkmates, the Spencer Davis Group, Charles Dickens and the Habits, the End and Unit Four + 2, 6:15 and 8:45 p.m.

**Friday, October 8:** ABC Theatre, Stockton-on-Tees, UK, with the Checkmates, the Spencer Davis Group, Charles Dickens and the Habits, the End and Unit Four + 2, 6:15 and 8:30 p.m.

    A rowdy fan at this show threw a coin at Mick, hitting him in the right eye. He continued the performance, but played the next few dates with a bandage over his bruised eye.

**Saturday, October 9:** Odeon Theatre, Leeds, UK, with the Checkmates, the Spencer Davis Group, Charles Dickens and the Habits, the End and Unit Four + 2, 6 and 8:30 p.m.

**Sunday, October 10:** Empire Theatre, Liverpool, UK, with the Checkmates, the Spencer Davis Group, Charles Dickens and the Habits, the End and Unit Four + 2, 5:40 and 8 p.m.

**Monday, October 11:** Gaumont Theatre, Sheffield, UK, with the Checkmates, the Spencer Davis Group, Charles Dickens and the Habits, the End and Unit Four + 2, 6:15 and 8:50 p.m.

    These shows were memorable for Charlie. In a *Tiger Beat* interview, he commented, "A huge stage and the only way up through a kinda footballers tunnel in the middle. I'm sitting there peacefully bashing away on 'The Last Time' when this well dressed geezer comes up the tunnel and starts whispering urgently in my earhole. I thought he was a manager tipping us off that there was to be a police raid. He wants my autograph! How daft can you get? Have you ever heard of a three-armed drummer? Still bashing away, I tell him to wait. Next moment he pulls me off my stool and I'm dumped on the floor with all the gear on top of me. And he's still insisting on an autograph!"

**Tuesday, October 12:** Gaumont Theatre, Doncaster, Yorkshire, UK, with the Checkmates, the Spencer Davis Group, Charles Dickens and the Habits, the End and Unit Four + 2, 6:15 and 8:30 p.m.

**Wednesday, October 13:** De Montfort Hall, Leicester, UK, with the Checkmates, the Spencer Davis Group, Charles Dickens and the Habits, the End and Unit Four + 2, 6:15 and 8:30 p.m.

**Thursday, October 14:** Odeon Theatre, Birmingham, UK, with the Checkmates, the Spencer Davis Group, Charles Dickens and the Habits, the End and Unit Four + 2, 6:45 and 9 p.m.

**Friday, October 15:** ABC Theatre, Cambridge, UK, with the Checkmates, the Spencer Davis Group, Charles Dickens and the Habits, the End and Unit Four + 2, 6:15 and 8:30 p.m.

**Saturday, October 16:** ABC Theatre, Northampton, UK, with the Checkmates, the Spencer Davis Group, Charles Dickens and the Habits, the End and Unit Four + 2, 6:30 and 8:45 p.m.

**Sunday, October 17:** Granada Theatre, Tooting, London, UK, with the Checkmates, the Spencer Davis Group, Charles Dickens and the Habits, the End and Unit Four + 2, 6 and 8:30 p.m.

This was the last show of the tour. Before embarking on another North American tour, the Stones engaged in promotional activities. On October 19 they performed "Get Off of My Cloud" on *Top of the Pops* at BBC TV Center. On October 22 they appeared on *Ready Steady Go Live*.

**Friday, October 29:** Montreal Forum, Montreal, Quebec, Canada, with the Vibrations, Patti Labelle and the Blue Belles and the Rockin' Ramrods

The Stones flew to New York with Andrew and Stu on October 27 to begin their fourth North American tour. Once again Bob Bonis acted as road manager. Also accompanying the group were Ronnie Schneider (Allen Klein's nephew) and Jerry Brandt and Mike Gruber of the William Morris Agency (which acted as the Stones' agents). In addition, Gered Mankowitz was commissioned to photograph the Stones on behalf of all the British press (he developed a good relationship with the band and continued to work with them for the next few years). On October 28 the Stones held a press conference at the Hilton, before heading to Montreal. Keith left his passport in New York and had to be "smuggled" in.

Opening for the Stones at most shows on this tour were the Philadelphia girl group Patti Labelle and the Blue Belles, who'd had a number of R&B hits including "I Sold My Heart to the Junkman" and "Down the Aisle," the Vibrations, an African American soul group from Los Angeles that reached the charts with "My Girl Sloopy" and the Rockin' Ramrods, a Boston group known for their garage-rock classic "She Lied." Bill described the concert that night, attended by 9,000 fans, in *NME* as "the wildest ever. The audience repeatedly broke through the security men and rushed us on stage. Charlie had a drum stolen and our road manager 'Stu' was only just in time to retrieve Keith's guitar from a boy halfway out of the Arena! Brian got a cut forehead and Charlie had a new jacket ripped. At the end we all ran but Keith and I were trapped on the stage and were finally relieved after 20 frightening minutes and a drive to the airport."

**Saturday, October 30:** Barton Hall, Cornell University, Ithaca, NY, and War Memorial Arena, Syracuse, NY, with Ed Wool and the Nomads, the Vibrations, Patti Labelle and the Blue Belles and the Rockin' Ramrods, 8 p.m.

The Stones made a rare university appearance in the afternoon. Charlie Nash of *The Cornell Daily Sun* commented, "The Stones are one of the evilest groups in town. No one screamed but college kids get more satisfaction than high school kids. Moments and things-beautiful bouffant Brian trying to get himself together: a mike dying on Mick and he, in one marvelous arc, throwing it on the floor, moving to the next and kicking the corpse into the audience; and Keith's satisfaction feedback." The Stones then headed to Syracuse to play for the kind of audience they were accustomed to: 8,000 screaming fans. The band played "Everybody Needs Somebody to Love," "Mercy Mercy," "Cry to Me," "Around and Around," "That's How Strong My Love Is," "I'm Alright," "The Last Time," "Get Off of My Cloud" and "(I Can't Get No) Satisfaction." *The Syracuse Herald Journal* had high praise for the group: "The Stones have a style of their own. They are very energetic performers and do not stand still for one minute. The full impact of their songs cannot be imagined when hearing one of their recordings. To fully appreciate their style, talent and tremendous vibrancy one must attend a live performance."

**Sunday, October 31:** Maple Leaf Gardens, Toronto, ON, Canada, with the Vibrations, Patti Labelle and the Blue Belles and the Rockin' Ramrods, 8 p.m.

The Stones flew into Toronto in the afternoon and departed for Rochester right after the gig. Before the show, they endured the now customary press conference. Mick complained, "I don't know why they come along. They know what they're going to say before they come and they just print what they like." About 11,000 screaming fans attended the concert. *The Toronto Globe* reported, "The darkened arena was lit continuously by popping flashlights. It was a weird effect of mass hysteria, with thousands of arms reaching for the stage and a thin blue line of police and ambulance men the meager protection between the performers and their admirers. Only one girl actually got her arms around one of the Stones, Mick Jagger. She was dragged off rudely, and none of the dozens of others who tried could break the strong defense line."

**Monday, November 1:** War Memorial Auditorium, Rochester, NY, with the Vibrations, Patti Labelle and the Blue Belles, the Rockin' Ramrods, 7:30 p.m.

An excited crowd of 3,500 fans went wild when the Stones appeared. *The Rochester Democrat and Chronicle* reported, "Some teenagers rushed to the stage while others stood on their chairs. They threw stuffed animals, candy and packages of gum at their heroes." Keith was even hit in the head by a flashbulb thrown by someone in the crowd. Nevertheless, he became irate when the police brought down the curtain midway through the show and began escorting the Stones offstage. Declaring Rochester "a hick town," he yelled, "They were twice as wild in Montreal. They (the fans) won't get hurt. You're too hard with them!" The angry fans rioted after the Stones left, hurling things at the police, while chanting "We want the Stones."

**Wednesday, November 3:** Rhode Island Auditorium, Providence, RI, with the Vibrations, Patti Labelle and the Blue Belles and the Rockin' Ramrods, 7:30 p.m.

**Thursday, November 4:** New Haven Arena, New Haven, CT, with the Vibrations, Patti Labelle and the Blue Belles, the Rockin' Ramrods, 7 and 9 p.m.

The Stones played for close to 8,000 people. Edward J. Leavitt of *The Journal Courier* noted, "Emotions soared as song after song was played. Everyone was either standing on a chair or in the aisle. Girls screamed so loudly lyrics were inaudible. The music continued to pour forth.... The grand finale: The Stones swing into a 12-minute rendition of 'I Can't Get No Satisfaction.' The audience stands up on its chairs again. Suddenly it's over. The audience quiets to a murmur. Rising they leave the Arena. They got a lot of satisfaction."

**Friday, November 5:** Boston Gardens, Boston, MA, with the Vibrations, Patti Labelle and the Blue Belles and the Rockin' Ramrods, 8 p.m.

Around 14,000 people attended this show. The set consisted of: "Everybody Needs Somebody to Love," "Have Mercy," "Cry to Me," "Around and Around," "That's How Strong My Love Is," "I'm Movin' On," "The Last Time," "Get Off of My Cloud," and "(I Can't Get No) Satisfaction." Bruce McCabe of *The Boston Record American* reported, "Onstage Jagger is the center of attention-doing all the singing.... During the seventh number, 'The Last Time,' he yields to the frantic pleadings of the crowd and, as the houselights turn an appropriate blue, peels off his jacket.... And teases the crowd by offering to throw his jacket to them.... He, like the rest of the group, rarely smiles.... Jagger of course had to do something constructive at the end, and he did. He tossed his tambourine into the crowd in front of him and whoever got it, I'm sure, was instantly clawed to pieces."

Backstage prior to the show, Mick granted McCabe a short interview. Asked about his future plans, he commented, "I suppose you'll laugh at this, but I'd like to be an actor.

Like Terry Stamp serious acting, I mean. My favorite actress is Sophia Loren, but there's nothing special in that. I mean she's everybody's favorite!" When McCabe inquired what Mick thought of Boston, he replied, "How much do you think I see of it through the back window of a police car?"

**Saturday, November 6:** Academy of Music, New York, NY, with the Vibrations, Patti Labelle and the Blue Belles, and the Rockin' Ramrods, 1 and 4 p.m., and Convention Hall, Philadelphia, PA, with the Vibrations, Patti Labelle and the Blue Belles and the Rockin' Ramrods, 8 p.m.

The Stones played two afternoon shows in New York and then high-tailed it to Philadelphia. Reporter Barbara Manzo of *The Bristol Daily Courier* captured some of the action: "Mick Jagger, the lead singer, wore a maroon velour suit and a brown tam on his head which he threw out into the audience. One girl caught it and sixty other jumped on her. One of the frantic fans squeezed through the barricades somehow and jumped onstage. She threw her arms around Mick's neck and kissed him. He kissed her back on the cheek before the police brutally grabbed her and escorted her to the door.… Things were getting wild when Mick picked up the microphone and turned it completely upside down during a wild number. He knelt down on the floor a few times hitting the tambourine on his head and only those in the first few rows could see.… I jumped on the first row seat and stood there until the end.… The show was even greater than their last one in Philadelphia on May 1!"

**Sunday, November 7:** Symphony Hall, Newark, NJ, with Herald Square, the Vibrations, Patti Labelle and the Blue Belles and the Rockin' Ramrods, 1 and 3:30 p.m.

The Stones were an hour late for the first of two afternoon shows, but fans were not disappointed. Alan Branigan of *The Newark News* reported, "Amplifiers turned up to a roar, the Stones rolled through their repertoire. One of the most popular bits featured Mick Jagger with a tambourine. Instantly, tambourines appeared in many hands all over the hall, with a beat the Spaniards never conceived." The second concert was halted near the end when a riot broke out during "(I Can't Get No) Satisfaction." Following the second show, the Stones headed back to New York. Brian met up with Bob Dylan and spent time with him in a recording studio. He was with Dylan on November 9, when a power outage caused a blackout across the city. In a candle-lit room, Brian, Dylan, guitarist Robbie Robertson and artist Bobby Neuwirth jammed through the night at the Lincoln Square Motor Inn.

**Wednesday, November 10:** Reynolds Coliseum, Raleigh, NC, with the Embers, the Vibrations, Patti Labelle and the Blue Belles and the Rockin' Ramrods, 8 p.m.

The Stones received $12,500 for their appearance in Raleigh. Asked by a reporter backstage if the Stones were really worth the money, Keith replied, "If people are willing to pay it, we're worth it." Jim Lewis of *The Raleigh News and Observer* reported, "Of course they did 'The Last Time,' 'Get Off of My Cloud' and 'I Can't Get No Satisfaction,' much to the satisfaction of the Stones' fans who were able to hear them." The Stones were hustled out of town after the show in a paddy wagon and flew to New York to tape an appearance on the TV show *Hullabaloo* the next day.

**Friday, November 12:** Coliseum, Greensboro, NC, with the Vibrations, Patti Labelle and the Blue Belles and the Rockin' Ramrods, 8 p.m.

About 5,000 fans attended this show. Pandemonium broke out when the Stones took the stage and broke into "Everybody Needs Somebody to Love." Owen Lewis of *The Greensboro Daily News* reported, "Mick Jagger, the leader and vocalist, brought down the house a few times with his gyrations. The other four 'musicians' played it pretty straight. 'Satisfaction' gave just that to the cheering, clapping, stomping crowd."

**Saturday, November 13:** Washington Coliseum, Washington, D.C., with the Vibrations, Patti Labelle and the Blue Belles and the Rockin' Ramrods, 3 p.m., and Civic Center, Baltimore, MD, with the Vibrations, Patti Labelle and the Blue Belles and the Rockin' Ramrods, 8:30 p.m.

The afternoon performance in DC attracted the press. One reporter tried to "gotcha" Mick by presenting him with the latest issue of the UK *Disc Weekly*, which featured the provocative headline "Mick Slams States." The reporter asked if it accurately represented Mick's views. He denied it with a chuckle and passed it to other members of the band. Asked his opinion of Otis Redding's cover of "(I Can't Get No) Satisfaction," Mick replied, "I like it very much." He explained that he hoped to meet Otis but "I just haven't been around the same time he was." Ronnie Oberman of *The Washington Star* reported that during the concert, "Wads of paper, oranges and toy animals were tossed at the fivesome and several female fans attempted to storm the stage, only to be repulsed by special policemen and ushers. The Stones went through such numbers as 'Mercy, Mercy,' 'The Last Time' and their latest 'Get Off of My Cloud,' before finishing with their biggest 'Satisfaction.'" Oberman also attended the Baltimore show that evening and noted, "it was more of the same, except that Mick had more maneuverability on the larger Civic Center stage. Fans there, though, were kept at a greater distance because of a 'moat' filled with policemen separating the stage from the first row of seats."

Advertisement for the Stones' appearance in Washington, D.C., in November 1965 (collection of Ira Korman).

**Sunday, November 14:** Civic Coliseum, Knoxville,

TN, with the Vibrations, Patti Labelle and the Blue Belles and the Rockin' Ramrods, 3 p.m.

The Knoxville concert was something of a fiasco. Despite the fact that the show was scheduled for 3 p.m., the Stones didn't arrive until early evening, by which time many frustrated fans had left the venue.

**Monday, November 15:** Coliseum, Charlotte, NC, with the Vibrations, Patti Labelle and the Blue Belles and the Rockin' Ramrods, 8 p.m.

The Stones attracted a disappointingly small crowd. The reporter assigned by *The Charlotte News* to review the show was distinctly unimpressed and reported: "What it was wasn't music, but it was harmless. Promoter Jim Crockett had hired 40 policemen to hold back the mob, but there wasn't any mob. Jagger looks like a teenage miss who's just washed her hair and can't find her curlers. His straggly brown locks swishing around his shoulders, Jagger wrestles with the microphone, does some fancy strutting and spinning and sings."

**Tuesday, November 16:** Municipal Auditorium, Nashville, TN, with the Vibrations, Patti Labelle and the Blue Belles and the Rockin' Ramrods, 7:30 p.m.

The Stones' trip to the country music capital wasn't reviewed, but Mick recalled in a 2015 interview with the *Tennessean*, "Nashville was very small. And I remember, when I got there, thinking how small it was. A lot of these towns were big names, but small places. They were very friendly places, intimate and friendly."

**Wednesday, November 17:** Mid-South Coliseum, Memphis, TN, with the Vibrations, Patti Labelle and the Blue Belles and the Rockin' Ramrods, 8 p.m.

A lively crowd of 6,000 fans attended this concert. James Kingsley of *The Commercial Appeal* reported, "Mick Jagger, leader of the five-member Rolling Stones, jumped into his show with 'Everybody Needs Someone' and rolled through 'Playing with Fire,' 'That's How Strong My Love Is,' 'Around and Around' and closed the show with the group's two biggest recordings 'Get Off of My Cloud' and 'Satisfaction.'" Following this show, the Stones flew to Miami, Florida, for a few days of relaxation.

A young reporter from *Teen Life* tracked down Mick and was invited to hang out with him and Brian. He was struck by the fact that there were no fans chasing them and asked Mick about it. "'Nobody knows we're here,' Mick said. 'The only people staying at the hotel are adults and they don't even know who we are. Most of them think we're dirty and sloppy just because we don't dress the way they do. Last night Brian and I we're walking around the lobby of the hotel. I was wearing one of my favorite outfits, a white shirt with striped pants and sneakers. All of the sudden two guards from the hotel staff came up to us. They told us we weren't dressed properly and we'd have to leave. When we wouldn't go,' Mick continued, 'they tried to throw us out bodily. It took an hour to convince them that we were guests at the hotel just like everybody else who was wearing a suit and tie!'"

**Saturday, November 20:** Hirsch Youth Center, Shreveport, LA, with the Vibrations, Patti Labelle and the Blue Belles and the Rockin' Ramrods, 8 p.m.

The Stones flew in from Miami to play one show. "You had to look fast to see them, though," wrote Welton Jones of *The Times*. "Their private plane arrived at the Greater Shreveport Municipal Airport after the opening acts had already taken the stage at Hirsch. They went on at about 9:40 p.m. and finished at about 10:05 p.m.… These guys don't fool around, During the 10 some-odd minutes they were on stage, they spoke only thrice—lead singer Mick Jagger said three 'thank yous.' It was a good show, actually. The Stones music is neither as complicated or as interesting as that, of say, the Beatles, but it has an elemental pull that was obvious in Hirsch Saturday night." Following the show, the Stones immediately left for Texas.

**Sunday, November 21:** Will Rogers Memorial Center, Fort Worth, TX, with the Barons, the Vibrations, Patti Labelle and the Blue Belles and the Rockin' Ramrods, 2:30 p.m., and Memorial Auditorium, Dallas, TX, with the Barons, the Vibrations, Patti Labelle and the Blue-Belles and the Rockin' Ramrods, 7:30 p.m.

The Stones played an afternoon show in Fort Worth, than headed to Dallas to appear before a crowd of 6,200. Francis Raffetto of *The Dallas News* reported, "The five young Englishmen sang for a half-hour after three other acts included in their countrywide tour had warmed up the audience. Best received were 'Get Off of My Cloud,' 'Satisfaction' and 'Play with Fire.'"

**Tuesday, November 23:** Assembly Center, Tulsa, OK, with the Vibrations, Patti Labelle and the Blue Belles and the Rockin' Ramrods

**Wednesday, November 24:** Civic Arena, Pittsburgh, PA, with the Byrds, We Five, Bo Diddley, Paul Revere and the Raiders, the Vibrations, Patti Labelle and the Blue Belles and the Rockin' Ramrods, 8 p.m.

**Thursday, November 25:** Milwaukee Arena, Milwaukee, WI, with the Vibrations, Patti Labelle and the Blue Belles and the Rockin' Ramrods

A small crowd of 3,343 turned out for this show. Michael Drew of *The Milwaukee Journal* reported, "Mick Jagger was the act's central figure…. Brian Jones, who missed the band's last Milwaukee visit due to illness, was Jagger's chief rival for girlish fervor. He wore orange pants and blonde bangs covered his eyes, sheepdog style. He played harmonica, organ and electric guitar, the last with a whining hum. The hum may have sounded intentional but was actually caused by a broken amplifier plug…. The Stones delivered nine songs, little of which was discernible above the din. The program included classics like 'Satisfaction,' 'Around and Around' and 'Get Off of My Cloud.'"

**Friday, November 26:** Cobo Hall, Detroit, MI, with Terry Knight and the Pack, Patti Labelle and the Blue Belles, the Rockin' Ramrods and the Vibrations, 8 p.m.

The Stones were scheduled to be on the CKLW TV show *Swinging Time*, but due to a mix-up they didn't appear, disappointing fans who had won a chance to meet them in a newspaper contest. But, they agreed to see them backstage at Cobo Hall. Loraine Alterman of *The Detroit Free Press* was also present and got a brief interview with Mick. Asked if he liked Detroit, he replied, "We wouldn't come here if we didn't like it." She also asked why people said the group were mean and he answered, "I suppose those rumors are from people who don't know us."

**Saturday, November 27:** Hara Arena, Dayton, OH, with the Vibrations, Patti Labelle and the Blue Belles and the Rockin' Ramrods, 4 p.m., and Cincinnati Gardens, Cincinnati, OH, with the Vibrations, Patti Labelle and the Blue Belles and the Rockin' Ramrods, 8:30 p.m.

The Stones returned to Dayton, where they'd appeared in 1964, for an afternoon concert, and then headed south to Cincinnati for an evening appearance before a crowd of 2,500. Dale Stevens of *The Cincinnati Post & Times-Star* reported, "Their 25-minute performance was somewhat marred by the audience. The police-who struck me as being rougher than they needed to be with the enthusiastic kids-stopped the show during the second number. And the microphone went dead at about the same time; only for a few minutes but long enough to hurt the pacing. Best thing about the Stones performance was their songs-especially 'Satisfaction' (Jagger forgot some of the words), 'This Could Be the Last Time' and their current 'Get Off of My Cloud,' good rocky, building bluesy tunes."

**Sunday, November 28:** Arie Crown Theater, Chicago, IL, with the Vibrations, Patti Labelle and the Blue Belles and the Rockin' Ramrods, 3 and 7 p.m.

Patty Faust of *The Daily Illini* captured the scene at the first of two concerts: "Mick Jagger ... grabbed the mike, jumped up and down, and did the splits. He was appropriately dressed in a cranberry jacket and striped pants. Brian Jones, 'a blonde bombshell,' wore a green turtleneck pullover with matching green pants. The rest of the group was dressed conservatively in non-matching coats and jeans.... The Stones were onstage for exactly 21 minutes but McCormick Place reverberated from the ecstatic screams for a full hour after the show ended."

**Monday, November 29:** Coliseum, Denver, CO, with the Vibrations, Patti Labelle and the Blue Belles and the Rockin' Ramrods, 8 p.m.

The Stones and the other acts on the tour flew from date to date on a chartered Martin 50-seater airplane. They occupied their time playing high stakes poker. The Vibrations usually joined in and they often kidded Charlie about his last name. The largely African American neighborhood of Watts in California had been in the news, due to the riots that took place there. As a joke, the Vibrations took to calling Charlie "Soul Brother."

**Tuesday, November 30:** Veterans Memorial Coliseum, Phoenix, AZ, with the Vibrations, Patti Labelle and the Blue Belles, the Rockin' Ramrods

Pete Marinovich of *The Arizona Republic* managed to get backstage before this gig, but received a remarkably hostile reception. The Stones had grown tired of answering the same boring questions. When he asked Charlie if there was a reason the Stones didn't dress alike, he received a curt "no." When he persisted, Keith snapped "Look, we dress like we bloody well please and that's it, cracker." Asked if it was true that the Stones were atheists, Mick replied, "Well I am, bucko. So what?" Keith chimed in, "So am I. Look what has that got to do with our being here? Nothing, nothing, nothing, so bug off!" Marinovich commented that he'd read Brian and Keith had been kicked out of school due to their behavior, which caused Mick to remark "Look, I don't think it's up to us to set examples for our fans and as long as we reach them and entertain them, we're happy." Asked whether they really reached anyone over the screaming, Mick snapped, "We bloody well reach them." Not deterred, Marinovich asked Mick if they had an original sound. He replied, "Certainly. Look, we work hard to give a good show. We say what we please, wear what we please, and we're just what we are, that's all."

**Wednesday, December 1:** Agrodome, Vancouver, Canada, with the Vibrations, Patti Labelle and the Blue Belles and the Rockin' Ramrods, 8 p.m.

About 5,500 turned out for this show, for which the Stones were paid $13,500. Reporter Jes Odam of *The Vancouver Sun* expressed little interest in the concert but noted, "The casually dressed Rolling Stones—one suit among them, the rest an assortment of pants, sweaters and jackets, could not be heard for the shouts, squeals and shrieks. When lead singer Mick Jagger jumped up and down with the microphone stand, the squeals reached a crescendo."

**Thursday, December 2:** Coliseum, Seattle, WA, with the Rockin' Ramrods, the Wailers, Paul Revere and the Raiders, the Liverpool Five, Ian Whitcomb, Patti Labelle and the Blue Bells and the Vibrations, 8 p.m.

The Stones headlined an all-star bill. The group took the stage at 10:15 p.m. and played "Mercy, Mercy," "That's How Strong My Love Is," "The Last Time," "Get Off of My Cloud" and others. For John Hinterberger of *The Seattle Times* the most interesting moment occurred when the amplifiers briefly lost power. "Turned off, the Stones were nothing if not resourceful. They used what they had. And it was one of the nicest harmonica and drum duets I ever heard too. The words were, as I recall, 'La, La, La,' an old favorite. With a crackle the amplifiers started again ... and the mop-tops launched noisily into 'Satisfaction,' their parting shot. The kids went berserk. A half a dozen tried to reach the stage but were nabbed (rather violently I thought) by jittery ushers over-responding.... It was a nice concert. There were no critical injuries."

**Friday, December 3:** Memorial Auditorium, Sacramento, CA, with the Vibrations, Patti Labelle and the Blue Belles and the Rockin' Ramrods, 7 and 9:30 p.m.

The Stones were scheduled to play two concerts, but the second show was cut short by a dramatic incident. Keith, dressed in brown pants and a white sweater, received a shock four songs into the show, when his guitar came in contact with an ungrounded microphone, knocking him unconscious. Fan Mick Martin recalled the event for *The Sacramento Bee* in 2013, "I was right there in the front row, in front of Keith. I saw the blue light. I literally saw Keith fly into the air backward. I thought he was dead. I was horrified. We all were. Silence fell over the crowd." The rubber soles of his Hush Puppies saved Keith. But, he had to be immediately taken to a hospital, forcing the show to end fifteen minutes early. Riots broke out amid the crowd of 4,500. A super-8 film of the incident shot by a fan exists.

**Saturday, December 4:** Civic Auditorium, San Jose, CA, with the Vibrations, Patti Labelle and the Blue Belles, the Rockin' Ramrods, 7 and 9:30 p.m.

The Stones spent Friday night in San Francisco and some writers from *KYA Beat* ran into Keith and Brian there on Saturday morning. Keith commented that he wasn't looking forward to playing that night, as he was shaken up from the shock he'd received in Sacramento. Finding Bill and Charlie calmly eating at a restaurant, Keith noted that he could never eat prior to a show as he got too wound up with nerves. About 2,000 fans attended the San Jose concert. The band performed "Everybody Needs Somebody to Love," "Mercy, Mercy," "Not Fade Away," "That's How Strong My Love Is," "Around and Around," "The Last Time," "Get Off of My Cloud," and "(I Can't Get No) Satisfaction." Like many reviewers, Jill Richards of *KYA Beat* was fascinated by Mick and commented, "He sings with his entire body, not just his voice.... He turns his back to the crowd and shakes his hips like his own maracas. He almost manages the splits. He gets down on his knees. He lifts the mike over his head. He jumps in the air. He does his 'will he throw it or won't he' bit with his jacket. He walks to each side of the stage, shades his eyes with his tambourine and looks at the people who pay to look at him. He sings and shakes and he makes thousands of girls and boys a little bit happier."

**Sunday, December 5:** Convention Hall, San Diego, CA, with the Rockin' Ramrods, the Vibrations and Patti Labelle and the Blue Belles, 2:30 p.m., and Sports Arena, Los Angeles, CA, with the Vibrations, Patti Labelle and the Blue Belles and the Rockin' Ramrods, 7:30 p.m.

The Stones concluded the tour with two concerts. The afternoon show in San Diego was a riotous affair. Jim McVicar of *The San Diego Union* reported, "The Rolling Stones were onstage for barely twenty minutes yesterday at Convention Hall but they managed to build a near capacity audience into a screaming, sobbing, frantic mob. At least a dozen young girls, squirming and struggling, had to be dragged from the hall. A glass door was broken as the Stones left the stage, when some of the 3,700 fans in the auditorium tried to rush out to get a last look as the entertainers were whisked away in a limousine."

Prior to their evening show in LA, the Stones held an end of tour press conference at the Beverly Rodeo Hotel. Asked about the new U.S. LP *December's Children*, Brian commented, "It's a mixture of very old stuff and some new things ... (basically) an album of rejects." Asked if they'd be getting MBEs from the Queen, like the Beatles, Keith quipped "No we've already been convicted of obscenity charges in England so we wouldn't get any MBEs." Discussing their hair, Keith stated, "We're not forced to wear our hair long. I wear mine long because I have big ears!" Asked if the Stones were being conformists by having long hair like other pop groups, Mick replied, "What's a conformist? I don't have to change just because everyone copies us." Brian added, "We conform to our own standards."

The show in LA attracted 15,000 fans and there were numerous attempts to storm the stage. Jim Conniff of *The KFXM Tiger* reported, "The Stones ... opened with 'Everybody Needs Somebody to Love.' Everything from keys to shoes went flying towards the stage. Standing five feet from Mick we could just about hear him, over the crowd's screams, screaming 'She Said Yeah.' We kept our cameras going, taking one picture every ten seconds through 'Mercy Mercy,' 'Not Fade Away,' 'Play with Fire' (and) 'That's How Strong My Love Is.' ... The Stones closed the show with 'Get Off of My Cloud' and 'Satisfaction.' Then they were gone." Following these shows, the Stones returned to LA to work on *Aftermath*. When the sessions ended, Brian's girlfriend Anita joined him and the two flew to South America for a three-week vacation. The other Stones went home. On December 31 they reunited to tape a special *Ready Steady Go!* at Wembley.

## CHAPTER 5

# 1966

The year 1966 began with the release of "19th Nervous Breakdown/As Tears Go By." The A-side, which featured Bill Wyman's diving bass and a loud fuzz guitar, hit number one on the British charts. Some wondered if the title represented the state of mind of band members, increasingly frazzled from endless touring. Keith Altham of *NME* tried to find out, but was quickly shot down by Mick, who exclaimed "We're not Bob Dylan, y'know. It's not supposed to mean anything. It's about a neurotic bird that's all. I thought of the title first, it sounded good." But even if the Stones dismissed questions about their lyrics' deeper meaning, they were aware rock was growing more sophisticated and that they had to progress to keep up with the Beatles (who released *Revolver* that summer), Dylan and the Beach Boys (who put out their masterpiece *Pet Sounds* in May). The Stones were at a disadvantage, as constant touring and promotion gave them little time to catch a breath. Nevertheless, in the midst of the madness, Mick and Keith found time to write an album's worth of material and the Stones squeezed in recording sessions in LA between tours.

Oldham initially planned to name the LP *Can You Walk on Water*, but Decca quashed that idea. The Stones fourth UK LP, *Aftermath*, released on April 8, marked a turning point. It was their first real attempt at an album, rather than just a collection of songs. It was also the first record to feature all Jagger-Richards material. Much of the credit for the album's high reputation, however, must be given to Brian Jones. Increasingly unhappy with his reduced role as second guitarist, he made his presence felt by contributing a host of new sounds, seldom heard up to that time on pop records. Brian's marimbas gave the vicious put-down "Under My Thumb" a lilting groove, while his skillful sitar on the single "Paint It Black" added a throbbing menace to Mick's dark lyrics. Jones also contributed dulcimer to the Elizabethan "Lady Jane" and the moody "I Am Waiting," as well as bluesy harp to the eleven-minute epic, "Goin' Home." As Mick later commented, Brian created a new, vital role for himself in the band: colorist. Bill Wyman commented to the BBC, "As a musician he was outstanding and he was able to walk into a studio and pick up anything that was laying about from a full grown harp, classical harp, and get something out of it…. So he was quite exceptional. And that's why in the '60s … there was so much variety of instruments."

Brian's renewed interest in the band was appreciated. Even Andrew admitted "Brian's contribution can be heard on every track of those recordings at RCA… In some instances it was more than a decorative effect. Sometimes Brian pulled the whole record together." Keith was equally fulsome in his praise. He told Robert Greenfield in 1971, "He was a gas. He was a cat who could play any instrument. It was like, 'There it is. Music comes out

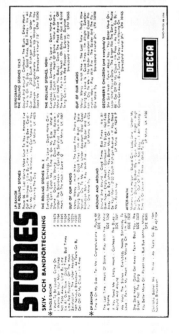

Nineteen sixty-six Scandinavian advertisement for the Stones (collection of Ira Korman).

of it, if I work at it a bit I can do it.'" The new esprit des corps brought Brian and Keith back together and they spent a lot of time hanging out and smoking copious amounts of grass in 1966 and early 1967, as Mick began spending his free time with new paramour Marianne Faithfull. Indeed, by the fall of 1966 Keith and his then girlfriend Linda Keith had practically moved in with Brian and Anita.

But, there was little time to relax. As soon as the band finished a summer tour of the States, they headed back to LA to work on their next album, *Between the Buttons*. They then headed off on vacations in late August (Brian broke his wrist in Morocco in a fight with Anita) but were back in the States in September to complete work on their fall single, "Have You Seen Your Mother Baby, Standing in the Shadow?" In an interview with Jonathan Cott, Mick called the song "the ultimate freak-out. We came to a full stop after that. I just couldn't make it with that anymore. What more could we say?" Indeed the song, which reached number 5 on the UK charts, moved at a speed driven, frenetic pace, the manic quality exacerbated by a full brass section. On September 10 and 11 the band shot a promo film for it in New York with director Peter Whitehead. The video featured the Stones parading around town in drag. Keith later recalled "It took a while to get the picture and going back, what do you do? Do you take half the stuff off and walk back or do you keep it on? Anyway, I'm thirsty, let's go and have a beer. We all zip down to this bar. Hey what voice do you do? We sat there and had a beer and watched TV and no one said anything. But it was just so outrageous because Bill stayed in his wheelchair and Brian was pushing him about."

Soon after their return home, the Stones launched another British tour with Ike and Tina Turner and the Yardbirds. London Records recorded a few dates for a U.S. only LP called *Got Live If You Want It*. However, the Stones were displeased with many of the tracks recorded. Bill later commented, "Don't forget in those day we didn't do very long shows. We used to play 25 minutes at the most, if you or we were lucky. Kids would get onstage and attack me, attack Brian, Charlie, Mick and Keith. So you would have the guitar go out for twenty seconds, drums, etc., half a minute where you would lose the bass or drums completely. Out of six shows you would be lucky to get a full set LP." As a result, "(I Can't Get No) Satisfaction" was doctored at IBC Studios later in the month, with Mick adding a new vocal and Keith redoing his guitar part. In addition, Andrew placed old studio versions of "Fortune Teller" and "I've Been Loving You Too Long" on the LP with overdubbed noise. All in all, it was a disappointing representation of the Brian Jones era, though the Stones played with an awe-inspiring energy that no later live album would ever replicate (especially on speed driven versions of "Get Off of My Cloud" and "I'm Alright").

## Concerts

**Friday, February 18, and Saturday, February 19:** Commemorative Auditorium, Sydney, NSW, Australia, with the Searchers, Max Merrit and the Meteors, Marty Rhone and the Four Fours, Friday at 6:45 and 8 p.m. and Saturday at 2:30, 6:45 and 8 p.m.

The Stones' second Australia/New Zealand tour came on the heels of frantic promotion for their new single, "19th Nervous Breakdown." They appeared on *Top of the Pops* (February 3) and *The Eamonn Andrews Show* (February 6) in the UK and then flew to New York to tape an appearance on CBS TV's *The Ed Sullivan Show* on February 13 before flying to Sydney. Once there they taped an appearance on the Channel 9 TV show *Bandstand* on February 17. Harry M. Miller, who'd brought the group down under in 1965, promoted the tour (emceed by game show host Tony Barber), teaming them with the Searchers, a Liverpool group who'd scored hits with "Needles and Pins" and "Goodbye My Love," and the New Zealand band Max Merrit and the Meteors. Miller hadn't allowed the Stones to bring their own equipment on the previous tour, but the group was more popular now and Miller agreed to pay for their equipment to be flown to Australia. One of the Sydney concerts on February 18 was broadcast on 2UW FM radio. The set consisted of "Mercy Mercy," "She Said Yeah," "Play with Fire," "Not Fade Away," "The Spider and the Fly," "That's How Strong My Love Is," "Get Off of My Cloud," "19th Nervous Breakdown," and "(I Can't Get No) Satisfaction."

**Monday, February 21:** City Hall, Brisbane, Queensland, Australia, with the Searchers, Max Merrit and the Meteors, the Purple Hearts, Marty Rhone and the Four Fours, 6 and 8:45 p.m.

Radio 4BH broadcast the second show in Brisbane. *The Courier Mail* reported, "Lead singer Mick Jagger and his band are experts in their chosen field of rhythm and blues and showed their capabilities well. With a string of hits such as 'Satisfaction,' 'Not Fade Away' and 'Get Off of My Cloud,' they could have been content to take it easy but their obvious love for their music drove them to give the 5,000 fans a taste of things to come. Jagger drew screams with his almost unbelievable stage antics." While the Stones were in Brisbane, they were filmed in bathing suits on the beach for a segment of *Top of the Pops* that aired in March.

**Tuesday, February 22:** Centennial Hall, Adelaide, South Australia, with the Searchers, Max Merrit and the Meteors, Marty Rhone and the Four Fours, 6 and 8:45 p.m.

**Thursday, February 24, to Saturday, February 26:** Palais Theatre, St. Kilda, Victoria, Australia, with the Searchers, Max Merrit and the Meteors, Marty Rhone and the Four Fours, daily at 6 and 8:45 p.m.

The Stones were so popular in the Melbourne area that they were booked for six concerts. The second show on Thursday was broadcast by Australian 3UZ radio, Melbourne. The set consisted of "The Last Time," "Mercy Mercy," "She Said Yeah," "Play with Fire," "Not Fade Away," "That's How Strong My Love Is," "Get Off of My Cloud," and "(I Can't Get No) Satisfaction."

**Monday, February 28:** Town Hall, Wellington, North Island, New Zealand, with the Searchers and the Four Fours, 6 and 8:45 p.m.

The Stones flew to Wellington on February 27. They weren't impressed with the "sleepy" vibe of New Zealand. The Beatles had also expressed complaints about the country and Mick told a reporter from the *NME*, "Tell John Lennon it's horrible here." Bill certainly had reason to dislike Wellington. His custom-made Vox Mark-IV teardrop bass was stolen after the gig (it was returned to him in 2004). The two shows provoked wild riots. *The Dominion* reported that during the first concert, "teenagers dashed to the stage continuously as the Rolling Stones were singing. … One of the girls who jumped from the balcony dashed 20 feet and threw her arms around Mick Jagger. A private security officer dashed after her. As he tried to drag her away, Jagger kept on singing. The girl, still clinging to him, pulled him with her for several yards." The second show was even wilder and had to be halted in the middle of "(I Can't Get No) Satisfaction." *The Evening*

Poster advertising the Stones' appearance in Adelaide, 1966 (collection of Ira Korman).

*Post* reported, "A group of about 30 teenagers surged onto the stage, grappling with the five Stones. Drummer Charlie Watts was attacked from the rear. The other members of the group, looking shaken, stopped playing as they were surrounded by screaming fans. Police hustled the Stones off the stage and out a side entrance, where they escaped in a van."

**Tuesday, March 1:** Civic Theatre, Auckland, North Island, New Zealand, with the Searchers, Sandy Edmondes, Mike Leyton, Ralph Cohen and the Four Fours, 6 and 8:30 p.m.

The set at the final shows in Auckland consisted of: "Mercy Mercy," "She Said Yeah," "Play with Fire," "Not Fade Away," "The Spider and the Fly," "That's How Strong My Love Is," "Get Off of My Cloud," "19th Nervous Breakdown" and "(I Can't Get No) Satisfaction." The group netted £7,063 each for the tour, though Harry Miller didn't pay them until months later. The Stones were quite angry and Keith allegedly knocked Miller out when he ran into him at a London club. With the tour over, Brian, Bill and Bob Bonis flew to LA, while the others took a holiday in Fiji. On March 6, the Stones reconvened in LA to continue work on *Aftermath* at RCA. Tracks recorded between March 6 and 9 included: "I Am Waiting," "Flight 505," "High and Dry," "Lady Jane," "Paint It Black" and "Out of Time."

**Saturday, March 26:** Brabanthal, Den Bosch, Netherlands, with the Bintangs, the Bumblebees, the Outsiders, the Ferraris and Peter and the Blizzards, 8 p.m.

The Stones launched a ten-day European tour accompanied by Andrew, road manager Mike Gruber and Stu. Interviewed by a TV reporter at the airport, Brian was asked if the Stones were still runner-up to Beatles. He replied, "Well you know, we have different scenes going. I don't know who's more popular in what part of the world. I don't know. I don't sort of worry about that." Asked why England had become a pop mecca, Brian replied, "It just happened that England had the right type of sound and the right sort of visual image that the kids over the world wanted at that particular time. It just happened. It could have been anywhere. It could have been France but it just happened to be England."

About 9,000 people attended the show that night. *De Telegraf* reported, "Despite the huge influx of people no serious disturbances occurred during the Rolling Stones' concert. Around a quarter to ten, Radio Veronica DJ Jan van Veen introduced the Stones and wild cheers rose from 9,000 throats. The enthusiastic crowd sang the first song, 'The Last Time,' with the band." The newspaper noted that a lot of potential violence was prevented by the decision of promoters to only allow soft drinks at the show: "Thus when the crowd got enthusiastic they could only throw crumpled paper cups at the Stones."

**Sunday, March 27:** Palais Des Sports, Schaarbeek, Belgium, with Ronnie Bird, the Squirrels, Peter Welch & the Jets and Little Jimmy and the Sharks, 3 p.m.

About 5,000 fans turned out for the Stones concert. The set consisted of "The Last Time," "Mercy, Mercy," "Play with Fire," "Not Fade Away," "That's How Strong My Love Is," "The Spider and the Fly," "Get Off of My Cloud," "19th Nervous Breakdown" and "(I Can't Get No) Satisfaction." Discussing this show with Keith Altham, Keith commented, "Good concert there. All the kids leaping and screaming about, with the police giving them plenty of truncheon." Opening act Little Jimmy, however, stated in an online interview that he felt the Stones "sounded a bit amateurish to me. Of course these guys could play, but somehow it didn't work that day."

**Tuesday, March 29:** L'Olympia, Paris, France, with the Sharkz, the Hou-Lops, J. B., Wayne Fontana and the Mindbenders and Ian Whitcomb, two shows

The Stones were scheduled to play at the Grugahalle in Essen, West Germany but it was canceled and they played Paris instead. They spent Monday relaxing at the Georges V Hotel, before playing two wild shows on Tuesday. Keith Altham reported in *NME*,

"The capacity audience reacted with football crowd verve, swaying in unison in their seats during 'Time Is on My Side' and chanting deafeningly through 'We Say Yeah' (She Said Yeah)… The entire audience at the finale stormed over the top of their seats in the stalls and were only just prevented from reaching the stage by a battalion of bouncers." Both concerts were broadcast on Musicorama. The set at both (though played in different order) consisted of: "The Last Time," "Mercy Mercy," "She Said Yeah," "Play with Fire," "Not Fade Away," "That's How Strong My Love Is," "I'm Moving On," "The Spider and the Fly," "Time Is on My Side," "19th Nervous Breakdown," "Around and Around," "Get Off of My Cloud," "I'm Alright," and "(I Can't Get No) Satisfaction." Following the concerts, the band headed back to their hotel for a party attended by Georgie Fame, Ian Whitcomb, Brigitte Bardot, Marianne Faithfull and Francoise Hardy.

**Wednesday, March 30:** Salle Vallier, Marseille, France, with Les Debs, Les Why Not, Jean-Christian Michel and Antoine, two shows

The Stones played for small but rowdy crowds. During the second concert, a piece of a wooden chair was thrown onstage and hit Mick above his right eye. According to Mike Grant of *Rave*, "His eye puffed up in a huge purple and pink bruise, and the cut required half a dozen stitches, but apart from a few colorful references to the chair thrower, he never complained once or even mentioned the injury. He just got on with the job and appeared at a concert in Lyon the next night wearing enormous dark glasses to hide the injury."

**Thursday March 31:** Palais d'Hiver, Lyon, France, with Antoine and the Problems, 5 and 9 p.m.

Following these shows, the Stones took a sleeper train to Paris. With a few days off, Mick, Keith and Charlie returned to London, but Bill and Brian stayed in Paris. Much to the annoyance of Andrew Oldham, who wanted to control such appearances, they attended a taping of *Ready Steady Go!* at La Locomotive Club and were interviewed by Cathy McGowan.

**Sunday, April 3:** Kungliga Tennishallen, Stockholm, Sweden, with Cecilia Stam, the Caretakers, the Defenders, the Hi-Balls and Lee Kings, two shows

On Saturday morning, Brian and Bill flew into Stockholm, minus the rest of the group, who only showed up on Sunday fifteen minutes before the gig. Mick appeared onstage in a striped jacket with large sunglasses, to hide the bruise he received in Marseilles. Brian was dressed in an outrageous polka dot shirt, white jacket and checkered pants. The set consisted of: "Mercy Mercy," "She Said Yeah," "Not Fade Away," "That's How Strong My Love Is," "I'm Moving On," "Time Is on My Side," "19th Nervous Breakdown," "Play with Fire," "I'm Alright" "The Last Time," and "(I Can't Get No) Satisfaction." Critic Ludvig Rasmusson reported in *Svenska Dagbladet* that the concert "was not a fun event. It was not just that the Stones themselves weren't at their best and the arrangements were bad-it was somehow something else that was lacking…. The Stones seemed listless and tired. They played most of their well-known songs and sounded just like the records. They dutifully pretended that they were having fun but really they were probably sick of it all. At least that's how the music sounded."

**Tuesday, April 5:** K.B. Hallen, Copenhagen, Denmark, with the Lions, the Hitmakers and the Defenders, 6 and 9 p.m.

About 150 fans were on hand to greet Brian, Bill and Charlie when they landed at

Kastrup Airport late on Monday afternoon (Mick and Keith opted to drive from Sweden and didn't arrive until the next day). Bill stayed in the hotel, but Charlie and Brian visited two nightclubs. The Stones reunited on Tuesday for two shows. *Berlingske Tidende* reported, "Last night, K.B. Hallen withstood a flood of enthusiasm as over 4,000 beat music followers poured out of chairs and benches to get as near as possible to their idol Mick Jagger of the Rolling Stones.... Jagger (in a red and green plaid jacket) got an enthusiastic response for every one of his movements." The next day, the Stones returned to England to promote *Aftermath*. They performed on *Top of the Pops* on April 14.

**Sunday, May 1:** NME Poll-Winners Concert, Empire Pool, Wembley, UK, with the Beatles, the Spencer Davis Group, Dave Dee, Dozy, Beaky, Mick and Tich, the Fortunes, Herman's Hermits, the Overlanders, the Alan Price Set, the Seekers, the Small Faces, Sounds Incorporated, the Walker Brothers, the Who, Dusty Springfield, Roy Orbison, Crispian St. Peters, the Yardbirds and Cliff Richards and the Shadows, 2 p.m.

Program for the Stones' concert in Stockholm, April 1966 (collection of Ira Korman).

The Stones again took part in the *New Musical Express*' annual awards show, which again featured an unbelievable bill of super talent. The Stones played "The Last Time," "Play with Fire" and "(I Can't Get No) Satisfaction." They also accepted an award for the single "(I Can't Get No) Satisfaction." Only the awards ceremony was televised. A week later, the Stones appeared on the ABC TV show *Thank Your Lucky Stars* to promote new single "Paint It Black." On May 12 and May 26 they appeared on *Top of the Pops*. They also appeared on *Ready Steady Go!* on May 27.

**Friday, June 24:** Manning Bowl, Lynn, MA. with the Mods, the Tradewinds, the Standells and the McCoys, 8:30 p.m.

The Stones flew to New York on June 23 to begin their fifth North American tour, accompanied by road managers Mike Cornwell and Mike Gruber and business representative Ronnie Schneider (Alan Klein's nephew). The Tradewinds (who'd had a minor hit with "New York Is a Lonely Town"), the Standells (on the charts with "Dirty Water") and the McCoys (of "Hang on Sloopy" fame) opened for them at all dates. After clearing customs, the Stones drove to West 79th Street to hold a press conference aboard the Sea Panther, a 110-foot yacht docked on the Hudson River. Following the conference, Bill and Brian met up with musician John Hammond, Jr., who was recording nearby. Bill ended up playing on three tracks on Hammond's 1967 LP *I Can Tell*. Bob Dylan visited the sessions and everyone went back to his apartment afterwards for a party.

More than 15,000 fans turned up in Lynn the next night and 85 police officers were needed to maintain order. The Stones performed their big hits, including "19th Nervous Breakdown," "Mother's Little Helper," "Lady Jane" and "The Last Time," without incident. But *The Boston Record American* reported that when they began "(I Can't Get No) Satisfaction," "The Stones hit a couple of notes then a wall of humanity descended on them. The police line crumpled. A tear gas grenade exploded in front of the stage and gave the quintet a few precious moments to make a dash for their Cadillacs parked in the rear." This was not the end of the story. *KRLA Beat* reported, "Groups from the audience completely surrounded the car, grabbed the bumpers and bounced the Stones around as they continued to scream and yell their devotion to the five Stones trapped inside a car which was unable to move without hitting crowds of teenagers pressed tightly around the suffocated car. Police finally cleared the mob away ... by popping more tear gas grenades near the cars as the 'fans' continued battering it with broken timbers."

**Saturday, June 25:** Cleveland Arena, Cleveland, OH, with the Tradewinds, the Standells and the McCoys, 2:30 p.m., and Civic Arena, Pittsburgh, PA, with the Tradewinds, the Standells and the McCoys, 8:15 p.m.

The Stones played an afternoon show in Cleveland for 6,000 fans. The set consisted of "The Last Time," "19th Nervous Breakdown," "Stupid Girl," "The Spider and the Fly," "I Am Waiting," "Mother's Little Helper," "Lady Jane," "Get Off of My Cloud," "Paint It Black," and "(I Can't Get No) Satisfaction." Jane Scott of *The Plain Dealer* reported, "As the show neared its end the whole thing became too much for the girls and they charged over, under and around police, attempting to touch the Stones as they rolled out the door." The evening show in Pittsburgh was memorable for Mick. According to *The Pittsburgh Post Gazette*, "Seven thousand shrieking teenagers turned out to drown out the electric shrieks of the five long-haired Britishers known as the Rolling Stones. Some of the electricity must have seeped into the hand microphone clutched in the sweaty paw of lead singer Mick Jagger for at one point in the program Jagger fell to the stage, grasping his hand and had to be helped to the wings by guitarist Keith Richard. The fans as they say in London 'went berserk.' ... But Jagger came back and the concert went on."

**Sunday, June 26:** Coliseum, Washington, D.C., with the Tradewinds, the Standells and the McCoys, 3 p.m., and Civic Center, Baltimore, MD, with the Tradewinds, the Standells and the McCoys, 8:30 p.m.

The performance in D.C. was relatively uneventful, but police halted the evening show in Baltimore during the final number, "(I Can't Get No) Satisfaction," after repeated stage invasions. Fan Jean Hill captured the excitement for *Fabulous 208*: "Bobbing heads and bodies of screaming, sweating fans ran toward the stage only to be driven back by police. All of this chaos was multiplied many times over as the fantastic Mr. Jagger breathed, 'I Can't Get No...' Everyone went wild as he kicked and twisted across the stage.

Official tour poster for the Stones' 1966 American tour (collection of Ira Korman).

When the Stones had gone they left stunned girls just sitting clutching crumpled posters or wads of their own hair."

**Monday, June 27:** Dillon Stadium, Hartford, CT, with the Tradewinds, the Standells and the McCoys, 8 p.m.

The Stones arrived right before show time in a station wagon. *The Hartford Courant* sent teenager Mary MacDonald to report on the show and she was there when they arrived. Asked what he'd do if he wasn't a performer, Mick, dressed in a blue coat and slacks, replied, "I don't know really. I haven't had time to plan and do other things." Keith was nearby and MacDonald asked him if he liked the title "The Aristocrat of Pop." Keith replied, "I never heard that before but I love it naturally. But, I don't go to fashionable parties in London." Brian didn't take part in the interview but caught MacDonald's eye due to his wild pink and blue striped jacket adorned with a button that said "I love the Beatles." After watching the show, she reported, "The range of the Stones music impressed me. They went from bitterness in 'Paint It Black' to super-blues in 'My Sweet Lady Jane' but the totality was very Rolling Stones. The crowd was getting close to the barricades and the Stones were told to leave. Shrugging, Mick Jagger began 'Satisfaction.' The audience screamed throughout the last line sung. Mick dropped the microphone off stage. The group ran to their station wagon and the driver hurtled out of Dillon Stadium."

**Tuesday, June 28:** War Memorial Auditorium, Buffalo, NY, with the Tradewinds, the Standells and the McCoys, 8 p.m.

The Stones took the stage around 9:30 with Mick decked out in a yellow and white pop painted jacket and blue shirt. *The Evening News* commented, "Next to their effervescent leader the other four Stones look quite grim. Almost stone faced you might say. They sang 'The Last Time,' '19th Nervous Breakdown,' 'Get Off of My Cloud,' 'Paint It Black,' 'Stupid Girl,' 'Lady Jane,' 'That's How Strong My Love Is,' 'The Spider and the Fly' and 'I Can't Get No Satisfaction.' There was the usual drawback—the screaming and the other look at me sort of foolishness."

**Wednesday, June 29:** Maple Leaf Gardens, Toronto, ON, Canada, with the Ugly Ducklings, the Rogues, the Standells and the McCoys, 8 p.m.

The Stones flew into Toronto at 12:30 a.m. It was so late that only two teenagers greeted them outside their hotel. But there were 13,000 excited fans the next night. Arthur Zeldin of *The Toronto Star* commented, "The audience passed through successive stages of desperation and exultation with 'Lady Jane,' 'Hey, Hey, Get Off of My Cloud' and 'Paint It Black.' Some mass consummation of the 60s was reached with the music-motion-lights of the Stones' universalized complaint, "Can't Get No Satisfaction."" Prior to the show, the Stones held a press conference backstage. Asked why they had such long hair, Mick replied, "Because we like it that way." Asked if they felt responsible for behavior of their fans, Bill answered, "We don't feel responsible to anyone but ourselves. We play our music and the kids come to hear it because they like it. That's all."

**Thursday, June 30:** Forum, Montreal, QB, Canada, with the Tradewinds, the Standells and the McCoys

Discussing the tour with Keith Altham, Mick commented, "In Montreal they employed wrestlers to beat the wild fans up and those toughs really seem to enjoy it. They hauled some little bloke out from the front row and about five of them were smashing him in the face. We stopped playing and booed them. Then the organizer came on stage and told me to get off." Luckily for the venue, the Stones ignored the request. But *The Montreal Gazette* reported that 100 young people received medical attention.

The Stones became friendly with the Standells and McCoys, but there was little opportunity to socialize. The Stones could barely leave their rooms. One night in Canada, Keith decided to try going out with Dick Dodd of the Standells and one of the McCoys. Dodd recalled in *Tiger Beat,* "There must have been at least 1,000 kids downstairs outside the hotel. Keith wanted to go out and he didn't think any of the kids would recognize us. We snuck out by the rear exit and walked to the side of the hotel. All of a sudden some kids saw us. So we started walking along slowly, whistling, and pretending that nothing was happening. We started walking faster and they started walking faster. It was just like that scene in *Hard Day's Night*. We didn't have anyplace to go because everything was closed. We thought the only way to make it back to the hotel was to split up, so we took off in all directions. I ran and hid behind this bank and I saw Keith trying to climb up a flagpole. They didn't catch us, but we had to hide out for about two hours and then we all snuck back to the hotel. It was the last time we tried going out!"

**Friday, July 1:** Marine Ballroom, Steel Pier, Atlantic City, NJ, with the Tradewinds, the Standells and the McCoys

**Saturday, July 2:** Forest Hills Tennis Stadium, Queens, NY, with the Tradewinds, the Standells and the McCoys, 8 p.m.

The band arrived in a helicopter to play a 35-minute set before 9,400 fans, for which they received $25,000. Robert Shelton reported in *The New York Times* that the Stones "were completely charming and very disciplined musicians.... Mick Jagger is a fascinating performer to watch. He does a nimble rock 'n' roll ballet, dancing around alone or with the microphone in another grand old Negro tradition. His antics and hand waving sent the young girls in the audience into paroxysms." Indeed, over fifty fans stormed the stage during the closing number, "(I Can't Get No) Satisfaction." The *Long Island Star Journal* reported, "A boy, ducking a police barricade and dodging special guards, managed to leap to the stage. He grabbed lead singer Mick Jagger around the leg and began to kiss his feet. Jagger continued to sing while policemen carried the boy away. Encouraged by his success, others leaped the barricade and ran towards the stage. For at least ten minutes fans grappled with police in front of and on the stage." The Stones hurriedly finished "(I Can't Get No) Satisfaction" and high-tailed it to a helicopter.

A *Hullabaloo* reporter accompanied the Stones to the gig. Mick commented to him, "'Here the kids scream but they're quiet. In France they break everything. I've never seen anything like that.' He shows me a little scar above his right eye. 'Some excited fan was throwing chairs at the cops who were guarding the stage at Marseilles. I got a whole load of it.'" Following the concert, the Stones went to a club to see a guitarist named Jimmy James, whom John Hammond had raved about. Jimmy James was in fact Jimi Hendrix, and the Stones' collective minds were blown. Hendrix soon headed to England, where he formed the Experience.

**Sunday, July 3:** Convention Hall, Asbury Park, NJ, with the Tradewinds, the Standells and the McCoys, 7:30 and 9:45 p.m.

A fan who attended one of these shows commented on the *It's Only Rock and Roll* website that the songs played were "Not Fade Away," "Get Off of My Cloud," "Stupid Girl," "Lady Jane," "The Last Time," "Paint It Black," "19th Nervous Breakdown," "Spider and the Fly" and "(I Can't Get No) Satisfaction." He also noted, "On 'Paint It Black' Brian sat cross-legged at the end of the stage playing the sitar. I don't remember him looking up once, all you saw was this head of golden hair, and all you heard were girls screaming out his name. On 'Lady Jane' he played the dulcimer.... It was a blazing hot day ... over

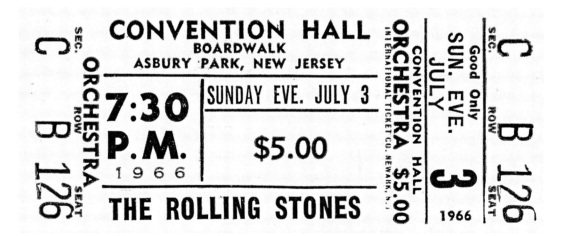

Concert ticket for the Stones' July 3, 1966, appearance in Asbury Park, New Jersey (collection of Ira Korman).

100 and humid. The fans in the front were actually handing up ice cream cones to the Stones."

Backstage Mick was asked by a reporter from the *Asbury Park Press* whether he cared that no one in the venue could hear him over the screaming and he replied, "If they want to hear me sing they can buy a record." The intrepid reporter then asked why girls screamed so much and Mick said, "I'm not a psychologist or a psychiatrist, I'm just a performer." A reporter then made the mistake of asking Mick when the success would end and Keith, sitting glumly with Brian, snapped at him, "The last question I would answer is that one. We don't think about that."

**Monday, July 4:** The Alan B. Shepherd Civic Center (The Dome), Virginia Beach, VA, with the Syndicate of Sound, the Tradewinds, the Standells and the McCoys, 7:30 and 10 p.m.

The Stones' plane landed at Norfolk Airport at 6:30 p.m. and police drove them to the venue. Backstage they gave a few brief comments to a reporter. Asked about the Beatles, Mick said they were "Nice Lads." Brian was asked if the Stones' music was serious and replied, "I think it is a serious threat to juvenile morals." As to the concert itself, *The Virginian Pilot* reported, "Some 3,500 screaming teenagers packed the house to see the five shaggy singers perform a 15-minute 'concert' showcasing their hits, 'I Can't Get No Satisfaction' and 'Mother's Little Helper.'"

**Wednesday, July 6:** War Memorial Auditorium, Syracuse, NY, with the Endless Knights, the Syndicate of Sound, the Tradewinds, the Standells and the McCoys, 8 p.m.

An enthusiastic crowd of 6,000 attended this show. *The Syracuse Post Standard* reported, "The Stones dressed in vari-colored jackets and pants, sang many of their hits, including 'This Will Be the Last Time,' (Paint It) 'Black,' 'Stupid Girl,' 'Get Off of My Cloud,' '19th Nervous Breakdown,' and of course 'Satisfaction.' Jagger also did the attractive, off-beat 'Lady Jane.'" The show was more memorable due to a bizarre backstage incident. While walking towards the stage, Brian saw a large American flag on a chair and grabbed it as a souvenir. An auditorium employee complained to the police that he was dragging the flag on the floor in a disrespectful manner. Though Brian and the Stones vehemently denied that they meant to show any disrespect to the flag, they had to profusely apologize to reduce the tension. Larry Tamblyn of the Standells recalled, in *Tiger Beat,* that Bill and Charlie were very surprised at the American attitudes: "They felt that the English people were a lot more broadminded than the Americans.... Charlie was telling me that the English don't think anything of touching their flag in England. They even cover up their amplifiers with them and make coats out of them. They couldn't understand how the Americans could get so upset over this incident."

**Friday, July 8:** Cobo Hall, Detroit, MI, with the Tradewinds, the Standells and the McCoys, 7:30 p.m.

Prior to the concert, Mick gave an interview to Loraine Alterman of *The Detroit Free Press*. Asked whether he worried about trying to be commercial, Mick replied, "We do what we like. Of course it's very difficult to make the distinction between a commercial and non-commercial sound. We try to do our best." Asked about changes in American teens, Mick commented that two years earlier "I don't think they thought that much about anything. They had no arguments except about petty things. Now they're more aware. On the West Coast especially they're very hung up about everything—much more so than on the East Coast."

**Saturday, July 9:** State Fairgrounds Coliseum, Indianapolis, IN, with the Tradewinds, the Standells and the McCoys, 8 p.m.

The Stones played before a rowdy crowd of 10,000 teens. During the show the band was continually pelted with paper cups and towards the end of the evening some cretins began hurling pieces of wooden chair slats, though none of the Stones were injured. There were also numerous attempts to storm the stage, but no one succeeded in breaking through security.

**Sunday, July 10:** Arie Crown Theatre, Chicago, IL, with the Tradewinds, the Standells and the McCoys, 3:30 and 7:30 p.m.

The Stones spent the day relaxing by the pool. As usual, many fans figured out where they were and besieged them with requests for autographs. One lucky one managed to get a short chat with Keith that appeared in *Datebook*. Asked if he was scared by the riot in Lynn, he answered, "No, not really, no.... I'd been through this type of thing before or I would have been." When the fan inquired what Keith liked to do on tour, he replied, "Laze around. Doesn't everyone?"

Advertisement for the Stones' July 1966 appearance in Chicago (collection of Ira Korman).

Dennis Leavy of *The Chicago Daily News* attended the shows that night and reported, "The Stones sang 'Satisfaction,' 'Get Off of My Cloud' (an old favorite) and their newest release, 'Lady Jane.' It's a sleeper. Jagger sang passionately and danced with gyrations that would do credit to a S. State Street stripper. The loudest shrieks of adolescent joy came when he turned his back on the audience and played the tambourine with his left foot." In between shows, Mick granted an interview to Ted Dziak of *The Chicago Tribune*. Asked about his favorite Stones LP, Mick replied "I feel our best album is our last one—*Aftermath*." Asked why the Stones recorded so much in America, he commented "The studios are better, and the engineers quicker. The English engineers always seem to be off having a spot of tea."

**Monday, July 11:** Sam Houston Coliseum, Houston, TX, with the Tradewinds, the Standells and the McCoys, 8 p.m.

About 6,500 fans turned out for the first Texas show since 1964. Dick Dodd of the Standells recalled, in *Tiger Beat*, a funny incident at the hotel: "The Stones were all very hungry. They ordered all this food, mostly pastries, to be sent to the room. They were all eating and their American business manager Mike Gruber got the idea that he'd like to put some chocolate cake in Brian's face. Then Brian thought it would be nice to put some chocolate pudding in Mike's face. It just got out of hand! Everyone was throwing everything at each other. There was chocolate pudding all over the walls and drapes—all over everything. It ruined the whole room!"

While in Houston, Mick gave an interview to Bruce Hathaway of KTSA radio (San Antonio). Asked if the Stones would still be performing in ten years, he said, "It's very unlikely, but we've been going four years now and that was very unlikely too, according to some people." Asked about Texas, he stated: "I do remember we were in your city about three years ago on our first trip to America. We were 'nobodies' then. We appeared at a show you were the MC of. You might say you were the first Texan we had ever met and as I recall we had a real nice time, thanks to you, as we were 'nobodies' and yet you took your time to show us around San Antonio and places."

**Tuesday, July 12:** Kiel Convention Hall, St. Louis, MO, with the Tradewinds, the Standells and the McCoys, 8 p.m.

The Stones arrived in St. Louis at 4 a.m. and spent the day lounging at their hotel, where they swam in the pool and played Monopoly. Perhaps the extreme heat in the city sapped some of their energy. William Woo of the *Post Dispatch* noted that the band seldom moved during the show that night, attended by 5,000 people. He commented, "The exception was the leader, Mick Jagger, who was all over the stage, dancing, strutting, jumping, mincing, pounding a tambourine and tossing a bump now and then for good measure…. The Stones sang for about 30 minutes, closed with 'I Can't Get No Satisfaction' and hurried off stage without an encore."

**Thursday, July 14:** Stadium, Winnipeg, MT, Canada, with the Ronettes, the Standells, the Hunts Man and the McCoys

The Stones performed on a seven-foot high stage separated from the capacity crowd by a 100-foot barrier. They barreled through "The Last Time," "Get Off of My Cloud," "Stupid Girl" and "Paint It Black" without incident, but during "19th Nervous Breakdown" an unidentified fan leapt from the balcony to the stage curtain to try and reach the group and fell 12 feet to the ground. He was unhurt, but this was the cue for numerous stage invasions. "Lady Jane" quieted everyone down, but Mick worked the audience into a fever pitch with the closing number "(I Can't Get No) Satisfaction." *The Winnipeg Free Press* reported, "Whatever section of the audience he faced came alive; he took one section of it at a time and played it as his own instrument, sitting, standing, pounding the floor, contracting his knees inside their tight-white pants, encouraging and enjoying audience sympathy. And then he was gone and his men with him-through the curtain, down a ramp and into a long black limousine."

**Friday, July 15:** Rosenblatt Stadium, Omaha, NB, with the Tradewinds, the Standells and the McCoys, 8 p.m.

Following this show, the Stones relaxed for three days in LA. They shopped in Beverly Hills and hit the clubs on the Sunset Strip, including the famous Whiskey A-Go-Go. Brian's electric dulcimer was stolen during the tour and he was forced to go on the radio and plead for its return. Luckily a kind-hearted fan turned in the thief and Brian got the instrument back in time for the West Coast shows.

**Tuesday, July 19:** PNE Forum, Vancouver, BC, Canada, with the Tradewinds, the Standells and the McCoys, 8 p.m.

This concert started ninety minutes late because the plane carrying the musicians broke down on the way from LA and had to be attended to in Portland. The show attracted 3,044, a far cry from the 16,000 that attended the Beatles 1964 concert in Vancouver. But despite fewer numbers, Stones fans were rowdier. Police temporarily halted the show after only five minutes. *The Vancouver Sun* reported, "At this point the youngsters were standing and swaying on ground floor benches and hundreds were attempting to smash through police lines and a crash fence to get at the mop haired musicians…. When the plugs were pulled, Mick Jagger, leader of the Stones, turned and pointed his finger at (Police Chief) Errington, then thumbed his nose. The audience screamed its approval." Keith felt that the police's actions were unwarranted. The police were equally upset with the Stones and vowed to prevent further shows. They only returned in 1972 after much pleading.

**Wednesday, July 20:** Seattle Center Coliseum, Seattle, WA, with the Tradewinds, the Standells and the McCoys, 8 p.m.

Only 6,000 turned up at the 14,000-seat Coliseum. Prior to the show, the press grilled the Stones about the show in Vancouver. Mick denied that he'd been rude to police. "If they give us a good time, we give them a good time. If they give us a bad time, we give them a bad time." He also insisted that the Stones had no message. "We're not trying to get anything across to people. The songs express what I feel. Too many people are trying to tell everybody what to do." Rolf Stromberg of *The Seattle Post Intelligencer* reported, "Accompanied by screams and hoarse exclamations, the Stones romped through such selections (lyrics largely inaudible) as 'Paint It Black,' 'Mother's Little Helper,' 'Get Off of My Cloud,' '19th Nervous Breakdown' and their big smash, 'Satisfaction.' If there were double meanings in the words of the last, it couldn't be heard in the general din."

**Thursday, July 21:** Memorial Coliseum, Portland, OR, with the Live Five, the Tradewinds, the Standells and the McCoys, 8 p.m.

The Stones arrival in Portland was such a well-guarded secret that there were only four fans to greet them when they landed. A reporter and a cameraman from a local TV station were present, but the Stones refused to cooperate. The cameraman almost got into a fight with Ronnie Schneider when he refused to move so he could get better photos. A fan reported on the concert for *Song Hits Magazine*: "I was seated quite close, in fact parallel to Brian Jones. He made faces at me. Mick waved at me several times. And at one point during 'Stupid Girl' (ironic, huh??) he pointed at me (I swear and will to my death that he did and nobody can persuade me otherwise!). Mick introduced Charlie, who got two screams, and said he'd do all the latest dance steps. Charlie just introduced 'Lady Jane.' And once—I could have kissed Mick—two cops were carrying out a little girl (two cops!!) who had run up to the stage and Mick said, 'Don't take her away!'"

**Friday, July 22:** Memorial Auditorium, Sacramento, CA, with the Tradewinds, the Standells and the McCoys, 6 and 9 p.m.

**Saturday, July 23:** Lagoon, Farmington, UT, with the Tradewinds, the Standells and the McCoys, 7 and 9:30 p.m.

The flight to Salt Lake City was intense. One of the airplane windows shattered where Brian was sitting, depressuring the plane and causing everyone's ears to pop. Dick Dodd of the Standells recalled, "Brian thought he was going to get sucked out of the airplane…. Brian jumped out of his seat really fast and he bruised his arm on the chair.

Then Keith just looked at the window like, 'well wow!' Then all of the sudden he figured out was happening and he jumped from his seat really fast. Then everyone just ran to the front of the plane and there was mass confusion. It was really scary!"

**Sunday, July 24:** Swing Auditorium, San Bernardino, CA, with the Tradewinds, the Standells and the McCoys, 2 p.m.,

The Stones played for an enthusiastic crowd of 5,000 fans, who rushed to the front when the group came on to begin their set. John Morthland of *The San Bernardino County Sun* reported, "When the Stones started singing one of their biggest hits, '19th Nervous Breakdown,' it became difficult to see them on the stage, as they became surrounded by girls, who had broken through the police lines. At least three girls were carried off stage during that song. Some had fainted-others began hugging their heroes.... The final song of the program, 'Satisfaction,' ... literally brought the house down. One girl got on stage, grabbed Wyman and wouldn't let go until two officers peeled her off."

**Monday, July 25:** Hollywood Bowl, Los Angeles, CA, with the McCoys, the Standells and Buffalo Springfield, 8 p.m.

About 17,000 fans turned out at the Bowl. For this show Buffalo Springfield (featuring Neil Young and Stephen Stills) replaced the Tradewinds. The Springfield was enthusiastically received, but the Stones were the main event. Tracy Thomas commented in *NME*, "The balmy summer evening found Mick in excellent voice and leaping about with his usual agility, the Bowl sound system in good working order and the boys a sight to behold—Mick in gold, black and white; Brian in red, white and wide black stripes; and Keith in purple! A highlight of the concert, completely sold out more than three weeks ahead, was Mick's charming 'Lady Jane.'"

**Tuesday, July 26:** Cow Palace, San Francisco, CA, with the Tradewinds, the McCoys, the Standells, the Jefferson Airplane and the Sopwith Camel, 8 p.m.

For this concert two Bay Area bands, the Sopwith Camel and the Jefferson Airplane, were added. The Stones, with Brian decked out in a black suit with pink pinstripes and Mick (who celebrated his twenty-third birthday that day) in a green and gold sports coat and white bell-bottoms, performed before a sell-out crowd eager to get close to them. The outnumbered police frequently looked as though they might lose control. Indeed, Jan Silverman of *The Oakland Tribune* declared "Picture the entire floor of the Cow Palace filled to the rafters with howling teenagers, nearly everyone standing on his chairs. It was a frightening sight." The Stones kept their cool, but *Tribune* reporter Gerri Looney commented, "There were instances when Mick Jagger ... was apparently unnerved by the violent happenings that surround them. He did repeat the first verse of 'Lady Jane,' while omitting the second. He did substitute several lines in 'Mother's Little Helper' for the original ones heard in the recording."

**Thursday, July 28:** HIC Arena, Honolulu, HI, with the Spirits, the King Bees and the Imports, 8 p.m.

A crowd of 8,360 attended the tour-ending Honolulu show. The *Star-Advertiser* reported, "It was an orgy as usual. The kids were screaming so loud you couldn't hear most of the songs. Except for 'Lady Jane.' Everybody was quiet for that." Although no one would have guessed it at the time, Brian, dressed in a broad-striped pink and black suit, had played his final U.S. concert. The show was broadcast live by K-POI Radio and the set consisted of "Not Fade Away," "The Last Time," "Paint It Black," "Lady Jane,"

Handbill for the Stones' concert in Hawaii on July 28, 1966 (collection of Ira Korman).

"Mother's Little Helper," "Get Off of My Cloud," "19th Nervous Breakdown," and "(I Can't Get No) Satisfaction."

Following the show, the Stones spent a few days in Hawaii and then headed to LA to work on their next LP, *Between the Buttons,* at RCA. Between August 3 and 11 they recorded tracks for "Backstreet Girl," "All Sold Out," "Connection," "Complicated," "Get Yourself Together," "Let's Spend the Night Together," "Miss Amanda Jones," as well as their next single "Have You Seen Your Mother Baby, Standing in the Shadow?" The Stones had tentatively planned to appear in the Philippines following the U.S. tour but scrapped the idea when they learned from the Beatles (who had a scary experience there in July) that the country was worth avoiding.

**Friday, September 23:** Royal Albert Hall, London, UK, with Ike and Tina Turner, the Yardbirds, Peter Jay and the New Jay Walkers, the Kings of Rhythm Orchestra, 8 p.m.

The Stones spent early September in the States completing work on "Have You Seen Your Mother Baby, Standing in the Shadow?" While in New York on September 11, the band taped an appearance on the CBS TV show *Ed Sullivan Show.*

After their return to the UK, the Stones launched a UK tour that included Ike and Tina Turner (who'd recently recorded "River Deep, Mountain High" with Phil Spector) and the Yardbirds (which now included both Jeff Beck and Jimmy Page on guitars). Brian had broken his wrist (allegedly in a fight with Anita) and had to play with his hand wrapped in bandages.

The opening show at Albert Hall was a wild affair. Norrie Drummond reported in *NME* "As soon as the group appeared onstage hundreds of screaming teenagers surged to the front of the stage, elbowed their way past the security men and climbed on to the platform. Keith Richard was knocked to the ground. Mick was almost strangled, while Brian Jones and Bill Wyman took to their heels, followed closely by dozens of determined fans. Charlie Watts sat quietly behind his drums watching the scene." The concert was halted until order was restored and then continued without further interruption. Director Peter Whitehead was on hand to film the Stones. B&W footage of them being attacked by teenage girls was used to make promo films for "Have You Seen Your Mother Baby" and "Lady Jane," to be shown on *Top of the Pops.* Some footage has popped up in documentaries (including Brian cackling as Keith is mauled by fans). Whitehead also filmed them being presented with gold records.

**Saturday, September 24:** Odeon Theatre, Leeds, UK, with Ike and Tina Turner, the Yardbirds, Peter Jay and the New Jay Walkers, the Kings of Rhythm Orchestra, 6 and 8:30 p.m.

Mick commented in *Melody Maker* that he enjoyed playing Britain. "When we toured last time, we'd done so much we had become blasé about it. But we haven't toured Britain for a year now, so it's fresh again. I'm very surprised at the fans—I thought they'd be older but they seem as young as ever. I never expected this sort of reception. It's a knockout."

**Sunday, September 25:** Empire Theatre, Liverpool, UK, with Ike and Tina Turner, the Yardbirds, Peter Jay and the New Jay Walkers, the Kings of Rhythm Orchestra, 5:40 and 8 p.m.

In order to avoid a mob, the Stones waited until the last minute to drive to the venue. They raced into the theatre just before showtime. Alan Walsh reported in *Melody Maker* "The Stones had the notoriously tough Liverpool fans going berserk all over the theatre....

This must be one of the best shows on the road for a long time. It's worth seeing for the Ike & Tina revue alone. Add the Stones and the Yardbirds and you can't afford to miss it."

**Wednesday, September 28:** ABC Cinema, Ardwick, Manchester, UK, with Ike and Tina Turner, the Yardbirds, Peter Jay and the New Jay Walkers, the Kings of Rhythm Orchestra, 6:30 and 8:45 p.m.

*Go Magazine* reported that Brian had to be treated by a doctor after these shows because "he was taking his guitar off carefully because of his healing injured hand when one of the strings grazed his eye."

**Thursday, September 29:** ABC Theatre, Stockton-on-Tees, UK, with Ike and Tina Turner, the Yardbirds, Peter Jay and the New Jay Walkers, the Kings of Rhythm Orchestra, 6:15 and 8:30 p.m.

During the second show, something thrown by a fan beaned Mick. The concert was briefly stopped while a bandage was applied to his bleeding forehead but the band then launched into "Get Off of My Cloud" as if nothing had happened.

**Friday, September 30:** Odeon Theatre, Glasgow, Scotland, UK, with Ike and Tina Turner, the Yardbirds, Peter Jay and the New Jay Walkers, the Kings of Rhythm Orchestra, 6:40 and 9 p.m.

**Saturday, October 1:** City Hall, Newcastle-upon-Tyne, UK, with Ike and Tina Turner, the Yardbirds, Peter Jay and the New Jay Walkers, the Kings of Rhythm Orchestra, 6:15 and 8:30 p.m.

Both shows were recorded for the U.S. only LP *Got Live If You Want It!* The versions of "Under My Thumb," "Get Off of My Cloud," "(I Can't Get No) Satisfaction," "The Last Time" and "19th Nervous Breakdown" on the album were taped this night (though some of the tracks were doctored in the studio).

**Sunday, October 2:** Gaumont Theatre, Ipswich, Suffolk, UK, with Ike and Tina Turner, the Yardbirds, Peter Jay and the New Jay Walkers, the Kings of Rhythm Orchestra, 5:30 and 8 p.m.

While on a tour break, the Stones appeared on *Ready Steady Go Live!* at Wembley on October 4. On October 5 they taped *Top of the Pops.*

**Thursday, October 6:** Odeon Theatre, Birmingham, UK, with Ike and Tina Turner, the Yardbirds, Peter Jay and the New Jay Walkers, the Kings of Rhythm Orchestra, 6:45 and 9 p.m.

The Stones genuinely enjoyed the UK tour. Despite playing with an injured wrist, Brian enthused to writer Keith Altham, "Youngsters, who had never seen us before, from the age of about 12, were turning up at the concerts. It was like it was three years ago when the excitement was all new." Keith added, "The tour has been an enormous success because it's brought the young people back again. In the 'It's All Over Now' period we were getting adults filling up half the theatre and it was getting all 'draggy' and quiet. We were in danger of becoming respectable! But now the wave has arrived, rushing the stage just like old times."

**Friday, October 7:** Colston Hall, Bristol, UK, with Ike and Tina Turner, the Yardbirds, Peter Jay and the New Jay Walkers, the Kings of Rhythm Orchestra, 6:15 and 8:30 p.m.

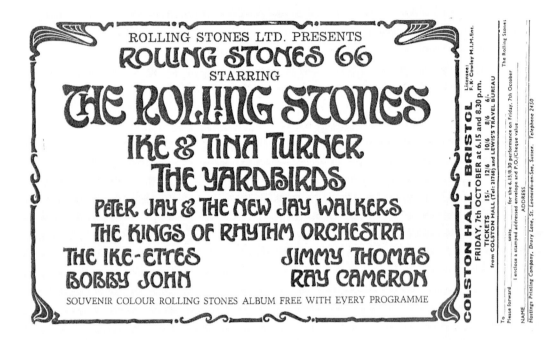

**Handbill for the Stones' appearance in Bristol in October 1966 (collection of Ira Korman).**

London Records recorded these shows for use on *Got Live If You Want It!* The versions of "Lady Jane," "Not Fade Away," "Time Is on My Side," "I'm Alright," and "Have You Seen Your Mother" on the album come from these concerts.

**Saturday, October 8:** Capitol Theatre, Cardiff, Wales, UK, with Ike and Tina Turner, the Yardbirds, Peter Jay and the New Jay Walkers, the Kings of Rhythm Orchestra, 6 and 8:30 p.m.

**Sunday, October 9:** Gaumont Theatre, Southampton, Hampshire, UK, with Ike and Tina Turner, the Yardbirds, Peter Jay and the New Jay Walkers, the Kings of Rhythm Orchestra, 6 and 8:30 p.m.

This was the last concert in 1966. After a lengthy break, the Stones reconvened in Olympic Studios to complete *Between the Buttons* in November. Around that time, they filmed promo videos for their upcoming single, "Let's Spend the Night Together/Ruby Tuesday." They taped an appearance on *Top of the Pops* televised on December 22. Mick also taped a cameo for the final episode of *Ready Steady Go!*

## Chapter 6

# 1967

The year 1967 began with the release of the fantastic single "Let's Spend the Night Together/Ruby Tuesday." The A-side was a classic pop song, enhanced by Charlie's frenetic drumming and Jack Nitzsche on piano, which reached number 3 on the UK charts. Disk jockeys in the States preferred the B-side, a wistful ballad, allegedly written by Keith and Brian, enlivened by Brian's haunting solo on the recorder. It went all the way to number one in the U.S. The Stones returned to New York to premiere the songs on the January 15 edition of *The Ed Sullivan Show*. The CBS censors objected to the risqué lyrics of "Let's Spend the Night Together" and insisted that Mick substitute "*Time* Together" instead. The Stones also performed the songs on the famed British TV variety show *Sunday Night at the London Palladium* on January 22. Again there was controversy, though it was not because of the songs themselves. The Stones, dressed in outlandish psychedelic gear, refused to take part in the old show-biz ritual of appearing at the end of the show with other performers to take a bow, despite the entreaties of an irate Andrew Oldham, who was photographed having an angry row with his former mates.

Indeed, the Stones may have refused to appear just to irritate him. The group and Andrew had grown apart and would part ways by the end of the year. The Stones no longer needed an image-maker and were disinclined to go along with his promotional schemes. His attempts to get things done in an organized manner were met with indifference by Mick, Keith and Brian, all of whom spent much of 1967 in an LSD and pot filled haze. The sessions for *Their Satanic Majesties Request*, which stretched on through much of 1967, were the final straw. The acid-drenched, psychedelic sounds the Stones were making in the studio had no allure for Andrew. Indeed, he told a reporter, "I want to produce good, progressive pop music but music which is still commercial. I'm not interested in this psychedelic trash, or taking trips." Oldham's last real production with the Stones was the *Between the Buttons* LP, released on January 20. It had a number of memorable tunes, including the pretty "Backstreet Girl," the rollicking "Connection" (which included Keith's first lead vocal) and the frenetically paced "Miss Amanda Jones," but some tracks, like "Cool, Calm and Collected" and "Something Happened to Me Yesterday," were criticized for aping the British music hall sensibilities of the Kinks. Only a year later, Mick was already dismissive of the LP. He commented to writer Jonathan Cott, "It just isn't any good. 'Back Street Girl' is about the only one I like."

The Stones had grown increasingly tired of the treadmill of recording and touring they'd been on since 1963 and spent much of the year attempting to enjoy some rest and relaxation. However, the British establishment wasn't happy that England was earning a reputation as the home of debauched, drug-taking millionaires and decided to "put the

Japanese advertisement for the Stones, with a photograph of the band taken in January 1967 (collection of Ira Korman).

boot in." Informed that a wild party was taking place at Keith's Redlands estate, police raided the home on February 12. In later interviews, the Stones insisted they'd been set up. Keith noted that George Harrison was also at the house, but police waited until the Beatle left to raid the home. In 2010 *The Daily Mail* appeared to confirm that it was planned. It reported that alleged drug dealer David Sniderman confessed before his death that he was an informant for U.S. and UK intelligence. In any event, police arrested Mick, Keith and art dealer Robert Fraser for drug possession.

While their management tried, unsuccessfully, to make the incident go away, the Stones were advised to get out of town. Brian was keen to record the musicians of Morocco and he and Anita set off for Tangiers in a Bentley in late February, with Keith and assorted companions. However, Brian grew ill in Southern France and Keith and Anita went ahead without him. On the way to Morocco, they launched an affair behind his back. Brian and Anita briefly reunited in Morocco, but she'd grown tired of his mercurial and abusive behavior and after a few days she left him permanently for Keith. The new couple took off together, leaving Brian to find his own way home. Brian and Keith's relationship was never the same.

The band's sole tour of the year, a three-week slog through Europe that commenced in mid–March, was a tense affair since the two guitarists weren't speaking to each other. On top of this problem, the Redlands bust had placed the Stones on the radar of custom officers, and they were subjected to stressful searches and scenes at every airport stop. Indeed, when the band was departing from Paris on April 12, a customs official physically assaulted Keith when the group failed to comply with his demands that they show him their passports individually.

Soon after the tour ended, Mick and Keith appeared in a London court to be officially charged with drug possession, stemming from the Redlands bust. On the same day, May 10, Brian and his friend Prince Stash were busted at his flat for drug possession. Many in the Stones' circle became convinced that the establishment was making an example of them. Such fears proved justified when Mick and Keith were found guilty on June 29. Mick received a three-month sentence and was taken to Brixton prison, while Keith received twelve months in jail at the notorious Wormwood Scrubs. The Stones were perceived by many young Londoners as martyrs to the cause of the revolution against the "petty morals" of the establishment. Thousands of fans staged a spontaneous protest against the police and the Who quickly rushed into the studio to record cover versions of "The Last Time" and "Under My Thumb" as a gesture of support. Even the conservative newspaper *The Times* weighed in. Editor William Rees-Mogg wrote a famous editorial, "Who Breaks a Butterfly on a Wheel?" in which he opined that the band was being punished simply for being counterculture leaders.

Mick and Keith were freed on appeal after only one night, but, with more court dates looming, the band was under a cloud. The stress proved unbearable for the always-sensitive Brian, who visibly declined as his trial approached. Alexis Korner, who'd not seen him in quite a while, was shocked when he bumped into Brian that summer. He later remarked, "He looked like a debauched version of Louis XIV. That's when I realized that acid-taking can cause casualties." Brian was in such a bad state that he checked into a psychiatric hospital. His doctor testified in court that Brian was extremely paranoid and capable of suicide. In the end, he was given a custodial sentence for possession of hash, reduced to a fine on appeal.

As a result of the busts and courtroom appearances, the Stones came to almost a total stop. But they continued to turn up at Olympic Studios to noodle around on what eventually became their psychedelic LP *Their Satanic Majesties Request*. As Keith explained in a 1981 interview, "We finished *Between the Buttons*, you know, 'Let's Spend the Night Together,' and boom we stopped working for like a year and a half. And in that year and a half we had to make another album. And that was insane-on acid, busted, right? It was like such a fractured business, a total alien way of working to us at the time." The Stones released their summer of love single, "We Love You/Dandelion," on August 18. The psychedelic A-side, which peaked at number 8 in Britain, featured Brian on spooky Mellotron keyboard and Nicky Hopkins on piano. Showing their support, Paul McCartney and John Lennon lent a hand on background harmonies. The Peter Whitehead directed promo (filmed on July 30 and 31) pointedly took place in court, with Mick posing as Oscar Wilde, Marianne as his lawyer and a be-wigged Keith as the judge. But if the Stones were attempting to show they'd been railroaded, footage of a zonked out Brian in the studio, barely able to keep his eyes open, did little to aid their cause.

To meet the insatiable demand for new material in the States, Andrew put together *Flowers*, an album of outtakes and tracks from their last few LPs that hadn't appeared in the U.S. (including "Out of Time" and "Please Go Home"). The unreleased tracks included "Sitting on a Fence," with Brian's lovely acoustic lead guitar, the driving "Ride on Baby" and a cover of the Temptations "My Girl." All in all it was a high-quality release. Indeed, many American fans still name the LP as their favorite. Keith later commented, "All that stuff had been cut a year or so before and rejected by us for not making it. I was really surprised when people dug it, when it even came out."

*Their Satanic Majesties Request* was finally released in December, having taken a year to complete. In a January 1968 radio interview Brian commented, "It's really like got together chaos. Because, we all sort of panicked a little, even as soon as a month before the release date we had planned we really hadn't gotten anything together. We had all these great things that we'd done but we couldn't possibly put out an album. So we just got them together and did a little bit of editing here and there.... We just strung them together with more instruments on top and voices and everything and they really work because whatever people might think about that album, I think it's very valid as a comment on the Rolling Stones as they were in 1967." The LP divided and continues to divide critics and fans. Even the band members themselves weren't sure what to make of it. (Mick maintained a soft spot for it. While on tour in 1972 he commented to Kid Jensen, "It was criticized a lot and when it was I guess we thought, well maybe it wasn't very good. There are some awful tracks on it, but there are some very good ones. I mean 'She's a Rainbow,' there are some really nice things on it.... It's not bad. I wouldn't mind having another departure like that. I like departures.") In any event, the Stones recognized that it represented a stressful period that the band had to put behind it.

## Concerts

**Saturday, March 25:** Idrottens Hus Paskafton, Helsingborg, Sweden, two shows
    The band's only tour of the year was a three-week European trek that took in a number of cities the Stones hadn't played before. Stu, road manager Tom Keylock and the Stones' personal assistant Jo Bergman accompanied them on the tour, which started off on a sour note. When the Stones flew into Malmo, customs officials forced them to submit

to a one-hour "head to toe" search. A frustrated Mick told a reporter, "They were looking for pot and they went through every bit of clothing we had—even our under clothes." The set was interesting. On most dates the Stones played a medley of "Get Off of My Cloud" and the rarely performed *Between the Buttons* track "Yesterday's Papers," as well as a mash-up of the *Aftermath* track "Goin' Home" (with Brian on harmonica) and "Satisfaction."

**Monday, March 27:** Vinterstadium, Orebro, Sweden, two shows

This concert was marred by the behavior of a few unruly fans who threw bottles and chairs at the group. Security had to briefly halt the show and send police with dogs to patrol the hall. Mick told Penny Valentine of *Disc*, "We still get a kick out of this kind of reception. The cops get up on stage and everyone throws seats around. You can't imagine what it's like unless you've seen it yourself. When they say there's a riot in Finsbury Park, Astoria it's nothing ... just some screaming fans. Here real bodily violence breaks out!"

**Wednesday, March 29:** Stadthalle, Bremen, West Germany, with the Easybeats, the Creations, the Batmen and Achim Reichel, 5:30 and 8:30 p.m.

The Stones flew to Hamburg on March 28 and made it their base of operations for the next few days. For the German leg of the tour the bill also included the Australian band the Easybeats (who had the hit "Friday on My Mind"), the Batmen (who'd appeared with the Stones in 1965 as Didi and the ABC Boys) and Achim Reichel (former leader of

Poster for the Stones' appearance in Bremen, March 1967 (collection of Ira Korman).

the Rattles). Prior to the first concert, the Stones attended a special ceremony at the Stadthalle, to receive gold records. Mick was asked what sentence he expected for his drug charge and replied dryly, "The death penalty." The concerts that night were somewhat disappointing. Only 2,600 fans attended the first show at the 7,000-seater arena. The second show attracted 5,000. *The Bremen Chronicle* reported, "The youthful fans screaming reached its climax when the 'hardest band in the world' played their newest hits 'Ruby Tuesday' and 'Let's Spend the Night Together.' The hall was cooking but didn't boil over. Then the beat-followers ... headed home satisfied and well-behaved."

**Thursday, March 30:** Sporthalle, Cologne, West Germany, with the Easybeats, the Creations, the Batmen and Achim Reichel, 4:30 and 8 p.m.

About 10,000 people turned out for the shows. *The Express* reported, "Mick Jagger threw red and white carnations into the audience at the Sporthalle. His enthusiastic fans promptly responded by throwing shirts and other pieces of clothing back. They jerked in rhythm with the hot beat, screeched, stomped and clapped. One managed to get through and leapt over the barrier in front of the stage and landed at the feet of Keith Richard."

**Friday, March 31:** Westfalenhalle, Dortmund, West Germany, with the Easybeats, the Creations, the Batmen and Achim Reichel, 8 p.m.

A short, silent film of this concert exists. The crowd was wild and there were numerous stage invasions. *The Ludenscheider News* reported, "During the song 'Let's Spend the Night Together,' Mick Jagger took off his gold shiny jacket and then there was no stopping it. The big stage invasions began.... The hall—previously in mystical semi-darkness—suddenly stood in a glaring spotlight. The great hour of the police had come.... But what the guardians of order could only have achieved with force, the Stones managed in a jiffy. The melancholy song 'Lady Jane' poured oil on the troubled waters of ecstasy, and the fans who were previously being cautioned by the house, now stood entranced, listening on their chairs."

**Saturday, April 1:** Ernst-Merck-Halle, Hamburg, West Germany, with the Easybeats, the Creations, the Batman and Achim Reichel, 5 and 9 p.m.

The reviewer from the *Hamburger Abendblatt* commented that the crowd was tamer than in the Stones' previous visit. "The first time the Rolling Stones performed in Hamburg the energy was as charged as the electricity in a storm cloud. However one already knew the show this time and thus only had to become "normally" excited.... Mick hopped, danced, gyrated, screamed and was once again the arrogant, charming, graceful, wild sorcerer of youthful ecstasy. Yeah! The police didn't need to step in."

**Sunday, April 2:** Stadthalle, Vienna, Austria, with the Easybeats, the Creations, the Batmen and Achim Reichel, 3:30 and 7:30 p.m.

About 13,000 people turned out for these shows. Unruly fans threw chairs, paint and eggs at the stage and there were violent clashes with police. Smoke bombs went off in the venue and over 154 people were arrested. Following the shows, Keith flew to Paris to see Anita, while the rest of the band returned to London for a few days.

**Wednesday, April 5:** Palazzo Dello Sport, Bologna, Italy, 5:30 and 8:45 p.m.

On April 4 the Stones flew to Milan, which they made their base of operations for their six-night stay in Italy. Mick was subjected to a rigorous search at the airport. The Bologna shows, before 7,000 fans, marked the Stones' first Italian appearances. At the

Ticket for the Stones' concert in Vienna on April 2, 1967 (collection of Ira Korman).

beginning of the sparsely attended afternoon show fans jumped the barriers to get close to the stage. The presenter warned them that the Stones wouldn't play if the audience didn't clear the space between the stage and the first chairs. Police had to push back stubborn fans so that the group could make their entrance. A debacle then ensued as Charlie made a rare mistake and played the wrong drum pattern on opener "The Last Time." Mick stopped the song and after a group huddle they started the song again. The *Corriere della Sera* reported, "They performed a dozen songs including 'Paint It Black,' '19th Nervous Breakdown' and 'Lady Jane.' During the last song, Jagger threw bouquets of flowers into the audience that the girls quarreled over. Throughout the Stones show, the screams of the girls drowned out the sounds of the instruments, despite abundant amplification."

**Thursday, April 6:** Palazzo Dello Sport, Rome, Italy, 4 and 9 p.m.

The Rome concerts were something of a letdown. Only 5,000 fans turned out to see the shows at the 15,000-seater venue (amongst the crowd were Ursula Andress, Brigitte Bardot, Jane Fonda and Roger Vadim). *La Stampa* reported, "The five musicians tried to get the crowd pumped up during the concert but the stalls and bleachers were relatively tranquil. The only incident occurred in between the first and second concerts when a group of 200 young men tried to storm the Stones' dressing rooms to get autographs and were rejected by a triple deployment of police."

**Saturday, April 8:** Palalido, Milan, Italy, with the Stormy Six, the New Trolls and Al Bano, 4 and 8 p.m.

The appearances in Milan attracted a wilder crowd then other Italian shows. The *Corriere della Sere* reported, "Between the music and suggestion, an uncontrollable excitement spread, which pushed the wave of fans towards the stage: the Rolling Stones were in danger of being overwhelmed on a number of occasions. Yesterday, the security had a tough job keeping the stage invaders in the Palalido in check." One of the two concerts was taped. The set consisted of "The Last Time," "Paint It Black," "19th Nervous Breakdown," "Lady Jane," "Get Off of My Cloud/ Yesterday's Papers," "Ruby Tuesday," "Let's Spend the Night Together," "Goin' Home" and "Satisfaction."

**Sunday, April 9:** Palazzo Dello Sport, Genoa, Italy, with the New Trolls and Al Bano, 5:30 and 8:45 p.m.

**Tuesday, April 11:** L'Olympia, Paris, France, two shows

The Stones were hassled by customs entering and leaving Paris but the band still put on good shows. The Stones were visited backstage by pop stars Johnny Hallyday and Sylvie Vartain. Musicorama broadcast one of the shows on radio. The set consisted of "Paint It Black," "19th Nervous Breakdown," "Lady Jane," "Get Off of My Cloud," "Yesterday's Papers," "Under My Thumb," "Ruby Tuesday," "Let's Spend the Night Together," "Goin' Home" and "Satisfaction."

**Thursday, April 13:** Sala Kongresowej, Palac Kultury i Nauki, Warsaw, Poland, with Czerwono-Czarni, 5 and 8 p.m.

The Stones wanted to play at least one show in Eastern Europe and had attempted to organize a show in Moscow. This proved impossible but two concerts were arranged in Poland. The Stones flew to Warsaw on April 12 and were met by smiling girls bearing flowers at Okecie Airport. But despite the calm greeting, the foray behind the Iron Curtain was a tense affair. Les Perrin of *NME* reported, "Tickets for the 2,701-seater hall had never been put in the box office for general sale, but had been sold through ministries, party officials and factories to 'selected audiences.'" Some fans who bought tickets from scalpers, managed to get in, filling the hall past its capacity, but police kept many out and there were massive riots outside the venue as angry students clashed with heavy-handed police.

A number of myths and legends surround these concerts, most of them made up by band members. It is true that the Stones were incensed when they looked into the audience and saw that party leaders' families took up the best seats. But the story Keith relayed to Robert Greenfield in 1971 is highly suspect. He fancifully recalled, "About three numbers and I say, 'Fucking stop playing Charlie. You fucking lot get out and let those bastards in the back down front.' So they went. About four rows just walked out. All the mamma's and daddy's boys." In actual fact, the band just played the show, though Mick told a Dutch reporter, "If we'd known, we would have played more concerts so we could get rid of the party people in the first concert and the other concerts would be (for non party members)." Bill supplied embroidered tales in his book, *Rolling with the Stones*, as well. Anticipating that many fans would be prevented from seeing the concerts, he alleged that the Stones arranged with Decca to have hundreds of LPs sent from London and drove around in a van giving them out. In actual fact Polish sources confirm that the band were confined to their hotel, venturing only as far as the downstairs bar. The story that they accepted a wagon full of vodka as payment is also farcical.

**Friday, April 14:** Hallenstadion, Zürich, Switzerland, with Les Sauterelles, 8 p.m.

The Stones' arrival at Zurich Airport created quite a scene. *KRLA Beat* reported, "2,000 fans showed up to welcome them. However, they attempted to get aboard the jet which carried the Stones and the police were forced to use water hoses to control the crowd and get the Stones out of the airport unharmed." Afterwards, a press conference was filmed, at which the usual silly questions were thrown at the group. Asked about acid, Mick laughingly commented, "What do I think about LSD? I think it's very nice." When quizzed if he liked to see young girls faint, Mick replied "No.... I don't care what they do. They can do anything. I just want them to do what they like." The concert that night, however, was no laughing matter. When the Stones took the stage at 9:30 all hell broke loose. Mick later commented in *Go Set,* "We were playing in a stadium—imagine somewhere with a capacity twice London's Royal Albert Hall—we had been put on a platform 30 or 40 feet above the crowd. As we walked on stage someone jumped on my

**Concert program for the Stones' appearance in Zurich, April 1967 (collection of Ira Korman).**

back. Ten of them nearly had me over the edge—yes I was frightened as I looked down." The fans nearly ripped Mick's shirt off and Tom Keylock's hand was broken trying to get them off him. The rest of the performance witnessed continual attempts to rush the stage by fans who were pushed back by overaggressive police. The band fled after the last song as vandals smashed chairs in the stadium.

Program for the Stones' concert in Athens, April 1967 (collection of Ira Korman).

**Saturday, April 15:** Houtrusthal, The Hague, Netherlands, with Armand, the Rangers, the Tykes, the Counts and Full House, 8 p.m.

After the madness in Switzerland, the show in The Hague was relatively uneventful, though police arrested fourteen fans. A poor quality tape exists. The set consisted of: "The Last Time," "Paint It Black," "19th Nervous Breakdown," "Lady Jane," "Get Off of

My Cloud/ Yesterday's Papers," "Ruby Tuesday," "Let's Spend the Night Together," "Goin' Home" and "Satisfaction."

**Monday, April 17:** Panathinaikos Stadion, Athens, Greece, with Loubogg, M.G.C., the Idols, Tasos Papastamatis, Dakis, We Five and Guidone, 8 p.m.

The Stones convened in Athens for the final date of the tour. Brian was jetlagged and missed a farcical press conference at the Hilton. At one point, Mick was asked if group members loved each other and replied, "Yes, the proof is that we all sleep in the same bed." When the reporter asked what Bill's wife thought about the arrangement, Mick answered, "She sleeps with us too." The Stones took the stage, placed in the middle of the stadium, at 9:30 p.m. They were met by the usual riotous reception when they kicked off the set with "The Last Time," but the concert passed uneventfully until the band launched into "(I Can't Get No) Satisfaction." Mick wanted to distribute red carnations to fans and Tom Keylock agreed to take them to the stadium tiers. But, as soon as he began to hand them out, six policemen started beating him. All five of the Stones stopped playing and rushed to help him. The event brought a premature end to the concert and the band was hustled backstage, while fans screamed their disapproval. In order to prevent them tearing apart the venue, police turned off the lights and plunged the stadium into darkness until everyone dispersed.

The next day Mick and Marianne headed to London; while Brian flew to Munich for the premiere of *Mord und Totschlag*, a film starring Anita that he'd written the music for. Keith planned to attend the premiere, but was subjected to a zealous drug search and missed the flight. He had Tom Keylock drive him to Munich instead. Bill and his family decided to stay in Athens for a holiday and ended up trapped in their hotel when the Greek government was overthrown by a coup. They finally were able to leave for England on April 23. A year would pass before the Stones played live again.

## Chapter 7

# 1968

The Stones recognized that they had to get their act together after a spacy year. In January, Brian commented in a radio interview, "We really did have a tough year with one thing and another. Brought about by, well you could call it persecution if you like or you could call it personal misconduct and the consequences thereof. However you approach it and however it's acceptable to other people … we were a little freaked out…. What we're trying to do now is get back into orbit…. You can't go so far out. That's like a one-way journey to flipping out." It was time to abandon psychedelic music and return to what they were best at, good, old-fashioned rock and roll. The Stones began preliminary work on what would become *Beggar's Banquet*, their first album with Jimmy Miller, an American producer who'd made a name for himself for his work with Traffic. Like *Satanic Majesties*, the LP would take almost a year to complete. As a result much of 1968 was spent out of the public eye. Indeed, it wasn't until May that the group released their next single, "Jumping Jack Flash/Child of the Moon." To promote it, they filmed two excellent promos. The video for "Jumping Jack Flash," directed by Michael Lindsey-Hogg, has rightfully achieved legendary status. The moody clip of the highly made up band performing the song on a dark stage perfectly captured the song's essence.

The band chose not to tour in 1968, though they did make a live appearance at the NME Poll-Winner's Show. They remained wiped out from the exhausting events of 1967. Brian, especially, was in a delicate and fragile state. The loss of Anita to Keith and the drug trial had crushed him. And British police compounded his paranoia by busting him a second time in May on cannabis possession. At his hearing on June 11, he decided to risk a jury trial. On September 26, with Mick and Keith looking on in the courtroom, he was found guilty and fined. The drug conviction created more problems for Brian, as it made it difficult for him to travel and tour with the Stones. But it was increasingly unclear if Brian cared about that. He'd become a sporadic presence at sessions. When he did show up, he often created problems. Jimmy Miller recalled, "We'd be doing let's say, a blues thing. He'd walk in with a sitar, which was totally irrelevant to what we were doing, and want to play it. I used to try to accommodate him. I would isolate him, put him in a booth and not record him onto any track that we really needed. And the others, particularly Mick and Keith, would often say to me, 'Just tell him to piss off and get the hell out of here.'" Depressed and frequently stoned, Brian often showed up in no condition to play anyway.

It was during sessions with Brian in June that the Stones were filmed by French director Jean-Luc Godard for his avant-garde movie *One Plus One*. He captured valuable footage of the band at work on one of their finest songs, "Sympathy for the Devil," featuring

Nineteen sixty-eight Japanese advertisement for the Stones (collection of Ira Korman).

a lilting samba groove, fantastic guitar work by Keith and a truly intense vocal by Mick. But, the film demonstrated how unimportant Brian had become. He was seen only briefly, weakly strumming an inaudible acoustic guitar and singing along on the chorus with Anita and other guests. Godard considered Brian so peripheral to proceedings that he mostly filmed the back of his head.

But Brian was still capable of magic if the mood struck him. He certainly contributed to *Beggar's Banquet*: adding Autoharp to "Jigsaw Puzzle," sitar to "Street Fighting Man," and harmonica to "Parachute Woman" and "Prodigal Son." He also picked up the slide guitar for one last hurrah. Mick recalled, "We sat around on the floor in a circle playing 'No Expectations.' And he picked up a guitar and played some very pretty lines on it, which you can hear on the record. And that was the last thing I remember him doing that was Brian, or the Brian that could contribute something very pretty and sensitive that made the record sound wonderful." But Brian's frequent absence made the once indispensable Stone increasingly superfluous. For the first time, on *Beggars Banquet* the group used session musicians in his place. Though the parts were tailor made for Brian, it was Dave Mason who played the shehnai (a double reed oboe) on "Street Fighting Man," guitar on "Dear Doctor" and mandolin on "Factory Girl," while Nicky Hopkins added the album's piano tracks.

The LP was completed and mixed by Mick and Keith at Sunset Sound in LA that July. However, it was held up when Decca objected to the Stones' cover idea, a photograph of a graffiti covered bathroom stall. Mick went to Italy to film the movie *Performance* with Anita, while the album languished. *Beggar's Banquet*, with a new blank cover, was finally released in the UK on December 6. The album reached number 3 on the UK charts and was hailed by critics as a stunning return to form. The Stones also thought highly of it. Both Mick and Keith have repeatedly referred to the LP as one of their favorites.

To promote it, they decided to film a TV extravaganza for the BBC called *The Rolling Stones Rock 'n' Roll Circus*. In addition to the Stones themselves, the show included the up and coming Jethro Tull, American blues singer Taj Mahal, Marianne Faithfull, the Who and a special performance by John Lennon with "the Dirty Mac," composed of Keith, Eric Clapton and Mitch Mitchell. The film features the last footage of Brian performing with the band he formed. He looked tired and peripheral to the proceedings, though he contributed slide on "No Expectations." His departure from the group was still six months away, but many in attendance sensed he wouldn't be with them much longer. Brian barely communicated with Mick and Keith during the taping. In a DVD commentary, Ian Anderson of Jethro Tull recalled that there was tension in the air, "which tended to drag things down. All of us felt, even those of who didn't know them, felt the Stones were in slightly shaky shape socially between them as a group. That was how it felt to me as an observer at the time."

Perhaps as a result, the Stones expressed dissatisfaction with their performance, filmed at almost 4 on the morning of December 12. Looking at the DVD today, it's clear that the Stones were in top form, despite problems with Brian. But this wasn't the opinion of the group and the decision was made to scrap the show. Keith related in *Mojo*, "We just didn't really think that we performed really well. Basically, I think, based upon the way we were feeling while we were doing it, because we were all so totally exhausted." The Stones expressed interest in re-filming their performance in Italy the following summer, but nothing came of it. After languishing in the vault, the film was released on video in 1996 and on DVD in 2004.

Advertisement for the Stones' 1968 single "Jumping Jack Flash" (collection of Ira Korman).

## Concerts

**Sunday, May 12:** NME Poll-Winners Concert, Empire Pool, Wembley, UK, with Status Quo, Don Partridge, Love Affair, the Showstoppers, the Association, the Paper Dolls, Tony Blackburn, Lulu, Cliff Richard and the Shadows, Amen Corner, the Herd, the Tremeloes, the Move, Dusty Springfield, Scott Walker and Dave Dee, Dozy, Beaky, Mick and Tich, 2 p.m.

With the exception of the taped *Rock and Roll Circus*, this would be Brian's last live appearance with the Stones. They performed their new single, "Jumping Jack Flash," and "(I Can't Get No) Satisfaction," while friends, including Anita Pallenberg and Marianne Faithfull, danced in the bleachers. The *NME* reported, "You could hear the Pool shaking to its foundations as the roar went up and onto the stage and into the light for their first British concert for nearly two years came Mick, Keith, Brian, Bill and Charlie.... 'Jumping Jack Flash,' their new single was inaudible above the din and 'Satisfaction' was only really recognizable because of its familiarity—but no one cared about that." Mick was excited by the appearance, but it didn't whet his appetite for further touring. He told *Rave Magazine*, "It was just like old times. In fact it was better than old times. We don't want to go leaping about all over every available stage because of it though. It was just a good thing to do at the time with our record coming out. I could carry on doing what I'm doing now for the next thirty years, but I don't want to end up playing 'Satisfaction' from my wheelchair! We have to look for new things."

**Wednesday, December 11:** *The Rolling Stones Rock 'n' Roll Circus*, Intertel Studios, London, with Taj Mahal, Jethro Tull, Marianne Faithfull, the Dirty Mac, Yoko Ono and the Who

Ticket for the *New Musical Express* Poll Winner's concert on May 12, 1968. This was Brian's last concert with the Stones (collection of Ira Korman).

Though not strictly a live concert, the Stones taped their TV special before a live audience (hence its inclusion here). The group performed a dress rehearsal of sorts by appearing on the LTV *Frost on Saturday Show* on November 29. They also held rehearsals at the Marquee Club on December 6 and at Intertel on December 10. The special, directed by Michael Lindsay-Hogg, was designed like a circus and the artists, decked out in outlandish attire, performed in the round before an invited audience. To give it more of a "circus" feel, a different Stone introduced each act and various acrobats and circus performers appeared during intermissions. Glyn Johns was present to record all the music for posterity with the Olympic Mobile Recording Truck.

Taping began at 2 p.m. but scheduling was poorly planned and there were interminable delays between acts. The cameras also broke down numerous times and as a result the Stones didn't take the stage until 2 in the morning. Their set consisted of "Jumping Jack Flash," "Parachute Woman" "No Expectations," "You Can't Always Get What You Want," and "Sympathy for the Devil" (with Mick stripping off his shirt to reveal a frightening satanic tattoo). Despite the late hour, the Stones insisted on taping multiple takes of each song. They also allegedly played other oldies in between, including "Route 66" and "Confessing the Blues," though these outtakes haven't surfaced. Finally at 5 a.m., the exhausted musicians and audience members gathered for a drunken mime-along to "Salt of the Earth."

## Chapter 8

# 1969

The year 1969 was a turning point in the history of the Stones. It had become clear that Brian was unable to work effectively with the band. His attendance at sessions continued to be sporadic. The Stones spent much of the spring working on what would become *Let It Bleed*. Brian is hardly to be heard on the album, even though the vast majority of it was recorded before he left the band. Mick later explained in *Mojo*, "We carried Brian for quite a long time. We put up with his tirades, and his not turning up for over a year. So it wasn't like suddenly we just said, fuck you.... We'd been quite patient with him. And he'd just gotten worse and worse. He just didn't want to be in it. He didn't want to be part of it. He didn't want to come out of this rather sad state." Even if Brian had been in better shape, the Stones' lawyer, Michael Havers, was unable to get his drug conviction overturned, which meant it would be very difficult to get him a visa to tour the States, something the band was intent on. As summer approached, Mick and Keith made the momentous decision to seek out a replacement. Stu suggested blues guitarist Mick Taylor and he sat in with the group at a session for "Live with Me" and "Honky Tonk Women" on May 31.

Michael Kevin Taylor (born January 17, 1949, in Welwyn Garden City, Hertfordshire) had been playing guitar since the age of 12 and had made a name for himself in the UK as Peter Green's replacement in John Mayall's Bluesbreakers. He'd toured all over Europe, and even moved to America with Mayall for a time, but by 1969 he was looking for a change and jumped at the chance to play with the Stones. His "audition" impressed them and they made him an offer to join. On Sunday, June 8, Mick, Keith and Charlie drove out to Cotchford Farm (former home of *Winnie the Pooh* author A. A. Milne) to talk to Brian. At the half-hour meeting they told him that, in light of the problems that had developed, he was being replaced. Mick recalled in the film *Crossfire Hurricane*, "It was a very difficult decision to make. This was someone that you've spent the beginning of the band with and it was horrible. We said to Brian, 'This isn't working out.' And he said, 'Yes, it isn't.' It was very sad and I felt awful afterwards. I remember I felt really terrible. He was the author of his own misfortunes really, but when you look back on it now, you think surely we could have done something more than just that." Charlie commented that he didn't recall much about the meeting, "but I remember it wasn't very nice."

Whether Brian was in agreement over his exit or not, he put a positive spin on it. In a letter to the press he stated, "The Stones' music is not to my taste anymore. I have a desire to play my own brand of music rather than that of others, no matter how much I appreciate their musical concepts. The only solution is to go our separate ways, but we shall still remain friends. I love those fellows." Brian reportedly remained in good spirits and talked about putting a new band together. But on July 2, while the Stones were recording a track called "I Don't Know Why," they received a phone call informing them that he'd drowned in his pool. That night Brian and girlfriend Anna Wohlin had dined with builder Frank Thorogood and a 22-year-old nurse, Janet Lawson. According to their accounts, Brian had been drinking and wasn't in a suitable condition to go swimming, but insisted on it. His guests joined him, but after a bit they went inside (Thorogood being the last one with him). When they came back out, they found Brian floating in the pool. Efforts to revive him were unsuccessful. The coroner ruled it "death by misadventure" but rumors persist that foul play was involved. Frank Thorogood died in 1993 and it was alleged that he had made a deathbed confession. But his friend Tom Keylock denied any such conversation took place. The truth will probably never be known.

Life for the Stones went on. Indeed, the day after Brian's death, the band appeared on *Top of the Pops* to promote their single "Honky Tonk Women." Released in the UK on July 4, the country infused tune, with its catchy chorus and great guitar riffs, was an instant classic and went to number one on both sides of the Atlantic. And on July 5 they played it at their first gig with Mick Taylor at London's Hyde Park. The free show was designed as a celebratory way to introduce the new lineup. But, Brian's tragic death changed it from a celebration to a memorial. The stage was decorated with photos of Brian, and Mick, attired in a flowing white dress, dedicated the concert to him. As a tribute, he read part of Shelley's poem "Adonais" from the stage and then released thousands of butterflies. However, many had died in storage and fell lifeless to the ground. Charlie later remarked that the butterflies "were a bit sad, there were casualties. It was like the Somme."

Following the Hyde Park show, Mick flew to Australia to begin filming his second movie, *Ned Kelly*, under the direction of Tony Richardson. Keith and Mick were already at odds over Mick's desire to do things separate from the Stones (an issue that would almost break up the band in the 1980s). Keith told *NME's* Ritchie Yorke, "We've often talked about it and I've asked him why the hell he wants to be a film star. He says, 'Keith you're a musician and that's a complete thing in itself but I don't play anything.' So I said anyone who sings and dances the way he does shouldn't need to do anything else. But he doesn't agree." From early July to September, Mick was in the Outback. As a result he missed Brian's funeral on July 10. Bill and Charlie were the only Stones in attendance. Asked fifty years later about his own non-appearance at the memorial, Keith remarked, "It was going to be too much of a circus. And anyways I never even went to my mother's funeral or my father's. We didn't have one. We're like that in my family…. Hyde Park was the funeral and the bit about burying and the shovels is not important to me. That was his funeral."

Mick's absence from England meant that the Stones weren't able to finish their album until he returned. They flew to LA on October 17 to do some last minute work on *Let It Bleed*, which was released on December 5. Brian appeared on only two tracks (percussion on the spooky "Midnight Rambler" and Autoharp on "You Got the Silver"). Despite the upheaval the band was going through, the LP is one of their best. The fantastic opening track "Gimme Shelter" features some of Keith's best guitar work and some positively eerie vocals by Mick and guest vocalist Merry Clayton. "You Can't Always Get What You Want" is also a bona-fide classic, with Mick augmented by a full choir. The LP came out towards the end of the Stones' 1969 American tour, which marked a new stage in their career.

When the group had last played the States in 1966, most of their audience had been screaming girls. Now, they played to more mature crowds interested in hearing music. And technology had caught up with the rock concert. For the first time, the band traveled with a state of the art sound system. Not only did the crowd hear the music better, but also the Stones had monitors on stage that allowed them to hear themselves. The financial side of touring had also changed. While Allen Klein was officially managing the Stones, he was too busy attempting to woo the Beatles to deal with the tour. His nephew Ronnie Schneider quit ABCKO to form his own company, Rolling Stones Limited. He handled the tour and formulated a new business model. To make touring more profitable, the Stones demanded from promoters 50 percent in advance against a percentage of the box office gross, so they always made money even if the house was smaller than expected. They also got more involved in marketing and exploiting the licensing of T-shirts, posters and tour books sold at gigs. By the 1970s every rock band in the world had adopted their model. More money was needed as the band now traveled with a larger entourage.

On the 1969 tour the group was accompanied by Stu, Jo Bergman (their personal assistant), Chip Monck (who oversaw sound and lighting), Sam Cutler (their British road manager, who introduced them onstage each night as "the greatest rock 'n' roll band in the world"), Michael Lydon of *Ramparts Magazine*, Stanley Booth (a young writer from Waycross, Georgia, who'd obtained a contract to write a book), photographer Ethan Russell, Ronnie Schneider, John Jaymes (who handled transportation and public relations), Klein's representative Al Steckler and assorted girlfriends (including Bill's ever-present Swedish wife, Astrid) and friends (notably Keith's new best mate Gram Parsons, lead singer of the Flying Burrito Brothers). The band required a chartered plane and a floor of hotel suites everywhere they went. A disgusted Stu told Michael Lydon, "We used to just do a bleeding tour ... get into town, get a room, hire a few local blokes to carry the gear, set up and do the gig—30, 40 cities like that. But when you start hiring whole houses and cars and have people like Ronnie Schneider and John Jaymes, for god sakes, around, you're bound to have trouble!"

The growing expenses led to higher ticket prices. As a result, the tour was mired in controversy before it even began. Ralph Gleason of *The San Francisco Chronicle* learned that the Stones intended to set ticket prices from $5.50 to $8.50. Most rock shows at that time ranged in price from $3.50 to $6.50 and an outraged Gleason accused the Stones of exploiting their fans. In an editorial he asked, "Can the Rolling Stones actually need all that money...? Paying five, six and seven dollars for a Stones concert at the Oakland Coliseum for, say, an hour of the Stones seen a quarter of a mile away because the artists demand such outrageous fees that they can only be obtained under these circumstances, says a very bad thing to me about the artists' attitude towards the public. It says they despise their own audience." At a press conference at the Beverly Wilshire on October 27, Mick responded, "We didn't say that unless we walk out of America with X dollars, we ain't gonna come. We're really not into that sort of economic scene. Either you're gonna sing and all that crap, or you're gonna be a fucking economist. I really don't know whether this is more expensive than recent tours by local bands. I don't know how much people can afford. I've no idea. Is that a lot? You'll have to tell me." However, the criticism stung and the Stones made the fateful decision to hold a free concert before they returned to England, if it could be worked out.

The tour itself was a triumph. After a warm-up show at Colorado State University, the Stones played sold-out shows at the LA Forum and slowly moved east. When they arrived in New York to play three shows at Madison Square Garden, filmmakers Albert and David Maysles were there to film them. The two were only contracted to record the Garden concerts, but convinced the group to let them film additional footage, including a recording session in Muscle Shoals, Alabama, that produced "Wild Horses" "Brown Sugar" and "You Gotta Move." Eventually the footage shot by the Maysles, edited by the brilliant Charlotte Zwerin, would form the 1970 film *Gimme Shelter*. But, by that time the nature of the movie had changed. Instead of being a documentary of the tour it had become a dark chronicle of the lead-up to the infamous free concert at Altamont Speedway on December 6.

The original idea was to hold it at Golden Gate Park in San Francisco, but when that plan fell through the group secured the use of Sears Point International Raceway and began constructing a stage. At the last minute, the deal collapsed and the concert was almost canceled. Then on December 4, Dick Carter offered the Stones his Altamont Speedway, between the towns of Tracy and Livermore, California. Michael Lang, who'd helped set up the Woodstock Festival, informed the Stones that the concert could be set up in time. But in actuality the haste needed to move equipment and set up in a day and a half created chaos. The stage constructed for use on top of a hill at Sears Point wasn't appropriate for Altamont. The performers ended up playing on a platform only a meter high, with nothing to separate them from the crowd that literally spilled onto the stage. Promoters also failed to anticipate how many people would show up. Over 300,000 poured in and shortages of parking spaces, toilets, medical facilities and other necessities quickly became apparent. Perhaps things could have worked out, but the Stones made the decision to employ the Hell's Angels motorcycle club as security. As Angel Sonny Barger later made clear on KSAN radio, the Angels weren't police and felt that the only promise they'd made was to guard the stage in exchange for all the beer they could drink. They arrived on their motorcycles, forcing the crowd to part like the Red Sea to make room for them. The Angels guarded the stage (and their bikes) but in a lot more aggressive fashion than the Stones hoped for.

From the start of the concert there was trouble. During sets by Santana and the Flying Burrito Brothers there were fights between members of the Angels, some armed with pool cues, and the spacy crowd. The musicians on stage found it hard to ignore the ugly scene going on. Marty Balin of Jefferson Airplane was knocked unconscious when he intervened to prevent a Hell's Angel beating on an audience member. Confined to their trailers, the Stones had little knowledge of what was transpiring but when they took the stage it became apparent that things were out of control. During "Under My Thumb" the violence reached a climax when a Hell's Angel stabbed an audience member armed with a gun to death (one of four people who died during the show).

The Stones were greatly affected by the carnage. At the airport the next morning, Mick was visibly depressed. He commented to an AP reporter, "If Jesus had been there, he would have been crucified. It was supposed to be lovely, not uptight. What happened? What went wrong?" One fan standing nearby tried to console him and remarked that he was "beautiful." Mick replied, "I don't think so. I wish I was then there wouldn't have been any trouble." Altamont was undoubtedly the most infamous concert in Stones' history and would follow them around for the rest of their career. It was a watershed moment in cultural history, signaling for many the symbolic end of the '60s love generation. *Rolling Stone* co-founder Ralph J. Gleason observed in *Esquire*, "If the name 'Woodstock' has come to denote the flowering of one phase of the youth culture, Altamont has come to mean the end of it." This was far too sweeping a statement, but it certainly marked the end of an era for the Stones. Their image and music had grown increasingly dark and foreboding, but the 1970s would see them move away from grand statements like "Sympathy for the Devil" and back to good old rock 'n' roll entertainment.

## Concerts

**Wednesday, June 25, and Thursday, June 26:** Coliseum, Rome, Italy, canceled

The Stones were scheduled to play their first concerts with Mick Taylor at the Coliseum. Mick told Chris Welch of *Melody Maker*, "We chose Rome for the concert because it is a very good visual thing. And the other reason is that I wasn't satisfied with the Rolling Stones part of the Rock 'n' Roll Circus film we made and we want to do it again in the Coliseum, the first ever circus." However, *NME* reported on June 28, 1969, that plans for the concert had run aground "because of technical difficulties with Italian TV, who were to have filmed the event."

**Saturday, July 5:** Hyde Park, London, UK, with Third Ear Band, King Crimson, Screw, Alexis Korner's New Church, Roy Harper, Family and Battered Ornaments, 1 p.m.

The Stones made their live debut with Mick Taylor at this free concert, filmed by Granada TV (after circulating in a poor quality edited version for years, the complete concert was released on DVD in 2006). The show was organized by Blackhill Enterprises, which had put on a number of free concerts, including a recent date by Blind Faith. The UK branch of the Hell's Angels handled security, terrifying fans in their German military helmets and studded garb. But the show passed without a hitch, despite a larger than expected crowd. As many as 500,000 people crowded into the park to hear the Stones, including Paul and Linda McCartney, Eric Clapton, Donovan and Steve Winwood. In a TV interview, Bill Wyman recalled, "The whole of London closed down. Nobody went shopping. People were in the streets, in Oxford Street, listening. It was an incredible day

Advertisement for the Stones' free concert at Hyde Park (collection of Ira Korman).

and the weather was beautiful. And the crowd! There were no problems. There was no fighting. And they cleaned the park up next day. It was amazing!"

The Stones took the stage at 5:30 and played a 50-minute set that consisted of: "I'm Yours and I'm Hers," "Jumping Jack Flash," "Mercy Mercy," "Stray Cat Blues," "No Expectations," "I'm Free," "Down Home Girl," "Love in Vain," "Loving Cup," "Honky Tonk Women," "Midnight Rambler," "(I Can't Get No) Satisfaction," "Street Fighting Man" and an epic, 18-minute version of "Sympathy for the Devil" (with Ginger Johnson's African Drummers and Rocky Dijon on extra percussion). However, although the show has taken on legendary status, most critics felt it wasn't the Stones' finest hour. They had not played a full set in two years and hadn't had time yet to develop a strong musical relationship with Mick Taylor. Chris Welch commented in *Melody Maker*, "Mick Taylor played very little lead guitar and I could barely hear Charlie or Bill, but it was a nostalgic out-of-tune ritual that summed up a decade of pop." Keith told Robert Greenfield a few years later, "We played pretty bad. Until near the end, cause we hadn't played for years. And nobody minded 'cause they just wanted to hear us play again. It was nice they were glad to see us because we were glad to see them."

**Friday, November 7:** Colorado State University, Fort Collins, CO, with Terry Reid and B.B. King

As a warm up for their first U.S. tour in three years, the Stones flew in from California to make an unadvertised appearance in Colorado. Journalist Michael Lydon captured an unforgettable scene at LA airport. Some businessmen with glasses of scotch approached Bill's wife Astrid and began hitting on her, before realizing she was with the Stones. "You the fellas who had the hockey game canceled for your concert?" they asked. When Bill informed them that it was just postponed, they replied: "Don't mind us we're from the manned space center in Houston, drinking up a little rest and relaxation in California." An incredulous Keith said, "You mean *you guys* are putting people on the moon?" "That's right, if Nixon will give us the money. You want to go to the moon?" "Sure" replied Keith. "Just lemme know when," the first man replied.

At the show that night, Mick premiered what would become his customary look for the tour, a tight-fitting black outfit with a silver omega on the chest and silver buttons down the sides of his pants, a red scarf around his neck and a red, white and blue hat perched on his head. The set consisted of "Jumping Jack Flash," "Carol," "Sympathy for the Devil," "Stray Cat Blues," "Midnight Rambler," "Under My Thumb," "Prodigal Son," "Love in Vain," "I'm Free," "Little Queenie," "Gimme Shelter," "(I Can't Get No) Satisfaction," "Honky Tonk Women" and "Street Fighting Man." A reviewer from *The Chinook* gushed, "Mick was great, incredibly great…. He handled all the famous songs of uptightness—'Satisfaction,' 'Honky Tonk Women,' etc., with such warmth and energy that they became expressions of exuberance rather than bitterness; his lyrics became secondary to his manner…. Mick Taylor, Keith Richard, and Bill Wyman played … a driving, singularly simple rock that did not interfere with Jagger's vocal trip…. This was by far the best rock and roll music ever to be played in Colorado."

**Saturday, November 8:** Inglewood Forum, Los Angeles, CA, 7 and 11 p.m.

The Stones opened the tour proper with two sold-out shows. The second concert was recorded and a fair quality tape makes the rounds. The Stones opened with a decent "Jumping Jack Flash," followed by rocking versions of "Carol," "Sympathy for the Devil" and "Stray Cat Blues." Mick then announced, "This sounds weird but we're gonna sit down," before performing a fantastic "Prodigal Son," a bluesy "You Gotta Move" and "Love in Vain." The band then played "I'm Free," with a nice guitar solo by Mick Taylor. Jagger may have sensed some apathy from the crowd, as he asked "Are you really grooving or are you too tired?" Following a tight "Under My Thumb," Mick announced that they were going to play some new tunes and the Stones launched into a menacing "Midnight Rambler," and "Live with Me." Keith than got a chance to shine on the Chuck Berry rocker "Little Queenie," before the band got everyone dancing with closers: "(I Can't Get No) Satisfaction," "Honky Tonk Women" and "Street Fighting Man."

**Sunday, November 9:** Oakland Coliseum, Oakland, CA, with Terry Reid, B.B. King and Ike and Tina Turner, 6:30 and 10:30 p.m.

The opening Oakland concert was plagued by problems. Midway into the second song, the amplifiers died and the Stones had to play an acoustic set. They finally got going again, but as soon as they started "Carol" the amps cut out and Keith smashed his guitar in frustration. Mick told the crowd, "Sorry about the amp problems. You'll just have to hear it in your heads." The Stones eventually got into a groove, but during "(I Can't Get No) Satisfaction" when kids crowded towards the stage, promoter Bill Graham raced out and started shoving them away. When Sam Cutler intervened, Graham tried to throw him off. The Stones headed to their dressing room after "Street Fighting Man" enraged.

The second show started late, but the crowd was enthusiastic. Writer Stanley Booth recalled, "When the band was playing 'Little Queenie,' as Mick was saying 'Come on, San Francisco, let's get up and dance, let's shake our asses,' Bill Graham was crouching below the stage, pointing to kids who were dancing, shouting, 'Down! Down!' Finally he took his cameras and left, as the crowd surged to the stage. There was no feeling of violence, only the desire to get close and boogie." One enterprising fan named "Dub" Taylor recorded the band's set and released it as *Live'r Than You'll Ever Be*, one of the first bootlegs. So hot was demand for live Stones product that it sold 250,000 copies and was even reviewed in *Rolling Stone*. Some prefer it to the official live LP *Get Yer Ya Ya's Out* because it has no studio doctoring and presents an honest, warts and all, performance.

**Monday, November 10:** Sports Arena, San Diego, CA, with Terry Reid, B.B. King and Ike and Tina Turner, 8:30 p.m.

The Stones took the stage at 11:30 p.m. The crowd was tense, as Bill Graham had been arguing with kids at the front of the stage to return to their seats or the Stones wouldn't play. But he finally surrendered and the show went on. *The San Diego Union* reported, "The highlight, musically, came when Jagger and Richard sat down and quietly did a couple of country-blues numbers, with Richard playing a dobro into a microphone and Jagger singing carefully. But the direct communication between artists and audience in 'Satisfaction,' despite the chaos is what the Stones are about." A good quality bootleg makes the rounds.

**Tuesday, November 11:** Coliseum, Phoenix, AZ, with Terry Reid and Ike and Tina Turner, 7 p.m.

The Stones played before a less than capacity crowd. Critics blamed high ticket prices, noting that many fans were heard complaining outside. The mood inside wasn't

*Opposite:* **Poster for the Stones' appearance in San Diego, 1969 (collection of Ira Korman).**

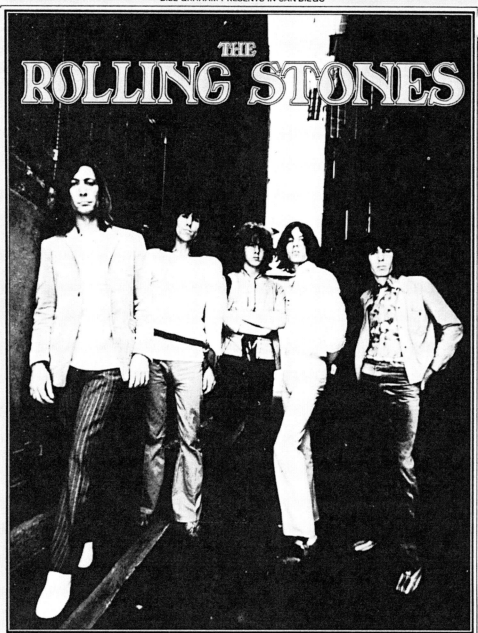

much better, as there were long delays before the Stones took the stage. But, all was forgiven when they appeared at 10:15 p.m. Jon Sargent of *The Arizona Republic* reported, "Jagger apologized to his fans for his hoarseness, blaming it on the desert. While it wasn't the highpoint of their 13-city tour of America, it was a high point for the 11,000 fans at the Coliseum."

**Thursday, November 13:** Moody Coliseum, SMU University, Dallas, TX, with Terry Reid and Chuck Berry, 8 p.m.

Opener Terry Reid celebrated his twentieth birthday and was followed by Chuck Berry, making his first appearance on the tour, in place of Ike and Tina and B.B. King. Writer Stanley Booth was unimpressed by Berry's backing band but noted that the old master occasionally showed flashes of brilliance. The Stones' set consisted of "Jumping Jack Flash," "Carol," "Sympathy for the Devil," "Stray Cat Blues," "Prodigal Son," "You Gotta Move," "Love in Vain," "Under My Thumb," "Midnight Rambler," "Live with Me," "Little Queenie," "(I Can't Get No) Satisfaction," "Honky Tonk Women" and "Street Fighting Man." Phillip Wuntch of *The Dallas News* reported, "As far as presence goes, Mick Jagger and the Rolling Stones proved a long time ago that they have it—in spades. The appeal of their iconoclastic music, compounded by the fury of their personal drive, is what kept the large teen-aged crowd as rapt and eager as if there was no school the next day."

**Friday, November 14:** Memorial Coliseum, Auburn University, Auburn, AL, with Terry Reid and Chuck Berry, 4:30 and 10 p.m.

The trip to Auburn was not pleasant. Owing to a mix-up by advance man Bill Belmont, the Stones' chartered plane left without them and the band had to jump on the only flight available to Columbus, Georgia. Michael Lydon noted, "It's a four hour flight and after take off they find there is no food, no drink and no cigarettes on board, plus no heat and stuck open vents under every seat that emit steady artic winds." Belmont almost lost his job over the incident. The concert itself went off without a hitch, though the Stones were annoyed by Chuck Berry's decision to play a longer set, delaying their performance. Despite such episodes, Mick Taylor enjoyed his first tour with the Stones. He told a reporter from *Beat Instrumental*, "The audiences were really great in America. They weren't as wild as they were when the Stones used to tour-the teeny element isn't as big now-but you always got the feeling they were enjoying it. Mind you, we had to work for it. We just couldn't go on and wait for it to happen, which was a good thing. And they were dancing by the end."

**Saturday, November 15:** University of Illinois, Champaign, IL, with Terry Reid and Chuck Berry, 4:30 and 8:30 p.m.

The band's equipment was late in arriving and the matinee show began two hours late. As a result, the second show was delayed and the Stones didn't take the stage until 11:45 p.m. *The Daily Illini* reported, "The audience merely stood and listened during most of the show, but when the opening chords of 'Satisfaction' were heard, the temptation to dance became too hard to resist. It was like *American Bandstand* all over again in the Assembly Hall as the couples continued to gyrate through 'Honky Tonk Women.'"

**Sunday, November 16:** International Amphitheater, Chicago, IL, with Terry Reid and Chuck Berry, 8 p.m.

Over 20,000 fans turned out for this show and *Chicago Tribune* reporter Robb Baker,

Handbill for the Stones' concert in Dallas, 1969. Note that the photograph shows Brian Jones rather than Mick Taylor (collection of Ira Korman).

who'd traveled with the band since the opening date in LA, declared it "the best crowd reaction yet." The Stones performed at the site of the infamous 1968 Democratic Convention. Taking note of the protests that took place there, Mick commented, "This one we dedicate to you and what you did in your town" before launching into closer "Street Fighting Man." Following the show, the group flew to Los Angeles to tape a final appearance on the CBS TV show *Ed Sullivan Show* on November 18. Keith told writer Michael Lydon, "We wanted to do Sullivan, not one of the new shows, 'cause there's nothing more far out than *The Ed Sullivan Show*. It's so old, it's funky." As usual, there was controversy. CBS censors bleeped out some "inappropriate" lyrics on "Honky Tonk Women." Asked about it a week later, Mick commented "Yeah they allowed us to sing the words and then they blocked them out. It doesn't really matter. It's all a joke. It's a washing machine and then it's you and then it's a soap powder."

Mick Jagger onstage at the University of Illinois, 1969 (courtesy *Illio* Yearbook and Illini Media).

**Monday, November 24:** Olympia Stadium, Detroit, MI, with Terry Reid and B.B. King, 8:30 p.m.

About 14,000 fans turned out to see the Stones at Olympia, where they'd played to only 619 people on their first U.S. tour. So great was demand that the promoter tried (unsuccessfully) to book the Stones for a second show. A good quality soundboard recording of this show exists. Jane Scott of *The Cleveland Plain-Dealer* gushed, "A cheer like a University of Michigan victory swelled the stadium as the quintet began 'Jumping Jack Flash.' Before they wound up with 'Street Fighting Man,' guitarists Mick Taylor and Keith Richard, bass player Bill Wyman and drummer Charlie Watts beat up enough heat to almost melt the ice under the cardboard coverings on the floor (this is a hockey stadium)."

**Tuesday, November 25:** Spectrum, Philadelphia, PA, with Terry Reid and B.B. King, 8 p.m.

The Stones were scheduled to play two shows but canceled the matinee when their equipment was delayed in arriving. The group took the stage at 11:15 p.m. and launched into "Jumping Jack Flash." But, they didn't get cooking until midway through the show when they played "Midnight Rambler." Jack Lloyd of *The Inquirer* reported, "The beat was hard, the rhythm pounded and Jagger's lyrics shot out like licks of brutal red-hot flames…. It was 12:05 a.m. Wednesday when the Stones tore into one of their biggest songs, 'Satisfaction.' Jagger chanted out the words—'I Can't Get No Satisfaction'—and that did it. Everyone in the Spectrum was on his feet, moving and clapping and shouting and screaming. Now the Stones were down to serious business and Jagger was going at top speed. Yes, it was like the old days. Well, almost."

Advertisement for the Stones' show in Baltimore, 1969 (collection of Ira Korman).

**Wednesday, November 26:** Civic Center, Baltimore, MD, with Terry Reid and B.B. King, 7:30 p.m.

Prior to flying to Baltimore, the Stones held a press conference at the Rainbow Room in New York, which was filmed by the Maysles. Mick was asked what he thought about John Lennon returning his MBE and replied, "At last. He should have done it as soon as he got it!" An interesting comment: considering that many years later Mick would come in for criticism from Keith for accepting a knighthood. He was also asked if the band was "more satisfied" and made his famous reply "Yeah, we're more satisfied sexually, financially dissatisfied and philosophically trying." Decca Records had decided to issue a live LP and Glyn Johns recorded the Baltimore concert that night and subsequent shows in New York and Boston with the Wally Heider Mobile Studio. The live version of "Love in Vain" heard on the LP *Get Yer Ya Ya's Out* was recorded this night.

**Thursday, November 27, and Friday, November 28:** Madison Square Garden, New York, NY, with Terry Reid, B.B. King and Ike and Tina Turner, one show Thursday and two shows Friday

The two-night stand at the Garden was arguably the musical highpoint of the tour. On the first night over 17,000 were present, including Jimi Hendrix and Janis Joplin, who came onstage during Ike and Tina's set to sing "Land of a Thousand Dances." Mick was in great form. The AP reported that he "pranced about the stage Thursday night in black jeans with silver buttons down the sides, black shirt and long red scarf. His leers, winks and smirks brought cheers and sighs." The New York shows are well documented. The

Maysles filmed them for *Gimme Shelter* (outtake footage appeared on the Criterion DVD) and Glyn Johns made soundboard recordings for *Get Yer Ya Ya's Out*. The live versions of "Jumping Jack Flash" and "Honky Tonk Women" on the album were taped Thursday night (versions of "I'm Free," "(I Can't Get No) Satisfaction," "Under My Thumb," "Prodigal Son," and "You Gotta Move" from that night were released in 2009). "Carol," "Stray Cat Blues," "Little Queenie," "Sympathy for the Devil" and "Street Fighting Man" from the LP were taped on Friday afternoon (the 2009 release also included "Under My Thumb," "(I Can't Get No) Satisfaction" and "I'm Free" from this show). Finally, the Stones selected "Live with Me" and "Midnight Rambler" from the Friday evening performance and versions of "Prodigal Son" and "You Gotta Move" from this show appeared in 2009.

**Saturday, November 29:** Boston Garden, Boston, MA, with Terry Reid and B.B. King, 5 and 9 p.m.

Glyn Johns made soundboard recordings of these shows, though none were chosen for the LP. The matinee attracted a sedate audience (B.B. King missed the show due to a flat tire). The only incident of note occurred when fans cut down an American flag hanging behind the stage during "Street Fighting Man." Police rushed out but were unable to catch the perpetrators. The 9 show, however, was (to my ears) one of the best of the tour, with Mick Taylor playing brilliant bottleneck guitar on "Love in Vain" and Keith shining on the semi-acoustic "Prodigal Son." As usual, "Midnight Rambler" kicked the show into high gear. Timothy Crouse of the *Boston Herald Traveler* gushed, "Jagger threw a huge invisible switch and set everyone in motion. He played a harp that hurt your ears. He forgot to drawl and articulated the ferocious lyrics. Midway through the song he unbuckled his belt and fell to his knees, moaning 'oh, baby.' A girl climbed halfway onto the stage and grabbed for him. Jagger snapped his belt at her. In most performances, he has only the stage to whip. The crowd appreciated the moment and howled."

**Sunday, November 30:** First Annual International Music & Arts Festival, International Raceway, West Palm Beach, FL, with Iron Butterfly, Sweetwater, Country Joe & the Fish, King Crimson, the Chamber Brothers, Pacific Gas & Electric, Johnny Winter, Vanilla Fudge, the Rugbys, Janis Joplin, Spirit, Rotary Connection, Sly & the Family Stone, the Byrds, Grand Funk Railroad, Steppenwolf, Rockin Foo and the Jefferson Airplane

The Stones played on the last day of this three-day festival for a payout of $100,000. Unfortunately, the day was a disaster. Due to problems with helicopter pilots shuttling bands to the venue, the concert didn't start until very late. Indeed, the Stones took the stage at 4 in the morning. It was freezing cold and many fans had gone home or were half asleep. Keith recalled in *Rolling Stone*, "You could enjoy the people for hanging around that long but it was too fucking cold to play properly and we tried to do the whole show ... too fucking cold. A bummer!" The Stones high-tailed it to Alabama to record at Muscle Shoals Studio. Footage of them recording "Wild Horses" appeared in the Maysles' film.

**Saturday, December 6:** Altamont Speedway, Alameda County, CA, with Santana, the Flying Burrito Brothers, Jefferson Airplane and Crosby, Stills, Nash and Young

The Stones' most infamous concert started with a set by Santana that ended after only four songs, due to the band's disgust with the behavior of the Hell's Angels. The Maysles and their crew (including a young George Lucas) captured ominous footage of Angels' swilling whiskey, wandering through the crowd with pool cues and scuffling with fans (some of whom, in fairness, were out of their heads on LSD). The Flying Burrito Brothers played an uneventful set, but the concert then took a startling turn when an Angel knocked out Jefferson Airplane singer Marty Balin. Paul Kantner and Grace Slick got into a shouting match with an Angel onstage, while more scuffles took place in the audience. Informed at the airport about what was taking place, the Grateful Dead (who were scheduled to play) sat out the show.

There was a long delay before the Stones took the stage, but they then launched into "Jumping Jack Flash" and "Carol" without incident. When they began "Sympathy for the Devil," however, all hell broke loose, as Angels battled with the crowd. The Stones had to stop the song, while Mick pleaded for sanity. They then restarted the song and followed it with some slow blues ("The Sun Is Shining," "Stray Cat Blues" and "Love in Vain"). But tensions again emerged and Mick asked the audience to chill out. The Stones then began "Under My Thumb,"

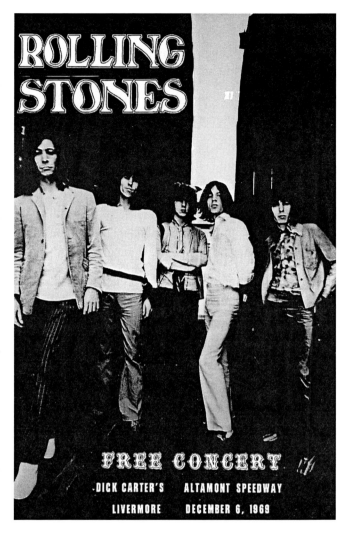

Poster for the Stones' infamous free concert at Altamont Speedway, 1969 (collection of Ira Korman).

which proceeded with fits and starts, until another scuffle began to the left of the stage. It was at this point that Meredith Hunter, a young African American attending the show with his girlfriend, became enraged by the Angels' behavior and took out a gun. Angel Alan Passaro pulled out a knife and killed him (all of which was captured on camera). He was later tried for the murder but acquitted when coroner's evidence was presented that Hunter was high on amphetamines and footage from the movie showed the gun in his hand.

The film makes it appear that the Stones then split and were spirited away on a helicopter. In actuality, they were unaware of what had taken place and proceeded with the rest of the set: "Brown Sugar," "Midnight Rambler," "Live with Me," "Gimme Shelter," "Little Queenie," "(I Can't Get No) Satisfaction," "Honky Tonk Women," and "Street Fighting Man." Some witnesses have declared that the Stones put on one of the best performances of their career, if only to distract the audience from further violence.

**Sunday, December 14:** Saville Theatre, London, UK, with Shakin' Stevens, David Berglas and Mighty Baby, 5 and 8:30 p.m.

Following their return to the UK, the Stones spent time polishing tracks they'd worked on at Muscle Shoals. On December 12 they performed "Gimme Shelter" for the BBC TV retrospective *Pop Go the Sixties*, "Honky Tonk Women" for *Top of the Pops* and "Let It Bleed" for the BBC2 Show *Ten Years of What?* The Stones found time to play some concerts. But the shows at the Saville were a disappointment. Mick Taylor commented to *Beat Instrumental*, "The Saville was a drag. It was one of those sophisticated London audiences and you got a feeling that a lot of people were there just to see a Stones audience." The undemonstrative crowd responded to the set with only tepid applause. A frustrated Mick Jagger screamed at them, "Now you are not just going to sit there—or I'm going to crown you!" He was still angry later that night when Chris Welch of *Melody Maker* ran into him. When Welch told Mick that he felt sorry for how hard he'd worked for such an unappreciative audience, Mick snapped, "Don't feel sorry for me. It was just another gig for me. I felt sorry for them. The most blasé audiences in the world are in our own country, which is why we don't play here." At least one of the shows was filmed. A color clip of the Stones performing "(I Can't Get No) Satisfaction" was televised on U.S. TV in 1984. Clips of "Jumping Jack Flash" and "Carol" also make the rounds.

**Backstage pass for the Stones' show at the Saville Theatre, 1969 (collection of Ira Korman).**

**Sunday, December 21:** Lyceum Theatre, London, UK, with Yes, 5 and 9 p.m.

The Stones received a warm welcome at the Lyceum. Mick Taylor commented, "The Lyceum was much better. There was a freer atmosphere, people were dancing and there was a younger audience. I felt that they let go at the Lyceum whereas they didn't at the Saville. English audiences tend to be a bit reserved, especially when you've just been to America." The set consisted of "Jumping Jack Flash," "Carol," "Sympathy for the Devil," "Stray Cat Blues," "Love in Vain," "Prodigal Son," "You Gotta Move," "Under My Thumb," "Midnight Rambler," "Live with Me," "Little Queenie," "(I Can't Get No) Satisfaction," "Honky Tonk Women" and "Street Fighting Man."

## CHAPTER 9

# 1970

The Stones took stock and considered the future in 1970. The band played only one tour and released no album of new material. However, they did make the momentous decision to sever ties with Alan Klein. The relationship had been strained for some time and the band had unfortunately paid little attention to business and signed contracts without analyzing them. Their lack of interest in such things now came back to haunt them. Advisors informed them in February that Klein's company ABKCO owned all their master recordings and the copyrights to the music they'd recorded for Decca since 1963. Thus, Klein was assured of continuing to make a fortune off the Stones by exploiting their back catalogue. The band launched a lawsuit, but it was clearly time to forget the past and look to the future. This meant breaking their ties to Decca. The Stones' contract with the label expired on July 31 and the band made it clear that they wouldn't sign a new one. They were eager to have more creative freedom and the only possibility was to have control of their own records. Mick told Nick Logan of *NME*, "We had decided in a very loose way that we were going to have a record company. We wanted to employ a few people to look after the Stones records.... So when it is running efficiently and when we are sure the services are good than other people can use the services we have to offer."

However, the Stones still needed a major label to distribute their product and much of the year was spent negotiating with various companies. The negotiations scuttled a plan to tour in the spring and it wasn't until late August that the band embarked on European dates. The Stones were far more involved in all aspects of touring than they'd been in the past. They personally selected Junior Wells and Buddy Guy as opening acts and brought along their own 173,000 watt lighting rig and aluminum stage-spanning proscenium arch. The group insisted that all venues have a stage 50 feet wide and 40 feet deep to accommodate it. Setting up all this required a traveling crew of 51 people. As a result, the Stones made little money on the tour. Mick commented to reporter Tom Donahue, "People are amazed, especially about that European tour because the tickets prices were rather high, but we actually had nothing at the end of it. We had a bigger crew and it was a much bigger presentation than anything we've done in America. And the places weren't as big and the tickets weren't as expensive and we came out with nothing."

The Stones intended to record some shows. Mick told *Record Mirror*, "It's going to be a fantastic undertaking. We're taking a mobile recording studio with sixteen-track equipment and a regular studio board and will probably record a live album on the tour." But the Stones ended up not doing anything with the tapes, as they were informed that Decca was releasing recordings of their 1969 tour that September. *Get Yer Ya Ya's Out* was an enormous hit, becoming the first concert LP to reach number one in the UK. As is often the case with live albums, the Stones couldn't resist fiddling with it. Mick re-recorded some of his vocals at Olympic Studios in January and February 1970, though no instrumental tracks were altered. The album is considered one of the top live albums of all time, ranking alongside such classics as the Who's *Live at Leeds*.

It was the last LP the Stones owed to Decca but the label informed the band that under their contract they were required to provide them with one more single. The Stones cheekily complied by recording the raunchy "Schoolboy Blues," better known as "Cocksucker Blues" due to its X-rated lyrics. Decca executives were horrified and refused to release it. Instead, they opted to put out a Mick Jagger solo single of "Memo from Turner." Mick had recorded the song in 1968 for the film *Performance*. Decca kept his original vocal but re-recorded the backing track with LA session musicians, including guitarist Ry Cooder and Randy Newman. It is today considered something of a lost classic. Mick, however, had nothing to do with the decision to release it and told *Record Mirror*, "I didn't do it as a single. It doesn't make any sense at all lyrically without the film to back it up…. I guess Decca just needed something to put out. It isn't the Rolling Stones. If I'd wanted a single, I'd have made a better one than that, although it's pretty good." Decca, however, seemed unconcerned about quality. That same year they put out *Gimme Shelter*, an odd compilation of recent singles, like "Honky Tonk Women" and "Street Fighting Man," and live recordings from 1966 that had only been released in America (on *Got Live If You Want It*). The album featured a recent photo of the band onstage with Mick Taylor, though he was not on any of the live tracks. It was clearly an attempt to cash in on the Maysles' film and did the Stones no critical favors. They ignored it and pressed on with finishing up work on their next LP.

## *Concerts*

**Sunday, August 30:** Baltiska Hallen, Malmo, Sweden, with Junior Wells and Buddy Guy

The Stones planned to tour Europe in the spring and tentatively booked dates at The Hague (May 8), Rotterdam (May 10), Vienna (May 12 and 13), Munich (May 15), Zurich (May 18), Berlin (May 21), Hamburg (May 24), Essen (May 26), Copenhagen (May 30 and 31), Gothenburg (June 2), Stockholm (June 4) and Helsinki (June 7). In the end, the tour was postponed and it was not until August 29 that the Stones flew to Copenhagen. Stu accompanied them on piano and the band added a two-piece brass section composed of Texans Jim Price and Bobby Keys. Mick expressed excitement about hitting the road. He told *NME* "I think musicians should live out of suitcases and not out of country houses." But the group chose to take it easier than in the past and played only one show a night. They also chose to highlight recent music and played nothing recorded before 1968, not even "(I Can't Get No) Satisfaction." Oldies consisted of three Chuck Berry covers. The set was basically the same for the whole tour and consisted of: "Jumping Jack Flash," "Roll Over Beethoven," "Sympathy for the Devil," "Stray Cat Blues," "Love in Vain," "Prodigal Son," "Dead Flowers," "Midnight Rambler," "Live with Me," "Let It Rock," "Little Queenie," "Brown Sugar," "Honky Tonk Women" and "Street Fighting Man." Blues legends Junior Wells and Buddy Guy opened at all dates. Singer Bonnie Raitt was then a twenty-year-old college student dating Buddy Guy's manager. She was invited to help out on the tour and has stated that traveling on the road with the Stones hooked her on becoming a musician.

**Wednesday, September 2:** Olympiastadion, Helsinki, Finland, with Junior Wells and Buddy Guy, 8 p.m.

The Stones' appearance in Helsinki was chaotic from the start. On their arrival at the airport, zealous customs officials subjected the band to a full drug search with specially trained dogs. Mick was furious and screamed, "Is this a police state or something? Let's go back to London. I've never seen anything like this before." When a TV reporter on the scene commented that the Stones had a reputation for drugs, Mick said, "It's not true that we use drugs. Who said we use drugs? They're full of shit. We don't use drugs.... I don't like those cops with those dogs. We're visitors here. We come here to be nice to people. We don't come to be with dogs." The concert itself was the scene of a riot. In addition to the close to 4,000 people who purchased tickets, thousands more descended on the stadium demanding free entry and barreled past the outnumbered security, who ultimately gave up and let everyone stay.

**Friday, September 4:** Rasunda Fotbollsstadion, Stockholm, Sweden, with Junior Wells and Buddy Guy, 7:30 p.m.

The Stones performed for a wild crowd of 9,000 fans. Hans Loven of *Svenska Dagbladet* reported, "They opened with 'Jumping Jack Flash' and ... after a few seconds a crowd stormed onto the field and pulled those who sat in the lower grandstand with them.... Mick Jagger asked everyone to sit down and was actually obeyed at first but as soon as the rhythm became heated, everyone again stood and pressed against the stage so that it looked really menacing. Police reinforcements arrived and took the stage. A team of more than 50 officers formed a barrier around the Rolling Stones. Some fans tried to get up on stage but were thrown headlong back into the sea of people. The music was never interrupted by the commotion. This kind of rioting is common for the Stones."

**Sunday, September 6:** Liseberg Amusement Park, Gothenburg, Sweden, with Junior Wells and Buddy Guy, 7 p.m.

**Wednesday, September 9:** Vejlby-Risskov Hallen, Aarhus, Denmark, with Junior Wells and Buddy Guy, 7 and 10 p.m.

The Stones had been using Copenhagen as base of operations for the tour but this was the first date in Denmark. *Berlingske Tidende* reported, "The Stones took Aarhus by storm.... There was small scale ecstasy from the moment Mick Jagger, with top hat and eye shadow, began singing 'Jumping Jack Flash' at the first Danish concert of the Rolling Stones in Vejlby Rilsskov Hall in Aarhus."

**Friday, September 11, and Saturday, September 12:** Forum, Copenhagen, Denmark, with Junior Wells and Buddy Guy, Friday at 10 p.m. and Saturday at 8 and 11 p.m.

Jørgen Kristiansen of *Berlingske Tidende* praised the Stones' shows in Aarhus but after witnessing them again in Copenhagen, he was disillusioned to learn that they weren't as spontaneous as he imagined. He commented, "When Mick Jagger pulls his belt back and with demonic zeal slaps it on the floor in 'Midnight Rambler' it is a subtle effect the first time you see it but after you've seen the same number three times in a row with the same movements encoded in the same pattern with exact precision, you lose all illusions that the Stones are an out of control steam engine bowling everyone over with raw, rhythmic music. It is called professionalism.... But the Rolling Stones' charm has always been their unpredictable reactions, their audacity and spirit.... This image has been singed at the edges by five musicians deliberate finger exercises at the Danish concerts."

Poster for the Stones appearance in Finland, 1970 (collection of Ira Korman).

**Monday, September 14:** Ernst-Merck Halle, Hamburg, West Germany, with Junior Wells and Buddy Guy, 9 p.m.

On the Sunday before their Hamburg concert, the Stones gave a press conference on a boat on the Elbe for 400 journalists. The Stones drank prodigious quantities of beer

Montag, 14. Sept. 70 Gemeinschaftsveranstaltung
21 Uhr (Einlaß 20 Uhr) Funke+Lippmann+Rau+SBA
Ernst-Merck-Halle

Einmaliges Gastspiel

# Rolling Stones

DM 22.– | STEHPLATZ

002759

**Ticket for the Stones concert in Hamburg on September 14, 1970 (collection of Ira Korman).**

and mumbled replies to the assembled press. Mick was asked if he felt responsible for the death of Meredith Hunter at Altamont and replied peevishly, "I should throw this beer bottle at your head! It's not as though we killed him. Damned, always the same questions!" Asked about the Beatles, he criticized their breakup but then stated diplomatically, "I'd like to stress that privately we are good friends with the Liverpudlians despite opposite musical views."

The concert itself was relatively sedate. Indeed, Mick was so surprised by the tepid response (considering how wild audiences had been when they visited with Brian) that he asked the crowd of 7,500 "Is this really Hamburg?" Perhaps, part of the reason for the lack of enthusiasm was the intense security. The *Hamburger Abendblatt* reported: "A wide perimeter was closed off and one had to pull out one's non counterfeited tickets at 3 checkpoints. Three groups of 100 police, outfitted by way of precaution with horses, guard dogs and water cannons, 100 security guards and several hundred meters of sturdy mesh netting were meant to insure that the public appearance of the 'Stones' didn't become a gigantic stone pit." The Stones were certainly playing well on the tour. Black and white footage shows them performing fantastic versions of "Honky Tonk Women" and "Brown Sugar."

**Wednesday, September 16:** Deutschlandhalle, Berlin, West Germany, with Junior Wells and Buddy Guy

The Stones arrived in Berlin on Tuesday, and Mick stirred up controversy by battering a photographer with a riding crop when he tried to take a picture at the airport. The concert was a disappointment for promoters, who'd hoped to attract as many as 20,000 fans. Only 6,500 people turned up but there were the usual chaotic scenes outside as students hoping to crash the show clashed with police, who used tear gas to restore order. The strange atmosphere intruded on the show. Mick and Keith were booed when they played an acoustic number. The *Berliner Morgenpost* reviewer seemed disappointed that there wasn't more violence in the hall. He reported, "It was as quiet as a mouse in the hall while the Rolling Stones played their first numbers. Afterwards, there was enthusiastic applause—but not wild."

**Friday, September 18:** Sporthalle, Cologne, West Germany, with Junior Wells and Buddy Guy, 9 p.m.

A good quality tape of this show exists. The Stones were in exceptionally good form and Mick Taylor played some exquisite solos, especially on "Love in Vain." Jimi Hendrix had died that day and, as a tribute, Jagger dedicated "Brown Sugar" to him. The full set consisted of "Jumping Jack Flash," "Roll Over Beethoven," "Sympathy for the Devil," "Stray Cat Blues," "Love in Vain," "Dead Flowers," "Midnight Rambler," "Live with Me," "Little Queenie," "Brown Sugar," "Honky Tonk Women" and "Street Fighting Man." *The Kolner Express* reported, "The Rolling Stones have definitively knocked the Beatles off their throne. They are now at the pinnacle. Even the somewhat restrained Mick Taylor … has blended in well musically with the Stones. The hardest beat group in the world understands how to push their drug and alcohol controversies into the background. They produce beat music which the listener can understand without imbibing a good portion of hash."

**Sunday, September 20:** Hohenpark Killesberg, Stuttgart, West Germany, with Junior Wells and Buddy Guy, 8:30 p.m.

**Tuesday, September 22, to Thursday, September 24:** Palais Des Sports, Paris, France, with Junior Wells and Buddy Guy, nightly at 9

The Stones were scheduled to play one show at L'Olympia but demand for tickets was so great that the group ended up playing four shows at the Palais des Sports instead. There were riots on opening night when fans who failed to get tickets became irate at the sight of jet setters emerging from limos to enter the venue. A "Maoist" even managed to get on the stage and deliver a harangue on how rock shows should be free, before security removed him. In addition, *Rolling Stone* reported, "When the Stones took the stage, there were bare-breasted chicks dancing on stage and Mick grabbed one by the most appropriate handles and danced her off." Eric Clapton was on tour with Derek and the Dominos and joined opener Buddy Guy onstage on opening night, but he didn't

**Ticket for one of the Stones' concerts in Paris, 1970 (collection of Ira Korman).**

come out to jam with the Stones. Glyn Johns recorded all three concerts and the first show was also broadcast on French radio.

**Saturday, September 26:** Stadthalle, Vienna, Austria, with Junior Wells and Buddy Guy

The Stones flew into Vienna on Friday night. Viennese police expected a large crowd and were out in force, but only 300 people turned up at the airport to greet them. Mick told a reporter "I like coming to Vienna. The fans here also didn't desert us at our last concert in the city hall." Over 12,000 fans attended the show on Saturday. *The Arbeiter Zeitung* reported, "The Stones sound has been honed through years of practice to absolute perfection. The start of the show was a hit parade of 'Jumping Jack Flash,' 'Roll Over Beethoven' and 'Sympathy for the Devil.' And on it went for twelve more numbers, but without 'Satisfaction.' … The Stones and their one man show Jagger are currently the best crafted and swingiest rock 'n' roll group in the world!"

**Tuesday, September 29:** Palazzo Dello Sport, Rome, Italy, with Junior Wells and Buddy Guy, 9 p.m.

Prior to this concert, the Stones held a press conference at the Parco del Principi. Things got heated when a reporter snidely noted that the Stones hadn't had a hit record in Italy in years and wondered if the band were losing popularity. Mick angrily dismissed the question and threw a glass of tomato juice at the reporter when he persisted. A reporter from *Variety* attended the show that night and commented, "Performance at the Sports Palace was the loudest ever. Noise submerged all artistry and got through only to the act followers in the rafters. Emphasis on souped-up guitar electronics smothered Jagger's vocalizing and his main performance, heavily repetitive, was limited to rhythmic stage movements that lost impact after their first two numbers."

**Thursday, October 1:** Palalido, Milan, Italy, with Junior Wells and Buddy Guy, 4 and 9:15 p.m.

These shows attracted over 26,000 people. About 2,000 who failed to score tickets rioted in the streets and Italian police had to use tear gas to get them to disperse. Daniele Caroli of *Record Mirror* reported, "At all concerts they impressed. From their opening number 'Jumping Jack Flash' to the closing 'Street Fighting Man,' they created the wildest excitement through a tight barrier of sound."

**Saturday, October 3:** Palais des Sports, Lyon, France, with Junior Wells and Buddy Guy, 5 p.m.

About 12,000 fans turned up to see the Stones. They took the stage at 9 p.m. and delivered a blistering set. Dan Yack of *La Vie Lyonnais* commented, "The Stones lived up to their reputations and for over seventy minutes offered us what many groups fail to provide: Rock 'n' roll! 'Carol,' 'Let It Rock,' 'Roll Over Beethoven,' with a greeting to Daddy Berry, '(Stray Cat) Blues,' and 'Love in Vain.'"

**Monday, October 5, and Tuesday, October 6:** Festhalle, Frankfurt, West Germany, with Junior Wells and Buddy Guy, Monday at 9 p.m. and Tuesday at 8 p.m.

A decent audio recording of one of these concerts exists. The set: "Jumping Jack Flash," "Roll Over Beethoven," "Sympathy for the Devil," "Stray Cat Blues," "Love in Vain," "Prodigal Son," "Dead Flowers," "Midnight Rambler," "Live with Me," "Let It Rock," "Little Queenie," "Brown Sugar," "Honky Tonk Women" and "Street Fighting Man."

Poster advertising the Stones' appearance in Frankfurt, Germany, 1970. The photograph shows them performing at Hyde Park in 1969 (collection of Ira Korman).

**Wednesday, October 7:** Grugahalle, Essen, West Germany, with Junior Wells and Buddy Guy, 9 p.m.

A color super 8 video of this show exists.

**Friday, October 9:** RAI Amstelhal, Amsterdam, Netherlands, with Junior Wells and Buddy Guy, 9 p.m.

About 20,000 fans attended this show, the largest crowd of the tour. Stephen Stills was in Europe and joined the band onstage. *The Leeuwarder Courant* reported, "The Stones mainly played songs from the last live LP.... 'Love in Vain' was a lingering and beautiful rendition. Jagger, accompanied only by Richard, on acoustic guitar, sang 'Live with Me' in a relaxed manner. 'Honky Tonk Women,' 'Midnight Rambler' and the finale, 'Street Fighting Man' were exhilarating and exciting." This was the last gig of the year. There were tentative plans for the group to play a show in London at the Roadhouse in November, but the band ultimately opted to do a UK tour in 1971 instead.

# Chapter 10

# 1971

As 1971 began the Stones were making plans to leave the UK and head into "tax exile" in France. The British government imposed a hefty tax of 83 percent on earnings over £24,000. As Prince Rupert Loewenstein, who took control of the band's business affairs, recalled, "the band had a burden of debt, which they would only be able to repay through future earnings if they left the United Kingdom." The band decided to do one more tour of England as a "farewell" to their homeland before leaving. It turned out to be their only tour of the year. Despite the fact that many of the songs the Stones played were from an album (*Sticky Fingers*) that wasn't even out yet, the band was already bored with the material (much of which had been recorded over a year earlier). Charlie commented in an interview in April, "This tour that we've just done was only nine dates. The first five were beautiful to do, but after that you were doing the same numbers. Maybe it was as good at the end, but it felt better at the beginning."

Much of the Stones' energies were taken up with the formation of their new label, Rolling Stones Records. The U.S. Kinney Group (which owned Atlantic, Warner Reprise and Elektra Records) made an offer that the band accepted to distribute their releases, through the Atlantic subsidiary Atco. The Stones appointed Marshall Chess to run their new enterprise. Mick, however, was quick to downplay the importance of it all. He told reporter Tom Donahue that the group wasn't trying to start another Apple Records. "This isn't like that. This is just our record label. Instead of putting Atlantic on it, we're just going to put Rolling Stones record number two … we're not going to make some big corporate image and build a skyscraper in a corner of Saville Row. It would be nice if we could have another act on the label … if it all goes well, we'll see how it goes."

The Stones continued to be at odds with their old label. In March, Decca put out a compilation album called *Stone Age*, which made it number 4 on the UK charts. The cover featured a close-up of a graffiti-covered wall remarkably similar to the one the label had rejected for *Beggar's Banquet*. The LP itself consisted of old tracks that had either never been issued in England (like "My Girl" and "Blue Turns to Grey") or only appeared as singles ("Paint It Black" and "As Tears Go By"). It was favorably reviewed in the March 20 *NME*, but the same issue featured a full-page letter from the Stones in which they vehemently objected to the record's release. The letter read, "We didn't know this record was going to be released. It is, in our opinion, below the standards we try to keep up, both in choice of content and cover design."

The Stones were also concerned that the compilation might clash with their own releases. On April 16 they finally put out their first single on Rolling Stones Records (with its now iconic tongue logo designed by John Pasche). "Brown Sugar," a rollicking rock song they'd recorded at Muscle Shoals in December 1969, was an instant classic. Mick was responsible for the risqué lyrics, which touched on such taboo subjects as slavery and interracial relationships. In a 1995 *Rolling Stone* interview he expressed some embarrassment over them, telling Jann Wenner, "God knows what I'm on about on that song. It's such a mish-mash. All the nasty subjects in one go…. I never would write that song now." The song was released in the UK as a maxi-single with "Bitch" and a live version of "Let It Rock," from a March show in Leeds. It went to number 2 in the UK and number 1 in America and has remained a fixture of concerts ever since.

The song led off the album *Sticky Fingers*, the Stones' first LP recorded entirely with Mick Taylor. Some consider it their best album. It certainly had some fantastic Jagger-Richards songs. In addition to "Brown Sugar," the album contained the hard rockers "Bitch" and "Can't You Hear Me Knocking," the lovely countrified "Dead Flowers," the haunting ballad "Wild Horses" (which the band had recorded at the same session as "Brown Sugar") and the beautiful "Moonlight Mile." The LP featured a cover designed by artist Andy Warhol, with a zipper that could be unzipped. It was a worldwide smash, hitting number one on both sides of the Atlantic, as well as in Australia and Germany.

In the meantime, the band had all settled in southern France. Headquarters became Keith and Anita's rented Villa Nellcote in the town of Villefranche-sur-mer. It was here that the Stones recorded *Exile on Main Street*, throughout the summer and fall. The band was, however, becoming more scattered. Mick married twenty-five-year-old Nicaraguan beauty Bianca Morena de Macias in St. Tropez on May 12 and she soon became pregnant, which meant that much of his time was taken up. With time on their hands, Keith and Anita began delving deeper into drugs and developed a serious addiction to heroin. Keith often disappeared for days, leaving the Stones to jam in his basement without him. The close bonds between Mick and Keith began to fray as the two led more differing lives.

In a 1987 interview, Keith recalled that the period set the seeds "for why we're not together right now. I mean Mick and I have different attitudes and throughout most of the '70s, I was living in another world from him. I didn't blame him. He'd earned the right to do what he wanted. It was just that I couldn't relate to (his lifestyle). And even if I could've related to it, I was too busy being busted—which, I mean, is equally as dumb, you know?" Even their musical relationship began to strain. Keith loved the relaxed atmosphere of the Villa, where one could record at any time of day. But, Mick told *NME* "I hated the basement where we recorded it…. It sounded bad. I like really big rooms to record in." Mick also began to feel constrained by Keith's definition of his role as "lyricist." He commented, "Keith thinks the same as when he started, but I don't. I used to be in a different position. At the very beginning I didn't contribute much except for the words. The more I got into it, the more my attitude changed. And I tried to write some of the melodies."

## Concerts

**Thursday, March 4:** City Hall, Newcastle, UK, with the Groundhogs, 6:30 and 9 p.m.

This was the opening date of the Stones' "Farewell Tour" of the UK. Prior to embarking on the tour, they taped an appearance on *Top of the Pops*. Mick sang live vocals on "Brown Sugar," "Bitch" and "Wild Horses," while the rest of the band mimed to the record. The footage aired in April when the album was released. For the tour, the Stones augmented their usual lineup with Nicky Hopkins on piano and Bobby Keys and Jim Price on horns. Also traveling with the group was the usual assortment of girlfriends and associates, including Gram Parsons, Chip Monck, Marshall Chess, writer Robert Greenfield, Bianca Jagger, Anita Pallenberg and Astrid Lundstrom.

The Stones took the stage after a short set by the Groundhogs and leapt into "Jumping Jack Flash," "Live with Me" "Dead Flowers" and "Stray Cat Blues." They followed this with "Love in Vain" and then Keith sat down on a stool for "Prodigal Son." Lon Goddard of *Record Mirror* reported that "Mick stood beside him, singing in the dim light, and the sound was fantastic. Following that they bashed 'Midnight Rambler,' 'Wild Horses' and the incredible 'Honky Tonk Women.' ... Then directly into 'Satisfaction' and 'Little Queenie' and the hall broke apart with ecstatic Northerners. They remembered. Last was the lively 'Street Fighting Man' which left the balcony dripping with people and the hall on its feet in an uproar.... One of the finest Stones' performances to date!" There was no encore at the show Goddard saw, but at the conclusion of the second show, the Stones returned for "Sympathy for the Devil" and "Let It Rock."

**Friday, March 5:** Free Trade Hall, Manchester, UK, with the Groundhogs, 6 and 9:15 p.m.

The Stones were scheduled to play at Strathclyde University in Glasgow on March 5 and they'd also agreed to appear at Manchester University on March 12, but the band found out that no one from outside the schools would be allowed entry and decided instead to play more inclusive venues. There was a forty-five minute delay after the Groundhogs' set because Keith was late getting to the venue. When they finally took the stage, most eyes were on Mick (dressed in a pink satin suit and wearing a multi-colored jockey cap). The Stones played a well-received set, but didn't return for an encore.

**Saturday, March 6:** Coventry Theatre, Coventry, Warwickshire, UK, with the Groundhogs, 6 and 8:30 p.m.

In Coventry, Mick was so incensed by the first house's passivity that he threatened not to play a second show. He remarked backstage, "They sold all the tickets here in three hours and then they come and just sit there." But the band eventually took the stage and Robert Greenfield reported, "Just like in the movies, the second show is a bitch and Mick and the boys incite the crowd to riot. Charlie cooks. The lights go all purple and green against a white painted wooden stage floor. Everyone sweats and goes home happy." The set consisted of "Jumping Jack Flash," "Live with Me," "Dead Flowers," "Stray Cat Blues," "Love in Vain," "Prodigal Son," "Midnight Rambler," "Bitch," "Honky Tonk Women," "(I Can't Get No) Satisfaction," "Little Queenie," "Brown Sugar" and "Street Fighting Man."

**Monday, March 8:** Green's Playhouse, Glasgow, Scotland, UK, with Merlin, 6:15 and 9:15 p.m.

The Stones flew to Glasgow minus Keith, who opted to take a train from London and only made it to the first concert ten minutes before show time. Scottish fans expressed wild excitement at the two shows that night. *The Daily Record* reported, "Many of the 3,000 fans danced in the aisles as Mick Jagger pelted them with rose petals. Boys pulled off their shirts and threw them in the air! Girls screamed and cheered their idols." Mick gushed to a reporter after the first show, "It is fabulous to play in Glasgow. I'm absolutely exhausted but it was fantastic to hear such audience appreciation. We will definitely come back!"

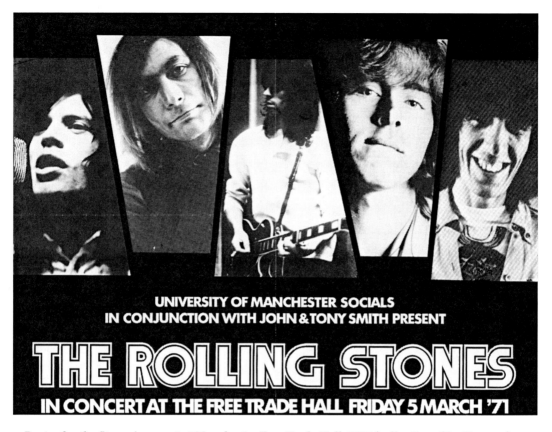

Poster for the Stones' concert at Manchester Free Trade Hall, 1971 (collection of Ira Korman).

**Tuesday, March 9:** Colston Hall, Bristol, UK, with the Groundhogs, 6 and 8:30 p.m.

**Wednesday, March 10:** Big Apple, Brighton, UK, with the Groundhogs, 10 p.m.
  This was the first show recorded by Glyn Johns for a possible live album. Writer Robert Greenfield noted in his book, *Ain't It Time We Said Goodbye: The Rolling Stones on the Road to Exile*, that Gram Parsons was on the road with Keith for this tour and was so stoned this night that he could barely walk. Greenfield spent much of the show taking care of him. The next day, the Stones took a break from the tour to tape an appearance on *Top of the Pops*.

**Friday, March 12:** Empire Theatre, Liverpool, UK, with the Groundhogs, 6 and 8:30 p.m.
  Glyn Johns recorded these gigs, but picked one of the worst nights. The Stones were in a bad mood and put on an uninspiring performance. Backstage afterwards Bill ranted, "I just want everyone to say it was shit…. We were shit." But Mick shut him down commenting, "I don't care. I don't give a shit. When I'm onstage maybe, but now I'm off."

**Saturday, March 13:** University of Leeds, Leeds, UK, with Noir, 8 p.m.
  The Stones performed at the venue made famous by the Who, who'd recorded *Live at Leeds* there the year before. Mick told the *Leeds Student*, "Everyone else seems to want to play here. This is the first time in the University for us, though we have played Leeds before." The Stones, however, nonplused reviewer Patrick Moss. He reported, "The performance on stage of both Jagger and the group as a whole was technically brilliant. The

music itself, however, did little for me, or the rest of the audience…. True they clapped in all the right places, even after Mick Taylor's rather uninspired solo, but there was no link, no rapport between the group and the audience."

Glyn Johns recorded this show and a portion of it aired on BBC Radio. In 2015 the full concert was released as a bonus feature on the "Super-Deluxe" European reissue of *Sticky Fingers* and provides evidence that, reviews to the contrary, the Stones really rocked that day. The set consisted of "Jumping Jack Flash," "Live with Me," "Dead Flowers," "Stray Cat Blues," "Love in Vain," "Midnight Rambler," "Bitch," "Honky Tonk Women," "(I Can't Get No) Satisfaction," "Little Queenie," "Brown Sugar," "Street Fighting Man" and "Let It Rock."

**Sunday, March 14:** The Roundhouse, London, UK, with the Groundhogs, 5 and 8:30 p.m.

The tour ending shows (recorded by Glyn Johns and partially released on the "Super-Deluxe" version of *Sticky Fingers* in 2015) attracted a celebrity crowd, including Eric Clapton, Rod Stewart and Chris Jagger. The first audience was fairly sedate, but the second crowd was wilder and the Stones responded with a great performance. *NME* reported, "Mick, stripped almost to the hips except for a tiny spangled bolero made for a kid of five, writhed and gyrated like a nudist in a nettle patch, and the rest kept the pulsating music on the same high pitched level of hysteria. 'Midnight Rambler' was one of the best numbers and to get some screams out of the girls, Mick took off his broad leather belt and flogged the stage with it. This never fails to get a screech or two."

**Friday, March 26:** Marquee Club, London, UK

The Stones returned to their old stomping grounds on Wardour Street to tape a TV special before 150 invited fans, friends and family, including Andrew Oldham, Jimmy Page and Mick's parents. The taping, however, was fraught with drama. Bill recalled that Keith didn't show up for four hours "and when he finally did, he looked awful. He was dirty, unshaven and very untogether." He was certainly in a foul mood and got into a fight with club owner Harold Pendleton because he'd put up a banner behind the stage that blocked a cameraman's view. Keith swung a guitar at Pendleton's head, though it wasn't captured on the video.

Mick, dressed in a ridiculous shiny lamé vest that stopped at his midriff and an odd multi-colored cap, was in sparkling form and the band rocked right from the opening number "Live with Me." The rest of the set consisted of "Dead Flowers," (which featured some tasty guitar by Mick Taylor), a towering version of "I've Got the Blues" (not played again until the 1990s), a nimble version of "Let It Rock," a slightly subdued but still powerful "Midnight Rambler," the classic "(I Can't Get No) Satisfaction," and a fantastic performance of "Bitch" featuring searing guitar work by Keith. The Stones closed the concert with a rocking "Brown Sugar," which in my opinion would never be equaled again. They hoped to sell the show to the BBC but the staid company inexplicably passed on it and the footage was not widely seen or heard until its release on DVD and CD in 2015. The Stones taped alternate versions of each song and outtakes of "I Got the Blues" and "Bitch" appeared as a bonus on the DVD, along with footage of the band playing "Brown Sugar" on *Top of the Pops*.

**Opposite:** Poster advertising the Stones' 1971 UK tour (collection of Ira Korman).

## Chapter 11

# 1972

As 1972 began the Stones were in France finishing work on *Exile on Main Street*. Once the tracks were recorded, Mick and Keith took them to LA for mixing. Decca took advantage of the gap to release the excellent *Hot Rocks* compilation in the U.S. and the *Milestones* collection in the UK, both of which sold very well. Rolling Stones Records put out an eccentric LP titled *Jammin' with Edward* that consisted of a 1969 recording session featuring Ry Cooder, Nicky Hopkins, Mick, Bill and Charlie. Asked about it by *208's* Kid Jensen, Mick commented "It was just a jam you know, that we held onto, then we put it out for a laugh because Nicky and Ry Cooder wanted to put it out." On April 14 the Stones put out the single "Tumbling Dice"/"Sweet Black Angel." Though it didn't rock at a frenetic pace, the A-side's infectious groove made it a hit and a set-list mainstay. It also served as a taster for *Exile*, which was released in May.

The Stones first double-album was unusual in that, with the exception of the rollicking "Happy" (featuring a lead vocal by Keith) it had few other stand-alone single possibilities. Most non–Stones fanatics probably wouldn't recognize many tunes on the album, like "Casino Boogie" and "Turd on the Run." Critics attacked the LP for being indulgent and sloppy and lacking variety. But many hard-core fans consider it their all-time favorite. The feelings within the band about the record remain divided. Keith is quite fond of it, while Mick has never rated it as high as other releases from the period.

The main event of 1972 was the Stones' long awaited North American tour. To prepare for it, they took over the Rialto Theatre in Montreux, Switzerland, in May for a week of rehearsals (some of which were filmed and can be seen on the DVD of *Ladies and Gentlemen: The Rolling Stones*), before flying to Los Angeles for further rehearsals at Warner Bros. Studios. The rehearsal was needed, as the Stones included many new recordings from *Exile* in the set, including "Tumbling Dice," "Sweet Virginia," "Happy," and "All Down the Line." The band played no songs from before 1968 except for some Chuck Berry covers. They also left out "Sympathy for the Devil," which many associated with Altamont. Gary Stromberg, the Stones' PR man, told an AP reporter, "They are bored with it. It incites people and they don't want to do that anymore."

The 1972 tour was more about excess. As Keith commented in his book *Life*, "The whole entourage had exploded in terms of numbers, of roadies and technicians, and of hangers-on and groupies…. We had become a pirate nation, moving on a huge scale under our own flag, with lawyers, clowns, attendants." Over thirty people were with them on the road, including girlfriends and children, assistants Jo Bergman and Alan Dunn, Rolling Stones Records president Marshall Chess, tour manager Peter Rudge (who'd

Poster for the Stones' 1972 tour (collection of Ira Korman).

previously worked for the Who) and the Stones personal physician, who gave out drugs to whoever wanted them. Also on the road was Motown superstar Stevie Wonder and his band Wonderlove. They opened for the Stones and towards the end of the tour began joining them onstage for a closing medley of "Uptight" and "Satisfaction."

The Stones remained at the peak of their performing powers. The 1974 documentary *Ladies and Gentlemen: The Rolling Stones,* filmed at shows in Dallas and Houston, remains one of the great concert films. However, show business played a larger part than it had in 1969. The 1972 concerts took place at giant arenas and needed to be far more visual. Mick pranced about the stage in specially designed sequined jumpsuits, with makeup and mascara. The lighting effects were also more dramatic. A 16 by 40 foot mirror was suspended on stage behind the band and Chip Monck developed light cues for each song. Prophetically, Mick commented in *Rolling Stone* that he could envision far more in the future. "It's the fact of people just standing on a bare stage playing that makes it funky. But there's so much more that could be done, with stages and ramps and balloons.... God, one would like to be able to do something conceptual as well."

The tour created a frenzy of media interest. But, many were more interested in the wild scene backstage, with cocaine flowing and groupies throwing themselves at anyone with access to the Stones. Filmmaker Robert Frank captured this excess for his unreleased documentary *Cocksucker Blues,* which included scenes of Keith tossing a TV out a hotel window and a groupie being ceremonially "sacrificed" on a plane. Tour manager Peter Rudge commented to writer Robert Greenfield, "The music's almost a byproduct. It goes on for an hour and a half and then it's not talked about. Fewer and fewer people seem able to get out of the dressing room to watch the show either. Makes me wonder what's going on here. Not rock and roll, surely."

In addition to rock 'n' roll debauchery; the backstage area was full of the denizens of high society that once ignored them. Truman Capote (commissioned by *Rolling Stone* to write a piece on the tour) mingled with Jackie Onassis's sister Princess Lee Radziwell (whom the Stones nicknamed "Princess Radish"), while Bianca Jagger chatted with writer Terry Southern in another corner. Mick enjoyed hobnobbing with the rich and famous, but Keith wasn't amused. He told journalist Nick Kent, "Personally I just don't want to know about 'em. I mean how they get in there and why they're there in the first place, I don't really know.... I mean, all those jetsetters must be bored or something."

In any event, the tour was a mammoth success. But the Stones had become more removed from their audience. A sense of intimacy had been sacrificed after Altamont, in the name of security. During the tour, Keith was excited to learn that over a half a million people had written to Madison Square Garden seeking tickets, but admitted to Don Heckman of *The New York Times,* "the perfect place for a band like this is a small place, like maybe a 300-seat cinema.... But now if you want to do it, you just run into all these problems.... If a million people are trying to get into a place that holds 300, you've got a freaking problem, man. And we can't be responsible for that." Success had turned the Stones into a stadium band, for better or worse, and that is what they'd remain for the rest of their career.

When the tour ended in July, the Stones set about compiling a killer concert album to be released at Christmas. But their plans ran aground due to another wrangle with Allen Klein and Decca. The parties were unable to agree to a deal that would enable the Stones to use older material and the band felt that without the showpiece numbers "You Can't Always Get What You Want" and "Midnight Rambler" the album wasn't worth putting out. A disappointed Keith told the *NME* in December, "Allen Klein and Decca are grabbing all they can because, being a live album, it has three old songs to which they have the rights. No doubt they won't let us put it out unless we give them the earth."

But the fate of the live album was not Keith's top priority. He and Anita's increasing addictions to heroin had not gone unnoticed by the staff at Villa Nellcote and they informed the French government. The authorities began extradition proceedings against them. The Richards' clan decamped to Switzerland, where Keith attempted to kick his habit. But there were too many people around with the same addictions, including producer Jimmy Miller and Gram Parsons, and he quickly relapsed. When Mick flew to Montreux in November to write songs for a new album, he found Keith uncommunicative and scattered. When the Stones gathered in Jamaica to start work on *Goats Head Soup* some songs simply weren't up to scratch. Mick explained to an AP reporter, "One of the benefits of recording away from home in an isolated place like Jamaica is there are no distractions. We can work without interruption and that is what we have been doing." The band had made it a goal to finish the album by the end of the year (though overdubs and mixing would continue in 1973) and they plowed ahead. But Keith continually disappeared and there were constant distractions. The French government insisted that Mick, Charlie, Bill and Mick Taylor make statements about what they observed at Villa Nellcote. They all dutifully flew to France in December to try and fix the situation, but Keith and Anita pointedly stayed away. Warrants were issued for their arrests. The Stones' residency in France was over. More troubling, Keith's drug use was beginning to threaten the future of the band, and the headlines probably contributed to Japan's decision not to let them into their country in 1973.

## Concerts

**Friday, January 21:** Hollywood Palladium, Los Angeles, CA

This was not actually a Stones show. Keith and Mick Jagger jammed with Chuck Berry at his concert at the Palladium. But Berry became annoyed by all the noise onstage and ordered them off after only three songs. He thought better of his decision, but by then the Stones had left the venue.

Keith told Nick Kent, "I was given this huge great amplifier and he had this tiny Jewel reverb, so there was no way I could turn down and still not overpower him. I was just trying to play as quiet as possible—anyway I came on with Dr. John and Mick (J) was standing at the back of the stage and it developed into a little ego thing where the people were taking more attention of his backing band than they were of him. It's a shame actually because the two numbers we actually played together were great."

**Saturday, June 3:** PNE Forum, Vancouver, BC, Canada, with Stevie Wonder, 8:30 p.m.

This was the opening date of the Stones' North American tour, which took in 29 cities. The touring band included Nicky Hopkins on piano and Bobby Keys and Jim Price on horns. Keys' nightly solo on "Sweet Virginia" was a tour highlight. The show in Vancouver almost didn't take place, as non-citizens with drug convictions weren't allowed in Canada. In addition the police had vowed to ban the band following their 1966 show. Eventually the authorities relented but refused to let the Stones' chartered plane land there. They had to fly to Washington and take limos across the border. The concert sparked riots, as 2,000 youths tried to crash the venue and clashed with riot police outside. People hurled rocks and bottles at cops, who called in reinforcements as tensions escalated. Many of the protesters complained that there weren't enough tickets available or that they had been scammed into buying counterfeit tickets and than denied entry.

**Sunday, June 4:** Seattle Center Coliseum, Seattle, WA, with Stevie Wonder, 4 and 10:30 p.m.

The set at both shows consisted of: "Brown Sugar," "Bitch," "Rocks Off," "Gimme Shelter," "Happy," "Tumbling Dice," "Love in Vain," "Sweet Virginia," "Loving Cup," "All Down the Line," "You Can't Always Get What You Want," "Midnight Rambler," "Bye, Bye Johnny," "Rip This Joint," "Jumping Jack Flash" and "Street Fighting Man." John Wendeborn of *The Oregonian* attended the afternoon show and reported, "Not everyone is capable of recreating tunes like Chuck Berry's 'Johnny B. Goode' with the utter intensity and attention to roots that the Stones offer…. By the end of the 90 minutes, the audience knew the Rolling Stones had performed their unique style of music with no hold barred."

**Tuesday, June 6, and Thursday, June 8:** Winterland, San Francisco, CA, daily at 4 and 8 p.m.

Despite some trepidation, the Stones returned to the Bay Area for the first time since Altamont to play at Bill Graham's 5,000-seat theatre. Robert Frank filmed the evening show on Tuesday for use in *Cocksucker Blues*. Portions of "Brown Sugar," "Happy" and "All Down the Line" appear in the movie. Peter Cowan of *The Oakland Tribune* reported, "The last three numbers were the Stones at their invigorating best. 'Rip This

Poster advertising the Stones' 1972 summer tour (collection of Ira Korman).

Joint' started it off, followed by 'Jumping Jack Flash.' From the upper balcony the audience swarming around the stage was a mass of bobbing bodies. Finally 'Street Fighting Man' ... brought it to a peak. Mick flung rose petals from a basket to eager fans. After a Chuck Berry encore, the Stones left."

Although he complained about having to play four shows to make as much money as one at Oakland Coliseum, Mick considered the Winterland engagement a tour highlight. He told Robert Greenfield, "The vibrations were just so good. We've always had strange times there. Altamont, yeah, everyone knows about, but Oakland too. It was just the start of the (1969) tour then and we played poorly and Keith blew two guitars ... but this time we just had fun."

**Friday, June 9:** Hollywood Palladium, Los Angeles, CA, with Stevie Wonder, 8 p.m.

Mick attended a number of shows at the Palladium while mixing *Exile* and was eager to play there. But critical consensus was that it wasn't the strongest show. Robert Hilburn of *The Los Angeles Times* reported, "The group played well, but not as consistently strong as in San Francisco and the audience, despite an enormous level of enthusiasm, didn't provide enough of a spark to make the evening the memorable occasion that many had sought." Chris Van Ness of *The LA Free Press* was harsher. In a review titled "The Rolling Stones: Are They Played Out?" he commented that the "new material is obviously not as good as their older stuff and they have gotten sloppy and less committed in performance.... The sound was mixed much like the record, so Jagger's voice was, for the most part, lost in all the noise. And finally, nobody bothered to tell Taylor and Richard that guitars occasionally have to be retuned between songs."

**Saturday, June 10:** Long Beach Arena, Long Beach, CA, with Stevie Wonder, 8 p.m.

Critical opinion divided on the Stones' performance at Long Beach. While singling out Mick for praise, John Mendelsohn of *Disc and Music Echo* expressed disappointment. He noted that Mick Taylor's "stage presence could only be described as comatose" and that the band sounded sluggish and uncohesive. "Jim Price's and Bobby Keys' horns ... all but completely obscured not only Nicky Hopkins but also, disastrously, the rhythm section.... What I have trouble working out is that in their current incarnation, Jagger's

**Ticket for the show at the Hollywood Palladium, June 1972 (collection of Ira Korman).**

presence is the only extraordinary thing about them, and his presence becomes extraordinary only when made so by the audience's energy." But Robert Hilburn argued, "everything worked.... Integrating Nicky Hopkins, Bobby Keys and Jim Price expertly into the group's basic lineup, the Stones music virtually sizzled on the up-tempo numbers and supplied all the tension Jagger-Richard wrote into the songs/arrangements of the slower, bluesy ones."

**Sunday, June 11:** Inglewood Forum, Los Angeles, CA, with Stevie Wonder, 4 and 8 p.m.

Demand for the LA dates was so great that scalpers sold tickets for as much as $750, an astronomical sum in 1972. At the evening show, the Stones opened with hard rocking versions of "Brown Sugar," "Bitch" and "Rocks Off," before launching into "Gimme Shelter." Keith than got a chance to sing "Happy," which was followed by the single "Tumbling Dice." The band then slowed things down for a bluesy "Love in Vain" with Mick Taylor on bottleneck and "Sweet Virginia" with Bobby Keys on sax. They then played "You Can't Always Get What You Want" and "All Down the Line" and an intense "Midnight Rambler." Danny Holloway of *NME* reported on the big finale, "Chuck Berry's 'Bye, Bye Johnny' is the sole survivor from the early Stones repertoire and is followed by Berry's 'Let It Rock.' The houselights come on and 'Jumping Jack Flash' is made to sound very much like 'Satisfaction.' Everyone is up and clapping once more and the band responds with 'Street Fighting Man.' Through sheer enthusiasm and appreciation, the crowd keeps applauding... (The Stones) finally decide to show their thanks by playing 'Honky Tonk Women' and the crowd is happy."

**Tuesday, June 13:** Sports Arena, San Diego, CA, with Stevie Wonder, 8 p.m.

A crowd of 16,000 attended (one fan complained that it was so crowded he didn't have room to light a joint). And there were riots outside the venue by a further 500 disgruntled fans who couldn't get tickets. The Stones were happy with the turnout and again played an encore of "Honky Tonk Women" (something that would only occur a few times on the tour). Mick was overheard telling Mick Taylor, "San Diego's a groove, they're hip here." Joe Cromwell of *The Evening Tribune* reported, "Their music cracked and sparkled on stage. Their fast tunes moved at a frantic pace.... If any disappointment was to be had, it was the fact that the Stones didn't delve back further into their past hits, playing such selections as 'Satisfaction,' 'The Last Time,' 'Let's Spend the Night Together,' etc."

**Wednesday, June 14:** Civic Arena, Tucson, AZ, with Stevie Wonder, 8 p.m.

Once again there was drama outside the Arena as 200 youths without tickets tried to crash the concert. Riot police used tear gas to disperse them and arrested many people outside venue. Inside the venue, however, everyone remained calm and they were treated to an hour and a half show.

**Thursday, June 15:** University Of New Mexico, Albuquerque, NM, with Stevie Wonder, 8 p.m.

The Stones made their first visit to New Mexico and 15,000 fans were on their feet from the opening number. Scott Beaven of the *Albuquerque Journal* reported, "Jagger's relationship to his audience is similar to a cobra's relationship to a snake charmer. In both cases it is difficult to tell who is in control. In addition to overt sexuality, he teases his audience with a callousness approaching the sadistic. When he sings 'You Can't Always Get What You Want' he points directly at the audience and you know he means it. And couldn't care less.... The Rolling Stones' show is an exercise in machismo and it's great fun."

**Friday, June 16:** Denver Coliseum, Denver, CO, with Stevie Wonder, 4 and 9 p.m.

**Sunday, June 18:** Metropolitan Sports Center, Bloomington, MN, with Stevie Wonder, 8 p.m.

The Sports Center was unbelievably hot and stuffy. Temperatures reached 100 degrees and fans fainted in the aisles. On the plane to Chicago after the show, Mick commented "Oooh, that hall! I remember one like it from back in Scotland. They'd erected an iron cage in front of the stage and these girls kept climbing up it, slowly, like insects going to their death. When we first arrived there we thought the place was on fire, but it turned out to be steam. That's how hot it was. Reminded me a lot of tonight. Course back then we only had to do a 15-minute set!"

**Monday, June 19, and Tuesday, June 20:** International Amphitheater, Chicago, IL, with Stevie Wonder, Monday at 8 p.m. and Tuesday at 2:30 and 8 p.m.

The Stones sold $198,000 in tickets for their shows at the cavernous Amphitheater. *Variety* reported, "Throughout the 88-minute show Jagger works extremely hard to please. His movements and singing are filled with the kind of honest, straightforward energy that has kept the Rolling Stones at the top of the rock pile since the beginning of the '60s. It's obvious that there is already some nostalgia over their earlier periods and it seemed rather appropriate that … the crowd's most enthusiastic response was reserved for somewhat older items, such as 'You Can't Always Get What You Want,' 'Street Fighting Man' and 'Gimme Shelter.'"

The Stones' stay in Chicago was non-stop insanity. They stayed at Hugh Hefner's Playboy Mansion, hobnobbing with Playmates and swimming in the giant pool. Keith called it basically "a whorehouse" and spent most of his time pilfering drugs from the doctor's bag with Bobby Keys. They were so high one night that they set fire to Hefner's "Red and Blue" room and had to be evacuated by staff. Hefner later sent the Stones camp a memo requesting reimbursement for damages.

**Thursday, June 22:** Municipal Auditorium, Kansas City, MO, with Stevie Wonder, 8 p.m.

**Saturday, June 24:** Tarrant County Convention Center, Fort Worth, TX, with the Dorothy Norwood Singers and Stevie Wonder, 3 and 8 p.m.

The Stones sold out both concerts within three hours of tickets going on sale. The Dorothy Norwood Singers, a gospel group, was added to the bill for the Southern dates. The shows were filmed for use in *Ladies and Gentleman the Rolling Stones*. The footage of "Gimme Shelter," "Dead Flowers," "Happy" and "Sweet Virginia" are from the first show, while "Bitch" and "Rip This Joint" were filmed at the second. Philip Wuntch of the *Dallas Morning News* declared, "The Stones throbbed mightily with 'Street Fighting Man' and 'Wild Horses' and lit dynamite with 'You Can't Always Get What You Want.' Jagger, his purple-pink silk scarf lashing the air to the music's vibrations, spun out a harmonica on 'Sweet Virginia' and invited the audience to sing along."

**Sunday, June 25:** Hofheinz Pavilion, Houston, TX, with the Dorothy Norwood Singers, 4 and 8 p.m.

Both concerts were filmed for use in *Ladies and Gentleman the Rolling Stones*. The footage of "Tumbling Dice," "Love in Vain," "You Can't Always Get What You Want," "Jumping Jack Flash" and "Bye, Bye Johnny" come from the first show, while "Brown Sugar," "All Down the Line," "Midnight Rambler," and "Street Fighting Man" comes from the second. Stevie Wonder and his band were unable to get to Houston and the Stones played without them. Robert Pincus of *The San Antonio Express* attended the afternoon show and commented, "When they broke into 'You Can't Always Get What You Want,' absolute pandemonium broke out. The magnetism and appeal those performers possess is difficult to describe. Jagger especially draws out audiences with his huge plunger like lips, his cocky strutting, jerky hips and rubbery legs. He still has the same image he had ten years ago, one of insolent rebellion and blatant eroticism."

**Tuesday, June 27:** Municipal Auditorium, Mobile, AL, with the Dorothy Norwood Singers and Stevie Wonder, 8 p.m.

Over 10,000 fans attended this show. Mick, dressed in a purple jumpsuit with silver studs, a cap and a jean jacket, was in command from the start. *The Mobile Register* reviewer noted, "The Stones moved quickly through their set, playing new and old songs with equal proficiency and temerity. Mick Taylor and Richard displayed a tightness when playing guitar together and Taylor was superb on his solos."

**Wednesday, June 28:** Memorial Coliseum, University of Alabama, Tuscaloosa, AL, with the Dorothy Norwood Singers and Stevie Wonder, 8 p.m.

The Stones flew from New Orleans, where they'd spent the previous night, to play one show attended by 16,000 fans. They opened with "Brown Sugar" and followed it with "Gimme Shelter," "Tumbling Dice," "Love in Vain," and "You Can't Always Get What You Want." Bob Wiggins of the *Crimson White* commented, "Midnight Rambler was one of the set's highs as Taylor and Richards were given more space to stretch out their leads. Keys, Price and Hopkins again blew in some steam and Jagger let us in on some of his legendary theatrics. Jumping Jack Flash was of course a 'Gas, Gas, Gas' and Street Fighting Man was the perfect sendoff."

**Thursday, June 29:** Municipal Auditorium, Nashville, TN, with the Dorothy Norwood Singers and Stevie Wonder, 7 p.m.

Over 9,600 attended this concert in the country music capital. *The Nashville Banner* dubbed the Stones "the raunchiest, flashiest, most exciting rock and roll band in the country.... Jagger gyrated throughout the show dressed in a one-piece membrane thin silk jumpsuit, white shoes, lavender sash and a denim jacket. He kicked it off with one of their most popular songs, 'Brown Sugar,' and the crowd didn't sit down until the show was over at 10 p.m." Following this show, the Stones took a break. Most of the group

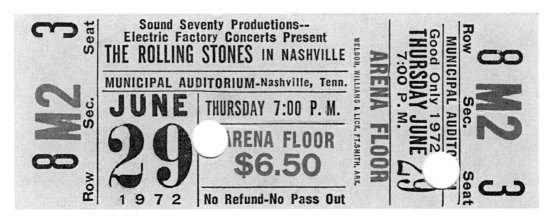

**Ticket for the Stones' concert in Nashville, 1972 (collection of Ira Korman).**

spent their time in the British Virgin Islands, where Mick and Keith tried to write a few songs.

**Tuesday, July 4:** RFK Memorial Stadium, Washington, D.C., with Stevie Wonder, 8 p.m.

About 40,000 attended the Stones' Independence Day concert, the biggest turnout at RFK Stadium since the Beatles. Frank Delano of *The Free Lance Star* noted that despite police fears that kids would throw firecrackers and cherry bombs, the show went off with hardly a hitch. "The Stones killed them, stopped the cherry bombs and absolutely wowed them in Our Nation's Capital on the 4th of July." But Mick told Robert Greenfield that he found the giant show "pretty frightening and a bit weird…. There was trouble in the front, people sitting on the stage, grabbing at your legs, getting tangled in the mike cables…. Just a few loons, really, among the 40,000, but still, I couldn't do my thing. I would have liked video blowups or something because there was no way for me to reach all them people, it being night and me unable to see 'em."

**Wednesday, July 5:** The Scope, Norfolk, VA, with Stevie Wonder

Mick considered this show, attended by 14,000, a tour highlight. A few months later he told Danny Holloway of *NME*, "I remember it was an especially good night for us in Norfolk, Virginia, where we had a tape made of it. It's really good. The ones in the South were funny—the people down there are very appreciative these days."

**Thursday, July 6:** Coliseum, Charlotte, NC, with Stevie Wonder, 8 p.m.

**Friday, July 7:** Civic Arena, Knoxville, TN, with Stevie Wonder, 8 p.m.

The Stones enjoyed their time down South. Mick commented in *Rolling Stone* "The best drive we've had so far has been through the Smokies—Charlotte down to Knoxville, very pretty going down these country roads, seeing little Baptist churches, revival tents and chain gangs." The show that night was reviewed by Chris Wohlwend of the *Knoxville Journal*, who noted, "Lead singer Jagger, looking like the devil in drag, opened with 'Brown Sugar.' His movement and dancing were in keeping with his image as the epitome of evil sexuality. The audience loved it."

**Sunday, July 9:** Kiel Convention Hall, St. Louis, MO, with Stevie Wonder, 2 and 8 p.m.

The Stones flew to St. Louis on Saturday and stayed through Monday. Lee Grinspan of *The River City News* attended the Sunday matinee and gushed, "After the third song they had the audience by the balls and didn't let loose for eighty-minutes…. Taylor and Richard, especially in their blues music, were so tight and augmented each other so beautifully that the combination made us lose the sense of listening to the music and we became it. 'Midnight Rambler,' 'Brown Sugar' and 'Bitch' had us all backed up against the wall. Then Jagger let loose with 'You Can't Always Get What You Want' and everybody was up on the chairs. As expected they concluded the show with 'Jumping Jack Flash' and it was strong enough to send all 10,000 of us into the aisles."

**Tuesday, July 11:** Rubber Bowl, Akron, OH, with Stevie Wonder, 8:30 p.m.

More than 40,000 attended this outdoor show and police prepared for the worst. But although a disturbance broke out during Stevie Wonder's set, the rest of the night was peaceful. Jane Scott of *The Plain Dealer* reported, "Jagger was as mean and magnificent as ever as he rocked into 'Brown Sugar,' 'Rocks Off,' 'Gimme Shelter,' the wild rocker 'Sweet Virginia' and the pounding 'Midnight Rambler.' 'I'd like to do one for anyone who doesn't have anyone to love anywhere,' he said, rolling into 'You Can't Always Get What You Want.' … Keith Richard's solos were beautiful."

**Wednesday, July 12:** Expo Center, Indianapolis, IN, with Stevie Wonder, 7:30 p.m.

**Thursday, July 13, and Friday, July 14:** Cobo Hall, Detroit, MI, with Stevie Wonder, nightly at 8

Over 12,000 fans attended the first show and another 1,500 attempted to gain entry but were thwarted by police. They took out their frustrations by smashing windows. When he took the stage, Mick swatted away a beach ball thrown at him by a fan and screamed "Hello Detroit! It's hot up here ... hotter than Alabama!" John Weisman of the *Detroit Free Press* noted, "For a concert that's been done before ... the music is beautifully fresh and alive. There is spontaneity, richness, soul and a whole lot of funk to what the Stones are doing at Cobo."

**Saturday, July 15:** Maple Leaf Gardens, Toronto, ON, Canada, with Stevie Wonder, 5 and 8 p.m.

As a result of riots in Vancouver on the opening night of the tour, Toronto police surrounded the venue with 500 officers and asked the Stones to fly on to Montreal afterwards, rather than spending the night there.

**Monday, July 17:** Montreal Forum, Montreal, Canada, with Stevie Wonder, 8 p.m.

The Stones spent three nights in Montreal relaxing and making surreptitious late nights strolls around town. Their visit, however, wasn't totally harmonious. Pro-French activists took advantage of their presence to gain media attention by blowing up a parked truck that contained the Stones' equipment. In addition, there were massive riots outside the venue on Monday as 3,000 people without tickets attempted to gain entry to the Forum. Over 20,000 ticketholders attended the concert, the Stones' fourth appearance in Montreal (though Mick commented to a reporter, "I think we've only been to Montreal once before"). Bill Mann of the *Montreal Gazette* reported, "If Bob Dylan be the soul of today's music, the Stones are its libido. Mick Jagger's stage presence is so irrationally overpowering that all the people who weren't dancing last night were gaping slack jawed as Jagger did his thing on a brilliantly spotlighted stage.... Just amazing, truly amazing, I've never seen an audience so totally involved with something they were watching."

**Tuesday, July 18, and Wednesday, July 19:** Boston Garden, Boston, MA, with Stevie Wonder

The Stones flew to Boston on Tuesday to play two sold-out shows. Due to fog, the plane was diverted to Warwick, Rhode Island. While going through customs, Keith took a swing at a photographer who kept snapping their picture. He was arrested. When Mick and Marshall Chess tried to intervene they were arrested too. The three and bodyguard Sam Moore sat in jail for a few hours, while the mayor of Boston struggled to convince authorities to let them out and prevent riots in his city. At Boston Garden, there was a three-hour delay, following Stevie Wonder's set. But fans were promised that the Stones would make every effort to appear. The 15,000 people waited patiently for their arrival (footballs were handed around for the crowd to toss while they waited). The group finally took the stage at 12:50 a.m. and launched into "Brown Sugar." Following the song, Mick apologized for being late, "we tried out the jail for awhile. Our thanks to the mayor of Boston, he helped to get us out of the jail." Despite the delay, Peter Herbst of *The Boston Herald Traveler* declared the Stones "Fantastic.... Keith Richard ... now ranks with Pete Townshend of the Who as a master of the overlooked art of rhythm guitar. Mick Taylor ... showed in his brilliant solo yesterday on 'Love in Vain' that he has the kind of sure, sensitive touch which made Eric Clapton's playing so great…. No one can pound the stage with a scarf like Mr. Jagger and no one can dance like him either."

**Thursday, July 20, and Friday, July 21:** Spectrum, Philadelphia, PA, with Stevie Wonder, Thursday at 8 p.m. and Friday at 2:30 and 8 p.m.

The Stones recorded the opening night in Philadelphia and the astounding tapes later aired on Radio Luxembourg. The blistering set consisted of "Brown Sugar," "Bitch," "Rocks Off," "Gimme Shelter," "Happy," "Tumbling Dice," "Love in Vain," "Sweet Virginia," "You Can't Always Get What You Want," "All Down the Line," "Midnight Rambler," "Bye Bye Johnny," "Rip This Joint," "Jumping Jack Flash" "Street Fighting Man," "Uptight/Satisfaction." Mick Taylor's solos on "Love in Vain" are really exceptional. The show was partially filmed for *Cocksucker Blues* (footage of the Stones jamming with Stevie Wonder on an exciting version of "Uptight/Satisfaction" is from this night).

**Saturday, July 22:** Civic Arena, Pittsburgh, PA, with Stevie Wonder, 8 p.m.

A record Pittsburgh crowd of 13,845 attended the concert and there were scuffles with police outside as additional fans tried to gain entry. *The Pittsburgh Press* commented, "The blaring music and the singing of Jagger, cavorting like a peacock in his skin tight purple jumpsuit, kept those able to gain admittance oblivious to the occurrences outside." The only note of violence in the Arena occurred when a fan threw a beer bottle on the stage and Mick yelled "Don't go throwing your bottles up here at me!"

**Monday, July 24, to Wednesday, July 26:** Madison Square Garden, New York, NY, with Stevie Wonder, Monday at 8 p.m., Tuesday at 2:30 and 8 p.m. and Wednesday at 8 p.m.

The Stones ended the tour with four sold-out shows, the last of which was recorded. The band was fatigued and Mick told the *NME*, "Madison Square Garden was a bit much by the time we actually got there. We were all so tired. I was falling on me feet and I couldn't move. It was horrible. And I knew that we had to look like we were really on top. But I think we were a bit wasted towards the end. We were doing two shows a day and getting up early in the morning." Nevertheless, critics and fans were united in praise of the performances. TV host Dick Cavett visited prior to the Tuesday afternoon show to interview them. Bill commented that the tour was different from previous ones: "There's never been so much energy as on this tour…. It always used to be screamers and they didn't seem to worry much about the music, but it was being played at the same time. But you never heard it. But now you hear everything and you see everything!" *The Cavett Show* also featured footage of the Stones performing "Brown Sugar" and "Street Fighting Man."

The final concert took place on Mick's 29th birthday. As the Stones completed closing number "Street Fighting Man," Confetti and beach balls fell from the rafters. A two-layer cake was wheeled on stage and Mick was given a big stuffed panda. AP writer Mary Campbell reported, "A very square recording 'Happy Birthday' was played and the audience sang along, a few banana-cream pies were thrown at the Stones by their stage crew … mostly missing, but one squishing custard on Jagger's left arm. He was handed a pie, which he threw towards his drummer Charlie Watts, a near miss." Following the concert, the Stones headed to the St. Regis Hotel for an end of tour celebration hosted by Ahmet Ertegun. Partygoers included Woody Allen, Diane Keaton, Andy Warhol, Bob Dylan, Lee Radziwell, Bianca Jagger, Tennessee Williams, Diana Vreeland, Count Basie and Muddy Waters (who was paid to perform). It broke up at 6 a.m., after a voluptuous woman popped out of a cake to sing "Happy Birthday."

## Chapter 12

# 1973

The year 1973 was the beginning of a new era for the Stones. They'd been the undisputed kings of rock 'n' roll, but suddenly some were calling them passé. The UK music scene had changed. There was a whole new crop of young rockers to divert the teens. As writer Mark Paytress recalled in *Mojo*, instead of the Stones vs. the Beatles, "It was Bolan vs. Slade on the school bus, Howe vs. McLaughlin in the rock press." In an age when most rock fans subscribed to Pete Townshend's famous mantra, "Hope I die before I get old," the Stones were suddenly dinosaurs at 30. There was much discussion in the music press about whether they really mattered anymore. But, the Stones didn't seem to spend anytime worrying about it. For all the talk of dwindling relevance, the band had no trouble filling venues or selling albums. They kept right on a rolling.

Indeed, in February they made their first Australasian trip since 1966. Though, as usual, there was controversy. The Stones planned to visit Hawaii, Australia, New Zealand, Hong Kong and, for the first time, Japan. Mick commented, "We've never been there so we thought it was obviously the place to go and we heard that they wanted to see us, so we thought we'd go." The Stones signed contracts with a Japanese promoter in October 1972 and by January 55,000 tickets had been sold for a seven-night residency at the Budokan in Tokyo. But the Stones had a bad reputation, owing to drug convictions, and at the last minute the Japanese government decided not to grant them permission to play. Mick attempted to resolve the matter by personally visiting the Japanese Consulate in America but the government wouldn't budge. As a result, the show in Hong Kong was also scuttled.

It looked as if the Australian government would follow suit. In early January the government announced they wouldn't let the Stones enter the country. The tour was on the verge of being canceled. Mick stated to the Australian press, "I really believe that bands and musicians and actors and ballet and opera and all that should be completely outside of government control. They shouldn't have anything to do with it. If there is an audience for a play or a band or a singer, they should be able to come and work or play or do whatever they want." Ultimately his argument (and complaints of promoters who stood to lose plenty) carried the day. The government relented and let the Stones in. It turned out to be a quiet and uneventful tour. There was almost none of the excess that had characterized the recent tour of the States. Few fans were interested in chasing the Stones or getting into their hotels. Most were content to just see the concerts. The set stuck fairly close to what they'd played in America in 1972. The Stones played some older numbers at their Hawaii shows, but dropped them when they reached Australia. Keith commented to *NME*, "One thing about working up the old numbers is that Mick (T) doesn't know them and would have to learn them from the beginning…. Another reason for us not doing old songs is that Decca have stopped us releasing new live versions of material recorded on their label."

Keith remained angry at his former label for preventing the release of a live album of the 1972 tour and continuing to exploit the band's catalogue. In late 1972 Decca put out the compilations *Rock 'n' Rolling Stones* in the UK and *More Hot Rocks* in the States. Both albums charted, with the latter LP reaching number 9 in America. Decca also released "Sad Day" as a single in April 1973. The track had never been issued in the UK but had been used as the B-side to "19th Nervous Breakdown" in the States. Keith told Nick Kent, "I don't really mind them packaging old stuff if they use a little bit of imagination, but putting out old flipsides as singles is shit. Decca are supposed to be making records but they might just as easily be making baked beans! A record to them is a piece of plastic and what's on there doesn't really matter." While Decca continued to scour the vaults, the Stones tried to finish *Goats Heads Soup*, but there were constant distractions, mostly due to Keith and Anita's dependencies.

In May while Keith was mixing the record with Mick in London, Anita was arrested for drug possession in Jamaica and put through a harrowing ordeal. No sooner was Anita released then she and Keith were busted in London in June (though their lawyer succeeded in getting the charges thrown out). In addition, the couple had to flee Redlands in July when the roof caught fire. But Keith told a Dutch reporter a few months later, "It's all been built up again…. I didn't lose much, just a Polaroid camera and a pair of boots. It always looks worse than it is." Eventually the album was completed and released on August 31. It was the last LP produced by Jimmy Miller, who'd learned the hard way that trying to live like Keith Richards can be dangerous for your health. He ended up addicted to heroin. Keith later commented to Victor Bockris, "Jimmy Miller went in a lion and came out a lamb. We wore him out completely. Jimmy was great, but the more successful he became the more he got like Brian." The Stones mixed the album without him or engineer Andy Johns, who also had developed a habit and stopped working with the band at the end of the year (according to Keith he got fired in Munich when the band was working on *It's Only Rock 'n' Roll*).

Critics have sometimes used *Goats Head Soup* to mark the moment that the Stones ceased being a relevant band. But in recent years many fans have recognized that it was quite a good album. It certainly contained some great songs, including "Can You Hear the Music" and the rocking "Doo Doo Doo Doo Doo (Heartbreaker)." The problem for the Stones was that, after four sublime albums in a row, anything less than perfection was perceived as a failure. The LP contained too many gentle ballads for some fans' tastes, including the mega-hit "Angie" (which Nick Kent called "a dire mistake" in *NME*) and Keith's beautiful "Coming Down Again." And some tracks were a bit lackluster. "Star, Star" was a silly (though enjoyable) throwaway and "Winter" and "Hide Your Love" were mediocre. The Stones didn't help the LP's reputation. As early as 1974 Keith had become disparaging of the record and took to calling it "Junkie music." Stu labeled the album "insipid."

The Stones quickly embarked on a European tour to promote it, supported by Kracker, an American band they'd signed to their label. While some jaded reviewers labeled the Stones "boring old men" (laughable today, considering most of the band were in their early thirties), most critics continued to rave about them. Bill Wyman told *NME*, "This is the best tour we've done really. You've got the craziness still, but everything is so much better organized than it was two or three years ago. The more you're in control, the better it all is." But under the surface, tensions were building. Keith and Mick seldom socialized anymore. Keith had little love for Mick's wife, Bianca, and spent most of his time hanging out with his own coterie of eccentric friends, such as Freddie Sessler, an elderly concentration camp survivor who supplied him with dope. Mick couldn't stand Freddie and avoided him when possible. Nor did he have much tolerance for Texas wild man Bobby Keys' unprofessional behavior (he was banned from the Stones for nine years after he missed a show in October). Mick Taylor was also becoming a potential problem. Never entirely comfortable in the Stones, he felt confined by his limited creative role and, like many in Keith's orbit, had developed an addiction to heroin.

## Concerts

**January 18:** Inglewood Forum, Los Angeles, CA, with Santana and Cheech and Chong, 8:30 p.m.

On December 23, 1972, a major earthquake hit Managua in Nicaragua. Over 6,000 people were killed and close to 250,000 people were made homeless, including Bianca Jagger's mother. Mick and his wife promptly chartered an airplane and flew to Nicaragua, via Jamaica, with a shipment of antibiotics and vaccinations for the victims. Mick then helped organize a Bill Graham-promoted benefit concert. To prepare for the show, the Stones came together in LA on January 16 for three days of rehearsal. The band was in a dispirited mood, as they'd hoped to visit Japan but received final word on their arrival in LA that the Japanese government wouldn't budge. Mick commented to *Rolling Stone* "It's just a minor sort of frustration. The main thing that bugs us is we got nothing to do for ten days, but that's about all. It's not a great financial loss."

The benefit show itself wasn't without problems. The Stones had sent all their stage and lighting gear to Hawaii to prepare for their tour and it all had to be repacked and sent to LA in time for the show. Tickets for the benefit were priced higher than usual, with the cheapest seats going for the then expensive price of $10. In an attempt to raise a large amount of money, Bill Graham reserved 1,975 of the Forum's 18,000 seats, for which he wanted $100 a piece. He was counting on generous record company executives buying them, but was disappointed. In the end, he was forced to sell 500 unsold tickets to fans for $25 each. A crowd of 18,625 turned out for the gig, despite having to queue in the pouring rain.

Mick (dressed in blue velvet pants with silver stars on the legs, a denim jacket and a rhinestone headband) and the band performed a set that consisted of: "Brown Sugar," "Bitch," "Rocks Off," "Gimme Shelter," "Route 66," "It's All Over Now," "Happy," "Tumbling Dice," "No Expectations," "Sweet Virginia," "You Can't Always Get What You Want," "Dead Flowers," "Stray Cat Blues," "Live with Me," "All Down the Line," "Rip This Joint," "Jumping Jack Flash," "Street Fighting Man" and an encore of "Midnight Rambler." Richard Cromelin of *The LA Free Press* was distinctly unimpressed. He commented, "It's extremely obvious that they're well over the hill, that the magic that once pulsated through the music is a faraway thing, that, in short, the Stones are a relic of a wonderful time, with very little relevance or immediacy." Robert Hilburn of the *Los Angeles Times*, on the other hand, while agreeing that it wasn't the best Stones show he'd seen, still called it "some of the most exciting rock n' roll in the world."

**Sunday, January 21, and Monday, January 22:** HIC Arena, Honolulu, HI, with ZZ Top, Sunday at 8 p.m. and Monday at 6 and 10 p.m.

The Stones played three shows with Texas rockers ZZ Top. Bill Graham, Barry Fey and Tom Moffatt of KPOI promoted the concerts. A sell-out crowd of 8,500 attended on Sunday and cheered when Mick appeared onstage, dressed in a rhinestone-encrusted headband, a white jumpsuit with shiny silver stars and a denim jacket, and launched into "Brown Sugar." Stephen Morley of *Record Mirror* reported, "Wyman, Taylor and Watts remained facially unexpressive as usual-but musically dynamic…. This concert (and indeed the whole tour) was evidence that the Stones are not living on nostalgia, but have introduced a new and vibrant spirit to their program."

The Stones had planned to play a residency at the Budokan in Tokyo from January 28 to February 1 and then one show at the Football Stadium in Hong Kong on February 5 but all these dates were canceled. With time on their hands, the band headed back to LA to work on *Goats Head Soup*. Mixing and overdub sessions were held at Village Recorders from January 27 to February 5. In order to work in peace, the staff was sworn to secrecy about the Stones' presence in the studio and the official log registered the sessions as for "Muddy Waters." Songs worked on included "Dancing with Mr. D," "Star, Star," and "Doo, Doo, Doo, Doo."

**Sunday, February 11:** Western Springs Stadium, Auckland, North Island, New Zealand, with Itambu, 3 p.m.

The Stones landed in Sydney on February 8 to begin a tour of Australia and New Zealand. Their arrival was such a closely guarded secret that not a single fan greeted them at the airport. A twenty-six person entourage accompanied the Stones: including Stu, Nicky Hopkins, horn players Jim Price and Bobby Keys, tour manager Peter Rudge, press rep Les Perrin and Mick's personal bodyguard Leroy Leonard. Chip Monck was no longer with the band and in his place Brian Croft manned the lighting system. At a filmed press conference on February 9, at the Old Spaghetti Factory near Sydney Harbor, the Australian media tried to bait the Stones. One reporter asked Mick, dressed in a pink cut-away jacket and white bow tie, "Don't you feel like a pansy dressed like that?" Keith snapped at him "No more than you must in that straight gear" and Mick chimed in, "Five years ago I would have walked out on that comment; today, thankfully, I am a little more mature than you." Keith was asked why he dressed like "the wreck of the Hesperus" which engendered the testy reply: "Probably for the very same reason you like to dress the way you do." Asked where his wife was, Mick replied "I'm here to work…. Do you take your wife to the office?" Mick later commented, in a private interview with an ABC TV reporter: "Some of them (the press) are rude, really rude. You spend a lot of time with them and they're really nice to you and then they turn out to be total hypocrites because all they want to do is write an article putting you down. So you say, 'Why? Why do I bother?'"

The Stones relaxed in Sydney for a few days before heading to New Zealand for one show. Due to the expense involved, the Stones left their lighting equipment in Australia, which necessitated playing Auckland in the afternoon. Promoter Phil Warren sold over 31,000 tickets for the gig at a price of $4.90 each, though eating into his profits were interesting provisos in the Stones' contract, including Bill being supplied with a bottle of Liebfraumilch in an ice bucket onstage, Keith having Cuervo Gold Tequila and Mick needing two bottles of bourbon. The set consisted of: "Brown Sugar," "Bitch," "Rocks

Poster advertising the Stones' appearance in Auckland, 1973 (collection of Ira Korman).

Off," "Gimme Shelter," "Happy," "Tumbling Dice," "Love in Vain," "Sweet Virginia," "You Can't Always Get What You Want," "All Down the Line," "Midnight Rambler," "Rip This Joint," "Jumping Jack Flash" and "Street Fighting Man." Phil Gifford of *The Auckland Star* raved, "Few legends survive close examination. Chalk up the Rolling Stones as an exception. 'The best rock and roll band in the world?' You can believe it!"

**Wednesday, February 14:** Milton Park Tennis Courts, Brisbane, Australia, 8 p.m.

The Stones arrived in Brisbane on Monday and were immediately driven to their motel. A controversy ensued when customs officials searched their plane and found two ounces of grass. The Stones suggested that the Australian government had planted the grass on the plane to entrap them. Sir Gordon Chalk, deputy premier of Queensland, angrily responded: "The statement alleged to have been made concerning police planting of drugs on the Rolling Stones is not only ridiculous but is without foundation…. But if this is the attitude of the Rolling Stones, then I think that the sooner they leave Queensland, the better it will be for the State." But the Stones were forced to remain in Brisbane an extra day when their show scheduled for Tuesday was delayed by torrential rain. There was another storm the next day but the show went ahead and the rain-soaked audience of 8,000 cheered the band.

**Saturday, February 17, and Sunday, February 18:** Kooyong Tennis Courts, Melbourne, Victoria, Australia, with Madder Lake, Saturday at 2:30 and 8 p.m. and one show Sunday

The Stones arrived in Melbourne on February 15 and held a press conference the next day at Montsalvat Castle. Things got heated when a TV reporter asked about whether the pot on the Stones plane to Brisbane had been smuggled in. Mick looked at him and replied, "I don't understand the question!" When the reporter fired back "I thought the question was quite clear," Mick angrily replied, "Someone smuggled…. I don't understand the question…. No I am very sorry sir but nobody tried to smuggle pot into the country, phone up anyone." The reporter called Mick rude and he commented, "I was so rude to you because you started on that. If you want to follow up in TV journalism the rubbish they dish out in the press than you're pretty low. So watch out, boy!"

The Stones performed three outdoor shows in Melbourne. The two afternoon shows were filmed by ABC TV Australia for use in a special on the Stones' tour. Performances of "Brown Sugar" and "Bitch" appeared in the special, though the producers opted to dub studio versions over the footage. The show also included B&W clips from their press conferences and extremely candid interviews, filmed outdoors, with Mick, Keith, Peter Rudge and other associates.

**Tuesday, February 20, and Wednesday, February 21:** Memorial Drive Park, Adelaide, Australia, nightly at 8 p.m.

The Stones played two shows before packed crowds. There were the customary riots outside the venue as 4,000 fans without tickets fought with police. Fencing was torn down and the authorities reported thousands of dollars in damages. The set on the first night consisted of: "Brown Sugar," "Bitch," "Rocks Off," "Gimme Shelter," "Happy," "Tumbling Dice," "Love in Vain," "Sweet Virginia," "You Can't Always Get What You Want," "Honky Tonk Women," "All Down the Line," "Midnight Rambler," "Bye, Bye Johnny," "Jumping Jack Flash" and "Street Fighting Man." On the second night the Stones omitted "Love in Vain" and replaced "Bye Bye Johnny" with "Little Queenie."

**Saturday, February 24:** Western Australia Cricket Ground, Perth, Australia, 2:30 p.m.

An excellent soundboard recording of the Perth show exists. The concert took place on Nicky Hopkins' birthday and Mick took note of it prior to "Little Queenie" with a quick and suitably cheesy rendition of "Happy Birthday." The Stones gave a truly exceptional performance that day. In my opinion, this is one of the greatest live performances by the Stones. The performance of "Bitch" truly rocks. Mick Taylor's solos are particularly

**Poster for the Stones' 1973 Australian tour (collection of Ira Korman).**

exciting, especially on "Love in Vain" and "Gimme Shelter." The full set consisted of: "Brown Sugar," "Bitch," "Rocks Off," "Gimme Shelter," "Happy," "Tumbling Dice," "Love in Vain," "Sweet Virginia," "You Can't Always Get What You Want," "Honky Tonk Women," "All Down the Line," "Midnight Rambler," "Little Queenie," and "Rip This Joint." Presumably "Jumping Jack Flash" and "Street Fighting Man" were also played but they were not recorded.

Keith related in *Life* that he and Bobby Keys had picked up two "outrageous Australian Sheilas" in Adelaide and decided to continue the fun in Perth. While on the commercial flight, the two ladies emerged from the bathroom almost naked, shocking everyone on board. Keith, Bobby and their ladies were detained at the airport and threatened with arrest, but eventually talked their way out of it.

**Monday, February 26, and Tuesday, February 27:** Royal Randwick Racecourse, Sydney, Australia, with Headband, nightly at 8 p.m.

For their Sydney shows, the Stones made a dramatic entrance in a blue horse driven coach. But Michael Symons of *The Sydney Morning Herald* complained that they'd become too professional: "The once shocking band has been tamed ... the music of the Rolling Stones neither had organized antics nor did it break its now respectable confines.... And the Stones played old favorites. They started with lesser known numbers from the middle late 60s before pleasing the people more with 'Honky Tonk Women,' 'Midnight Rambler,' 'Jumping Jack Flash' and 'Street Fighting Man.'"

**Saturday, September 1:** Stadthalle, Vienna, Austria, with Kracker and Billy Preston, 7:30 p.m.

After a six-month break, the Stones hit the road for their second tour of the year. The touring operation was larger than ever. Peter Rudge had a veritable army of staff: There was a reconnaissance man, whose job it was to go to each venue a day in advance and make sure it was ready for the show, and a Danish travel agent, who made sure the band's travel accommodations were up to snuff. Keith had his own guitar-mechanic from Arkansas (Newman E. Jones), whose job it was to ensure that his instruments were tuned and Mick had his own Parisian makeup artist to make sure he looked his best. Prior to the tour, the Stones rehearsed in Rotterdam. Mick told Dutch TV, "We thought it was a nice place and that we'd have less distractions

Poster for the Stones' appearance in Vienna on September 1, 1973 (collection of Ira Korman).

than in England." The rehearsal was necessary as there were shakeups to the touring band. Pianist Nicky Hopkins decided to do his own album and was replaced by Billy Preston, who'd made a name playing with Ray Charles and Little Richard as a teenager, before recording with the Beatles on *Let It Be*. He was given a solo spot prior to the Stones' set each night. Also absent was trumpeter Jim Price, who was replaced by Steve Madaio. Saxophonist Trevor Lawrence was another new face on the tour.

The band updated the set with five songs from *Goats Head Soup*, but dropped the older numbers played in Hawaii. The set in Vienna consisted of: "Brown Sugar," "Bitch," "Gimme Shelter," "Happy," "Tumbling Dice," "100 Years Ago," "Star Star," "Angie," "Sweet Virginia," "You Can't Always Get What You Want," "Dancing with Mr. D.," "Midnight Rambler," "Silver Train," "Honky Tonk Women," "All Down the Line," "Rip This Joint," "Jumping Jack Flash" and "Street Fighting Man." Many shows on this tour were taped and can be found in fairly high quality.

**Monday, September 3:** Eisstadion, Mannheim, West Germany, with Kracker and Billy Preston, 7 p.m.

Only 12,000 fans could fit into the ice rink to hear the Stones, but many more waited outside. *The Hamburger Abendblatt* reported: "Fans even hung in the trees of the castle garden to hear the music of the Rolling Stones." This show was partially filmed by a German TV crew and portions of "Brown Sugar" and "Star Star" appeared on the show *Treffpunkt*.

**Tuesday, September 4:** Sporthalle, Cologne, West Germany, with Kracker and Billy Preston, 6 and 10 p.m.

About 14,000 people attended the Cologne shows. A poor quality but exciting video of one of the concerts exists. It includes performances of "Brown Sugar," "Happy," "Star Star," "Doo Doo Doo Doo Doo (Heartbreaker)," "Midnight Rambler," "Honky Tonk Women," "Rip This Joint" and "Jumping Jack Flash." Wolfgang von Schmitt reported in the *Kölner Express* that many of the fans at the show wanted the Stones to sing more of their older numbers. Mick was philosophical about it when interviewed backstage. "I always see a concert from two sides. On the one hand the listeners have to be satisfied—which is why I play the old songs which they demand. But it also has to be fun for me when I'm standing onstage and that's why the people should also listen to our new songs. Thank God things remain balanced here in Cologne."

**Friday, September 7, to Sunday, September 9:** Empire Pool, Wembley, London, UK, with Kracker and Billy Preston, Friday at 8 p.m., Saturday at 3 and 8 p.m. and Sunday at 7:30 p.m.

The Stones first "hometown" shows in years attracted great crowds (fans who failed to get tickets tried to storm the gates) and quickly sold out. But the band seemed unwilling to get caught up in the excitement. The night before the first gig, the Stones attended a party in their honor at Blenheim Palace, but Charlie commented, "This is just another tour and London is just another show." The set for the opening show consisted of: "Brown Sugar," "Gimme Shelter," "Happy," "Tumbling Dice," "Star Star," "Angie," "You Can't Always Get What You Want," "Dancing with Mr. D.," "Doo Doo Doo Doo Doo (Heartbreaker)," "Midnight Rambler," "Silver Train," "Honky Tonk Women," "All Down the Line," "Rip This Joint," "Jumping Jack Flash" and "Street Fighting Man."

Rick Sanders of *Record Mirror* reported, "Their evil image, in England at least, has gone, replaced by theatrics. In the middle of 'Midnight Rambler,' Mick was saying—at

Ticket for the Stones' show at Wembley on September 8, 1973 (collection of Ira Korman).

the highest point of drama—that he needed an oxygen mask, thus blowing any sense of menace. 'It's nice to be back in England, nice to see our smiling faces after so long,' he says, and, sure enough, it's always nice to see the Stones. In a way it's sad to see the days of aggressive psychic violence on their way out. On the other hand, it seems that the band have managed to accomplish reentry after the incredible brave madness of the sixties, for which we should be happy." Mick seemed somewhat put off by the reviews in the music papers and suggested that they'd seen the wrong show. He commented to Bob Harris on *The Old Grey Whistle Test*, "The first one was really quiet, which was the one that was reviewed. It was really a quiet audience. But the last one was really not at all. It was completely different." The Stones recorded that one and a listen to the tapes proves Mick right. The Stones were on fire and the audience (which included Ron Wood and David Bowie) very involved. The versions of "Gimme Shelter" and "Happy" are both fantastic, with Mick Taylor playing some incredible riffs.

**Tuesday, September 11, and Wednesday, September 12:** Kings Hall, Belle Vue, Manchester, UK, with Kracker and Billy Preston, nightly at 7:30

The Stones embarked on a short UK tour. In addition to the concerts played, they planned to perform in Wales, but the city council rejected requests to perform at Cardiff Castle or Pembroke Castle. Touring the UK for the first time in two years, they discovered that not much had changed. In Manchester, the band were forced to stay at a nondescript motel outside the city because no other hotel would take them due to their reputation. By this point in the tour, the Stones had dropped "Silver Train" from the set, because, as Mick Taylor explained, "It sounds just a little too much like 'All Down the Line' when played live." They'd also ditched the seldom-performed "100 Years Ago."

**Thursday, September 13:** City Hall, Newcastle, UK, with Kracker and Billy Preston, 5 and 8:45 p.m.

The first show was recorded and performances of "Brown Sugar," "Star Star" and "Angie" aired later in the year on UK and French radio. *The Newcastle Chronicle* reported, "The Rolling Stones proved last night that after a decade they are still the world's top rock 'n' roll band.... The whole audience was on its feet, clapping and swaying as the Stones burst through songs like 'Honky Tonk Women,' 'Jumping Jack Flash' and 'Street Fighting Man'... The audience unsuccessfully chanted for more for a full 10 minutes. An unforgettable evening."

**Sunday, September 16, and Monday, September 17:** Apollo Theatre, Glasgow, Scotland, UK, with Kracker and Billy Preston, nightly at 7:30

The Stones performed two sold-out shows, which attracted 6,000 rabid fans. On the first night the crowd were on their feet from the opening number. *The Daily Record* reported, "At the end, they were all-and I mean all-on their feet for five minutes clapping and shouting: 'We want more.' ... (Mick) exuded not only sexual excitement but also musical excitement.... This is the magic of Jagger. He works and he sings, tosses his hair back and covers every inch of the stage in a show in which he is not only Punch but also Judy."

**Wednesday, September 19:** Odeon Theatre, Birmingham, UK, with Kracker and Billy Preston, 5 and 8:30 p.m.

A good quality tape of one of theses shows exists. The version of "Brown Sugar" with the horn section is exceptional, as is Mick Taylor's playing on "Angie." When he was interviewed for the *Old Grey Whistle Test* a few weeks after these concerts, Mick commented, "In Birmingham, the first show was undeniably quiet. I mean they had a good time. We just played rather than trying to rip it to bits.... But the next audience was totally different.... They were very up and very young, whereas the first audience was really quite staid, God bless 'em. I mean I don't mind. You can't choose your audience. That's one you can't do. You have to take the audience that comes and pays and be grateful that you get them."

**Sunday, September 23:** Olympiahalle, Innsbruck, Austria, with Kracker and Billy Preston

While in Innsbruck, Keith learned that Gram Parsons had died of a drug overdose. He was understandably distraught at the loss of his friend and decided that the worst thing in the world he could do was sit in the hotel brooding. Already drifting apart from Anita, he decided to rent a BMW and drive to Munich to try and meet German model Uschi Obermaier, who he fancied. He spent a wild night in Munich with Bobby Keys, searching the German clubs for her. The two wound up having an on and off affair for the rest of the decade.

**Tuesday, September 25, and Wednesday, September 26:** Festhalle, Bern, Switzerland, with Kracker and Billy Preston, Tuesday at 7 Wednesday at 7:30 and 10:30 p.m.

The Stones traveled to Bern on the train. The shows were poorly attended and tempers flared due to Keith's behavior. When the band left for the opening gig, he was nowhere to be seen, but arrived on his own ten minutes before they took the stage. The gigs on Tuesday were apparently underwhelming. However, on Wednesday when the Stones took the stage the crowd rose to their feet and stayed up until the end. The *Nouvelle Revue de Lausanne* reported that during the first half of the show the Stones performed flawlessy, "But something was missing.... Then the Stones return to their older songs ...

Poster for the Stones' concert in Bern, 1973 (collection of Ira Korman).

less polished than the latest ones, but more vivid, more vulgar, more raging! The group is running at full speed when the fantastic 'Midnight Rambler' begins, where Mick Jagger, the sorcerer, packs all his machinery on a frightful rhythm to the limits of fury… When one sees Jagger, one understands better why the majority of the concerts given by the Stones degenerate into a collective brawl…. It is enough that the listener has a hot temperament for Jagger to provoke him and bring out all the violence buried deep within."

**Friday, September 28:** Olympiahalle, Munich, West Germany, with Kracker and Billy Preston, 6 and 10:30 p.m.

Prior to these sold-out shows, Bob Harris interviewed a very stoned Mick (dressed in a pinstripe suit) for the *Old Grey Whistle Test*. When asked if he was still motivated to tour, Mick replied, "Yeah, the motivation's still there, otherwise I wouldn't be out here. I mean I just like doing it. The simple answer to that is: that's what I do. So if I don't do that then I don't do anything. It's a great part of what I want to do: which is to sing live. So this is what we do. This is what I do. That's why we tour."

**Sunday, September 30:** Festhalle, Frankfurt, West Germany, with Kracker and Billy Preston, 5:30 and 10 p.m.

The performance of "Street Fighting Man" at one of the shows was filmed for *The Old Grey Whistle Test*. The Stones certainly rock, though the song is played much too fast, forcing Mick (in a blue unitard with stars on it) to rush the vocal. The song is enhanced by Mick Taylor's decision to play some tasty melody lines on the chorus.

**Tuesday, October 2:** Ernst-Merck-Halle, Hamburg, West Germany, with Kracker and Billy Preston, 4 and 8 p.m.

Over 26,000 attended these shows but despite the turnout, Horst Lietzberg of *The Hamburger Abendblatt* insisted the Stones' popularity was waning. After attacking them for being spoiled prima donnas (they allegedly insisted on fifty security men, two limos, South American papaya to eat, two personal waitresses, a doctor and a couch for backstage), he commented: "The Stones lack new ideas. Glorifying veils of color from enormous spotlights, over dimensional mountains of speakers and ear deafening clouds of sound are not enough to sell 'old hats' to the musically spoiled Hamburg audience. Jagger's gags, such as throwing rose petals on himself and the audience or a bucket of water into the watching crowd, were met with muted responses."

**Thursday, October 4:** Vejlby-Risskov Hallen, Aarhus, Denmark, with Kracker and Billy Preston, 6 and 9 p.m.

The Stones remained in Denmark on Friday and journalist Erling Bundgaard tried to interview them for Danish TV. But the Stones weren't in the mood and began taking the piss. When he asked if they were "big business now," Mick, dressed in a Chinese communist hat and sunglasses, replied, "We're small business … like a sweets shop on the corner." Bundgaard countered, "But you make more money" to which Mick replied "How do you know?" Bundgaard answered, "I think so" and Mick replied, rather truculently, "You don't think nothing till you know about it."

**Saturday, October 6:** Scandinavium, Gothenburg, Sweden, with Kracker and Billy Preston, 3 and 7:30 p.m.

The Stones landed in Gothenburg on Saturday afternoon and were met by customs officials, who zealously searched for drugs. Over 22,000 fans saw the Stones that day. The set for the second show consisted of: "Brown Sugar," "Gimme Shelter," "Happy," "Tumbling

Ticket for the Stones' October 6, 1973, concert in Gothenburg (collection of Ira Korman).

Dice," "Star Star," "Doo Doo Doo Doo Doo (Heartbreaker)," "Angie," "You Can't Always Get What You Want," "Midnight Rambler," "Honky Tonk Women," "All Down the Line," "Rip This Joint," "Jumping Jack Flash" and "Street Fighting Man." Some rowdy fans marred the show. One of them threw a whiskey bottle at Mick. He waved it angrily at the crowd, many of whom thought the show would be stopped. It continued, but there was no encore. Immediately after the show, the Stones took a rented bus to the airport (while friends drove there in a limo to try and deceive the media) and headed to Copenhagen.

**Sunday, October 7:** Brondby-Hallen, Copenhagen, Denmark, with Kracker and Billy Preston, two shows

The Stones arrived in Copenhagen on Saturday. Keith went on a bender, hitting the bars until 2:30 the next morning. His condition may have affected the concerts that night. Jørgen Kristiansen of *Berlingske Tidende* declared the shows "disappointing." He reported, "It was an apathetic and routine performance, without musical highlights, that they presented in both concerts last night in Brøndby Hall…. There was a widespread feeling that the Rolling Stones had to live up to something they could not live up to. The concert ended lamely without the long applause that used to follow the top performers on the road."

**Tuesday, October 9, to Thursday, October 11:** Grugahalle, Essen, West Germany, with Kracker and Billy Preston, nightly at 8

**Saturday, October 13, and Sunday, October 14:** Ahoy Sportpaleis, Rotterdam, Netherlands, with Kracker and Billy Preston, Saturday at 8 p.m. and Sunday at 4 and 8:30 p.m.

The Stones flew to Amsterdam on October 12 and Mick, Keith and Mick T took part in a press conference for Dutch TV. Keith commented that he considered touring "vital" to the band. Asked why, if touring was so vital, they toured so little, Mick replied, "We don't. This is our second tour this year." Keith stated, "We do four or five months a year on the road" to which Mick added, "That's enough!" Over 22,000 fans attended the shows in Rotterdam. The *Dagblad Van Het Noorden* reported, "On stage the Stones are nothing more and nothing less than a first rate rock 'n' roll band…. The Stones are at their live best on old rhythm and blues classics like 'Midnight Rambler,' 'Honky Tonk Women' and 'All Down the Line' and 'Jumping Jack Flash.' During these last four rockers the hall reached a boiling point…. It was an impressive concert by a group of thirty-something's, who for the time being are still the voice of current pop."

**Monday, October 15:** Sportpaleis Merksem, Antwerp, Belgium, with Kracker and Billy Preston, 8:30 p.m.

Bobby Keys' increasingly erratic behavior led to his dismissal from the band. Like many people who ran with Keith, he'd become addicted to the fast life. He allegedly missed this gig because he was enjoying a bathtub full of champagne with a French woman and refused to leave, despite pleading from Keith, who knew Mick wouldn't tolerate more bad behavior. It was a number of years before Mick allowed Keys back on the road.

**Wednesday, October 17:** Forest National, Brussels, Belgium, with Kracker and Billy Preston, 5 and 9 p.m.

Andy Johns recorded these shows with a mobile recording unit and the Stones belatedly released a live album, *The Brussels Affair* in 2011. It consists of exciting performances of: "Brown Sugar," "Gimme Shelter," "Happy," "Tumbling Dice," "Star Star," "Dancing with Mr. D.," "Doo Doo Doo Doo Doo (Heartbreaker)," "Angie," "You Can't Always Get What You Want," "Midnight Rambler," "Honky Tonk Women," "All Down the Line," "Rip This Joint," "Jumping Jack Flash" and "Street Fighting Man." Most of the tracks come from the first show, though "Brown Sugar" and "Midnight Rambler" derive from the second. Many fans consider it the greatest live album by the band. The LP illustrates how the Stones, when truly inspired, were able to transform songs in a live setting. "Angie" accompanied by Mick Taylor's exceptional guitar playing is ten times better than the studio version.

**Friday, October 19:** Deutschlandhalle, Berlin, West Germany, with Kracker and Billy Preston, 8 p.m.

The Stones concluded their tour with a sold-out show in Berlin. The set consisted of: "Brown Sugar," "Gimme Shelter," "Happy," "Tumbling Dice," "Star Star," "Dancing with Mr. D.," "Angie," "You Can't Always Get What You Want," "Midnight Rambler," "Honky Tonk Women," "All Down the Line," "Rip This Joint," "Jumping Jack Flash" and "Street Fighting Man." The concert was a historic event: Although no one foresaw it at the time, it turned out to be Mick Taylor's last appearance as a Stone. Nick Kent of *NME* reported, "And there it all is. Oozing out in the passionate rhythm guitar-trumpet introduction to 'Gimme Shelter' or the bumping, kicking ending of 'Starfucker' (which, along with 'Mr. D' sounds so much better live that it doesn't even bear comparing with the recorded version); or that time when Keith ripped out a chord on 'Mr. D' which cracked like a grown man pulling a muscle … or when Jagger goes through the motions while smearing his larynx over 'Midnight Rambler.' Rock 'n' roll deluxe, for the connoisseurs and the crazies."

## Chapter 13

# 1974

The year 1974 was a fallow year for the Stones. They played no concerts together and spent much of their time apart. Keith commented, "I would like to work on the road a lot more. But I have to respect the fact that there are other members of the band, say Bill and Charlie, who have a need for a really stable home life in one place. They need that anchor, whereas my old lady and myself are very nomadic sort of people." As it turned out, 1974 also marked the end of the Mick Taylor era. By the end of the year, the talented guitarist had quit the group amid some acrimony.

The Stones spent the earlier part of the year sporadically working on their next album in Munich and London. Bill Wyman used the considerable downtime to record a fun solo album titled *Monkey Grip* with musician friends including Dr. John, Leon Russell and Dallas Taylor. He told reporter Roy Carr, "Loving—as I do—old blues records, R&B, hillbilly and Cajun music, I needed an outlet. I felt that I had written some nice songs, but there wasn't any way I could perform them with the Stones.... So the only alternative left to me was to record this album." The LP was released on Rolling Stones Records in May, but Wyman chose not to do any concerts or TV appearances to promote it and it soon disappeared.

The biggest event of 1974 for Rolling Stones' fans was the release of their concert film, *Ladies and Gentlemen: The Rolling Stones,* directed by Rollin Binzer. Filmed at concerts in Texas in 1972, it captured the Stones at the peak of their powers and remains a captivating experience for viewers to this day. In the absence of a tour, the film itself was treated like a concert. It was released for an initial run in Quadrasound, which was designed to replicate the experience of seeing the band on stage. Engineers were hired to accompany the film to these theaters and insure the listening experience lived up to expectations. The distributors hyped the fact that the film would only be shown in this manner in select cities and turned the showings into theatrical events. Following a limited run, the film was released worldwide in the usual monoaural manner of most films of the time. After many years of unavailability, the movie was released on DVD and Blu-ray in 2010.

The Stones released a single of "It's Only Rock 'n' Roll"/"Through the Lonely Nights" in July. Mick and Faces guitarist (and future Stone) Ron Wood had held a few sessions together the previous December and recorded the A-side with little input from Keith. The song was certainly catchy and became a mainstay of the Stones' set, but there was something calculated about its sentiments. Indeed, Mick admitted in a contemporary interview "I don't like oldies or nostalgia. I don't like rock 'n' roll." Mick Taylor described the song as a failure in *NME*: "On the one hand it was Mick and Keith maybe trying to

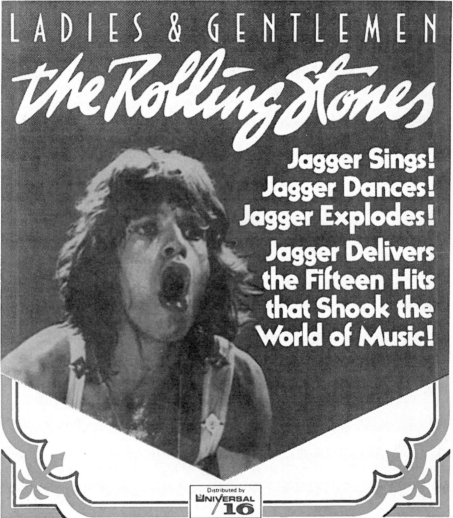

Poster blank for use in advertising special screenings of the 1974 film *Ladies and Gentlemen: The Rolling Stones* (collection of Ira Korman).

Ticket for a screening of *Ladies and Gentlemen: The Rolling Stones* (collection of Ira Korman).

write something in the classic Stones style and on the other, it was a parody—and I don't think it really worked on either level, unfortunately." Nevertheless, the promo video of the Stones dressed as sailors, performing amidst a sea of bubbles (which threatened to drown Charlie and his drum kit) is fondly recalled. The accompanying album *It's Only Rock 'n' Roll* was released in October. It was the first LP produced entirely by Mick and Keith (using the pseudonym "The Glimmer Twins"). Keith told reporter Steve Turner, "Mick and I felt that we wanted to try and do it ourselves because we really felt we knew much more about techniques and recording and had our own ideas of how we wanted things to go." Like *Goats Head Soup*, it was generally favorably received, but no one suggested it was a classic. The LP lacked any thematic unity. It contained an eclectic mix of reggae ("Luxury"), pop ballads ("If You Really Want to Be My Friend" and "Till the Next Goodbye"), soul covers ("Ain't Too Proud to Beg") and dance music (the fantastic "Fingerprint File.")

The LP marked Mick Taylor's swan song with the group. Like Brian before him, Taylor grew frustrated with his limited role as "lead guitarist" and wanted to play a greater role in the creation of the music. He frequently contributed melodic arrangements and guitar lines to Stones' songs but despite promises to the contrary, they always ended up credited to Jagger-Richards. By 1974 Taylor was no longer willing to remain silent. In an interview with Nick Kent he admitted that he'd been "rather annoyed" when he wasn't credited with helping Mick compose 1971's "Moonlight Mile" or 1973's "Hide Your Love." And he expressed genuine surprise when Kent informed him that he wouldn't receive a credit on *It's Only Rock 'n' Roll* for his contributions to "Till the Next Goodbye" and "Time Waits For No One." In addition to these problems, Taylor later admitted he'd developed a sizable drug addiction and needed to clean up.

When the Stones met up in Geneva in late November to discuss future plans, Taylor did not voice his concerns. But, when the two Micks met up soon after at an Eric Clapton concert, Taylor let Jagger know he was thinking of leaving. When the Stones reunited in Munich a few weeks later to begin work on their next LP, *Black and Blue*, he was nowhere to be found. He soon released a statement that said: "The last 5½ years with the Stones have been very exciting and proved to be a most inspiring period. And as far as my attitude to the other four members is concerned, it is one of respect for them, both as musicians and as people. I have nothing but admiration for the group, but I feel now is the time to move on and do something new." The Stones wished him well, but Mick and Keith were annoyed by the surprise move, as they were in the midst of planning a new tour and LP and had to scramble to find a replacement. Nevertheless, when asked about Taylor's announcement, Mick made light of it: "No doubt we can find a brilliant 6'3" blond guitarist who can do his own makeup!" When pressed by writer Derek Johnson on who would actually replace him, Mick stated: "I don't know about permanently finding someone. It's going to take a little while…. I've played with Ron (Wood) a lot. I had one very good night playing with Jeff Beck recently. There's Eric (Clapton) too. They're all great friends of mine."

## Concerts

**Saturday, July 13, and Sunday, July 14:** Gaumont Theatre, Kilburn, UK

During the course of 1974, Keith became good friends with Ron Wood of the Faces. He joined Wood and his other friends, Rod Stewart, organist Ian McLagan, bassist Willie Weeks and drummer Andy Newmark, for these two concerts, which were billed as "Woody and Friends." The July 14 show was professionally filmed and shown on American television in 1975. It was also recorded and released on Ron Wood's Wooden Records in 2007, along with a DVD of the show, as *The First Barbarians: Live from Kilburn*. The set consisted of: "Am I Grooving You," "Cancel Everything," "Mystifies Me," "Take a Look at the Guy," "Act Together," "Shirley," "Forever," "Sure the One You Need," "I Can't Stand the Rain," "Crotch Music," and "I Can Feel the Fire." The DVD also had "If You Gotta Make a Fool of Somebody," which was not on the CD.

**Monday, December 23:** Gaumont Theatre, Kilburn, UK, 8 p.m.

Keith made a guest appearance at a Rod Stewart and the Faces concert, once again in Kilburn. He played guitar on Chuck Berry's "Sweet Little Rock 'n' Roller," Bill Foster's "I'd Rather Go Blind" and Sam Cooke's "Twistin' the Night Away." The show was filmed and the footage appeared on the ITV special *Rod Stewart & the Faces,* which aired in November 1975. Keith commented in *Record Mirror*: "I enjoyed it. It was something different, something to get me chops together, considering we did one and a half hours of music nobody had ever heard before. Even with the Stones we get the horrors of doing more than three unknown songs."

## Chapter 14

# 1975

When 1975 started, the Stones were a four-piece band for the first time since 1962. But they had no inclination to remain that way. When sessions for *Black and Blue* took place in Rotterdam in January and February, a number of guest guitarists took part. In a sense the sessions for the next LP were also an audition process. Wayne Perkins (lead guitar on "Hand of Fate" and "Fool to Cry") and Harvey Mandel ("Hot Stuff") can both be heard on the album and Rory Gallagher and Jeff Beck jammed with the band in the studio. But, it was Ron Wood who proved to be the best fit. He got on well with both Mick and Keith and showed a willingness to simply be a band member. Some critics have charged that this was the problem with him: He simply blended into the mix rather than providing something discernible or different. But he certainly added a sense of fun to the band that had sometimes been lacking in the Taylor years.

Ronald David Wood (born June 1, 1947) had been part of the UK music scene since the mid 1960s. He'd played with the Jeff Beck Group on two acclaimed albums, before joining the Faces in 1969. Wood was a talented player, but, perhaps due to his fondness for clowning around and acting the lad, he had never attracted as much attention as guitar "gods" like Clapton and Page. But he was always ready to lend a hand and had taken part in Stones sessions in 1974. Rod Stewart's solo ambitions had created tension in the Faces and Wood was ready for a change. With his band on a hiatus, Ronnie joined the Stones for more recording sessions for *Black and Blue* in March and April in Munich.

The album, however, was left on hold as Atlantic had already scheduled a greatest hits package called *Made in the Shade* for release that summer. Indeed, *Made in the Shade* was rushed out to compete with *Metamorphosis*, a compilation put out by Allen Klein's ABKCO label that consisted of unreleased material from the band's Decca years. Many of the songs on the record were demos that Mick and Keith had recorded of their early songwriting efforts, such as "I'd Much Rather Be with the Boys" and "Sleepy City." The duo had shown good judgment in not giving them to the band. While an alternate version of "Out of Time" (which Mick recorded with a symphonic orchestra) and a cover of Stevie Wonder's "I Don't Know Why" were fun, most critics agreed that the majority of tracks should have been left in the vaults. Nevertheless, the album made it to number 8 on the U.S. charts.

With nothing new to promote, the Stones turned their attention to touring. After three years, it was time for another massive North American trip and, while no permanent decisions were made, Ron Wood agreed to take part (allegedly for £50,000). The band flew to New York on April 26 and announced the tour on May 1 in unforgettable fashion. Their publicist told the media that the Stones would be holding a press conference at a

Fifth Avenue Hotel in New York, but instead the band rented a flatbed truck and drove by the hotel performing "Brown Sugar" while the media chased after them. In a promo interview some years later, Mick recalled, "Obviously people looked as we passed. But being New York they didn't really care that much. They just gave it a glance probably!" Nevertheless, it was a brilliant bit of PR that let everyone know the Stones were back in town. Due to Ron Wood's involvement, extensive rehearsals were needed. He later commented in *Mojo*, "I had to learn 151 songs. Of course you really can't do that, so you get a rough sketch and fill in the rest."

The tour began in Baton Rouge on June 1 and concluded with a giant show at Rich Stadium near Buffalo on August 8. The Stones had initially planned to also play shows in Latin America (the tour was to conclude in Caracas on August 31) but the plans fell through. The tour was well attended and most critics heaped praise on the band but a few noted that the Stones were less intensely focused than on past tours. There was plenty of acrobatics by Mick, but the passion he and the Stones brought to their performances in 1969 and 1972 was missing. Robert Hilburn of *The Los Angeles Times* commented: "'It's Only Rock 'n' Roll' best exemplifies the spirit of the group's current tour.... The mysterious even occasionally satanic undercurrents from past Stones tours have disappeared. The emphasis now, strictly, is on fun and, of course, music." In a sense, the Stones went back to basics for the tour, dispensing with a horn section, and utilizing only Stu on piano, organist Billy Preston and percussionist Ollie Brown. But, the tour still had plenty of '70s style theatrics, including a confetti-spewing dragon (wheeled out for closing number "Jumping Jack Flash"), a massive lighting system and a six-sided star shaped stage that, when viewed from the audience, resembled a lotus flower.

As in 1972, the band played little from the "Brian Jones Years." The only pre–1968 songs in the set were "Lady Jane" and a throwaway version of "Get Off of My Cloud" played in a sloppy medley with "If You Can't Rock Me." But they added a few covers, including the Temptations' "Ain't Too Proud to Beg" and the bluesy "You Gotta Move." Unusually, the band opted to give Billy Preston (wearing his trademark Afro-wig) a solo spot in the middle of the show. He usually played "That's Life" and then "Outa-Space," on which he was joined onstage by Mick for some funky dancing. Mick also used this opportunity to swing out into the crowd on a circus rope.

To drum up some controversy, the shows also featured a giant inflatable penis (dubbed "Tired Old Grandfather" by the band, for its habit of deflating at the wrong moment). Mick released it from a trapdoor during "Star, Star" and gave it a ride. No one seemed to mind in Louisiana, but in Texas it was branded obscene and the Stones had to temporarily put it in mothballs. The police in Memphis also objected to the phallus and even threatened to arrest the group if they performed "Star, Star." But, the rebellious Stones chose to sing it anyways, reciting the "Star Fucker" chorus with extra relish, as local police watched impotently.

Keith's reputation and dubious choice of friends also created problems. Following a July 4 show in Memphis, he decided it would be nice to drive to Dallas. He took off in a rented Chevrolet accompanied by Ron Wood, security man James Callaghan and mate Freddie Sessler. They were partying a bit too hard and police in the tiny town of Fordyce, Arkansas, stopped the car. Keith was taken into custody for reckless driving and possession of a concealed weapon (a knife). But more trouble was created when police found a controlled substance in Sessler's luggage. Luckily for all concerned, the cops didn't search the car too closely. Keith later admitted that it contained a lot of cocaine, the drug of choice on the tour. When the national media got wind of the story the Arkansas police decided they didn't want the headache. Keith and Freddie were released after seven hours in jail and took off with Woody in a plane.

"Ronnie" and Keith had become fast friends. Keith enjoyed playing with Wood more than he had with Mick Taylor. He commented to Barbara Charone in *Sounds*, "With Mick Taylor, the role of the guitar player was very fixed because Mick plays lead solos and I play rhythm. Because Mick is that kind of guitar player you'll never get the kind of thing you get with Ronnie, which is throwing it around between us.... I prefer it this way because I don't like rigidly defined rules for playing. I don't agree that so and so is a lead guitar and so and so is a rhythm guitar." Ronnie was also one of the few guys that could outdo Keith when it came to imbibing and was always up for a good time. The only stumbling block was his loyalty to his mates in the Faces. But Rod Stewart showed little interest in doing anything with the group, as his solo career gained momentum. In December Ron Wood officially became the fifth Stone and he's remained with the band to the present day.

## Concerts

**Sunday, June 1:** Assembly Center, Louisiana State University, Baton Rouge, LA, with the Meters, 3:30 and 9 p.m.

After a few weeks of rehearsal in Montauk and Newburgh, NY, the Stones flew to New Orleans on May 30 with a 40-person entourage that included tour manager Peter Rudge, lighting technician Jules Fisher, Mick's personal make-up artist, Pierre Laroche, stage manager Brian Croft, press rep Lisa Robinson and ex-cop Tom Phelan, hired to take care of security. The Stones rented a 727 for the tour (it had just been used by Elton John and was painted red, white and blue). The interior of the plane was done in red and gold and contained a private bedroom for Mick and Bianca (who traveled along for many dates). The band had a VCR and fifty videos (mostly old comedies like the Marx Brothers and Laurel and Hardy) to watch on the flights, as well as an ample supply of liquor and even a wine cellar. Traveling with the Stones was a local New Orleans band called the Meters. They opened most nights.

The concerts in Baton Rouge, which marked Ron Wood's debut, were well received by a festive crowd. Charlie Watts sported a

**Mick Jagger performing in Baton Rouge, 1975** (collection of Louisiana State University Gumbo Archives).

radically short military-style haircut, which he admitted was due to his "going bald." Mick had 21 stitches on his right hand and wrist, due to an incident at Gosman's Restaurant in Montauk. His hand went through a glass door. He told an AP reporter, "I was leaving the restaurant. I had my left hand on the door handle and my right hand on the window for support. The window just gave way." However, the injury didn't hamper him much. One of the shows was filmed and a clip of "Honky Tonk Women" aired on the ABC TV show *Goodnight America*. The set consisted of opener "Honky Tonk Women," followed by "All Down the Line," a medley of "If You Can't Rock Me/Get Off of My Cloud," the bluesy "You Gotta Move," "Rocks Off," "Ain't Too Proud to Beg," a fast-paced "Star Star," with Mick riding the giant phallus, "Gimme Shelter," a slow "You Can't Always Get What You Want," Keith's lead on "Happy," "Tumbling Dice," "Luxury," "Fingerprint File," with Mick taking over electric guitar and Ron Wood briefly strapping on a bass, then "Angie," followed by Billy's Preston two-song set of "That's Life," and "Outa-Space," and then the big finish of "Dance Little Sister," "Brown Sugar," "It's Only Rock 'n' Roll," "Jumping Jack Flash," "Rip This Joint," "Street Fighting Man" and "Midnight Rambler." The show remained basically the same on future dates, though "Dance Little Sister" and "Rocks Off" were soon phased out and "Wild Horses" added.

**Tuesday, June 3, and Wednesday, June 4:** Convention Center, San Antonio, TX, with the Meters, nightly at 8

The Stones' return to San Antonio, where they'd last played in 1964, wasn't completely harmonious. *The San Antonio News* (owned by Australian tycoon Rupert Murdoch) urged local police to bust the Stones and the band was warned by their management to be extra careful. Indeed, they dropped the inflatable phallus for the second night of the two-day engagement. When quizzed by Chet Flippo, Mick commented "I just thought it would be better if we didn't use it because if we were arrested we wouldn't be able to use the fucking thing at all anymore. They'd be waiting for us everywhere. The cock has now reached minimal proportions, rather than if we'd said 'Oh fuck 'em.' I thought of that, of course I did. You just have to realize where you are and if it's really worth it."

**Friday, June 6:** Arrowhead Stadium, Kansas City, MO, with Rufus and the Eagles, 3 p.m.

About 35,000 fans watched Rufus (with Chaka Khan), the Eagles and the Stones. Marshall Fine of *The Lawrence Journal World* reported, "There may be other groups that can do to a crowd what the Rolling Stones do, but there is none that has the impact of the aggregation which has been called 'the greatest rock 'n' roll band in the world.' … Jagger danced and sang demonically, now kidding coyly with the audience, now aiming punches and kicks at Ron Wood, now blowing kisses to Keith Richard. Wood … provided a blazing counterpoint to Richards' searing rhythm and lead work."

**Sunday, June 8:** County Stadium, Milwaukee, WI, with Rufus and the Eagles, 2 p.m.,

A huge crowd of 54,000 attended this concert, the largest attendance in the stadium's history. The set consisted of: "Honky Tonk Women," "All Down the Line," "If You Can't Rock Me/Get Off of My Cloud," "Star Star," "Gimme Shelter," "Ain't Too Proud to Beg," "You Gotta Move," "You Can't Always Get What You Want," "Sure the One You Need," "Tumbling Dice," "Luxury," "Doo Doo Doo Doo Doo," "Angie," "Wild Horses," "That's Life," "Outa-Space," "Midnight Rambler," "Brown Sugar," "Rip This Joint," "Street Fighting Man" and Jumping Jack Flash." Damien Jacques of *The Milwaukee Journal* was underwhelmed and reported, "The band lacked the edge that always set them zooming towards the stars. It is evident that they miss guitarist Mick Taylor, who has left the group. The expert heavy guitar work that is a Stones trademark was absent too often Sunday.... The crowd was happy but subdued and the Stones seemed less energized than in the past."

**Monday, June 9:** Civic Center, St. Paul, MN, with Rufus and the Eagles, 6 p.m.

Mick took the stage in a panama hat, leather jacket, blue jeans and sneakers to play for a crowd of over 17,000 fans. Michael Anthony of the *Star Tribune* commented, "Musically the show was tight and well paced, even though the opening numbers, 'Honky Tonk Women' and 'All Down the Line' were bass-heavy and muddled instrumentally. The horn section used in the '72 tour, which added definition and thrust to the up-tempo songs, was missed Monday night. But the guest players—guitarist Ron Wood of the Faces, keyboard player Billy Preston, percussionist Ollie Brown—contributed mightily."

**Wednesday, June 11, and Thursday, June 12:** Boston Garden, Boston, MA, nightly at 9

The Stones played to two sell-out crowds. Dave Marsh reported on one unexpected event in *Rolling Stone*: "Overzealous fans grabbed the writhing, confetti-spitting dragon that appears at the end of 'Jumpin' Jack Flash,' yanking its head off. Jagger and percussionist Ollie Brown lost their grip on the head as it skittered across the stage, and the flying skull bumped Billy Preston into the front row seats." The crowd helped him get back on stage.

**Saturday, June 14:** Municipal Stadium, Cleveland, OH, with Vitale's Madmen, Tower of Power and the J. Geils Band, 2:30 p.m.

To throw off fans, the Stones drove to the Stadium in a mobile home. They performed before 81,700, the largest crowd at an outdoor structure up to that time. Jane Scott of *The Plain Dealer* remained impressed by the Stones. She commented, "The old punk, raunchy image of the Stones has faded a bit, but the basic raw power remains." But her colleague Anastasia Pantsios was less excited: "This particular Stones tour reminded me of the last concert that the Moody Blues did. Both concerts were balanced recitals of past glories spread evenly over all phases of the groups' careers. Both were extremely well done reminders of the groups' contributions, competent but bloodless recounting of essentially past splendors."

**Sunday, June 15:** Memorial Auditorium, Buffalo, NY, with the Crusaders, 8 p.m.

The Buffalo audience apparently took a long time to build up their enthusiasm and the first half of the concert lacked energy as a result. Anthony Bannon of *The Buffalo Evening News* commented that it was Billy Preston who finally got the crowd out on its feet with "an instrumental that had him in a bump dance with Jagger.... Jagger laid out 'Brown Sugar,' 'Midnight Rambler' and a few more and tied it up with 'Jumping Jack Flash,' signing off with some signature piece movements: kicking over the mikes, pulling a huge dragon head from the floor which spewed cut paper on the crowd, ripping off his shirt and dousing himself with buckets of water and sharing the water with the people."

**Tuesday, June 17, and Wednesday, June 18:** Maple Leaf Gardens, Toronto, Canada, nightly at 8

**Sunday, June 22, to Friday, June 27:** Madison Square Garden, New York, NY, nightly at 8

The Stones settled into New York for a week of concerts. The set for the first show consisted of: "Honky Tonk Women," "All Down the Line," "If You Can't Rock Me/Get Off of My Cloud," "Star Star," "Gimme Shelter," "Ain't Too Proud to Beg," "You Gotta Move,"

Poster for the Stones' 1975 tour (collection of Ira Korman).

"You Can't Always Get What You Want," "Happy," "Tumbling Dice," "It's Only Rock 'n' Roll," "Doo Doo Doo Doo Doo," "Fingerprint File," "Angie," "Wild Horses," "That's Life," "Outa-Space," "Brown Sugar," "Midnight Rambler," "Rip This Joint," "Street Fighting Man," "Jumping Jack Flash," and an encore of "Sympathy for the Devil" with special guest Eric Clapton. The set remained basically the same on subsequent nights. The Stones added the *Black and Blue* reggae track "Cherry Oh Baby" on Monday and Friday and Mick sang a quick verse of "Lady Jane" on Tuesday while the musicians were tuning up. On the last night, Carlos Santana played with them on "Sympathy for the Devil." Keith, however, was exhausted from a week of partying and skipped the epic closer.

While *Rolling Stone* declared the New York concerts "mediocre," Chris Charlesworth of *Melody Maker* was more charitable: "The latest lineup of the group is a crude primitive rock band who generate a raw excitement rarely seen as rock becomes more and more sophisticated…. Highlights were 'You Can't Always Get What You Want,' distinguished by a fine guitar solo from Wood, 'Brown Sugar,' when the house lights were raised to reveal a house full of raving dancers and 'Midnight Rambler' which still retains the masochistic trivialities as Jagger cracks his belt and whips the stage."

**Sunday, June 29, and Monday, June 30:** Spectrum, Philadelphia, PA, with the Commodores, nightly at 8 p.m.

Close to 40,000 people attended these shows, which were opened by Motown superstars the Commodores (led by Lionel Ritchie).

Ticket for the Stones' concert in Toronto, 1975 (collection of Ira Korman).

**Tuesday, July 1, and Wednesday, July 2:** Capitol Center, Largo, MD, with the Mighty Clouds of Joy, nightly at 8 p.m.

The Stones performed for over 36,000 fans, including President Ford's son Jack, who came backstage to meet Mick. But the opening show was marred by long delays and a set by the gospel-tinged soul group Mighty Clouds of Joy was met with indifference. It took the Stones a large part of the night to get the crowd re-engaged. Mick was annoyed and made occasional sarcastic remarks, such as "I suppose you all do know how to put your hands together and clap, don't you?" Boris Wentraub of *The Washington Star* commented, "What was surprising was that the Stones played as well as they did without feedback from the crowd. In a set that was trimmed of four songs, including 'Luxury' and 'Angie,' they did wonderful versions of 'Star, Star,' 'Can't Always Get What You Want,' 'Gimme Shelter' and 'It's Only Rock 'n' Roll,' which had Jack Ford and Bianca Jagger up and clapping along."

**Friday, July 4:** Memorial Stadium, Memphis, TN, with the Meters, the Charlie Daniels Band, the J. Geils Band and Furry Lewis, 2 p.m.

The Stones arrived in Memphis at 1 a.m. on Friday morning and headed to the Hilton. The nervous night manager demanded a deposit for the numerous rooms the large entourage had reserved and a furious Peter Rudge, who could be an intimidating figure, roared, "So you want a deposit, eh? I'll show you a bloody deposit!" He raced out to his limo and returned with a giant satchel of cash, which he dumped on the desk. He screamed, "There's your bloody deposit!" as dollars flew around the room.

The Stones were in town to play an Independence Day show before 50,000 people. To make it more special, Mick wanted the Stones to enter the stadium on elephants, but the animals refused to go onstage, causing a two-hour delay. Eventually the band simply walked on at 8:40 p.m. without them. The set consisted of: "Honky Tonk Women," "All Down the Line," "If You Can't Rock Me/Get Off of My Cloud," "Star Star," "Gimme Shelter," "Ain't Too Proud to Beg," "Lady Jane," "You Gotta Move," "You Can't Always Get What You Want," "Happy," "Tumbling Dice," "It's Only Rock'n Roll," "Doo Doo Doo Doo Doo (Heartbreaker)," "Fingerprint File," "Angie," "Wild Horses," "That's Life," "Outa-Space," "Brown Sugar," "Midnight Rambler," "Rip This Joint," "Street Fighting Man" and "Jumping Jack Flash."

**Sunday, July 6:** Cotton Bowl, Dallas, TX, with Montrose, Trapeze and the Eagles, 2 p.m.

Over 50,000 people crowded the Cotton Bowl to see the Stones (who'd been all over the evening news the night before as a result of Keith's bust in Arkansas). It was close to 100 degrees and many fans were near exhaustion by the time the band took the stage. Jan Hubbard of *The Dallas Morning News* reported: "The start was plagued partially by a faulty sound system fading in and out and partially because the Stones weren't exactly playing together—separated only by a beat or two and by the dumb system.... Then midway through the 23-show set everything combined into pleasant brilliance. The music, the weather (highlighted by the sun setting and a nice breeze), the sound system, which was steady and booming 'Its Only Rock 'n' Roll,' made the audience appreciate why it was there."

**Wednesday, July 9, to Sunday, July 13:** Forum, Los Angeles, CA, with the Meters, nightly at 8 except for Sunday at 7 p.m.

Most of the Stones spent their week in LA relaxing. Unlike past tours, there were no wild parties, though the Stones ventured out on their first night in town (July 7) to attend Ringo Starr's 35th birthday. Keith opted to stay at pal Freddie Sessler's home and apparently didn't sleep the entire week. His personal bodyguard Jim Callaghan told a reporter after the first LA gig, "Last night, we went to the gig, then to the party, then to another place and 'e's still up, 'e's still bouncin' and 'e's still got his 'ead together. And this ain't for a couple of days, this is through the fuckin' tour. 'E's brilliant, Keef Richards." Despite his lack of sleep, Keith was present for all five nights at the Forum, though his condition probably didn't aid their performances. Opening night attracted the usual star-studded crowd, including two Beatles (George and Ringo), Neil Young and Neil Diamond. A gleeful Mick ended the show by dumping a bucket of water on Liza Minnelli, her sister Lorna Luft and Bianca, who were in the front row. Drummer Keith Moon joined them on the encore of "Sympathy for the Devil." The Stones' old horn section of Steve Madaio, Bobby Keys and Trevor Lawrence also played with them on the last three nights.

The LA shows were all recorded for a possible album, but the Stones opted to shelve the tapes. A soundboard recording of the July 13 show became a popular bootleg (the bootleggers believed the recording was from the Friday show, hence the LP's title *LA Friday*) and the Stones eventually put out a higher quality version in 2012, keeping the catchy but misleading title. As a bonus on a deluxe version of the release, the Stones put out a DVD with footage of the July 11 concert. The album captures a strong performance, but the DVD illustrates that the Ron Wood era Stones could be very sloppy on an off night. Keith seems completely out of it and out of tune on "Happy" and the band is all over the place on a tired "Sympathy for the Devil." Mick's vocals are raspy and shouted throughout. "You Can't Always Get What You Want" particularly lacks fire and is dragged down by uncohesive playing.

**Tuesday, July 15, and Wednesday, July 16:** Cow Palace, San Francisco, CA, with the Meters

The Stones were supposed to fly out of LA on Monday afternoon but Keith was nowhere to be found so they had to wait for him at the airport, delaying their arrival in San Francisco until 2 a.m. Rather than sleeping, he and Mick headed to the Orphanage to hang with reggae band Toots and the Maytals. Todd Tolces of *Melody Maker* was disappointed by the Cow Palace show: "Jagger's vocals were rough … and harsh: almost a cough away from as hoarse as the crowd sounded…. Richard was uninspired most of the evening as far as solos went. Ron Wood, however, traded off his solos with real finesse, making it look all too easy as he waltzed slowly around the stage tearing off Claptonesque riffs with the greatest of ease."

**Friday, July 18:** Seattle Center Coliseum, Seattle, WA, with the Meters, 8 p.m.

Mick drove to Seattle with a friend on Thursday. The rest of the Stones opted to fly there the next day. The band took the stage at 10 p.m., with Mick dressed in a blue taffeta jacket, on top of an all-black zippered outfit, with an orange diamond on the front. He also wore a silver belt and bright red socks. As usual, the group quickly launched into "Honky Tonk Women." Mick seemed to be having fun on this night. He introduced Ron Wood by telling the crowd "I think this chap is in the wrong band!" Patrick MacDonald of *The Seattle Times* enthused, "Although the group has never played better, and Keith Richard proved himself indispensable on guitar, the night belonged almost entirely to Jagger, the Stones charismatic lead singer. He leapt and danced and wiggled and sassed for almost two hours, while at the same time singing better than ever."

**Sunday, July 20:** Hughes Stadium, Fort Collins, CO, with the Charlie Daniels Band and Rufus, noon

About 38,500 attended this show. Elton John, who was recording at Caribou Ranch during this period, joined the Stones on piano for opener "Honky Tonk Women" and remained onstage for most of the show. He can be glimpsed in backstage footage shot for the TV show *All You Need Is Love*. Reviewer Ruth Pelton-Roby of *The Denver Post* commented, "Jagger's attitude was the only significant change since the group's last couple of tours. He has gone from being seething and demonic to flippant."

**Tuesday, July 22, to Thursday, July 24:** Chicago Stadium, Chicago, IL, with the Crusaders, nightly at 8

**Mick Jagger performing at Hughes Stadium in Fort Collins on July 20, 1975 (Archives and Special Collections of Colorado State University).**

The Stones played three nights with jazz-funk fusion group the Crusaders, led by trombonist Wayne Henderson. Blues legend Howlin' Wolf attended one of the shows. He was weak from several heart attacks and had kidney problems, which would result in his death six months later. Bill Wyman recalled in the *Express*, "I gave him tickets for a Stones concert and, as I'd heard in the media that he didn't have any money, I arranged a limo to collect him and his wife Lillie. He came backstage then when he went into the auditorium, they all stood and applauded him. His wife said it was one of the most wonderful moments of his life and the next night he invited the whole band to his house. Can you believe that nobody wanted to go except me?" Ron Wood recalled in the *Chicago Tribune*,

"His movements were restricted by old age and all that, I guess, and apparently he wasn't taken care of very well when he came to the show. But we were busy getting ready to go on, and we really didn't know what was going on. We really dug him."

**Saturday, July 26:** Indiana State University, Bloomington, IN, with the Crusaders, 8 p.m.

Mick celebrated his 32nd birthday in Indiana, playing before 18,000 people. Tom Healy of *The Indianapolis News* called it "a good mixture of old and new material, over two hours of just plain rock and roll, injected with Rolling Stones fire. To hear anyone else play tunes like 'Jumping Jack Flash' or 'Midnight Rambler' is a farce, because it seems too easy. The Stones alchemy charges each song with a burst of power that overwhelms audiences."

**Sunday, July 27, and Monday, July 28:** Cobo Hall, Detroit, MI, with the Crusaders, nightly at 8

The Stones were all showing signs of exhaustion from the long and grueling tour and were given vitamin B-12 shots to give them stamina. But when they took the stage for the first of two nights in Cobo Hall they showed no signs of tiredness. Christine Brown of *The Detroit Free Press* commented, "The legendary Jagger … sounded stronger than ever; more mature as he teased the audience with the opening number 'Honky Tonk Women.' … He slurs the famous lyrics but makes songs like 'Get Off of My Cloud' have a 70s sound. Part of the Stones' greatness is that they play their roots but always bring them up to date. Keith Richard's guitar playing has never had more swagger."

**Wednesday, July 30:** Omni Coliseum, Atlanta, GA, with the Meters, 8 p.m.

**Thursday, July 31:** Coliseum, Greensboro, NC, with the Meters, 8:30 p.m.

The Stones received a roaring welcome from the crowd of 17,000. Mick was dressed in a bizarre combination of rolled up jeans, pink jacket and purple cape, and led the band through a rousing if hoarse "Honky Tonk Women." But the band seemed to lose their groove after that and the medley of "If You Can't Rock Me/Get Off of My Cloud" had little fire. "Star, Star" started strong but problems with "Tired Old Granddad" soon ensued. Glenn Brank of *The Greensboro Record* commented: "Fans burst into laughter when the infamous phallic-symbol balloon rising from a stage trapdoor collapsed…. It was up to the black-leathered Richard to turn the show around. First on 'Ain't Too Proud to Beg' and then on 'You Can't Always Get What You Want' his guitar licks smoldered. Wood picked up the lead and the pair left the audience breathless.'"

**Saturday, August 2:** Gator Bowl, Jacksonville, FL, with Atlanta Rhythm Section, Rufus and the J. Geils Band, 2 p.m.

The Stones played before a massive crowd of 71,000, who waited in sweltering heat until 6 p.m. for them to take the stage. Despite the wait, Bob Ross of *The St. Petersburg Times* praised the show and singled out Keith for special mention: "Keith now plays those searing rock and raunch leads that were left out in the recent past. Not only did he kick out some jams on 'Honky Tonk Women' but Richard also stood out on 'All Down the Line,' 'Star Star' and 'Happy,' on which he also did his only singing verse. Keith even played an outstanding blues lead on 'You Gotta Move,' the sort of thing he wouldn't touch when Taylor was around."

**Monday, August 4:** Freedom Hall, Louisville, KY, 8 p.m.

Mick, resplendent in a pink and white striped silk jacket and matching pants topped off with red shoes, walked out at 9:45 p.m. and pandemonium ensued as young people rushed to the front of the stage. Billy Reed of the *Courier Journal* was impressed by Mick's energy and showmanship but complained that, "musically, the show probably could have been better. Sometimes the songs seemed to run together, one indistinguishable from another. Old-timers probably wish the Stones had done more of their 1960s hits. Yet what the Stones did they did well enough."

**Wednesday, August 6:** Coliseum, Hampton, VA, 9 p.m.

The Stones flew to Norfolk on Tuesday, and checked into the 1776 Inn in Williamsburg, to relax away from the crowds. The sleepy town was not prepared for a visit by a rock band. Their entourage required 32 rooms. A waitress at a local restaurant was stunned that night when Mick and some companions wandered in and ordered a few beers. About 11,000 people attended the show the next night. C.A. Bustard of *The Richmond Times* commented: "Musically the evening's best moment was the Stones pungent reworking of 'Ain't Too Proud to Beg,' the Temptations rhythm and blues classic. This is stage matter suited to Jagger's frenetic style: the song had a strong beat, lingering chords and shouted lyrics, all crashing together into chorus."

**Friday, August 8:** Rich Stadium, Orchard Park, NY, with the Outlaws and Bobby Womack, 5 p.m.

About 70,000 people turned up for the tour finale at Rich Stadium, just south of Buffalo. Sixty-five people were arrested for drug possession, but the concert itself was incident-free. The set consisted of: "Honky Tonk Women," "All Down the Line," "If You Can't Rock Me/Get Off of My Cloud," "Star Star," "Gimme Shelter," "Ain't Too Proud to Beg," "You Gotta Move," "You Can't Always Get What You Want," "Happy," "Tumbling Dice," "It's Only Rock 'n' Roll," "Fingerprint File," "Wild Horses," "That's Life," "Outa-Space," "Brown Sugar," "Midnight Rambler," "Rip This Joint," "Street Fighting Man" and "Jumping Jack Flash." Dale Anderson of the *Buffalo Evening News* reported that the show was "less intense" than the Stones' June concert in Buffalo: "After 45 concerts in 27 cities, the Stones seemed to be in this one for the fun of it. Vocals were enthusiastic but sloppy: Jagger, in poor voice, slurred and curlicued lyrics into unintelligibility."

The Stones were scheduled to play their first shows in Latin America following the

**Ticket for the Stones' final show of the 1975 tour (collection of Ira Korman).**

## ROLLING STONES – SOUTH AMERICA

| Seating Capacity | AUGUST: | Day | Date | City |
|---|---|---|---|---|
| | | Saturday | 2 | Jacksonville, Fla. |
| | | Sunday | 3 | Day Off |
| | | Monday | 4 | Day Off |
| | | Tuesday | 5 | Day Off |
| | | Wednesday | 6 | Day Off |
| 14,600 | | Thursday | 7 | Mexico City, National Aud. |
| | | Friday | 8 | Mexico City |
| | | Saturday | 9 | Mexico City |
| | | Sunday | 10 | Mexico City |
| | | Monday | 11 | Travel to Rio |
| | | Tuesday | 12 | Day Off |
| | | Wednesday | 13 | Press Reception |
| 16,700 | | Thursday | 14 | Rio de Janeiro, "Maracanazinho" |
| | | Friday | 15 | Rio de Janeiro |
| | | Saturday | 16 | Rio de Janeiro |
| | | Sunday | 17 | Rio de Janeiro |
| | | Monday | 18 | Travel |
| 3,500 | | Tuesday | 19 | Sao Paulo, Conv. Hall |
| | | Wednesday | 20 | Sao Paulo " " |
| | | Thursday | 21 | Sao Paulo " " |
| | | Friday | 22 | Day Off |
| | | Saturday | 23 | Setup |
| 150,000 | | Sunday | 24 | Sao Paulo, Anhembi Hall |
| | | Monday | 25 | Day Off |
| | | Tuesday | 26 | Day Off |
| | | Wednesday | 27 | Setup |
| 13,000 | | Thursday | 28 | Caracas, El Poliedro |
| | | Friday | 29 | Caracas " " |
| | | Saturday | 30 | Caracas " " |
| | | Sunday | 31 | Caracas " " |
| | SEPTEMBER: | Monday | 1 | Home |

**Document detailing tentative plans for a 1975 tour of South America. The tour did not take place (collection of Ira Korman).**

U.S. dates but the proposed tour, that was to start in Mexico City (August 7–10), take in Rio (August 14–17) and Sao Paulo (August 19–24) and end in Caracas (August 28–31), was canceled in June. One reason for the cancelation was that Ron Wood had promised the Faces he'd take part in an August tour with them and therefore couldn't play with the Stones.

## Chapter 15

# 1976

As 1976 began the Stones were again officially a five-man band. With the Faces having called it quits, Ron Wood became a full-time member. Mick commented, "Yeah he's got his badge and his membership card…. It was nice to work with Ronnie this last tour. He's good for the band, I think." But Wood spent early 1976 recording with other musicians while the Stones took a hiatus. He took part in recording sessions with Eric Clapton, Bob Dylan, Rick Danko and Kinky Friedman. Bill Wyman used the break to release a second solo LP, *Stone Alone,* in February. It was a solid effort with contributions from an all-star cast including Van Morrison, Joe Walsh and Dr. John, but it failed to chart and disappeared quickly. Keith was typically dismissive of Bill's solo foray. He commented to Barbara Charone of *Sounds,* "Bill is a great bass player. With Charlie, he's a great rhythm section. But it's the Mick Taylor syndrome. OK, you're a guitar player but that's not enough. Then you also want to be a great songwriter…. It's the case of someone who can do something really well insisting they can do a lot of other things well. And they can't."

That April the Stones released their next LP, *Black and Blue,* most of which had been recorded the previous year. Ron Wood played on half of the tracks. Perhaps, as a result of the lineup changes, it was another uneven album. The Stones embraced a number of musical styles including funk ("Hot Stuff") and reggae ("Cherry Oh Baby") but some of the tunes floundered and lacked melodic structure. "Hand of Fate" was an incredibly tough rock song with a great Wayne Perkins guitar solo and "Hey Negrita" was equally good, but "Crazy Mama" and "Cherry Oh Baby" were forgettable. The two most memorable tunes were probably the ballads, "Fool to Cry" (which reached number 10 on the Billboard charts in America) and the meandering "Memory Motel." Reception for the LP was mixed. While Dave Marsh of *Rolling Stone* praised it, Lester Bangs of *Creem* called *Black and Blue* "the first meaningless Rolling Stones album." Charles Shaar Murray of *NME* dubbed the LP "a letdown of hideous proportions." As usual, the Stones proved immune to criticism. The LP spent four weeks at number one in the States and was in the top ten all over Europe.

To promote it, the band played their first European tour in three years. It started in Frankfurt on April 28 and ended on June 23 in Vienna. The Stones were at the height of their extravagance. They traveled on their own private plane with a massive entourage. Mick brought along a $70,000 wardrobe, which included many sequined jumpsuits, while Keith insisted on having each hotel room he stayed at decorated floor to ceiling with Persian carpets and drapes from his collection, which he said were necessary to give him peace of mind. As had become the norm, he also brought along eighteen guitars and his own personal guitar tech to tune them. It was a far cry from 1962. The band played numerous songs from the new album, including "Fool to Cry," "Hot Stuff, "Hey Negrita" and "Hand of Fate," as well as set regulars "Brown Sugar," "Honky Tonk Women" and "Street Fighting Man." They continued, however, to ignore their early hits. The only number in the set recorded before 1968 was a quick version of "Get Off of My Cloud" played (as they had on the 1975 U.S. tour) as a medley with "If You Can't Rock Me." "(I Can't Get No) Satisfaction" remained absent. Keith was unapologetic. He told *Sounds*, "That's the problem with all these people relating to 'Satisfaction.' They just want you to take them back. They just want to drag you back.... If people aren't trying to drag us back they're just looking for someone else to do it and pretending those bands are the Stones."

The Stones played in some countries that they'd never before visited, including Yugoslavia and Spain. The tour also included a week of sold-out shows in London. However, the UK shows were overshadowed by Keith's continuing problems with the law. His heroin addiction had not gone away and he was arrested on May 18 after crashing his car on the way home from a show in Stafford. Once again, Keith was fortunate. Despite being found guilty of possession of LSD and cocaine, he spent no time in jail and only had to pay a £2,000 fine. Unfortunately this was not the end of Keith's problems. In June, while the Stones were performing in Paris, he received word that his 10-week old son, Tara (born on March 26), had suffocated in his crib in Switzerland and died. Fortunately, Keith had taken his then seven-year-old son Marlon on the road with him. As Keith related in *Life*, "I don't have enough time to cry about this, I've got to make sure this kid is all right. Thank God he was there." The show went on, but Keith and Anita's relationship never recovered. It also only increased their use of heroin and other narcotics to ease the pain. Keith's domestic troubles were reaching a climax and would finally boil over in 1977.

## Concerts

**Wednesday, April 28, and Thursday, April 29:** Festhalle, Frankfurt, West Germany, with the Meters, nightly at 8

After two weeks of rehearsals in France, the Stones headed to Frankfurt for the opening date of their European tour. A large entourage that included tour manager Peter Rudge and musicians Ian Stewart, Ollie Brown and Billy Preston accompanied them. The Stones again gave Preston a short solo segment. He performed "Nothing from Nothing" and "Outa-Space" in the middle of the show. The group continued to employ the stage designs and props from their tour of the States, including the inflatable phallus and confetti-spewing dragon. There were the usual opening night kinks (Keith and Ron's guitars weren't plugged in until the third number) but John Ingham of *Sounds* reported, "You Can't Always Get What You Want' is when things really took off, maintained through a wildly rocking 'Midnight Rambler' and the last two numbers 'Jumping Jack Flash' built and built into so much jangling noise and 'Street Fighting Man' just compounded it. It sounded really great."

The full set for the first show consisted of: "Honky Tonk Women," "If You Can't Rock Me/Get Off of My Cloud," "Hand of Fate," "All Down the Line," "Hey Negrita," "Tumbling Dice," "Ain't Too Proud to Beg," "Fool to Cry," "Star Star," "Hot Stuff," "You Gotta Move," "You Can't Always Get What You Want," "Midnight Rambler," "Nothing from Nothing," "Outa-Space," "It's Only Rock 'n' Roll," "Brown Sugar," "Jumping Jack Flash" and "Street Fighting Man." The second show consisted of the same set, minus "All Down the Line," which was replaced by "Happy" on most future dates.

**Friday, April 30:** Munsterlandhalle, Munster, West Germany, with the Meters, 7 and 10:45 p.m.

**Sunday, May 2:** Ostseehalle, Kiel, West Germany, with the Meters, 8 p.m.

The Stones initially planned to play in Hamburg but the show was moved to Kiel at the last minute. The band traveled there a day earlier to shoot promotional films for "Fool to Cry," "Crazy Mama," "Hey Negrita" and "Hot Stuff" with British director Michael Lindsay-Hogg. *The Kiel News* reported, "A dragon spewed Confetti into the audience, Mick Jagger grabbed a water bucket and cooled the fans, before pouring the last bucket over himself: 'Good night!' The biggest rock music event in the history of the Ostseehalle was finished. Impatient fans had stood for hours in front of the Ostseehalle ... and waited until just before 11 p.m., before the Rolling Stones opened their program with 'Honky Tonk Women.' For ninety minutes, Mick Jagger danced around the stage, raising his voice and movement in harmony with the rhythm of his band.... About 8,000 fans listened to old and new songs.... The Stones offered a perfect rock show, showing that they are still the greatest after 14 years, the 'bad boys' of rock music—loud, wild and aggressive."

**Monday, May 3:** Deutschlandhalle, Berlin, West Germany, with the Meters, 8 p.m.

Part of this concert was filmed by German SFB TV, including portions of "Hey Negrita," "Hot Stuff" and "Star Star."

**Tuesday, May 4:** Stadthalle, Bremen, West Germany, with the Meters, 9 p.m.

The Stones arrived in Bremen from Hamburg in six limousines to play before 8,000 fans. It was their first appearance in the city since 1967 and authorities were convinced a riot would occur but *The Weser Kurier* reported that "In fact, the Bremen 'beat friends' behaved by and large in a civilized manner last evening. Just like nine years ago, when The Rolling Stones last performed in the hanseatic city, the crowd generally knew to reign in their spirits despite their excitement about the explosive show. Probably also in order not 'to miss' some of the gentler songs, and thus see their quick acquisition of the tickets (which have been sold out for weeks) rewarded."

**Thursday, May 6, and Friday, May 7:** Forest National, Brussels, Belgium, with the Meters, Thursday at 8:30 p.m. and Friday at 7 p.m.

**Monday, May 10, to Wednesday, May 12:** Apollo Theatre, Glasgow, Scotland, UK, with the Meters, nightly at 7:30

After a short break, the Stones began the UK leg of the tour. The venue was tiny by current Stones standards and Bill joked to a reporter, "It's really cramping my style. I just can't jump about like I usually do." Thames TV filmed the show on May 12 for the TV special *Stones on the Road*, though only a portion of "Street Fighting Man" ended up in the broadcast. The Stones and their crew also filmed interviews that appeared in the show on that day. The set list on Monday consisted of "Honky Tonk Women," "If You Can't Rock Me/Get Off of My Cloud," "Hand of Fate," "Hey Negrita," "Ain't Too Proud to Beg," "Fool to Cry," "Hot Stuff," "Star Star," "You Gotta Move," "You Can't Always Get What You Want," "Happy," "Tumbling Dice," "Nothing from Nothing," "Outa-Space," "Midnight Rambler," "It's Only Rock 'n' Roll," "Brown Sugar," "Jumping Jack Flash" and

Poster for the Stones' concert in Berlin on May 3, 1976 (collection of Ira Korman).

"Street Fighting Man." *The Glasgow Herald* reported "Blues-based, unrelenting rock is still dominant…. The Stones still deliver the goods though. The band is tight, working well, and augmented last night by the worthwhile addition of keyboards wizard Billy Preston-whose own solo spot was alas too short-plus percussionist Ollie Brown. Mick Jagger is the front man and he hasn't mellowed. Rock's the thing and Mick's the king."

In his book *Life*, Keith commented that Billy Preston's presence in the band sometimes created tension, as Preston was used to showing off. At the first show in Glasgow, Keith felt he played too loud and drowned out the band. He confronted him in his own inimitable fashion: "I took him backstage and showed him the blade. 'You know what this is Bill? Dear William. If you don't turn that fucking thing down right now, you're going to feel it!'" Preston's reaction is unrecorded, but he must have complied enough to please Keith, as he remained with the band.

**Friday, May 14, and Saturday, May 15:** Granby Hall, Leicester, England, UK, with the Meters, nightly at 8

Thames TV filmed the second show and portions of "Honky Tonk Women," "Star Star," "Midnight Rambler," "Brown Sugar," "It's Only Rock 'n' Roll" and "Jumping Jack Flash" appeared on the broadcast. Eric Clapton guested on guitar for concert closers "Jumping Jack Flash" and "Street Fighting Man." Simon Frith of *Creem* was impressed enough to declare, "The Stones were the best rock 'n' roll band I've ever seen and they were hard and harsh and nonsense-free. Keith Richard is back in his chunky lead role and Charlie Watts was wonderful beyond words."

**Monday, May 17, and Tuesday, May 18:** New Bingley Hall, Stafford, England, UK, with the Meters, nightly at 8

While on tour, the Stones gave extensive interviews for the documentary *Stones on the Road*. Asked his views on touring, Charlie commented: "I love playing the drums and I love playing with the Rolling Stones. I mean my wife always says I like them more than I do her. Which isn't true! … But I think they're great and I love playing with them…. I thought I packed up four times doing gigs, I mean to myself I have and my family. I thought that's it. But I don't know what to do. I don't know what I'd enjoy as much. It's very difficult. I wish I were a writer or painter because, you know, you've got it all there." Asked about life on the road, Keith commented, "You must be fit just to do it every night. You've got to be in pretty good condition to go from three or four months in the studio and living at home to leaping onstage out of nowhere. If you weren't in good shape, you wouldn't make it. I've never had to worry about my body. I've been used to punishing it."

**Friday, May 21, to Sunday, May 23, and Tuesday, May 25, to Thursday, May 27:** Earl's Court Arena, London, England, UK, with the Meters, nightly at 8

To drum up interest for their London shows, Keith leaked a phony story to the media that he planned to marry Anita live on stage. In reality the Stones needed no publicity. Demand in the UK was so great that they ended up adding extra shows. Keith told *Sounds*, "Frankly England surprised us. Nobody in this band expected to play Earl's Court more than one night. There was no reaction in 1973 to indicate we'd be in that kind of demand. It really surprises you." The set was basically the same as on the rest of the tour, but London audiences were treated to a rare encore of "Sympathy for the Devil" that included clowns and circus performers onstage.

The full set on Friday consisted of: "Honky Tonk Women," "If You Can't Rock Me/Get

Special admission ticket for the Stones' 1976 European tour (collection of Ira Korman).

Off of My Cloud," "Hand of Fate," "Hey Negrita," "Ain't Too Proud to Beg," "Fool to Cry," "Hot Stuff," "Star Star," "You Gotta Move," "You Can't Always Get What You Want," "Happy," "Tumbling Dice," "Nothing from Nothing," "Outa-Space," "Midnight Rambler," "It's Only Rock 'n' Roll," "Brown Sugar," "Jumping Jack Flash," "Street Fighting Man" and "Sympathy for the Devil." Nick Kent was pleasantly surprised by changes to the band since he'd seen them in 1973. He'd felt that Keith was becoming peripheral due to his relegation to rhythm guitar by Mick Taylor and was happy to see that with the addition of Ron Wood, "It was Keith ... who played the solo on 'Honky Tonk Women,' who paced the thing, who damn near called all the heavy guitar shots while Ron Wood chunked away merrily on rhythm." However, critics noted that the sound at Earl's Court was abysmal. There were so many complaints that the Stones played an extra show in August to appease their loyal fans. Despite these problems, the gigs were recorded and a performance of "If You Can't Rock Me/Get Off of My Cloud" heard on *Love You Live* comes from the May 27 show, though it was "fixed" in the studio.

**Saturday, May 29, and Sunday, May 30:** Stadion F.C. Den Haag, The Hague, Netherlands, with Robin Trower, the Meters and Kokomo, daily at 4 p.m.

The Stones performed two well-attended shows. The newspaper *Het Vrije Volk* reported, "The first real highlight of the concert was a long version of 'You Can't Always Get What You Want.' Keith Richards and Mick Jagger sang into the same microphone and the audience sang the chorus. But Keith Richards then sang 'Happy' from *Exile on Main Street* in such a bad voice that the momentum was lost... 'Midnight Rambler' was the next highlight.... It was followed by 'It's Only Rock 'n' Roll,' with Ron Wood and Keith Richards singing the chorus and Jagger screaming "I like it.' ... A swinging version of 'Brown Sugar' was then followed by 'Jumping Jack Flash' and the finale 'Street

Fighting Man.' The Stones sounded much better at the end than in the middle of the concert."

**Tuesday, June 1:** Westfalenhalle, Dortmund, West Germany, with the Meters, 8 p.m.

The Stones performed in Germany on Ron Wood's birthday and Mick got the crowd to sing "Happy Birthday" to him at the gig.

**Wednesday, June 2:** Sporthalle, Cologne, West Germany, with the Meters, 5 and 9 p.m.

The Stones played two concerts in sweltering heat for 13,000 fans. At the first show, Mick greeted the crowd by shouting "Hello, Cologne, how are you?" *The Kölner Express* reported that Mick "vehemently threw himself into the role of a clown that no one should take seriously. Then every audience member forgot that he had resented having to wait forty minutes for the star group to make its appearance after the end of the supporting program."

**Friday, June 4, to Monday, June 7:** Pavilion De Paris (Les Abattoirs), Paris, France, with the Meters and John Miles, nightly at 8

The Stones performed four shows under trying circumstances. While there, Keith learned that his young son Tara had died. But the shows went on anyway. The Stones chose to play at Les Abattoirs, situated in the northern part of the city because, as Mick told *The Old Grey Whistle Test*, "It was the only place that was unfashionable. The trouble with the French is that they try to make everything into an occasion, which is laudable. But they turn up in evening dress and diamonds, even when we did the Palais Des Sports, which is like the equivalent of Wembley Pool. Anyways, the Abattoir was sufficiently disgusting that we thought we could obviate that. But even then we had to make a special section for people dressed in evening dress and diamonds." The set for the opener consisted of: "Honky Tonk Women," "If You Can't Rock Me/Get Off of My Cloud," "Hand of Fate," "Hey Negrita," "Ain't Too Proud to Beg," "Fool to Cry," "Hot Stuff," "Star Star," "You Gotta Move," "Angie," "You Can't Always Get What You Want," "Happy," "Tumbling Dice," "Nothing from Nothing," "Outa-Space," "Midnight Rambler," "It's Only Rock 'n' Roll," "Brown Sugar," "Jumping Jack Flash" and "Street Fighting Man." The set remained the same all four nights, though the Stones added "Cherry Oh Baby" at the last show.

The band recorded all the Paris concerts. Most of the material on the LP *Love You Live* came from these gigs. The performances of "Honky Tonk Women," "Happy" and "You Gotta Move" were recorded at the June 5 show. "Hot Stuff," "Brown Sugar," "Jumping Jack Flash" and "Star Star" were taped on June 6 and "Tumbling Dice" and "You Can't Always Get What You Want" were taped on June 7. All apparently received studio overdubs in 1977. In addition to recording the gigs, the Stones allowed a French crew to film them for a television show titled *Les Rolling Stones aux Abattoirs* that aired in 1977. It featured performances from all four nights.

**Wednesday, June 9:** Palais Des Sports, Lyon, France, with the Meters and John Miles, 5 p.m.

A tape of this show makes the rounds and is one of the best concerts from this period that I've heard. Ron Wood plays exceptional guitar throughout and Billy Preston adds fantastic energy to the proceedings. Mick was in strong voice as well. *The Progress* reported, "For lovers of rock and pop music, last night was a milestone.... Thirteen years after their first success, the Stones remain faithful to their influences, they remain into their music … they are still vibrant, sometimes touching and deliberately challenging....

The crowd of 15,000 listened to (Mick) singing old and newer hits with a calm, almost worshipful air."

**Friday, June 11:** Plaza Des Toros Monumental, Barcelona, Spain, with Inconnu and the John Miles Band, 9 p.m.

The Stones performed in Spain for the first time. Asked by a Spanish TV crew why they'd never played there before, Charlie bluntly replied, "You're just a bunch of fascists!" But Franco was gone and the Stones made the trip at the urging of promoter Gay Mercado. Only 11,000 fans turned out to see them but Mercado later recalled "the electric atmosphere" at one of the first big rock concerts in Spain. The country was just emerging from years of repression and the Stones encountered a few problems. There were massive protests outside the venue by the Grays a group that felt the show should be free. Smoke bombs went off and authorities clashed with the people outside. Spain was a very Catholic country as well and Mick and Ronnie had a fight with the concierge at their hotel when he refused to let them bring two ladies to their rooms because they weren't married. Robin Trower and the Meters were advertised as appearing but were both absent. *La Vanguardia* reported, "They did their usual show, more or less, a selection of their well known songs ... highlighted by the constant contortions of Mick Jagger, the conscientious playing by Charlie Watts on drums, the dedication of Keith Richard, the imperturbable Bill Wyman and, now, the clarity of new guitarist Ron Wood, who has become one of the stars of the band. The work of these musicians ... was irreproachable." *El Pais* commented, "The best moments were with songs like "You've Got to Move" that included the audience's participation in the chorus, 'Midnight Rambler' with Mick Jagger's incredible performance and the final songs 'It's Only Rock 'n' Roll,' 'Brown Sugar,' 'Jumping Jack Flash' and 'Street Fighting Man,' with which they ended."

**Sunday, June 13:** Stade De L'Ouest, Nice, France, with Robin Trower and the Meters, 7 p.m.

The Stones played before a crowd of 20,000 fans.

**Tuesday, June 15:** Hallenstadion, Zurich, Switzerland, with the Meters, 7 p.m.

The show in Zurich started very late. Despite this, the reviewer from *Die TAT* praised, "The quality of the show, the hard work the Stones put into their performance (and) the spontaneity and excitement of Mick Jagger.... Most of the songs from the Rolling Stones were sung by the fans at the concert ... starting with the blockbuster "Honky Tonk Women." For around 90 minutes the Stones strove to bring their audience to a inspiring frenzy, until the half-naked Mick Jagger reached the final medley and emptied a water bucket into the audience and onto himself."

**Wednesday, June 16, and Thursday, June 17:** Olympiahalle, Munich, West Germany, with the Meters, nightly at 8

The two nights in Munich proved stressful, as the militant Baader-Meinhof Group threatened to blow up the Olympiahalle. Nothing ultimately happened but the Stones were rattled.

**Saturday, June 19:** Neckarstadion, Stuttgart, West Germany, with the Meters, the John Miles Band and Little Feat, 4 p.m.

The Stones weren't at their best when they played before a crowd of 43,000. A number of songs simply trailed off when members of the band stopped playing. Keith was apparently in poor shape.

Poster for the Stones' appearance in Stuttgart on June 19, 1976 (collection of Ira Korman).

**Monday, June 21, and Tuesday, June 22:** Sportska Dvorana, Zagreb, Yugoslavia, with the Meters, nightly at 8

The Stones made their first appearance in a Communist country since 1967. Zagreb had witnessed Jethro Tull and Frank Zappa, but the Stones' appearance was a big moment for a country still quite isolated. The shows attracted large crowds and passed without incident. But Mick had doubts about safety and opted not to swing on a rope over the crowd as he usually did on the tour. The Stones ultimately returned to Zagreb in 1998.

**Wednesday, June 23:** Stadthalle, Vienna, Austria, with the Meters, 7:30 p.m.

This concert attracted 10,000 fans. The *Arbeiter Zeitung* reported, "From the first moment 'The Bad Boys of Rock' had the fans in the palm of their hands.... Nevertheless, some songs were a little too slick, some were performed too routinely; some arrangements did not quite convince the crowd. But on songs like 'Fool to Cry,' 'Star Star,' 'You Got to Move' or 'Midnight Rambler' the audience went berserk. When Mick Jagger, dressed in red pants and a green jacket, danced with the excellent Billy Preston on the stage, jumped, vulgarly wiggled his hips or rolled on the ground, he knew that he had the young people in the audience as excited as the fans who have remained loyal for a decade."

This was the last show of the tour and the Stones headed home to rest. However, the band had discussed playing a U.S. tour after the European one ended. Mick particularly wanted to play in the U.S. on July 4, as part of the bicentennial celebrations and a venue was booked in LA. The Stones tentatively booked other dates as well. The dates planned were: Seattle (July 1), Los Angeles (July 4), Cincinnati, Chicago or St. Louis (July

THE ROLLING STONES U.S. TOUR

| DATE | TOWN | VENUE | CAPACITY |
|---|---|---|---|
| July 1 | SEATTLE | DOME STADIUM | 75-85,000 Not set,'cos no show before but will limit cap. |
| July 2nd | OFF | | |
| July 3rd | OAKLAND | STADIUM | 55,000 |
| July 4th | LOS ANGELES | COLISEUM | 100,000 |
| July 5th | OFF | | |
| July 6th | OFF | | |
| July 7th | CINCINNATTI | RIVERFRONT STADIUM | 40,000 |
| | ST. LOUIS | BUSCH STADIUM | 40,000 |
| | CHICAGO | SOLDIERS FIELD | 70,000 |
| July 8th | OFF | | |
| July 9th | WASHINGTON | RFK STADIUM | approx. 50,000 dome expansion |
| July 10th | PITTSBURG | THREE RIVERS STADIUM | TBA |
| JULY 11th | PHILADELPHIA | JFK STADIUM | 125,000 |
| July 12th | OFF | | |
| JULY 13th | OFF | | |
| July 14th | ATLANTA | BRAVES STADIUM | 55,000 poss. More |
| July 15th | OFF | | |
| July 16th | TORONTO | CNE STADIUM | 70,000 |
| July 17th | MONTREAL | | |

**Document outlining a tentative tour of the United States that would have followed the 1976 European tour. The tour did not take place (collection of Ira Korman).**

7), Washington, D.C. (July 9) Pittsburgh (July 10), Philadelphia (July 11), Atlanta (July 14), Toronto (July 16) and Montreal (July 17). However, by the time the European tour wound down the Stones were too exhausted. They still considered playing a July 17 show at the Montreal Forum, in conjunction with the opening of the Olympics, but negotiations collapsed. Mick did, however, attend some of the games with his father. On July 31 Ron

Wood joined Eric Clapton onstage at London's Crystal Palace Bowl for a version of "Further on Up the Road."

**Saturday, August 21:** Knebworth Park, Stevenage, England, with the Don Harrison Band, Hot Tuna, Todd Rundgren, Lynyrd Skynyrd and 10cc, 2 p.m.

Promoter Fred Bannister had begun staging shows at Knebworth, on the grounds of the Lytton-Cobbold family, in 1974 and it had become an annual event. He'd tried to get the Stones in 1975 but they were busy and Pink Floyd played instead. Bannister remained persistent, however, and met with the Stones in Munich in June, where they agreed to do it. A crowd of 130,000 people attended the concert, the biggest audience the Stones had played for in the UK since Hyde Park. Many celebrities showed up, including Jack Nicholson, Van Morrison, Jim Capaldi, Paul and Linda McCartney and John Phillips. This was one of the first UK shows to feature video screens, so the audience could see the performers up close even from far away. The technology was so new that Michael Lindsay-Hogg was called on to direct the whole thing.

The Stones took the stage four hours later than scheduled, at 11:30 p.m., and the audience was tired. But many perked up when they opened with "(I Can't Get No) Satisfaction," which they hadn't played since 1972. In fact, the Stones dipped into their Decca catalog quite a bit, playing songs they hadn't played in years, as well as a few (such as "Country Honk") they'd never performed. Many critics, however, felt that the Stones were sloppy and under-rehearsed. To my ears, they also sound a little stoned but it was still clearly a fun show. The full set consisted of "(I Can't Get No) Satisfaction," "Ain't Too Proud to Beg," "If You Can't Rock Me/Get Off of My Cloud," "Hand of Fate," "Around and Around," "Little Red Rooster," "Stray Cat Blues," "Hey Negrita," "Hot Stuff," "Fool to Cry," "Star Star," "Let's Spend the Night Together," "You Gotta Move," "You Can't Always

Ticket for the Stones' concert at Knebworth on August 21, 1976 (collection of Ira Korman).

Get What You Want," "Dead Flowers," "Route 66," "Wild Horses," "Honky Tonk Women," "Country Honk," "Tumbling Dice," "Happy," "Nothing from Nothing," "Outa-Space," "Midnight Rambler," "It's Only Rock 'n' Roll," "Brown Sugar," "Rip This Joint," "Jumping Jack Flash" and "Street Fighting Man."

While the Stones played no shows in the fall, on November 25 Woody made a guest appearance at The Band's final concert at Winterland in San Francisco. He joined Bob Dylan, Van Morrison, Neil Young, Eric Clapton and other musicians for the encore "I Shall Be Released." The performance was filmed by Martin Scorsese and appeared in the 1978 film *The Last Waltz*.

## Chapter 16

# 1977

The year started off promisingly but 1977 became something of a lost year for the Stones, though it was not necessarily intended that way. The band's contracts with Atlantic and WEA were up and the Stones negotiated a stunning new deal. Atlantic Records won the right to continue to distribute the Stones records in the U.S. and Canada by offering them the (then) astronomical sum of $21 million for six albums, but EMI became the Stones' label in the rest of the world by shelling out £7 million. The Stones were busy compiling a live album for the last release of their old contract. There were many tapes from the 1975 and 1976 tours to listen to and cull songs from but most of the recordings on the LP *Love You Live* came from their shows in Paris in 1976. However, the Stones felt that the album was missing something and opted to record a few new shows at a small club in Toronto to give the LP more variety. The band flew to Canada in February to rehearse for the gigs, their first club appearance since the Marquee taping in 1971. But, things did not go according to plan. When Keith arrived in Canada on February 24, customs officers searched Anita and found 10 grams of hashish and a small amount of heroin on her. She was charged with drug possession. Anita was released on bail, but the Royal Canadian Mounted Police knew that where there was smoke there was probably also fire and on February 27 they raided Keith and Anita's room at the Harbour Castle Hotel. Keith was asleep, but next to his bed was a bag with an ounce of heroin in it. He was arrested and charged with possession of drugs with intent to traffic. He and Anita were ordered to remain in Canada until the trial date.

Although Keith tried to put a positive spin on the arrest, the situation was very troublesome for him and for the Stones. Drug trafficking was a serious crime and Keith was potentially facing a life sentence if convicted. He had already been charged with possession in the past, which meant the judge might not go easy on him. Even if he only got a few months, another drug conviction would affect his ability to travel and pass through customs in other countries. Verne Jervis of U.S. Immigration Service commented, "Mr. Richards has obtained waivers on prior convictions enabling him to tour the U.S. with his band. Obviously, the more offenses you pile up, the harder it is to get a visa." Countries like Japan refused to allow people with major drug convictions into the country. The Stones' ability to tour with Keith was in doubt but Mick remained outwardly calm. He told Nick Kent of *NME*, "It could be anything from him being landed with a life sentence, to him having to report to the Canadian authorities every week…. They could do just anything. They could put him in a hospital for months, they could … oh, anything. And I seriously haven't made any plans for any of these eventualities."

The Stones could have canceled the club gigs but they were already there and Keith was happy to have something to do. He told CBC Radio "For me it was a great relief to get up and do it, after all that other shit (happened) that was unintended." So on March 4 and 5 the Stones played at the tiny El Mocambo Club. But the gigs were overshadowed by a new brouhaha that developed. Mick had become acquainted with Canadian Prime Minister Pierre Trudeau's wife, Margaret, and she was invited to the gig. Afterwards, she left with Mick in his limo and the Canadian press went bananas. Although it later became public knowledge that the Trudeaus were estranged (and that she was actually spending time with Ron Wood), at the time the media thought that Margaret was cheating on her husband with Mick. The Stones eventually flew home, but Keith and Anita remained "prisoners" in Toronto. On March 14 Anita was let off with a small fine, but Keith was ordered to stand trial on June 27. The media attacked him for being a druggie and "setting a bad example" for youth. But Keith explained to Barbara Charone, "Nobody gets up and says 'I'm taking dope and you should too' ... they say that the Rolling Stones and rock musicians in general are corrupting the kids but if they just left us alone, and didn't come looking for drugs, no one would know if we had a drug problem or not."

Button produced by fans to support Keith Richards during his drug trial in Toronto in 1977 (collection of Ira Korman).

To keep from going stir crazy, Keith spent some time with Stu in a local studio, recording country tunes like "Apartment No. 9" and "Worried Man Blues." Fortunately for Keith, the Canadian government eased the pressure by allowing him to leave the country in April, provided he returned for the trial. The Jimmy Carter administration in the United States had a liberal policy on drug addiction and helped Keith get a visa to come to Philadelphia to receive an experimental treatment with Dr. Meg Patterson. The Canadian courts gave Keith an extension to complete his treatment. Keith continued to fool around with heroin but slowly weaned himself off it. By the time his case came to court in October 1978 he was able to tell the judge that he had "kicked" it. Anita, however, was allegedly not ready for "the cure" and Keith made the decision to make a clean break from her.

In the meantime, *Love You Live* was released on September 23. It had some strong moments. Mick's vocals on the El Mocambo side were quite good (especially on a reggae inspired "Crackin' Up") and the Stones' sounded strong on rockers like "Happy" and "Star Star." But the playing was sloppy and lacked the energy of *Got Live If You Want It* or the finesse and commitment of *Get Yer Ya Ya's Out*. Ron Wood certainly had guitar-playing ability but didn't add anything notable to songs Mick Taylor had shined on, like "You Can't Always Get What You Want." Jagger sounded less interested than he had in 1969, even like a parody of himself. The LP seemed to demonstrate that the band had been transformed for good or ill from a tight blues-based band into a shambolic, anything goes, rock 'n' roll band like the Faces.

As the year drew to a close, the Stones holed up in Pathé Marconi Studios outside

Paris to begin work on their next LP. The UK music scene had been transformed by the punk revolution. Bands like the Stranglers and the Sex Pistols now took up the charts. Many people were questioning whether the Stones still had relevance. The punks sought to obliterate all that had come before and the decadent Stones seemed an easy target. Johnny Rotten declared that the Stones were over the hill and "should've retired in 1965!" Mick professed not to mind. He told Chet Flippo, "Everything Johnny Rotten says about me is only 'cause he loves me 'cause I'm so good.... But they've got something different, in a way, they've got lots of *energy,* and that's what rock and roll needs. And I would prefer to hear those bands than a lot of shit that goes on the Hollywood rock awards." But the Stones needed to prove they mattered. The year 1978 would put them to the test.

## Concerts

**Friday, March 4, and Saturday, March 5:** El Mocambo Club, Toronto, Canada, with April Wine

The Stones played these club dates accompanied by Billy Preston and Ollie Brown for their upcoming live album. They tried to appear under the radar by sneaking into town and billing themselves as the Cockroaches. The venue was chosen by Mick, who explained to Goldrush Radio, "I just happened to go there one night.... But we went specifically to record there, it wasn't just to play (a club). We wanted to record some different numbers for this album." Asked how it was to play in a club in 1977 versus 1963, Mick said "Well it's very similar but we didn't have such high powered critics (sitting there) in 1963... It's easier in a way playing in clubs than it is in big halls. You can hear people. You can relate to people, you can talk to people very easily. There's not the pressure to dance as much. It's easier. (But) I was a bit apprehensive the first night because I didn't know how it was going to be. I don't know what the people would be like.... But they were very warm and it was very easy to get into it." Keith was happy to be in a club setting and to play some old R&B numbers. He told the CBC, "They're the sort of things that you don't get to do much in concert because they're real club numbers and you need to be filling the room completely.... Also, those are the sort of numbers that we use to do two or three times a night when we started off. So it was a good opportunity

Ticket for the Stones' appearance at the El Mocambo Club in Toronto in 1977. The band was billed as the Cockroaches (collection of Ira Korman).

to put down (on vinyl) some of the other sort of things that we'd missed out (on recording) in the beginning."

The set on March 4 consisted of "Route 66," "Honky Tonk Women," "Hand of Fate," "Fool to Cry," "Crazy Mama," "Crackin' Up," "Around and Around," "Melody," "Star Star," "Worried About You," "Let's Spend the Night Together," "Little Red Rooster," "Luxury," "Brown Sugar" and "Jumping Jack Flash." The set on March 5 consisted of "Honky Tonk Women," "All Down the Line," "Hand of Fate," "Route 66," "Fool to Cry," "Crazy Mama," "Mannish Boy," "Crackin' Up," "Dance Little Sister," "Around and Around," "Tumbling Dice," "Happy," "Hot Stuff," "Star Star," "Worried About You," "Let's Spend the Night Together," "Worried Life Blues," "It's Only Rock 'n' Roll," "Rip This Joint," "Little Red Rooster," "Luxury," "Brown Sugar" and "Jumping Jack Flash." The Stones ultimately opted to include "Mannish Boy," "Crackin' Up," "Little Red Rooster" and "Around and Around" on the LP. It is not certain which of the two nights the songs were recorded, but according to Bill Wyman the band felt that they were better on the second night so most likely the recordings come from that show. Keith told Chet Flippo, "The first night, the band sounds like it was playing for something in New Delhi; there were these weird sort of quarter tones, out of tune, very frantic; it was all adrenalin."

While the Stones as a band stayed away from the concert stage for the rest of the year, individual members continued to play the occasional gig with their mates. On March 18, Ron Wood joined the Eagles at Madison Square Garden in New York for an encore performance. He also played a show for charity in London at the Halfmoon with Jimmy Page on September 17. Bill Wyman joined Muddy Waters for a gig on July 23 at the Montreaux Jazz Festival.

## Chapter 17

# 1978

As 1978 began the Stones were in Paris completing their next album, *Some Girls*. The punk challenge gave the Stones a much-needed kick in the ass. The band rose to the occasion with one last great LP. Keith credited engineer/producer Chris Kimsey for making the album special. In *Life* he recalled, "We had to pull something out, not make another Stones in the doldrums album. He wanted to get a live sound back and move away from the clean and clinical recordings we slipped into." Kimsey convinced the band to record in a primitive "rehearsal studio" with an old-fashioned sound console. It gave the LP a real rock 'n' roll feel. Mick and Keith composed some fast, energetic songs in the punk mode like "Lies," "Shattered," "Respectable" and "When the Whip Comes Down." But the Stones refused to be confined to one style. Mick had been spending time in New York at the clubs and was keen to record a song in the disco style, which became the funky classic "Miss You." And Keith's renewed interest in country music led to the hilarious but oddly moving "Far Away Eyes." He also recorded arguably his best lead vocal on the autobiographical "Before They Make Me Run." And the Glimmer Twins composed one of their best-ever ballads, "Beast of Burden."

The album was released on June 9 to mostly excellent reviews. It quickly raced up the charts, spending 32 weeks on the U.S. *Billboard* charts and reaching number one. In the UK, despite the punk invasion, it made it to a respectable number 2. To promote it the Stones headed out for another North American tour. But Mick dithered about how many dates he wanted to play and the itinerary continued to be changed until the first concerts commenced in Florida. Indeed, the tour was booked so late that the Stones had to travel on commercial planes, as they couldn't find a private plane to charter on such short notice. The tour was relatively short, with 25 shows scheduled. As a result there was less hype and excess than on previous tours. The stage setup was noticeably stripped down. It was just the Stones and a few extra musicians with no giant props, backing singers or synthesizers in sight. Even Mick seemed deglamorized. He dispensed with his outrageous jumpsuits in favor of a simple cap and a blazer. Mick was uneasy about the prospect of playing just stadiums so they played some small halls as well. It was as if the Stones had momentarily tired of all the glitz and excess and just fancied playing some old-fashioned concerts.

As usual, the Stones were uncompromising in their set lists. The band usually played seven or eight new songs from *Some Girls* at the shows and dispensed with many crowd-pleasing tour staples, like "Midnight Rambler" and "You Can't Always Get What You Want." This worked well in smaller venues, where fans were excited to be so close to the band and willing to listen to new music, but brought the energy level down in stadium shows, where rowdy audiences tuned out when oldies weren't played. The new songs featured the debut of Mick playing guitar. He seemed to enjoy dueling with Ronnie and Keith, but looked more comfortable without the restraints of the instrument. Each night he also sat down and played piano on country tune "Far Away Eyes." The reggae artist Peter Tosh, who'd recently been signed to Rolling Stones Records, served as opening act for most of the dates and Mick sometimes came out to perform "Don't Look Back" with him.

The tour received many negative reviews from rock critics. Dave Marsh of *Rolling Stone*, who attended early shows in New York and Philadelphia, spoke for the naysayers. He called the Stones "awful" and argued that they were past their prime. In an article entitled "The Rolling Stones: Just Another Rock Band?" he questioned whether the Stones were still deserving of the title of greatest rock 'n' roll band. He stated that most of the new songs were derivative of past glories and commented "What the program really did point up is how much the quality of the group's material has slipped: anyone who can listen to 'Star Star,' hardly the greatest Stones song, back to back with 'Whip,' which is near the top of the new crop, and not think the band has lost a great deal in the past five years just isn't paying attention." Asked about the tour's critics by *Rolling Stone's* Chet Flippo, Mick was dismissive: "I don't care about them. The kids are what I want. We don't want critics. They ought to fuck off. The stuff they write is rubbish…. I mean, one of the reviewers reviewed the 1975 show. They think 'Let It Rock' is 'Johnny B. Goode.' They don't even ask for a song list. You don't need those people." But Mick clearly was upset by the reviews. Indeed he denied *Rolling Stone* access to the Stones after Marsh's review was published.

To be fair to Marsh, it's clear that your opinion of the Stones in 1978 depended on what night you saw them. Tapes of some shows are indeed listless and sloppy. The Stones seemed burned out on arena shows and their performances at many of them were subpar. But other concerts in smaller venues, like the Capitol Theater in Passaic or the filmed show at Fort Worth, are a wonder to hear with tight playing and high energy. If Ron Wood was not the melodic soloist Mick Taylor had been, he nevertheless brought a punk like energy to the Stones and Bill and Charlie continued to supply incredible rhythm behind them. Many fans hold concert tapes of the 1978 tour in high regard, recognizing that it was one of the last times the Stones discarded the bullshit and just concentrated on music. Critic Lisa Robison declared, "The Stones have never played better than they have been playing on this tour. It's as simple as that."

Following the tour, Keith headed back to Toronto for his trial. The future of the Stones hung on the decision of a judge. On the advice of his lawyer, Keith pleaded guilty to heroin possession and, much to his relief, was given a suspended sentence and a year of probation. He agreed to continue his substance abuse treatment and to play a concert for the Canadian Institute for the Blind. The prosecution appealed the "light" sentence but in 1979 an appeals court confirmed the lower court's ruling. Keith was off the hook. To end the trying year on an upbeat note, he released his first solo single at holiday time. It was a fun cover of Chuck Berry's Christmas classic "Run Rudolph Run" that he'd recorded in November 1976, backed with a version of Jimmy Cliff's reggae anthem "The Harder They Come," recorded at the end of the tour.

## Concerts

**Saturday, June 10:** Civic Center, Lakeland, FL, with the Henry Paul Band, 8 p.m.

The Stones headed to Bearsville Studios in upstate New York in late May to rehearse

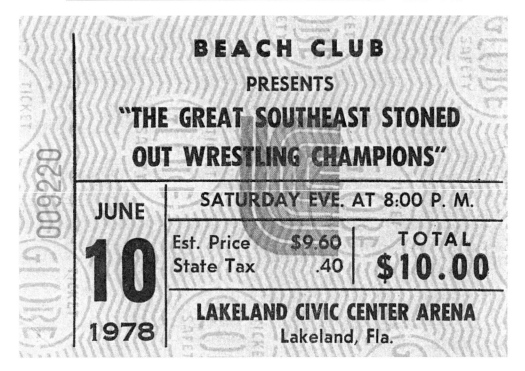

Ticket for the Stones' concert in Lakeland, Florida, on June 10, 1978. The Stones were billed as "The Great Southeast Stoned-Out Wrestling Champions" (collection of Ira Korman).

for the tour. It was a streamlined band, without extra percussion or synthesizers. Only Stu and Ian McLagan of the Faces, who'd agreed to play organ in place of Billy Preston, accompanied them. During rehearsals, ABC TV's *20/20* filmed interviews for use in a show that aired after the tour had begun and these are available as a bonus on the *Some Girls Live in Texas* DVD/Blu-ray. The opening show in Florida was not announced until the last minute, but a crowd of over 9,000 still turned out. The Stones chose to open away from the spotlight. Keith told *The London Sun*, "We've gotta get back to the people, to the audiences that made us. A lot of other rock and roll groups talk about this but it's all crap. We mean it." The Stones were billed as "The Great Southeast Stoned-Out Wrestling Champions!" The set consisted of: "Let It Rock," "All Down the Line," "Honky Tonk Women," "Star Star," "When the Whip Comes Down," "Miss You," "Beast of Burden," "Respectable," "Far Away Eyes," "Love in Vain," "Shattered," "Tumbling Dice," "Happy," "Brown Sugar," "Jumping Jack Flash" and "Street Fighting Man."

*The Lakeland Ledger* reported, "Few fans remained seated. They all stood, hands clapping over their head, screaming along with songs such as 'Honky Tonk Women.' The ebullient Jagger, microphone in hand, ranged over the stage, discarding his coat and tossing kisses to the women in the first row. They threw back scarves, which Jagger accepted to the accompaniment of their delighted screams." *The St. Petersburg Times* added, "Despite some crackling equipment (wireless microphones and guitars seemed to be the culprits) and the Civic Center's naturally atrocious acoustics, the Stones immediately established rapport…. A new selection 'Shattered' proved that Jagger and Richard remain a top writing team."

**Monday, June 12:** Fox Theater, Atlanta, GA, with Patti Smith, 8 p.m.

This was an unannounced "warm-up" gig at one of Atlanta's most famous movie palaces (the Stones were billed as "The Cockroaches"). Mick told Chet Flippo, "The smaller dates were added quickly, because we just wanted to get away from playing only the big places." About 4,000 people were treated to an opening set by Patti Smith. She told Lisa Robinson, "I saw the Rolling Stones on the Ed Sullivan Show and it changed my life…. No matter what happens, this night represents the completion of a cycle for me." Smith stood enrapt by the stage during the Stones' performance and Mick rewarded her by dousing her with a bucket of water. The Stones' set was different from the previous night, as the band tested out "Lies" and "Just My Imagination." The full set consisted of: "Let It Rock," "All Down the Line," "Honky Tonk Women," "Star Star," "Lies," "Miss You," "When the Whip Comes Down," "Beast of Burden," "Just My Imagination," "Respectable," "Far Away Eyes," "Love in Vain," "Shattered," "Tumbling Dice," "Happy," "Brown Sugar" and "Jumping Jack Flash."

**Wednesday, June 14:** Capitol Theater, Passaic, NJ, with Etta James, 8 p.m.

This show was again unannounced. Tickets were sold at the last minute at bars and record stores. The theater had a sign on the marquee that said, "Closed for repairs." About 3,500 lucky people attended. The band clearly enjoyed playing at this intimate venue and put on (in my opinion) one of the best shows of the tour. An enthusiastic Mick, dressed in a yellow sports coat, white cap, brown plastic pants and red socks, commented conspiratorially to the crowd, "It's nice to be here instead of the usual barns! I guess will have to play a few barns though." The set contained a rare encore of "Street Fighting Man." *Relix Magazine* reported, "No star shaped stages; no ten-foot rubber pricks; no distractions. Just basic rock and roll; and the show was that much better for it…. The greatest rock and roll band in the world is also a pallid description. In sixteen years the Rolling Stones have gathered no moss; instead they've learned the art of totally commanding a crowd. Any band that plays shows like that as regularly as they do deserve any praised heaped upon them."

**Thursday, June 15:** Warner Theater, Washington, D.C., with Etta James, 8 p.m.

This was the last "warm-up" show. Tickets went on sale on Tuesday and were quickly snatched up. The Stones played for 2,000 excited fans. The set was similar to the previous night, but they dropped "Lies" and added "Sweet Little Sixteen." Mick was run down and was given a shot of antibiotics by a doctor before going onstage. He told a reporter, "I have the flu. I feel terrible. I'll be all right tomorrow. Other than that, I feel great. The tour's going well, everyone's playing well, the audiences have been excellent. I'm very happy with the tour. Once I get rid of this cold, it'll get better." Nevertheless, *The Evening Star* reported, "The Stones put on the finest show they have ever given in Washington. Jagger is singing with authority. Richard, who usually looks like the grim reaper, actually smiles and does a little dancing of his own. Bass player Bill Wyman, the dime store Indian of the group, moves more in one night than he has in the previous three tours. Ron Wood is superb on guitar and Charlie Watts provides the sort of excellent rock drumming of which he is capable." The Stones were in the midst of final number "Jumping Jack Flash" when the power cut out in the building. When it did not come back on, they left the venue while boos rained down, marring an otherwise fantastic show.

**Saturday, June 17:** JFK Stadium, Philadelphia, PA, with Peter Tosh and Foreigner, 1 p.m.

Although Mick was still feeling the affects of the flu, the Stones played a huge stadium date in front of 90,000 people. The show was not one of their best. The full set consisted of: "Let It Rock," "All Down the Line," "Honky Tonk Women," "Star Star," "When the Whip Comes Down," "Miss You," "Just My Imagination," "Respectable," "Beast of Burden," "Far Away Eyes," "Love in Vain," "Shattered," "(I Can't Get No) Satisfaction," "Sweet Little Sixteen," "Tumbling Dice," "Happy," "Brown Sugar" and "Jumping Jack Flash." The band added crowd pleaser "(I Can't Get No) Satisfaction" to the set, but still got booed for playing too many new songs and no encore (the crowd seemed unaware that the Stones seldom played one). Indeed, the angry drunken crowd began pelting the stage with beer bottles and tore down the stage.

**Monday, June 19:** Palladium, New York City, NY, with Peter Tosh

The Stones made a last minute decision to play the 3,386-seater Palladium on 14th Street (formerly the Academy of Music, where they played in 1965). Indeed, many in their entourage were unaware that the gig was taking place until the night before. As he would occasionally do throughout the tour, Mick (dressed in red pants, white jacket and gold socks) joined Peter Tosh for his performance of "Don't Look Back" prior to the Stones' set. John Rockwell of *The New York Times* commented, "The set sprang to life with a fierce and desperate account of the new single 'Miss You' and sustained that intensity nearly the entire rest of the night…. Mr. Jagger was performing with a sense of personal involvement that was always compelling and sometimes almost frightening in its intensity."

**Wednesday, June 21:** Coliseum, Hampton, VA, with Peter Tosh, 8 p.m.

**Thursday, June 22:** Convention Center, Myrtle Beach, SC, with Peter Tosh, 8 p.m.

Showing their commitment to playing a fair number of small halls, the Stones appeared at the 2,100-seat Convention Center in Myrtle Beach, where they remained for the weekend. Dave Doubrava of *The Charleston News* reported, "Jagger danced. He pranced. He lunged around the stage screaming into the microphone to the beat of the English rock group's big bass guitars. And the audience loved it. For their part the audience was equally wild. They danced and pranced atop their seats and in fact didn't sit down for the first 35 minutes of the concert."

**Monday, June 26:** Coliseum, Greensboro, NC, with Peter Tosh, 8 p.m.

About 16,000 people attended. Tickets sold out quickly, as scalpers gobbled them up to resell them at exorbitant prices. Many thought it might be their last chance to see the band before Keith went to jail and were willing to pay. There was the usual controversy as the organization Women Against Violence Against Women protested outside the venue, due to anger over the band's sexist advertising for *Some Girls*.

**Wednesday, June 28:** Mid-South Coliseum, Memphis, TN, with Etta James, 8 p.m.

The set consisted of "Let It Rock," "All Down the Line," "Honky Tonk Women," "Star Star," "When the Whip Comes Down," "Miss You," "Lies," "Beast of Burden," "Just My Imagination," "Respectable," "Far Away Eyes," "Love in Vain," "Shattered," "Hound Dog" (a tribute to Memphis' favorite son Elvis Presley at this show and the next night at Lexington as well), "Tumbling Dice," "Happy," "Sweet Little Sixteen," "Brown Sugar," and "Jumping Jack Flash." Bob Clearmountain made a soundboard recording of this show and ten songs aired in 1979 on the *King Biscuit Flower Hour*.

**Thursday, June 29:** Rupp Arena, Lexington, KY, with Eddie Money, 8 p.m.

The Stones played to a record crowd (for Lexington) of 23,000. A soundboard recording exists and portions aired in 1979 on the *King Biscuit Flower Hour*. Opener Eddie Money (a New York singer who'd scored big with "Two Tickets to Paradise") joined the Stones to play sax on "Miss You" but many in the audience couldn't hear him because of technical difficulties. Indeed, Mick's vocals on opener "Honky Tonk Women" were nearly inaudible and problems continued throughout the night. Still the audience remained mesmerized by the band. Barry Bronson of *The Lexington Herald* commented, "Jagger played guitar and seemed to enjoy the interplay with Wood and Richard…. Songs from the past included 'Love in Vain' (performed with Woody on slide guitar), 'Tumbling Dice' (marred by Jagger's faulty wireless mike), 'Honky Tonk Women' and 'Brown Sugar.'"

**Saturday, July 1:** Municipal Stadium, Cleveland, OH, with Kansas and Peter Tosh, 1 p.m.

Concert poster for the Stones' 1978 U.S. tour (collection of Ira Korman).

The Stones sold all 82,000 tickets for their appearance at the annual "World Series of Rock," grossing $1,186,500. They were in a good but sloppy mood, missing the opening chords of "Let It Rock." Mick was particularly boisterous (and allegedly drunk). It rained continually throughout much of the show and Mick muttered "Rain, rain, rain" between songs. At one point during "Shattered" he slipped and fell to the floor but quickly brushed it off with the comment "I can't play standing up and I can't play sitting down." Commenting on the end of the show, Jane Scott of the *Plain Dealer* reported that during the finale of "Jumping Jack Flash," Mick "whipped off his shirt and strode topless to the wings of the stage, carrying an American flag. He wound up, after vigorous kicking and jumping; sitting on the floor, bending his head down so his forehead touched the floor. He gave a scissors kick and jump as he left the stage. The audience didn't need to see the flash across the scoreboard, 'Let's hear it for the Stones, ladies and gentlemen.'"

**Tuesday, July 4:** Rich Stadium, Orchard Park, NY, with April Wine, Journey and the Atlanta Rhythm Section, 2 p.m.

The Independence Day show attracted a huge audience of 80,000. The crowd arrived early and sat through six hours of music, while drinking and taking various substances. The Stones played their usual set consisting of "Let It Rock," "All Down the Line," "Honky Tonk Women," "Star Star," "When the Whip Comes Down," "Lies," "Miss You," "Beast of Burden," "Shattered," "Just My Imagination," "Respectable," "Far Away Eyes," "Love in Vain," "Tumbling Dice," "Happy," "Sweet Little Sixteen," "Brown Sugar" and "Jumping Jack Flash." But the rowdy crowd wanted more oldies and many were rude and inattentive when the Stones played new songs. Inevitably, things got out of hand. At one point Mick had to ask people to refrain from throwing bottles at Keith while he sang 'Happy.' Things got ugly when the Stones refused to return for an encore. The crowd angrily stormed the stage and began wrecking the sound and lighting equipment, while the Stones crew attempted to fight them off with two-by-fours.

**Thursday, July 6:** Masonic Auditorium, Detroit, MI, with Etta James, 8 p.m.

The Stones made a surprise appearance at this 5,000-seat venue. The show was announced only one day before tickets went on sale. The Stones were driven to the show in a police paddy wagon, except for Mick who arrived in a vintage Thunderbird. Members of the Michigan football team escorted them into the auditorium. Timothy Yagle of *The Michigan Daily* reported, "In numbers like 'Honky Tonk Women' they affirmed that their ability to mesmerize an audience has not been withered by the years. The show was overpoweringly loud and much of the music, not to mention the obligatory slurred lyrics, was unintelligible. But such technical rough edges never seemed to matter much, Jagger's perpetual motion can still keep an audience hopping." Portions from this show, too, were heard on the *King Biscuit Flower Hour*.

**Saturday, July 8:** Soldier Field, Chicago, IL, with Southside Johnny and the Asbury Jukes, Peter Tosh and Journey, 11:30 a.m.

Over 75,000 fans turned out, but in contrast to the rowdiness at Rich Stadium, peace and harmony prevailed. Lynn Van Matre of *The Chicago Tribune* reported that the set "was about as satisfying as it could be considering that to almost all of the crowd—except those in the very front rows—the band were virtually indistinguishable. … There is no doubt that after 15 years the Stones still retain enough of the magic to entertain all but the most critical." NBC TV partially filmed part of the concert, including the final two songs: "Jumping Jack Flash" and a surprise version of "(I Can't Get No) Satisfaction," played for the second time on the tour.

Later that night, Mick, Ronnie, Keith and Charlie ventured out to the Chicago clubs and jammed with Muddy Waters and Willie Dixon at the Quiet Knight Club. Ron Wood was in the mood for more playing and jammed with Lefty Dizz at the Kingston Mine Club and Junior Wells at the Wise Fools Pub until the sun came out. The Stones flew to Minneapolis the next day and Mick and Keith briefly joined Peter Tosh onstage at the Cabooze Bar that night.

**Monday, July 10:** Civic Center, St. Paul, MN, with Peter Tosh, 8 p.m.

The Stones played to a mellow audience of 17,500 that showed little enthusiasm for non-oldies. Bill Wyman fell from the stage as the band was exiting the arena and had to be taken to a hospital. The Stones' spokesman told the press that he "was waving to fans after the performance and leaned his left hand against what he thought was a wall but turned out to be a black curtain. He fell off the stage, was unconscious for about eight minutes and was taken to Saint Paul Ramsey Medical Center." It turned out that Bill had suffered a slight concussion and injured his left hand. He continued the tour nonetheless.

**Tuesday, July 11:** Kiel Opera House, St. Louis, MO, with Peter Tosh, 9 p.m.

The Stones didn't roll onto the stage until 11:15. However, to whet their appetites Mick, dressed in a white cap, pink shirt and yellow jacket, came out during Peter Tosh's set to join him on "Don't Look Back." During the Stones' set, fans hung a large banner from the balcony that said "Free Keith Richards," referring to his legal problems in Canada. Bill Wyman was in tremendous pain from his accident the night before but played the gig anyway. The *St. Louis Post* reported that midway through the show, "with the first notes of the Stones' current single, 'Miss You,' the audience collectively jumped to its feet and stayed that way through 'Imagination' and 'Shattered,' which is a real screamer for Jagger." The band then played "Respectable," after which Mick moved to the piano for "Far Away Eyes." The reporter noted, "Only in that song, the bluesy 'Love in Vain' and the rock 'n' roller 'Sweet Little 16' were all the words distinguishable."

Copy of the band's set list for their show in Detroit on July 6, 1978 (collection of Ira Korman).

**Thursday, July 13:** Superdome, New Orleans, LA, with Van Halen and the Doobie Brothers, 7:30 p.m.

A crowd of 80,173 people attended this massive show, which also featured the mellow rock of the Doobie Brothers and Van Halen, promoting their eponymous debut LP. The concert grossed $1,060,000. The Stones played a rare encore of "Street Fighting Man." A private film of the concert titled the "The Stones in the Dome" exists.

**Sunday, July 16:** Folsom Field, Boulder, CO, with Eddie Money, Kansas and Peter Tosh, noon
About 60,000 fans turned out for this event in sweltering 90-degree heat.

Press box pass for the Stones' concert in Boulder on July 16, 1978 (collection of Ira Korman).

**Tuesday, July 18:** Will Rogers Auditorium, Fort Worth, TX, with Peter Tosh and Doug Kershaw, 8 p.m.

The Stones flew into Dallas on Monday and attended Bobby "Blue" Bland's concert at the Longhorn Ballroom that night. The show on Tuesday (billed as "The London Green-Shoed Cowboys") at the 3,000-seat auditorium was professionally filmed by director Lynn Lenau and released in 2011 on DVD/Blu-ray. The set consisted of: "Let It Rock," "All Down the Line," "Honky Tonk Women," "Star Star," "When the Whip Comes Down," "Beast of Burden," "Miss You," "Just My Imagination," "Shattered," "Respectable," "Far Away Eyes," "Love in Vain," "Tumbling Dice," "Happy," "Sweet Little Sixteen," "Brown Sugar" and "Jumping Jack Flash." Doug Kershaw guested on fiddle for "Far Away Eyes." The concert, in my opinion, was quite good. Mick, dressed in a bright yellow jacket, leather pants and a red cap, was in energetic form and the band played flawlessly. Mick was quick, though, to excuse any imperfections by commenting, "If the band is lacking energy, it's because we've been out fucking all night." Pete Oppel of *The Dallas Morning News* agreed with Mick. He commented, "The band seemed ragged and tired…. Mick Jagger was not in good form Tuesday night. His voice was thin and weak." He also criticized the Stones' decision to play so many new songs in a row and argued "I don't think the Stones would have compromised their integrity by substituting 'Cloud' or 'Satisfaction' for either 'Shattered' or 'Respectable.'"

**Wednesday, July 19:** Sam Houston Coliseum, Houston, TX, with Peter Tosh, 8 p.m.

After exerting themselves for the cameras in Fort Worth, the Stones probably should have taken a night off. Critical consensus was that the show in Houston was a letdown. Dale Adamson of the *Houston Chronicle* called it, "One of the most painful disappointments I've ever encountered in live rock 'n' roll—aggravated all the more by the fact that the Rolling Stones rank very close to the top of the list of my all-time favorite bands. It was a dismal experience—to be endured, not enjoyed.... Starting off a bit sloppy, that's exactly how they continued for the duration of the show." This show was recorded and portions of it aired the following year on the *King Biscuit Flower Hour.*

**Friday, July 21:** Community Center, Tucson, AZ, with Etta James, 8 p.m.

The 11,000 people who crowded the auditorium cheered wildly when Tucson native Linda Ronstadt, dressed in short shorts with the Stones' tongue logo, joined the band for "Tumbling Dice." Mick seemed to enjoy himself and told the crowd, "I never thought I'd play Tucson again.... Tucson, you're really good!" Reporting on the new songs from *Some Girls* Jane Kay of *The Arizona Daily Star* noted, "'Miss You' ... had Wood and Richard alternating riffs in an impressive jam that gave life to a song that could be their 'Melancholy Baby.' The Stones were into it, clustering around drummer Watts to play a tight, exciting arrangement.... The crowd loved it when Jagger, Richard and Wood traded off mikes and licks on 'Faraway [sic] Eyes,' another new one. Jagger played piano and Wood played [pedal] steel for the country joke of a song."

**Sunday, July 23, and Monday, July 24:** Anaheim Stadium, Anaheim, CA, with Etta James, Peter Tosh and the Outlaws, daily at 1 p.m.

The Stones played to massive crowds. Over 60,000 turned out on the first show alone. Many showed up early in the morning and had to stand in the heat until 5:45 p.m. when the Stones took the stage. Fred Rath of *Record Mirror* was underwhelmed by the performance of old favorites like "Honky Tonk Women" and "Star Star," which were performed "rather as a matter of course rather than out of inspiration" but he felt the Stones came alive when playing new material. "'Beast of Burden' features some great interplay between Wood and Richard. 'Miss You' is greeted with a massive cheer and is a winner-its long loping shuffle pounding out in true Stones style. 'Just My Imagination' is another song in the classic Stones mold; its heavy chords a perfect backdrop to Jagger's vocal and body gyrations."

**Wednesday, July 26:** Alameda Coliseum, Oakland, CA, with Santana, Eddie Money and Peter Tosh, 11 a.m.

Mick celebrated his thirty-fifth birthday before a crowd of 60,000 at the tour-ending show. Bobby Keys joined the band for "Beast of Burden" and "Miss You." The set consisted of "Let It Rock," "All Down the Line," "Honky Tonk Women," "Star Star," "When the Whip Comes Down," "Beast of Burden," "Lies," "Miss You," "Just My Imagination," "Shattered," "Respectable," "Far Away Eyes," "Love in Vain," "Tumbling Dice," "Happy," "Sweet Little Sixteen," "Brown Sugar," "Jumping Jack Flash" and "(I Can't Get No) Satisfaction."

The Stones didn't play any more shows that year. However on October 7 they appeared before a studio audience on NBC TV's *Saturday Night Live*. On October 25 Keith got onstage at the Bottom Line in New York with Rockpile, the British band led by Dave Edmunds and Nick Lowe, to perform a few Chuck Berry tunes. The concert was

Handbill for the Stones' appearance in Anaheim on July 23, 1978 (collection of Ira Korman).

recorded and parts of it aired on the U.S. radio show *The King Biscuit Flour Hour*. On December 16 Mick again appeared on *Saturday Night Live,* before a live audience. This time he dueted with Peter Tosh on "Don't Look Back," a song from Tosh's *Bush Doctor* LP that Mick had helped produce.

# CHAPTER 18

# 1979

The uncertainty about the outcome of Keith's drug trial meant that the Stones' management made no touring plans for 1979. As it turned out the Stones would play only one live show that year as a unit. However, the band was hot to put some new music on tape and flew to the Bahamas to record at Chris Blackwell's Compass Point Studios in January. The 1980 LP *Emotional Rescue* was begun there, though additional recording took place in France between June and October. Mick and Keith had written too many songs for one album and numerous outtakes were left on the cutting room floor, some of which ended up on the 1981 LP *Tattoo You* and the 1983 LP *Undercover of the Night*. Ron Wood had spent his downtime the previous year recording his third solo album, *Gimme Some Neck*, which was released on April 20 by Columbia Records. The album included vocal and instrumental contributions from Mick, Keith and Charlie and featured the song "Seven Days," which Bob Dylan had given to Ron to record. While not a tremendous success, it reached a respectable number 45 on *Billboard* during its thirteen weeks on the U.S. charts. Many people wondered why Wood chose to release a solo record but, as he explained to Lynn Van Matre of the *Chicago Tribune*, "It kind of catches me by surprise when people don't realize that there could be a lot of stuff that I'd written that just doesn't fit in that well with the Stones, or songs I'd had on my mind for years and wanted to express."

As the Stones had no intentions of hitting the road, Ron put together a makeshift band called the New Barbarians to promote his LP. He told a reporter that Neil Young had coined the name. "He was interested in the group and one day he just rang me up and said why not the New Barbarians? And I figured, 'Why not?'" The band consisted of Stones confederates Bobby Keys on saxophone and Ian McLagan on keyboards as well as Stanley Clarke on bass and Joseph Modeliste, of the Meters, on drums. Keith was itching to tour and decided to join the band as "guest guitarist." He

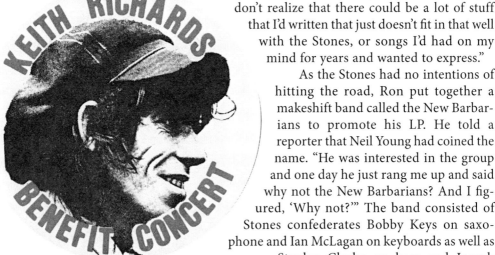

**Button advertising the Stones' benefit concert for the blind in Oshawa, Ontario (collection of Ira Korman).**

told a reporter in Wisconsin that he was eager to stay "off the junk" and thought he was better off on the road. "I had never really thought about touring with anybody else. But I figured as long as the Stones weren't working I'd keep my chops in shape with Ron. Besides my big problem in rock has always been the sudden stops and starts—the rushes and the lulls…. I knew that if I could keep working it'd be easier."

The New Barbarians spent two weeks rehearsing in California in early April. They agreed that their first shows would be the charity concerts Keith had agreed to play for the blind, as part of the terms of his court sentencing. The shows took place near Toronto on April 22. The crowds that attended got a fantastic surprise when the full Stones came onstage for a ten-song set. The New Barbarians then embarked on their tour, performing eighteen dates. While the main purpose was to promote *Gimme Some Neck*, the band played tracks from all of Ron's solo albums as well as tackling a number of Stones classics, including "Honky Tonk Women" and "Jumping Jack Flash," the Chuck Berry classic "Sweet Little Rock and Roller" and even some country songs that Keith had become fond of, like the Tammy Wynette tune "Apartment No. 9." While Ron Wood sang the majority of songs, Keith took more vocal leads then he ever did with the Stones.

While the tour was a fun experience for the participants, the Canadian shows created unrealistic expectations on the part of fans that the full Stones would appear at other dates. However, the two Canadian concerts were the only shows the other Stones played. In addition, the dates were billed as "The New Barbarians & Friends" and in pre-tour interviews Ron Wood suggested that mates like Neil Young, Rod Stewart, Jeff Beck and Jimmy Page might make appearances. However, none of these stars ultimately took the stage. Ron admitted in an interview that at first he "encouraged the rumors. I was a bit a worried about how I was going to sell all those tickets." Some fans felt cheated. Promoters in Milwaukee made the mistake of advertising that the concert would definitely have a surprise guest and when one failed to appear attendees rioted. Seats at the venue were smashed and hurled at the stage and the rioters chanted: "Ripoff! Ripoff!"

Despite the lack of big name guests, the shows were full of exuberant good time rock and roll. Photographer Henry Diltz commented in *Goldmine*, "It was just like a Stones tour except that Mick wasn't there, so there was a certain looseness and freedom because the boss was absent."

However, many journalists criticized the tour for exactly that reason. Rob Patterson commented in *The Republic*, "Part of the problem is that Wood is a charmingly raw singer whose Dylanesque voice just can't carry a whole show as a front man. And neither Keith's contributions as a singer nor rather long-winded instrumental jams could spark the show to become something special." It didn't really matter. The New Barbarians was never anything more then a temporary side project. Woody and Keith reconvened with the other Stones in France that June to continue work on *Emotional Rescue*. The Barbarians played together one more time in August, supporting Led Zeppelin at Knebworth and then called it a day.

However, other band members took the opportunity to play some non–Stones shows as well. Ian Stewart and Charlie Watts formed a boogie-woogie band with former mentor Alexis Korner, jazz saxophonist Dick Morrissey, pianists Bob Hall and George Green and trumpeter Colin Smith. The band, which also included Cream bassist Jack Bruce, performed at the Bracknell Jazz Festival on July 8 and then flew to Holland to play at the Northsea Jazz Festival at The Hague on July 14. Billed as Rocket 88 they also embarked on a short tour of Germany and the Netherlands in November and December. Their

November 17 concert in Hannover at the Rotation Club was recorded and released by Atlantic Records in 1981. A December 13 show in London was also partially released in 2013. Bill Wyman also found time to jet to America to perform a few numbers with Ringo Starr, Todd Rundgren, Dave Mason, Doug Kershaw and Kiki Dee at the annual televised Jerry Lewis Muscular Dystrophy Telethon, held at the Convention Center in Las Vegas on September 11.

## Concerts

**Sunday, April 22:** Civic Auditorium, Oshawa Ontario, Canada, 4 and 8:30 p.m.

Keith had agreed to play two benefit concerts at an ice hockey arena near Toronto as part of his court settlement, with 2600 tickets reserved for the blind. The remaining tickets at the 5,000-seat venue were sold with only Keith's name mentioned. Tickets were listed at $10 but scalpers had a field day selling exorbitantly marked up tickets to fans who gambled the other Stones would appear. They were correct. All the Stones flew in to Toronto at their own expense. On Saturday night they rehearsed at the Centre Studio for a few friends and invited guests, including *Saturday Night Live* star John Belushi, who'd volunteered to emcee. The shows were also warm-ups for the New Barbarians tour and the band, consisting of Keith, Ron Wood, Ian McLagan, Stanley Clarke, Bobby Keys and Joseph Modeliste, opened both concerts.

At the first show the Barbarians opened with "Breathe on Me," from Ron Wood's second solo LP, *Now Look,* and then performed "Come to Realize," "Infekshun," and "Lost and Lonely" from *Gimme Some Neck*. After playing "Am I Grooving You" from Woody's first LP, they performed "Seven Days," an unreleased Dylan song recorded for *Gimme Some Neck*, before concluding with Keith's, "Before They Make Me Run." To the jubilant excitement of the crowd, Mick then came on stage and joined Keith for "Prodigal Son," after which all of the Stones appeared and performed a *Some Girls* heavy-set that consisted of: "Let It Rock," "Respectable," "Star Star," "Beast of Burden," "Just My Imagination," "When the Whip Comes Down," "Shattered," and "Miss You." The full New Barbarians band returned to the stage to join the Stones for the rousing closer, "Jumping Jack Flash." Chet Flippo reported, in *Rolling Stone,* that the concerts "were the most blistering, manic and high-powered they have performed in years" and that "Keith, now healthy and energetic after his cure from heroin addiction, had never played better or cockier." Paul McGrath of the *Globe and Mail* also was struck by the change in Keith. "At the El Mocambo about two years ago … he was slack-jawed and passive, playing his rhythms as well as he ever had, but leaving the tough solo work to colleague Ron Wood. Last night was something entirely different; he bounded on stage, practically kicking up his heels, and launched into a parade of tough rock and roll songs with his new band, the New Barbarians." The Stones performed the same set at both concerts, but the Barbarians dropped "Come to Realize" and "Lost and Lonely" in the second set in favor of the Berry classic "Sweet Little Rock and Roller," the *Gimme Some Neck* number "F.U.C. Her," and "I Can Feel the Fire" from Wood's first solo LP, *I've Got My Own Album to Do*. The shows were professionally recorded but remain unreleased.

## New Barbarians Tour

**Tuesday, April 24:** Crisler Arena, University of Michigan, Ann Arbor, 8 p.m.

Ron Wood wasn't used to acting as front man. Mick criticized Woody's decision, at the first Canadian show, to open with one of his own songs and advised him instead to open with the Chuck Berry number "Sweet Little Rock and Roller." Wood commented to the *Los Angeles Times*, "Mick said it was important that you open with a familiar song so that the audience can identify with what you're doing. Then you can branch off." The feeling that the Stones might appear at any moment hung over the gig and led to some frustration when it became clear that they wouldn't. R. J. Smith of the *Michigan Daily* noted, "Many of the people that I talked to after the Barbarians concert last week wanted to see Keith Richards' and Ron Wood's heads skewered on twin poles all because Mick Jagger didn't show." Smith argued that it still was a fun show, despite Mick's non-appearance but noted that the Barbarians goodtime rock 'n' roll was more suited to a small club then an arena. "As a bar band I'd rather see the Barbarians then George Thorogood and the Destroyers, but I would have swapped it all for a hint, even, of the Rolling Stones' excitement."

**Thursday, April 26, and Saturday, April 28:** Cobo Arena, Detroit, MI, 8 p.m.

The Barbarians played two nights in Detroit. Commenting on the April 28 show, Brad Flory reported in the *Daily Tar Heel*, "Richards ... was in top form, trading licks with Wood in sizzling guitar duels and jamming fiercely to Clarke's incredibly fast bass.... The Barbarians play a brand of all-out rock that puts most contemporary rockers in the shade."

**Sunday, April 29:** Milwaukee Arena, Milwaukee, WI, 8 p.m.

A tape of this concert exists. The band started off with "Sweet Little Rock and Roller," "Buried Alive," "Infekshun," "Mystifies Me," "F.U.C. Her," "Rock Me Baby," "Sure the One You Need," and "Breathe On Me." These were followed by Keith's first lead of the night on "Let's Go Steady Again." He then moved to the piano to sing "Apartment No. 9," and joined Ron on the chorus of "Honky Tonk Women." The show continued with "Love in Vain," "Lost and Lonely," "I Can Feel the Fire," "Come to Realize," "Am I Grooving You," and "Seven Days." Keith then again took center stage to sing "Before They Make Me Run," and the show ended with a manic "Jumping Jack Flash." As discussed, irate fans who had been promised a "surprise guest star" were disgruntled throughout the show. When the band failed to come out for an encore they rioted and severely damaged the venue.

Keith was allegedly furious and blamed the fiasco on Ron's manager, Jason Cooper, whom he felt was responsible for spreading the stories about guest stars to drum up publicity. In Rob Chapman's book *New Barbarians: Outlaws, Gunslingers and Guitars*, Bobby Keys recalled, "When Keith found out what had happened and how come the papers were saying all these bad things, he grabbed Jason Cooper and put a knife to his throat and told him to get the fuck out and if he saw him again he was going to put a bullet between his eyes." Cooper was off the tour the same day. The state of Wisconsin ultimately sued the band; the promoters and the booking agent. Ron Wood later agreed to recompense them for the damages by playing a special make-up show in Milwaukee on January 16, 1980.

**Monday, April 30:** International Amphitheater, Chicago, IL, 8 p.m.

The setlist for this show was basically the same as the night before but the band played two extra songs with a special guest, blues legend Junior Wells, who had opened for the Stones in 1970. The songs performed with Wells were "Key to the Highway" and "Hoodoo Man Blues."

**Wednesday, May 2:** Civic Arena, Pittsburgh, PA, 8 p.m.

A less-than-capacity crowd turned out. The *Post Gazette* reviewer disparaged Woody's singing as "only adequate" but singled out Bobby Keys for praise: "He is a powerful man with a horn and can convey a surprising amount of emotion with the instrument. He seized every opportunity he had to solo with gusto."

**Thursday, May 3:** Riverfront Coliseum, Cincinnati, OH, 8 p.m.

This show was marred by a 53- minute delay before the band took the stage, which put the crowd in a sour mood. The mood wasn't aided by a poor sound system that made it nearly impossible to hear the vocals. However the Barbarians soldiered on with a two-hour show. The band then headed to New York, which served as their base of operations for most of the next week. Portions of this show were released in 2017 as a bonus CD with purchase of Rob Chapman's book, *New Barbarians: Outlaws, Gunslingers and Guitars*. The songs on the bonus CD from this night were: "Breathe on Me," "Let's Go Steady Again," and "Worried Life Blues."

**Saturday, May 5:** Capital Centre, Largo, MD, 8 p.m.

The Barbarians flew to Maryland from New York and returned immediately after the show. The concert was professionally recorded and belatedly released on Ron Wood's record label, Wooden Records, in 2006 as *Buried Alive: Live in Maryland*. The set consisted of "Sweet Little Rock and Roller," "Buried Alive," "F.U.C. Her," "Mystifies Me," "Infekshun," "Rock Me Baby," "Sure the One You Need," "Lost and Lonely," "Love in Vain," "Breathe On Me," "Let's Go Steady," "Apartment No. 9," "Honky Tonk Women," "Worried Life Blues," "I Can Feel the Fire," "Come to Realize," "Am I Grooving You," "Seven Days," "Before They Make Me Run" and "Jumping Jack Flash."

The Capital Centre was one of the first venues to film performers so they could be seen on monitors above the stage. A videotape of this feed exists. Wood's vocal delivery worked best on his own material and the show suffered when he took on the task of singing Stones classics. He was stuck between a rock and a hard place. The band needed some crowd pleasers but when they played them everyone was reminded of what was missing: Mick Jagger. Ron displayed little charisma as a front man. His between-song patter was slight. His solo tunes also lacked the dynamism of the best of the Stones. However, the guitar interplay between Keith and Ron sparkled on tunes like "Buried Alive" and "Before They Make Me Run" and the band was tight and rocking. Bobby Keys' solos especially were a wonder to behold.

**Monday, May 7:** Madison Square Garden, New York, NY, 8 p.m.

This show was professionally recorded and two songs performed on this night ("Am I Grooving You" and "Seven Days") were released as a single on record store day in 2016, along with a version of Eddy Grant's song "Hello Africa," recorded at a rehearsal in April. Further portions of the show were released in 2017 as a bonus CD with purchase of Rob Chapman's book, *New Barbarians: Outlaws, Gunslingers and Guitars*. The songs on the bonus CD were: "Sweet Little Rock and Roller," "Buried Alive," "F.U.C. Her," "Mystifies Me," "Infekshun," and "Rock Me Baby." The concert was marred by the band's decision not to come back out for an encore, which led to yet another riot.

**Tuesday, May 8:** Richfield Coliseum, Cleveland, OH, 8 p.m.

Almost 10,000 fans turned out. Many bought tickets in the hope that superstars would appear. Ron felt obliged after the fourth number to make it clear no one else was

Ticket for the New Barbarians' concert at Madison Square Garden, May 1979 (collection of Ira Korman).

coming. He announced, "There will be no special guests. I hope this band is good enough for you." Mark Faris of the *Akron Beacon* noted that Keith "appeared to be in a lethargic stupor" when he took the stage but still singled out his playing as the highlight of the night. He felt that the band simply lacked fire. "Everybody just sort of stood around and played. It was high-class rock. But even the musicians didn't seem too enthusiastic about it all."

**Thursday, May 10:** Omni, Atlanta, GA, 8 p.m.

The band was tentatively booked to play on Birmingham on this night, but the show ultimately took place in Atlanta.

**Saturday, May 12:** The Summit, Houston, TX, 8 p.m.

**Sunday, May 13:** Tarrant County Convention Center, Fort Worth, TX, 7:30 p.m.

The show was marred by a poor sound system and by the band's occasionally sluggish behavior. Pete Oppel of the *Dallas News* complained that "Ron Wood seemed to be spending the first half of the show waking up. They never started a song at the same time, although they came close once in a while. And they never finished one together either- and they never came close to doing that" but he still declared that the concert "was rock 'n' roll the way its supposed to be-raw, rough and exciting."

**Tuesday, May 15:** McNichols Arena, Denver, CO, 8 p.m.

**Thursday, May 17:** Salt Palace, Salt Lake City, UT, 8 p.m.

**Saturday, May 19:** Forum, Los Angeles, CA, 7:30 p.m.

Billy Preston joined the band on keyboards for part of this show but many were clearly expecting the big LA show to be more star-studded. Once again Woody had to announce that no one else was expected. Mark Williams of *Melody Maker* enjoyed the show but opined, "In the 14,000-seat Forum you need a sense of purpose, and to me that's what they lacked."

**Sunday, May 20:** Coliseum, Oakland, CA, 8 p.m.

Keith enjoyed the tour and singled out playing with bassist Stanley Clarke as one of the highlights. He told Lisa Robinson, "He's amazing and even if we never work together again, it's been an experience. Doing this tour is like getting my chops together. Rather then not play a Stones tour and get rusty, this gives me a chance to get in shape."

**Handbill for the New Barbarians' appearance in Denver on May 15, 1979 (collection of Ira Korman).**

A performance of "Apartment No. 9" from this night appeared on a bonus CD released in 2017 in conjunction with Rob Chapman's book, *New Barbarians: Outlaws, Gunslingers and Guitars.*

**Tuesday, May 22:** Sports Stadium, San Diego, CA, with Bob Welch, 8 p.m.

Former Fleetwood Mac guitarist Bob Welch, who had a hit with "Ebony Eyes," opened. He also joined the Barbarians on one number. Robert Laurence of the *San Diego Union* commented, "As guitarists, Woods and Richards were as, as always, spirited, involving performers, trading off leads, interweaving and in general keeping spirits high…. But it faltered when Wood or Richards approached the microphone as lead vocalist. They had neither the compelling stage presence nor the vocal force required of a leader, and the band seemed like a powerful foundation without a structure to support." This concert was apparently filmed with the permission of the band, but the whereabouts of the footage is unknown. This was the final date of the tour and tentative dates in Seattle and Phoenix were canceled.

**Saturday, August 11:** Knebworth Park, Stevenage, Hertfordshire, UK, with Led Zeppelin, Todd Rundgren and Utopia, Southside Johnny and the Asbury Jukes, the New Commander Cody Band, Chas & Dave and Fairport Convention

The Barbarians reconvened for one UK gig, supporting Led Zeppelin (at their last concert appearance before the death of drummer John Bonham). Jamaican reggae musician Phil Chen replaced Stanley Clarke on bass. The band rehearsed for one day at Shepperton Studios. They were supposed to take the stage at 6:30, following a set by Todd Rundgren, but didn't arrive until 8 p.m., apparently due to financial squabbles with the

Poster for the New Barbarians' concert at Knebworth, August 1979 (collection of Ira Korman).

promoter. Ronnie insisted that they get the £35,000 they'd been promised before they went on. The set consisted of "Sweet Little Rock and Roller," "F.U.C. Her," "Breathe On Me," "I Can Feel the Fire," "Let's Go Steady," "Worried Life Blues," "Honky Tonk Women," "Come to Realize," "Am I Grooving You," "Seven Days," "Before They Make Me Run" and "Jumping Jack Flash"

Keith played no more shows in 1979 but Woody joined Bob Marley and the Wailers onstage at the Oakland Auditorium on November 30 and jammed with them on five numbers.

# Chapter 19

# 1980

As the 1980s began, the Stones were in a strange place. They seemed uncertain whether they should bother to continue. They had been playing music together for almost twenty years, something unheard of in rock up to that point. Bill Wyman, the oldest member of the band, was seriously considering retiring in 1982 when the Stones reached that magic number. He told Chet Flippo, "I am going to retire from the Rolling Stones. I really do want to do other things, you know. I don't want to wait until I am sixty; that'd be too late." Like Brian Jones and Mick Taylor, Bill had begun to express some bitterness about his role in the band. Although he'd recorded numerous solo albums and felt he had more to offer, his role remained limited. "You do get frustrated in a band like the Stones because it can be restrictive." That fall he recorded the soundtrack to the sci-fi film *Green Ice*.

The interpersonal dynamics within the group were becoming frayed. One reason for the strain may have been their changing personal lives. Keith's fractious relationship with longtime muse Anita Pallenberg had come to an end and he found stability in a twenty-two-year-old American model, Patti Hansen. She would eventually become his wife. Keith suddenly had a reason to go home. He began to spend much of his time in New York. Mick had also gotten serious with an American model, Texan Jerry Hall, and spent much of his time in New York as well. Despite often being in the same city, neither Mick nor Keith felt much desire to hang out with each other. As Bill Wyman noted in *Rolling with the Stones*, "We were all concentrating on our own projects and personal lives and the Rolling Stones seemed to be taking a back seat. Mick and Keith could not agree on anything without a fight." Keith's decision to clean up his act (to a degree) meant that he was now more involved in facets of the Stones recording and business ventures. These had been largely left to Mick to deal with for much of the 1970s. Mick allegedly wasn't thrilled by Keith's renewed interest and tensions developed. As Keith noted in his autobiography, "I realized that Mick had got all the strings in his hands and he didn't want to let go of a single one." During the mixing of *Emotional Rescue* in November 1979, they had a major disagreement over a song and briefly stopped work on the album. They'd patched up their differences enough by December to again begin work on the LP at Electric Lady Studios in New York, but they continued to bicker. Bill Wyman recalled that when he met them in New York that March, all they did was argue with each other. Unfortunately, the relationship between the Glimmer Twins would become more strained as the decade progressed.

Some of this strain showed on the resulting album, *Emotional Rescue*, which was released in June. The album sold over five million copies and yielded two hit singles

("Emotional Rescue" and "She's So Cold") but it was a mixed bag that seemed to pull in disparate directions. The Mick-led "Dance (Part 1)," written with Ron Wood, and the discofied "Emotional Rescue" seemed far removed from Keith's tastes. Album closer "All About You," written by Keith, was at least partly a pointed attack at Mick. In retrospect, the LP's reputation has suffered due to its being overshadowed by the inspired *Some Girls* and the entertaining *Tattoo You*. The album was full of solid but workmanlike rock 'n' roll songs. "Where the Boys Go" and "She's So Cold" were fun up-tempo numbers but neither was a classic. There were definitely some weak tracks on the LP, like the faux-reggae "Send It to Me" and the odd blues tune "Down in the Hole." Illustrating that artists aren't always the best judge of their own work, the Stones left a number of better tracks on the cutting room floor, which eventually found release on *Tattoo You*. In June Mick told Cherry Ripe on the Australian show *Countdown* that the album took "far too long. We're a bit late with this one. We're supposed to have put it out last year. I don't know what happened. Last year doesn't seem to exist for us so this year we hope is going to be more active." He commented that he hoped to do a short tour of Europe and then come to Australia "in the next six months." But no tour took place and the Stones did not play a single show as a group the entire year, for the first time in their career. However, individual members made numerous appearances.

On January 16 Ron Wood played in Milwaukee at the Uptown Theater, a makeup show for the promoters of the 1979 concert that ended in a riot and cost them thousands of dollars. Keith was not present. The lineup was Woody, Ian McLagan, Bobby Keys, Johnnie Lee Schell (on guitar), Andy Newmark (drums), Reggie McBride (bass) and Mackenzie Philips (backing vocals). About 1,200 fans turned out for the low-key event. Mick and Keith were both living in New York and couldn't resist getting on stage in the clubs they frequented. On March 18 Mick sang a few numbers with the Jimmy Rogers Blues Band at the nightclub Trax and two days later Keith followed suit by jamming with the Dead Boys at the 80's Club. He also played with the Jim Carroll Band at Trax in June. Charlie Watts also played a few gigs with Rocket 88 in London in June and at the Bracknell Jazz Festival in July.

# Chapter 20

# 1981

As 1981 began, all of the Stones were busy with solo pursuits. Mick was in Peru. Twelve years after filming Ned Kelly, he had again gotten the acting bug. Mick agreed to appear in German director Werner Herzog's *Fitzcarraldo*, the story of an Irishman determined to transport a steamship over a steep mountain to gain access to a rich source of rubber in the Amazon. In January Mick joined the cast, led by American actor Jason Robards, but the shoot was dogged by bad luck. Robards eventually contracted dysentery and had to drop out of filming in February. Klaus Kinski agreed to replace him but this necessitated that Herzog begin a total reshoot. Mick, cast as Fitzcarraldo's assistant Wilbur, abandoned the film as he had already made plans to tour with the Stones. He can, however, be glimpsed in outtake footage shown in the 1982 documentary *Burden of Dreams*.

Ron Wood spent part of January in the studio with Ringo Starr, helping him produce his album *Stop and Smell the Roses*. Woody had taken part in fun sessions the previous September at Cherokee Studios in Hollywood. He collaborated with Ringo on a song called "Dead Giveaway." He again joined Starr in January but the mood was greatly altered. John Lennon was supposed to attend the January sessions, but his tragic murder in December 1980 made it impossible. Ron, however, joined a depressed Ringo to help him finish the LP, released to mixed reviews in October. Woody remained in Hollywood until the end of March, working on his own LP *1234*, which was released in September. The record was recorded with an all-star cast that included Ian McLagan, Bobby Keys, Nicky Hopkins, Bobby Womack and Charlie. I like the title track and the song "Outlaws" but prefer his '70s releases over this one. However, there are some fans who consider it their favorite.

Bill Wyman was also busy working on a solo LP, but it was not released until 1982. However, he released a single in July called "(Si Si) Je Suis un Rock Star" that was a surprise hit in the UK, reaching number 14 on the charts. Bill sang the song in silly French accent and clearly had a ball. Charlie also kept busy. Besides contributing to Ron Wood's album, he continued to play occasional gigs in the UK with Rocket 88. Keith was in New York that winter and itching to perform again. He took the stage as a guest performer a number of times early in the year. On January 22 he joined the Shaboo All Stars at Trax nightclub to perform "Johnny B. Goode" and on February 9 he got onstage with Etta James to perform "Miss You" at the Lone Star Café. He also did some intermittent solo recordings in Los Angeles that March with longtime partner-in-crime Bobby Keys and traveled to Jamaica to contribute to Max Romeo's LP *Holding Out My Love to You*.

On April 14, the compilation album *Sucking in the Seventies* was released. The LP was a successor to *Made in the Shade* and featured edited and remixed tracks from the

Stones' post–1973 albums. For completists, the LP contained three rarities: a live version of "When the Whip Comes Down" (recorded in Detroit on the 1978 tour), "Everything Is Turning to Gold," (the B-side to "Shattered") and the previously unreleased "Dance (Part 2)." It reached number 15 on the *Billboard* charts. Around the time of its release, Mick was in Paris to finish a new Stones record, *Tattoo You*. Mick and Keith had spent very little time together and had written almost no new material. Instead, the LP consisted of outtakes from various sessions, dating as far back as *Goats Head Soup*, that producer Chris Kimsey had pulled out of the vaults the previous winter. He told an interviewer, "I spent three months going through like the last four, five albums finding stuff that had been either forgotten about or at the time rejected. And then I presented it to the band and I said, 'Hey, look guys, you've got all this great stuff sitting in the can and it's great material, do something with it.'" Many of the songs already had basic tracks and Mick had laid down most of his overdubbed vocals at solo sessions the previous winter. It was only necessary to polish up a few songs and add additional instrumentation (including a great sax solo by jazz legend Sonny Rollins on "Waiting on a Friend") and voila, a new LP was completed.

Despite its grab-bag origins, the resulting album, released on August 24, was surprisingly solid. Indeed, in my opinion it is the last album the Stones recorded that every fan must own. The LP kicked off with a bona fide classic rocker, "Start Me Up." The song had been kicking around since the *Black and Blue* sessions but had been left on the cutting room floor in 1978. It was released as the first single from the LP in August and rocketed up the charts, reaching number 2 in the States. Two more songs from the LP also charted: the mellow classic "Waiting on a Friend," tracked in 1973 (and thus featuring Mick Taylor on guitar), reached number 13 in November, and the fun, up-tempo "Hang Fire," recorded mostly at the *Some Girls* sessions, scraped the top twenty in 1982. The LP also included Keith's rocker "Little T&A," which had been demoed for *Emotional Rescue*, the pretty falsetto ballad "Worried About You," which dated from the *Black and Blue* sessions, the soulful "No Use in Crying" and the funky "Slave," featuring Sonny Rollins on sax.

With the album finished it was time to start planning the band's first U.S. tour since 1978, but this proved difficult. Relations between Mick and Keith continued to be strained. Indeed, when Mick tried to gather the band in New York in late May, Keith opted to remain in Florida with Freddie Sessler. In addition, a new wrinkle had been added to the already strained dynamics within the band. As Ron Wood later admitted, he had developed a serious cocaine habit, just as Keith was straightening up his act. According to Bill Wyman, Woody "didn't look very good" when he showed up at Mick's house to discuss the state of the band. Wyman eventually flew back to London, though not before fielding a drunken phone call from Charlie, who insisted that the band was finished. However, things were patched up enough by late June for the Stones to gather together in New York to film music videos for "Start Me Up," "Hang Fire," "Worried About You," "Neighbors" and "Waiting on a Friend," directed by Michael Lindsay-Hogg, who'd helmed the Rock and Roll Circus in 1968. The Stones had been making promo videos for years but with the launch of MTV in August they now became a required part of promotion for rock bands. The *Tattoo You* videos remained in heavy rotation on the fledgling station for the next few years, introducing the band to a new audience.

While in New York, heavy discussions took place about what to do if Ronnie wasn't in a condition to tour. According to Keith, everyone except him wanted Ron off the tour.

The band informed him that he needed to clean up and offered him $500,000 as an incentive. Woody promised to do so but his addictions put a strain on his relationship with newly clean Keith and led to tension with Mick, who was insisting on a drug-free tour. He even put signs up backstage warning all and sundry not to give any drugs to Ronnie. It was clear that the 1970s were over. Mick had decided that the Stones were now to be run in a more professional manner. The band began rehearsals for the tour in mid July but after ten days in New York Mick headed to India on vacation. On his return, the band rented the 145-acre Long View Farm in North Brookfield, Massachusetts, where rehearsals continued from mid–August into mid–September. There continued to be a great deal of tension within the band. According to Bill, "There were frequent arguments and many absences from the guitar section of the band." They were usually nowhere to be found in the daytime, which meant rehearsals often didn't start until 11 p.m. and lasted until everyone was falling over from tiredness at 6 a.m. When Ronnie missed one rehearsal, a furious Keith attacked him and had to be pulled away by security. Possibly because he and Woody were partners in crime, the band debated about whether to use Ian McLagan on keyboards. They rehearsed for a few days with David Sancious and then tried out Chuck Leavell of the Allman Brothers. Ultimately they chose to again employ McLagan. As usual, Stu was also there on piano.

Mick announced the tour at a press conference at JFK Stadium in Philadelphia on August 26, where he was joined by San Francisco legend Bill Graham. He had won the contract to promote the tour, which ended up being an enormous windfall, grossing over $30 million. Graham was beloved by the musicians he promoted but famous for his large ego. He had butted heads with the Stones in the past. Tour coordinator Greg Perloff told writer Pete Fornatale of one memorable encounter between Bill and Mick on the road: "Early in the tour there was this wonderful article about Bill. And Mick asked to see Bill and Bill went into the suite and Mick had the newspaper laid out and said, 'Bill what's the name of this tour?' The answer being the Rolling Stones.... It was one of the few times I ever saw Bill shook up!" The press was informed that the blockbuster tour would consist of 50 dates, mostly of large arenas and stadiums. Mick called it, "The biggest tour we've ever done." It was certainly one of the most expensive to put on. Since the Stones were mainly playing outdoor stadiums, a giant stage was built at great expense. The set measured sixty-four feet wide and it had two eighty-foot ramps that stretched out on each side. Japanese artist Kazuhide Yamazaki was commissioned to design the large, colorful stage scrims. Mick later commented, "Most concerts that took place outdoors at the time were played during the day.... So we had the bright, bright primary colors and we had these enormous images of a guitar, a car and a record—an Americana idea—which worked very well for afternoon shows." For the indoor shows, a second stage was designed in the shape of a flower, which would open. To pay for all this, the Stones agreed to corporate sponsorship. Jovan Musk became "the official aftershave of the tour" and got its name on all merchandise in exchange for paying the band $1 million. Keith commented, "It's like a happy medium: Jovan is getting what they want out of it and we're getting some cash up front to pay for gigs that we're gonna work at a loss."

The Stones had now been a band for nineteen years and were all pushing forty (Bill Wyman, the oldest Stone, turned 45 during the tour). Almost every journalist they encountered felt obliged to ask if they'd be hanging up their rock and roll shoes after the tour. Mick told Robert Palmer of *The New York Times*, "That's rubbish. I'm sure we'll be carrying on for years. It's quite easy to. People think that because you're white and it's rock and roll somehow it's different. But all the performers that I love and admire, who are mostly black, went on until they literally died." Asked by the Associated Press about his oft-quoted assertion that he wouldn't want to still be singing "(I Can't Get No) Satisfaction" when he got older, Mick replied, "I never meant it. I just said it. People say 'well can you see yourself doing this at 32?' This was when I was 25. They say, 'Can you see yourself doing this at 38?' I'd say no. So what am I going to say? No, I can't possibly see myself doing this at 39!"

The 1981 tour is extremely well documented. By this time Jumbotron screens had become common at stadiums, so crowds in the bleachers could get a view of the musicians onstage. As a result video of most of the shows exist in varying quality. In addition, the Stones professionally recorded several concerts for yet another concert album, *Still Life*, and director Hal Ashby was hired to make a film of the tour entitled *Let's Spend the Night Together*. Neither the LP (released in 1982) nor the movie (released in 1983) holds a candle to earlier concert albums and films by the Stones. The problem was that the 1981 tour was the Stones at their most professional, not their most inspired. Large daytime shows at stadiums were not the recipe for magic, though the crowds had a great time. In addition, while the band still had fun, the tension evident in rehearsals did not go away. The length of the tour, which lasted almost to Christmas, didn't help. Charlie had not wanted to tour in the first place and grew more morose as time went on. Ronnie was on good behavior, but still was a source of concern. Mick tried to keep things organized and thereby succeeded in irritating Keith, who liked things casual. It was hard, however, to be casual when the Stones were traveling with an entourage of over sixty people. It was far cry from the 1960s, when they traveled in a rented car with only Stu and a road manager. The logistics of moving from place to place was quite stressful and the pressure of taking care of everything took its toll on Mick. According to Bill, he began to drink a lot as the tour progressed. As it turned out, it would be the last American tour for eight years.

## *Concerts*

**Monday, September 14:** Sir Morgan's Cove, Worcester, MA

In the midst of rehearsals, the Stones played a warm-up gig at this 300-seat venue. Tickets were given away to selected fans with the aid of radio station WAAF-FM. Although the Stones tried to keep the site of the gig a secret, words got out and people without tickets camped outside the venue. Seventy-five police officers patrolled outside but the crowd remained calm, listening to the sound emanating from within. The band was billed as Little Boy Blue & the Cockroaches and showed up in a 35-foot Winnebago, with Stu, Ian McLagan and Keith's twelve-year-old son, Marlon, in tow. The Stones allegedly played for about ninety minutes. The eclectic set included "Under My Thumb," "Let It Bleed," "When the Whip Comes Down," "She's So Cold," "Start Me Up," "All Down the Line," "Sympathy for the Devil," and "Honky Tonk Women." They also allegedly played "I Just Want to Make Love to You," "Everybody Needs Somebody to Love," and "Mona," none of which had been performed in concert since the 1960s. The show ended with a stripped to the waist Mick belting out "Jumping Jack Flash."

Keith told reporter Kurt Loder, "It was great. Probably better then we thought, because it was our first gig, and technically it was real rough.... But the audience was great; we all had a good time and it really helped us, you know? Afterward we knew exactly which songs worked onstage and which ones we didn't know well enough and needed to rehearse." The band intended to play two more warm-up show at Boston's Orpheum Theatre on September 18 and 19 but city authorities nixed the plan due to security concerns. Their management then lined up a gig at the Ocean State Theatre in Providence for September 19 but when word leaked out that the Stones were coming it was called off.

**Friday, September 25, and Saturday, September 26:** JFK Stadium, Philadelphia, PA, with George Thorogood and the Destroyers and Journey, daily at 11 a.m.

The tour was the event of the year, thanks to massive publicity. Demand for tickets was overwhelming and the group played to sold-out houses everywhere. Indeed, an astounding 180,000 fans attended the shows in Philadelphia. Even Mick was taken aback by the interest, commenting backstage, "It's amazing isn't it? I mean we were a pretty hot attraction back in 1978, I thought." The Stones picked George Thorogood and his band the Destroyers to open. Their fast paced boogie-blues complemented the Stones' sound. The San Francisco band Journey, fronted by Steve Perry, also performed. They were high on the charts with their signature song, "Don't Stop Believin.'" At the opening show, management made both openers leave the stage after short sets, which meant the audience sat on their hands for two and a half hours until the Stones appeared at 4 o'clock. Nonetheless, when Mick, dressed in a lemon yellow jacket, red T-shirt and white leotards, and the band launched into opener "Under My Thumb," all was forgiven.

The Stones included a number of songs from the Decca years that they'd rarely played since the '60s, including "Time Is on My Side" and "Let's Spend the Night Together." They also performed seven numbers from *Tattoo You*, as well as a few tracks from *Emotional Rescue*. In what would become a standard part of the tour, Mick climbed onto a cherry picker during the finale of "Jumping Jack Flash" and was lifted forty feet. The crane carried him out over the audience, as he threw flowers. The shows ended with balloons raining down on the stage and audience, followed by fireworks. The full set at the opening show consisted of: "Under My Thumb" "When the Whip Comes Down," "Neighbors," "Just My Imagination," "Shattered," "Let's Spend the Night Together," "Black Limousine," "She's So Cold," "Time Is on My Side," "Beast of Burden," "Waiting on a Friend," "Let It Bleed," "You Can't Always Get What You Want," "Tops," "Tumbling Dice," "Hang Fire," "Let Me Go," "Little T&A," "Start Me Up," "Miss You," "Honky Tonk Women," "All Down the Line," "Brown Sugar," "Jumping Jack Flash," "Street Fighting Man" and an encore of "(I Can't Get No) Satisfaction," with Mick draped in a Union Jack. On the second day the band dropped "Tops," "Let Me Go" and "(I Can't Get No) Satisfaction." They replaced those songs with three oldies: "Down the Road Apiece," "Mona," (played for the only time on the tour) and the Eddie Cochran classic "Twenty Flight Rock." Recordings of both shows make the rounds.

**Sunday, September 27:** Rich Stadium, Orchard Park, NY, with George Thorogood and the Destroyers and Journey, noon

This show, attended by 75,000 people, was beset by mishaps. The Stones had commissioned a second stage-set, so that a crew could dismantle one while the other crew set up at the next venue. However, the fierce winds and rain at Rich Stadium wrecked the second stage and the band was forced to have another one hastily built at great expense. The strong winds also repeatedly blew Mick's microphone into his teeth and he had to see a dentist after the show. A good quality tape of this show exists.

**Thursday, October 1:** Metro Center, Rockford, IL, with the Go-Go's

About 35,000 fans wrote a petition begging the Stones to play in Rockford, a city seldom visited by rock legends. They responded by sending a telegram that said, "To the music fans of Rockford: We are overwhelmed by your gracious invitation by petition. We accept. See you on October 1, 1981. Tattoo You." This was the first indoor show and the band easily sold out the 9,000-seat venue. The Stones had initially intended not to utilize a horn section, but after three concerts they decided that something was missing and tenor saxophonist Lee Allen of the Blasters joined them for this show and subsequent dates in Boulder. Ernie Watts took his place starting on October 7. *Chicago Tribune* critic Lynn Van Matre reported, "Jagger presided over proceedings in his usual coquettish style, though his movements seemed less energetic and less mannered then a few years ago, when they bordered on self-parody.... Thursday night's concert featured most of the Stones' classics, with the exception of 'Satisfaction' ... as well as a number of songs from the new album, none of which was as impressive as the vintage material."

**Saturday, October 3, and Sunday, October 4:** Folsom Field, University of Colorado, Boulder, with George Thorogood and the Destroyers and Heart, daily at noon

About 120,000 people attended these outdoor concerts. The full set on Saturday consisted of: "Under My Thumb" "When the Whip Comes Down," "Let's Spend the Night Together," "Shattered," "Neighbors," "Black Limousine," "Just My Imagination," "Twenty

Backstage pass for the Stones' appearance at Folsom Field on October 3, 1981 (collection of Ira Korman).

Flight Rock." "Let Me Go," "Time Is on My Side," "Beast of Burden," "Waiting on a Friend," "Let It Bleed," "Tops" (which wasn't played again on the tour), "You Can't Always Get What You Want," "Tumbling Dice," "Little T&A," "She's So Cold," "All Down the Line," "Hang Fire," "Star, Star" (making its first appearance on this tour), "Miss You," "Start Me Up," "Honky Tonk Women," "Brown Sugar," "Jumping Jack Flash," and an encore of "(I Can't Get No) Satisfaction." *The Colorado Daily* reported, "After its 'Ladies and Gentlemen: The Rolling Stones' intro, the 'greatest rock and roll band in the world' proves the validity of its reputation and excites anyone who loves rock at its best. The Stones are by now so professional and entertaining in their stage show that all of a sudden those two hours have passed and as Ron Wood, Keith Richards and Bill Wyman stand beside a shirtless Mick Jagger for a bow, he is already saying goodbyes to the audience."

**Wednesday, October 7:** Jack Murphy Stadium, San Diego, CA, with George Thorogood and the Destroyers and the J. Geils Band, 3 p.m.

The Stones played to another gargantuan audience of 70,000. Although the sound in the cavernous stadium was abysmal, the crowd rocked along on oldies like "Brown Sugar," though they occasionally grew restless during new tunes. Robert Laurence of the *San Diego Union* reported, "Of these newer songs, it must be said only the hard rocking 'Start Me Up' and heavily bluesy 'Black Limousine' at the moment seems to match up with the best of the Stones' early material.… In this concert, only 'Start Me Up' really reached the crowd with the intensity of say, 'Street Fighting Man.' But 'Black Limousine' needs to be heard in close quarters."

**Friday, October 9, and Sunday, October 11:** Memorial Coliseum, Los Angeles, CA, with Prince and the Revolution, George Thorogood and the Destroyers and the J. Geils Band, daily at 1 p.m.

Rumors spread in Los Angeles that the Stones would play a surprise club date on Saturday but a member of their entourage commented, "Forget it. There's no way the Stones can do a club in this town. We'd have to rent the (3,000-seat) Santa Monica Civic just to handle the guest list!" Instead Keith and Ronnie spent Saturday hanging out with Bob Dylan at Woody's home, while Stu sat in with George Thorogood at a club and Bill shot a video for his solo album. Over 180,000 fans turned out for the Coliseum shows, including celebrities like Dylan, Robin Williams and Jack Nicholson. Brian Jones' son Julian also visited.

The shows were opened by Prince, then near the start of his career. For whatever reason, the audience on Friday wasn't impressed when he came out to play in a bikini and trench coat. They began booing at him and his band. Bottles and cans were hurled at the stage. Bill Graham tried to calm the crowd, but the boos continued and a tearful Prince left the stage in the middle of his fourth number. Allegedly it took much pleading from his management to get him to turn up on Sunday. Mick recalled in 1983, "I talked to Prince on the phone once after he got two cans thrown at him in L.A. He said he didn't want to do any more shows.… I told him, if you get to be a really big headliner, you have to be prepared for people to throw bottles at you in the night." Keith was less sympathetic. He commented in *Musician*, "That's the trouble with conferring a title on yourself before you've proved it. That was his attitude when he opened for us on the tour, and it was insulting to our audience.… He's a prince who thinks he's a king already." The crowds were kinder to George Thorogood and the J. Geils Band, but the audience was there to see the Stones. Large crowds pushed up against the stage when they came on and Mick

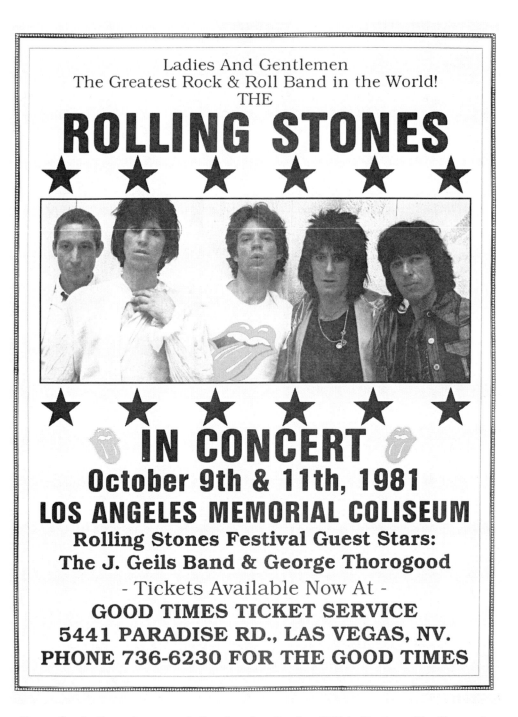

Poster for the Stones' concerts in Los Angeles, October 1981 (collection of Ira Korman).

had to repeatedly advise people to move back. The shows, however, went off without a hitch and Bobby Keys came out to aid Ernie Watts on "Brown Sugar" and "Jumping Jack Flash" both nights.

**Wednesday, October 14, and Thursday, October 15:** Kingdome, Seattle, WA, with the Greg Kihn Band and the J. Geils Band, Wednesday at 8 p.m. and Thursday at 3 p.m.

These concerts were broadcast on the Jumbotron screens and a good video exists. The full set at both shows consisted of: "Under My Thumb" "When the Whip Comes Down," "Let's Spend the Night Together," "Shattered," "Neighbors," "Black Limousine," "Just My Imagination," "Twenty Flight Rock." "Let Me Go," "Time Is on My Side," "Beast of Burden," "Waiting on a Friend," "Let It Bleed," "You Can't Always Get What You Want," "Little T&A," "Tumbling Dice," "She's So Cold," "All Down the Line," "Hang Fire," "Star, Star," "Miss You," "Start Me Up," "Honky Tonk Women," "Brown Sugar," "Jumping Jack Flash," and the encore of "(I Can't Get No) Satisfaction."

**Saturday, October 17, and Sunday, October 18:** Candlestick Park, San Francisco, CA, with George Thorogood and the Destroyers and the J. Geils Band, daily at 11 a.m.

About 140,000 people turned out to see these massive concerts. The band continued to have trust issues with Ronnie, despite his promise to stay clean. In his book *Life*, Keith related that things got ugly while the band was staying at the Fairmont Hotel when he learned that Woody and his mates were doing coke in his room. "He'd promised me he wouldn't be doing that shit on the road.... I got there, he opened the door and I just socked him. You cunt, boom! So he fell backwards over the couch and the rest of my punch carried me over on top of him, the couch fell over and we both nearly fell out the window. We scared ourselves to death!" Despite the behind-the-scenes tension, Bill Wyman professed to be enjoying himself on tour. He told a reporter, "Even the weather has been great to us. Everywhere we go it clears up just in time for the shows—even in Boulder, where it rained until 11 o'clock the day of the concert. Somebody up there likes us."

**Saturday, October 24, and Sunday, October 25:** Tangerine Bowl, Orlando, FL, with the Henry Paul Band and Van Halen, daily at noon

The Stones played to over 120,000 fans. Van Halen, concluding their *Fair Warning* tour, opened along with southern rocker Henry Paul (formerly of the Outlaws). It was Bill's 45th birthday and during the Saturday show, a plane flew overhead with the words "Happy Birthday Bill!" Mick then got the whole crowd to sing to him. The next day, Bill told the BBC, "It was wonderful because yesterday the whole audience of 60,000 people sang 'Happy Birthday' to me. (It was) one of the highlights of my career no doubt! No really ... it was really very emotional. And we had a great party in Disneyland last night." Noel Holston of *The Orlando Sentinel* attended the Sunday show and commented, "Led by the indefatigable Jagger, a dervish in orange football togs, they put on a high energy two-hour show that was far more exciting then their Lakeland concert three years ago—and better even, in the opinion of dual concert-goers, than their first Orlando show on Saturday."

**Monday, October 26:** Fox Theatre, Atlanta, GA, with the Stray Cats, 8 p.m.

As a change of pace from the stadiums, the Stones returned to the tiny Fox Theatre, where they'd played a memorable show in 1978. About 3,900 lucky fans, including former first daughter Amy Carter, got to see them in an intimate setting. Keith and Ronnie, however, were out partying and almost missed the gig. They arrived as the opening act was finishing their set. Woody, somewhat the worse for wear, walked straight onto the stage to set up his gear and had to make a quick disappearance when he realized the rockabilly band the Stray Cats were still performing. Mick sardonically commented, "Now that's professionalism!" Despite the smaller setting, the group played basically the same show, but did not do an encore of 'Satisfaction.' They did, however, perform "Street Fighting

Man" for the last time on the tour. Chuck Leavell, who'd auditioned for a spot in the band in August, guested on keyboards. John Smyntek of the *Detroit Free Press* reported, "From the opening 'Under My Thumb' to the closing 'Jumping Jack Flash' the aging rockers gave spirited performances on every tune. Even the usually dour Watts smiled when Jagger made a quick sortie into the crowd late in the show during a sizzling version of 'Miss You.' All night long, Richards and Wood traded guitar work like juicy gossip. And bassist Wyman looked as bored as ever, twanging away in his yellow suit, which is de rigeur on this tour."

**Wednesday, October 28, and Thursday, October 29:** Astrodome, Houston, TX, with the Fabulous Thunderbirds and ZZ Top, nightly at 6

The Stones put together a great bill in Houston, including ZZ Top, who'd opened for them in Hawaii in 1973. The Jumbotron screen captured a spirited performance. However, Marty Racine of the *Houston Chronicle* felt that the Stones didn't live up to the hype. He commented, "Whether it was the laid back atmosphere, the Astrodome logistics or the task of fulfilling great expectations, the Stones did not elicit a wild response. Something was missing…. After a three-year layoff, they've rehearsed and geared themselves into rock 'n' roll once more. But only at peak moments were they capable of dissolving the Astrodome echo into a unified rhythm, and never did the Dome's audience coalesce into one great vibration."

Considering the huge crowds that squashed into stadiums to see the Stones, the tour was remarkably riot free. The first show, however, was marred by some unfortunate occurrences. Two people were stabbed, one fatally, at the concert. Many in the media were quick to bring up Altamont and the Stones' satanic image but their spokesman Paul Wasserman commented, "I just think that's a false cliché. I just think it's people searching for an angle when they say it has something to do with the aura (of the band)."

**Saturday, October 31, and Sunday, November 1:** Cotton Bowl, Dallas, TX, with the Fabulous Thunderbirds and ZZ Top, daily at noon

The Stones played before 160,000 people. The first show was played in pouring rain, but no one left. Mick made light of the situation when he sang, 'She's So Cold' and 'I'm so wet.' The driving rain gave "Jumping Jack Flash" a great visual but prevented Mick from doing his usual cherry-picker routine. Pete Oppel of *The Dallas News* reported one unusual occurrence. During "Beast of Burden" Mick "ran down a ramp on the west side of the stage and snapped Polaroid pictures of the crowd. After his camera spewed out the instant snapshots, which fell to the stage, Jagger picked them up and handed them to a security man stationed between the stage and the crowd. The security guy flung the pictures into the crowd." Some lucky fans probably have a framed Polaroid of them taken by Mick. The full set at the first show consisted of: "Under My Thumb" "When the Whip Comes Down," "Let's Spend the Night Together," "Shattered," "Neighbors," "Black Limousine," "Just My Imagination," "Twenty Flight Rock," "Let Me Go," "Time Is on My Side," "Beast of Burden," "Let It Bleed," "You Can't Always Get What You Want," "Little T&A," "Tumbling Dice," "She's So Cold," "All Down the Line," "Hang Fire," "Miss You," "Start Me Up," "Honky Tonk Women," "Brown Sugar," and "Jumping Jack Flash." The show on Sunday was the same, except for the addition of "Waiting on a Friend" and encore of "(I Can't Get No) Satisfaction," which ended all future shows.

**Tuesday, November 3:** Freedom Hall, Louisville, KY, with the Neville Brothers, 8 p.m.

The Stones played before a comparatively small crowd of 18,000. Since it was the first show with their new secondary stage set (rebuilt after being wrecked at Rich Stadium), they scheduled a full rehearsal for 7 p.m. on Monday, which in typical Stones fashion didn't start until 1 a.m. and ended at 6:30 in the morning. They added a new song to the set, Smokey Robinson's 1960s classic "Going to a Go-Go," which remained in the show for the rest of the tour.

**Thursday, November 5, to Saturday, November 7:** Brendan Byrne Arena, the Meadowlands, East Rutherford, NJ, with Tina Turner, nightly at 8

Tina Turner opened for the Stones as a last-minute replacement for Garland Jeffreys. She also joined Mick for "Honky Tonk Women" on all three nights. All three of these shows were filmed by Hal Ashby for his concert film, which first premiered in Germany in 1982 under the title *Rocks Off* and then in slightly edited fashion as *Let's Spend the Night Together* in 1983. The footage of "Little T&A," "Tumbling Dice," "She's So Cold," "All Down the Line," "Hang Fire," "Let It Bleed," "Start Me Up," and "Brown Sugar" in the film comes from the Thursday show, while the footage of "Going to a Go-Go," "You Can't Always Get What You Want," "Miss You," and "(I Can't Get No) Satisfaction" comes from the Friday show. Nothing was used in the film from the Saturday concert. The full set on Thursday consisted of: "Under My Thumb" (the version on the LP *Still Life*, comes from this show), "When the Whip Comes Down," "Let's Spend the Night Together," "Shattered," "Neighbors," "Black Limousine," "Just My Imagination," "Down the Road Apiece" "Going to a Go-Go," "Let Me Go," "Time Is on My Side," "Beast of Burden," "Waiting on a Friend," "Let It Bleed," "You Can't Always Get What You Want," "Little T&A," "Tumbling Dice," "She's So Cold," "All Down the Line," "Hang Fire," "Miss You," "Start Me Up," "Honky Tonk Women," "Brown Sugar," and "Jumping Jack Flash" and "(I Can't Get No) Satisfaction." At the following two shows, the Stones dropped "Down the Road Apiece" in favor of "Twenty Flight Rock."

**Monday, November 9, and Tuesday, November 10:** Civic Center, Hartford, CT, with Garland Jeffreys, nightly at 8

The Stones returned to Hartford for the first time since 1966. Fans descended on the city in hopes of gaining access to the shows and there were fights between crowds and the police outside the Civic Center. However, inside the venue order was maintained. The *Hartford Courant's* Colin McEnroe noted, "The material from 'Tattoo' the band's newest album, was, not surprisingly, the freshest and most exciting. 'Start Me Up' given a sexy, pounding treatment near the end of the show, seems destined to become a Stones standard for as long the band continues to play; and the propulsive 'Neighbors,' spiced up by the pyrotechnics of sax player Ernie Watts, was one of the evening's most musically satisfying moments."

**Thursday, November 12, and Friday, November 13:** Madison Square Garden, New York, NY, with Screaming Jay Hawkins, nightly at 8

The legendary Screaming Jay Hawkins, of "I Put a Spell on You" fame, opened these shows. *The White Plains Journal News* noted, "The Stones are far from tired or retired. They're getting better musically and more entertaining and innovative in stagecraft all the time.... The concert was fun. During the encore, 'Satisfaction,' ripcords were pulled on 20 clear plastic sacks full of orange, yellow and black balloons hanging from the ceiling, where they looked like huge sacks of jellybeans."

**Monday, November 16, and Tuesday, November 17:** Richfield Coliseum, Richfield, OH, with Etta James, nightly at 8

**Thursday, November 19:** Checkerdome, St. Louis, MO, with Lamont Cranston, 8 p.m.

This show was opened by the Minneapolis blues-band Lamont Cranston, who'd made the charts with "Upper Mississippi Shakedown."

**Friday, November 20:** UNI Dome, Cedar Falls, IA, with the Stray Cats, 7:30 p.m.

The Stones performed before a crowd of 24,000 at this indoor show. Water from the cold roof leaked onto the stage and Mick quipped, "I didn't know it rained indoors." UPI reported, "The 38-year-old Jagger pranced onto the stage wearing a green jersey and white football knickers and the band led the concert with the controversial tune, 'Under My Thumb.' Despite the dripping water, the Stones played for more than two hours, reeling off hits like 'Shattered,' Honky-Tonk Woman,' and 'Brown Sugar.'" A low-quality video from the Jumbotron screen exists.

**Saturday, November 21:** Civic Center, St. Paul, MN, with the Stray Cats, 8 p.m.

The set consisted of: "Under My Thumb," "When the Whip Comes Down," "Let's Spend the Night Together," "Shattered," "Neighbours," "Black Limousine," "Just My Imagination," "Twenty Flight Rock," "Going to a Go-Go," "Let Me Go," "Time Is on My Side," "Beast of Burden," "Waiting on a Friend," "Let It Bleed," "You Can't Always Get What You Want," "Little T & A," "Tumbling Dice," "She's So Cold," "Hang Fire," "Miss You," "Honky Tonk Women," "Brown Sugar," "Start Me Up," "Jumping Jack Flash," and the encore of "Satisfaction."

The Stones performing at the UNI Dome in Iowa on November 20, 1981 (Special Collections and University Archives, Rod Library, University of Northern Iowa).

**Sunday, November 22:** Checkerboard Lounge, Chicago, IL, with Muddy Waters

According to the DVD notes, the decision to get on stage at this club on the south side of Chicago, owned by Buddy Guy, was impromptu. However, other sources suggest it had been arranged in advance. While Muddy Waters was performing "Baby Please Don't Go," Mick, Keith, Ronnie and Stu entered the small club and were invited to the stage (Bill was absent and Charlie, according to Buddy Guy, "was laying out on the bar" when he walked in. He later told him he had no memory of the night). They performed with Muddy and his band and were joined by blues Legends Buddy Guy, Junior Wells and Lefty Dizz. A camera crew was on hand to film the encounter between the Stones and their mentor and David Hewitt recorded the show, which was later mixed by Bob Clearmountain. A DVD and a CD of the show was released as *Live at the Checkerboard Lounge, Chicago 1981* in 2012. The set consisted of blues classics: "Baby Please Don't Go," "Hoochie Coochie Man," "Long Distance Call," "Mannish Boy," "Got My Mojo Working," "Next Time You See Me," "One Eyed Woman" "Baby Please Don't Go" (instrumental), "Clouds in My Heart," and "Champagne and Reefer."

**Monday, November 23, to Wednesday, November 25:** Rosemont Horizon, Chicago, IL

These shows were recorded and the Stones opted to use versions of "Start Me Up" and "Beast of Burden" recorded on Wednesday for the *Still Life* LP. While the band was in Chicago a fun after-gig party was arranged for the crew at Park West. Mick and Ronnie served as bartenders and Mick's girlfriend, Jerry Hall, acted as a waitress, along with Keith's girlfriend Patti. The Stones treated the crew to performances by strippers and the Neville Brothers.

**Friday, November 27, and Saturday, November 28:** Carrier Dome, Syracuse University, Syracuse, NY, with the Henry Paul Band and Molly Hatchet, daily at 4 p.m.

**Monday, November 30, and Tuesday, December 1:** Silverdome, Pontiac, MI, with Iggy Pop and Santana, Monday at 7:30 p.m. and Tuesday at 6 p.m.

Over 150,000 fans turned out for the two shows. On Monday night the crowd embraced opener Santana but showed hostility towards Michigan native Iggy Pop. Boos and catcalls led him to end his show after only twenty-five minutes. Iggy's sound was allegedly muddled and fans were impatient to see the Stones, who didn't take the stage until 10 p.m. NBC TV filmed the opening concert for the program *Television: Inside and Out*. The show also contained backstage footage from before and after the concert. The Stones allowed producers to have unrestricted access and footage exists (much of it not broadcast) of Bill playing ping-pong and Mick doing Pilates to warm up.

**Saturday, December 5:** Superdome, New Orleans, LA, with the Neville Brothers and George Thorogood and the Destroyers, 6 p.m.

The Stones flew into New Orleans on Wednesday to relax before their appearance at the Superdome. On Thursday they held a private bash aboard the riverboat President, attended by Stephen Stills, Dr. John, Bill Graham, Ahmet Ertegun, Jerry Hall and other invited guests. The Stones didn't play, but the Neville Brothers, the Meters, Clarence "Frogman" Henry and Toots Washington did. The New Orleans show, before a record crowd of over 87,000, was professionally recorded, though nothing was used on the *Still Life* album. *The Baton Rouge Advocate* reported, "Jagger is still the rocker's Peter Pan. He is still the best rock showman on any stage…. There were closeups of Jagger on the

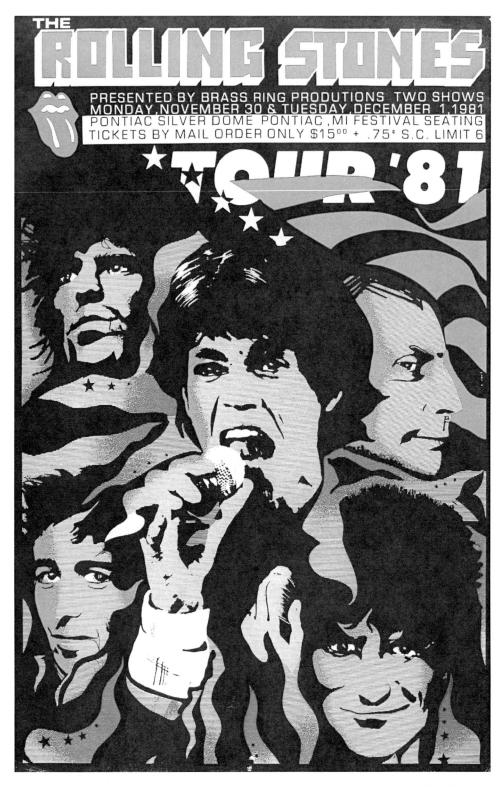

Poster for the Stones' appearance at the Pontiac Silverdome, 1981 (collection of Ira Korman).

Dome's TV screens. Jagger didn't need the television screens. He reached out to the farthest seats in the Dome with his patented gestures. He played the great audience as though it were a great bass fiddle. He flew over the crowd in a crane bucket during 'Jumping Jack Flash' to ecstatic cheering."

**Monday, December 7, to Wednesday, December 9:** Capital Centre, Largo, MD, with Bobby Womack, nightly at 8

The Stones recorded these shows. The set on December 9 consisted of: "Under My Thumb," "When the Whip Comes Down," "Let's Spend the Night Together," "Shattered," "Neighbours," "Black Limousine," "Just My Imagination," "Twenty Flight Rock," "Going to a Go Go," "Let Me Go," "Time Is on My Side," "Beast of Burden," "Waiting on a Friend," "Let It Bleed," "You Can't Always Get What You Want," "Tumbling Dice," "She's So Cold," "Hang Fire," "Miss You," "Honky Tonk Women," "Brown Sugar," "Start Me Up," "Jumping Jack Flash," and "(I Can't Get No) Satisfaction." The Stones opted to use the versions of "Going to a Go-Go," "Let Me Go," and "Twenty Flight Rock," taped that night, for the *Still Life* LP.

**Friday, December 11:** Rupp Arena, Lexington, KY, with the Meters, 8 p.m.

The Stones played before a tiny crowd of 23,400. *The Lexington Herald* reported that the crowd "Loved it. They were on their feet through all 26 songs, clapping hands, stomping feet, jumping on fast songs and swaying on slow ones." This show was professionally recorded, though nothing was used on *Still Life*.

**Sunday, December 13:** Sun Devil Stadium, Arizona State University, Tempe, with Joe Ely and George Thorogood and the Destroyers

This show, before 80,000 fans, was recorded and the version of "(I Can't Get No) Satisfaction" heard on *Still Life* comes from this performance. Hal Ashby also filmed the show for his documentary. The performances of "Under My Thumb," "When the Whip Comes Down," "Let's Spend the Night Together," "Shattered," "Neighbours," "Black Limousine," "Just My Imagination," "Twenty Flight Rock," "Let Me Go," "Time Is on My Side," "Beast of Burden," and "Waiting on a Friend" "Honky Tonk Women" and "Jumping Jack Flash" seen in the German version of the film were taped on this day. The U.S. release of the film does not include "When the Whip Comes Down."

**Monday, December 14, and Tuesday, December 15:** Kemper Arena, Kansas City, MO, with George Thorogood and the Destroyers, 8 p.m.

Mick Taylor made a guest appearance at the Monday show, his first appearance with the group since 1973, but things did not go well. Ron Wood later commented, "He was so loud—I don't know if it was out of nerves or what—that Keith was about to wring his neck. I had to try and block Keith's path a few times during the songs. He was going, 'I'm going to kill him!'" Bill noted in his diary, "I regarded this as our worst show of the tour."

**Friday, December 18, and Saturday, December 19:** Hampton Coliseum, Hampton, VA, with George Thorogood and the Destroyers, Friday at 9 p.m. and Saturday at 8 p.m.

The Friday night show was broadcast via satellite as "The World's Greatest Rock and Roll Party" to television viewers as a pay-per-view event. This was a new concept, but soon became common in the industry. Hal Ashby, already filming the Stones for his movie, directed the program with Tom Trbovich. By this time the band was exhausted and some members were not thrilled about more filming. Bill especially was angered

```
HAMPTON RDS, VA.        DEC. 18, 1981

1.  THUMB
2.  WHIP
3.  SPEND NIGHT
4.  SHATTERED
5.  NEIGHBORS
6.  BLACK LIMO
7.  IMAGINATION
8.  20 FLIGHT
9.  GO GO
10. LET ME GO          [AUDIENCE - M.J]
11. TIME ON MY SIDE    STAGE TO STGE LEF
12. BEAST              BACK SCISSOR - M.J.
13. FRIEND             STAGE TO CENTER
14. LET IT BLEED
15. CAN'T ALWAYS GET   WOODY TO STG. LEFT SCIS
                       MICK TO STGE RIGHT SCISSO
16. T & A
17. DICE               STGE TO STGE RIGHT
18. COLD
19. HANGFIRE
20. MISS YOU           STGE TO CENTER
21. HONKY TONK         MICK & WOODY TO STG RIGHT
                                       SCISSO
22. BROWN SUGAR
23. START ME UP
24. J.J. FLASH         MICK - CHERRY
    SATISFACTION
```

**Copy of the band's set list for the December 18, 1981, show in Hampton Roads, Virginia (collection of Ira Korman).**

that Mick and Prince Rupert cooked up the idea with little band input. In any event, the Stones put on a good show for the cameras (which also captured a backstage jam). One infamous moment occurred during the gig when a fan ran onto the stage as balloons were falling and Keith hit him with his guitar. In the booklet accompanying the DVD of this show, he commented, "Security was a bit slow and I saw some guy heading straight for Mick. I do have a weapon in my hands. The damn thing stayed in tune and this is the greatest advertisement for Fender that I can give you."

The set consisted of: "Under My Thumb," "When the Whip Comes Down," "Let's Spend the Night Together," "Shattered," "Neighbours," "Black Limousine," "Just My Imagination," "Twenty Flight Rock," "Going to a Go Go," "Let Me Go," "Time Is on My Side," "Beast of Burden," "Waiting on a Friend," "Let It Bleed," "You Can't Always Get What You Want," "Little T & A," "Tumbling Dice," "She's So Cold," "Hang Fire," "Miss You," "Honky Tonk Women," "Brown Sugar," "Start Me Up," "Jumping Jack Flash," and "(I Can't Get No) Satisfaction." The Stones used the versions of "Time Is on My Side," "Shattered," and "Let's Spend the Night Together" taped that night for the *Still Life* LP. The version of "Just My Imagination" heard on the album was taped the following night. The entire performance was released on DVD and CD in 2012. The tour ended the following night and a party was held to celebrate, which included cake for Keith and Bobby Keys, both of whom had birthdays on December 18.

## Chapter 21

# 1982

As 1982 began the Stones were unwinding after the long U.S. tour. Mick and Keith spent some time in Los Angeles with director Hal Ashby in February to look at the footage of the 1981 tour and help shape his documentary, which was first released as *Rocks Off* in Germany later in the year and then premiered in America in 1983 as *Let's Spend the Night Together*. Ron Wood was across the country in New York and got on stage at the Ritz with Bobby Womack on February 18 and Chuck Berry on February 21.

Bill Wyman used the time to promote his third solo album, *Bill Wyman*. In addition to featuring his 1981 hit "(Si Si) Je Suis un Rock Star," the LP also included a second top forty single, "A New Fashion," which was released in March. Bill did numerous radio and television interviews in the UK early in the year and then embarked on a promotional tour of Australia and Japan in late February and early March. After a quick trip to New York, he traveled to Germany in April. Bill also filmed a music video for "A New Fashion" that got a lot of television airplay. Bill's trip to New York in March was to work with the band at the Power Station. While the Stones did not record new music, they gathered in New York in March and April to mix and record overdubs for the planned live album of the 1981 U.S. tour. While in New York, Ron Wood joined Toots and the Maytals on stage at the Ritz on April 17 and Keith got onstage with Etta James at the Other End nightclub on April 26.

The live LP *Still Life* was released in June. It reached the top ten in both the U.S and UK but was, to my ears, a disappointment. The live performances captured on the single LP in no way outclass the original versions, though it is nice to have the Stones' covers of "Going to a Go-Go" and "Twenty Flight Rock" for posterity. The LP sounds overproduced, with the guts taken out of it in the process. I know a number of people who saw fantastic shows by the Stones on that tour and none of them feel that the overly slick LP captures the rough energy and enthusiasm they experienced. Indeed, the CD of the December 1981 Hampton show released in 2012 is far superior, perhaps because it all comes from one night and thus has a unity of sound and mood.

By the time the live LP was released, the Stones had already embarked on the European leg of their tour, again promoted by Bill Graham. Rehearsals took place in England in May. Keith and Mick continued to disagree on just about everything. Mick wanted to rehearse for a month, while Keith only wanted to do one week. Mick wasn't even keen to do the tour, as the band usually made little money on their European trips. The rest of the band, however, wanted the money and were keen to play. The 35-date tour began on May 26 in Scotland and ended at Leeds on July 25. There was great demand for tickets and the band ended up making more money than expected. The set differed little from the American shows, though the Stones did add a cover of the Big Bopper's 1958 hit "Chantilly Lace." By this time many European venues featured the Jumbotron screens above the stage so that the audience in the back could see the band. Many video feeds of the concerts exist.

Following the tour, Mick and Keith made an attempt to reconnect and write some new songs at a basement studio in Paris. However there remained some unspoken tensions that were obvious to other band members when the full band reconvened in November at EMI's Pathé Marconi Studios to begin work on *Undercover*. Ron Wood recalled in *According to the Rolling Stones,* "Mick was not a very good drinker and drugger, and when he decided to quit or cut down his intake, generally change his personality and try and be a more responsible person, Keith didn't really like the change in him." Keith was also unhappy with Mick's desire to make a 1980s record that embraced new technology like synthesizers and sequencers. Mick, on the other hand, felt constrained by the limitations of the band and was probably already planning to make a solo album when *Undercover* was completed. Ron Wood found himself playing the role of diplomatic intermediary between the two warring camps and as Keith recalled in *Life*, things reached such a low point that he took to only coming into the studio at night when Mick had already left.

Ultimately the band took a break for Christmas and the rest of the *Undercover* LP was not recorded until 1983. Miraculously the band would complete the LP and a 1985 follow-up *Dirty Work* in the next three years. The 1982 tour, however, had marked the end of an era. The tension between Mick and Keith continued to build and touring became impossible to contemplate. Both men opted to make solo albums during the period and to tour with their own bands. The Stones had entered "the wilderness years" and wouldn't play another full concert together until 1989.

## Concerts

**Wednesday, May 26:** Capitol Theatre, Aberdeen, Scotland, UK, with TV21, 7:45 p.m.

The Stones opened their first European tour since 1976 with a few warm-up shows. The opening concert took place at a 2,000-seat cinema, the kind of venue they'd played so often in the 1960s. The band for the tour included former Allman Brothers keyboardist Chuck Leavell, who took the place of Ian McLaglen. The band also was augmented by a horn section composed of Bobby Keys and saxophonist Gene Barge, who'd played on many Chess sessions in the 1960s. The tour would also be the last in which Ian Stewart played piano before his untimely death in 1985.

As usual the British press was far more critical of the Stones than their American counterparts, with much talk of the band's declining relevancy. Paolo Hewitt of *Melody Maker* expressed great boredom with the concert, declaring "What the Stones show suffered from most was sheer, unremitting tedium.… Only Keith Richards seemed excited, genuinely excited by the occasion, cutting a sharp contrast with Jagger's forced performance, smiling, dancing and seemingly gaining true pleasure from his playing."

**Thursday, May 27:** Apollo Theatre, Glasgow, Scotland, UK, with TV21, 7:30 p.m.

The Stones performed for 3,000 happy fans at this intimate venue. Iaian Gray of the *Glasgow Herald* reported, "The Rolling Stones, in the second of a three day Scottish tour, could do no wrong. Despite acoustics which reminded one of listening to early

Rolling Stones records on a Dansette record player, the energy generated was more than enough to feed the nostalgia of the fans, some of whom paid more then three times the face value of the tickets."

**Friday, May 28:** Playhouse Theatre, Edinburgh, Scotland, UK, with TV21, 8 p.m.

Fans welcomed the Stones back to the UK and the press opined that they'd become a grand tradition in England. Keith was delighted and told writer Robin Denselow, "After we'd done the Scottish shows I read a piece suggesting that there was now no reason why the Stones couldn't be like Sinatra and Crosby. I thought that was an amazing comparison!"

**Monday, May 31:** 100 Club, London, UK

The Stones played another warm-up show at this 400-seat club. The band advertised the concert by putting up six posters in the city four hours before showtime. Alexis Korner was in attendance, as well as assorted wives and girlfriends. The show included a rare performance of "Mona," which did not show up again on the tour. Mick told Andy Peebles of BBC Radio 1, "We'd played some clubs in America but this one was much more unannounced and last minute. I enjoyed it; it's just a very different atmosphere. You can relax in between numbers and it doesn't matter if you want to do a different number. You tend to get locked into a certain show in stadiums."

**Wednesday, June 2, Friday, June 4, and Saturday, June 5:** Feyenoord Stadion, Rotterdam, the Netherlands, with George Thorogood and the Destroyers and the J. Geils Band, Wednesday and Friday at 4 p.m. and Saturday at 2 p.m.

The Stones played three shows for 135,000 fans. On the first night, the Stones did

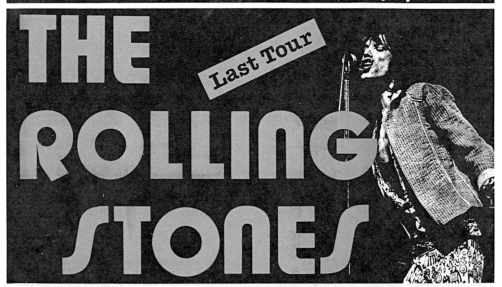

Advertisement for the Stones' concert in Rotterdam in 1982 (collection of Ira Korman).

not take the stage until 9 p.m. The *Nieuwsblad Van Het Noorden* reported, "While thousands of balloons were lauched into the the air, the band started Under My Thumb, a song from their early days. After that, twenty-five numbers followed, forming a cross-section from their almost twenty-year career. Let's Spend the Night Together (sung by everyone), Time Is on My Side and You Can not Always Get What You Want (where thousands of burning lighters were kept up in the air) and Satisfaction, they were all played.... A well rehearsed Mick Jagger was fantastic.... The rest of the band remained in his shadow. Even Keith Richards, as always with a cigarette in the mouth, was barely noticed despite some of his well known cutting guitar solos and what to do back and forth on the gangway."

**Sunday, June 6, and Monday, June 7:** Niedersachsen Stadion, Hannover, West Germany, with Peter Maffay and the J. Geils Band, Sunday at 1 p.m. and Monday at 2 p.m.

About 63,000 fans witnessed the opening show in Hannover. Over six hundred police were on hand to maintain order, but the days of wild riots at concerts had passed and both shows passed uneventfully.

**Tuesday, June 8:** Waldbühne, Berlin, West Germany, with Peter Maffay and the J. Geils Band, 8 p.m.

The Stones occupied the entire top floor of Berlin's best hotel with an entourage of 130 people. An audience of 22,120 people attended the band's outdoor concert. Peter Hillmore of *The Observer* opined, "The group does not let any of their audience down, from the moment they come on before 40,000 people in an open-air stadium to the time that a firework finale erupts two and a half hours later.... Without a break, without even a pause or interval, the group plays number after number.... All the audience's favorite songs are played/performed in a way that the audience seemed to want them to be... 'One of the reasons why we have to play for so long,' Jagger tells me, 'is that even playing just our hits of twenty years takes a while and the audience still want our hits.'"

**Thursday, June 10, and Friday, June 11:** Olympia Stadion, Munich, West Germany, with Peter Maffay and the J. Geils Band, daily at 2 p.m.

**Sunday, June 13, and Monday, June 14:** Hippodrome D'Auteuil, Paris, France, with the J. Geils Band and George Thorogood and the Destroyers, daily at 1 p.m.

The two-day residency in Paris was attended by close to 140,000 fans. Even this did not satisfy demand. Two fires were set by those without tickets to protest the high price for shows. The arsonists left a note at the scene that stated, "If you want to save your racetrack, bring down the price of Rolling Stones tickets!" The first show was also marred by heavy rain, which suddenly cleared before the band took the stage at 4:30 p.m. *Rolling Stone* reported that "the band ... seemed to get better and better as the show progressed. Jagger, dressed in red and white striped tights, pranced up and down the stage, tossing asides to the crowd in barroom French. Keith Richard and Ron Wood pumped out the group's trademark licks and huddled together at one mike to share their occasional vocals, while the sturdy rhythm section of Bill Wyman and Charlie Watts kept everything rolling."

**Wednesday, June 16:** Stade de Gerland, Lyon, France, with Jean-Marie and the Butcher Boys, George Thorogood and the Destroyers and the J. Geils Band, 4 p.m.

Mick performed in a red and white football outfit before 45,000 fans. It was boiling hot in the stadium and over 400 people fainted. The stadium officials turned on sprinklers to cool down the crowd. Despite the heat, *Le Progres* reported, "Mick Jagger was in great

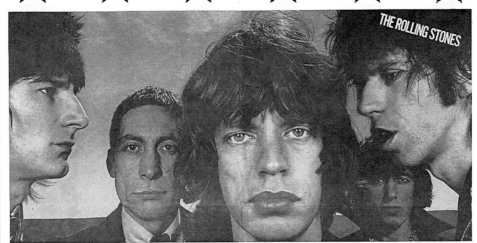

Handbill for the Stones' appearance in Hannover in 1982 (collection of Ira Korman).

shape and was continually jumping, running, dancing and walking up and down the stage. He had no trouble exciting the crowd. For all those who were there, June 16 was an opportunity to be together for a large party. Much more then the music itself, the crowd came to Gerland mainly to see those characters of legend in the flesh."

**June 19 and June 20:** Ullevi Stadium, Gothenburg, Sweden, with Kim Larsen & Jungle Dreams and Thomas Ledin, daily at 1 p.m.

The Stones maintained their popularity in Sweden. All 110,000 tickets for these shows sold out in six and a half hours.

**Wednesday, June 23:** St. James Park Newcastle, England, UK, with the J. Geils Band and George Thorogood and the Destroyers, 2 p.m.,

The Stones were one of the first bands to play at St. James Park, home of the Newcastle United football team. They arrived at the stadium in a luxury coach at 7 p.m. and entertained Sting and members of the group Genesis backstage. The band played before a crowd of 38,000 fans. *The Newcastle Chronicle* reported, "Their sell out concert at St James' Park was a mesmerizing spectacle, a non-stop musical party, an unqualified success.... Jagger is still the most charismatic live performer in rock. He cuts a striking figure, making full use of the 240ft-long stage, running from end to end to tease and torment in fine athletic form. (Keith) Richards seemed to be only marginally less popular than Jagger, eliciting huge cheers every time he moved to one side of the stage, with the inevitable cigarette jammed in his mouth."

**Friday, June 25, and Saturday, June 26:** Wembley Stadium, London, UK, with the J. Geils Band and Black Uhuru, Friday at 2 p.m. and Saturday at 1 p.m.

The Stones' concerts attracted 140,000. The celebrity studded crowd included John McEnroe, Michael Caine, the Who's John Entwhistle, Sting and Christopher Reeve. Many of the band members' parents were also on hand to see their children on stage "at home." Mick's mom commented, "Each performance is different and I promise I never tire of it." Many aristocrats also attended the shows and requested permission to meet the Stones backstage. Keith, never a great admirer of such folk, proposed that signs be put up backstage that declared, "Dandys, enter at your own risk!"

Mick admitted to Paula Yates, "London was a big up for us in our hometown. No one had ever played in Wembley very well before, so they say. I've never actually seen a group play there but the Who didn't do well there.... It was great to get it over because we were scared to death of it being a bad sound and raining and it nearly was." Barney Hoskyns of *NME* opted to review the show in the guise of an alien from another planet, but was clearly unimpressed. He commented that "the greater part of the noise performed by the five ... was dire in the extreme and never more so than when their pace (makers) quickened, uncomfortably, on droning anthems like 'When the Whip Comes Down,' 'Let Me Go,' 'Neighbors,' 'She's So Cold' and 'Hang Fire.' All of these seemed to me identical and equally fatuous, despite the marvelous rhythm provided by the melancholy, long-faced drummer (Charlie Watts) and the deep, looping structures built under the sound by the four-stringed player (Bill Wyman)."

**Sunday, June 27:** Ashton Gate Stadium, Bristol, England, UK, with Talisman and the J. Geils Band, noon

About 36,000 fans turned out in pouring rain to see the Stones' first concert in Bristol since 1971.

**Tuesday, June 29, to Thursday, July 1:** Festhalle, Frankfurt, West Germany, with Peter Maffay and the J. Geils Band, nightly at 8 p.m.

**Saturday, July 3:** Prater Stadion Vienna, Austria, with the J. Geils Band, 2 p.m.

In the book *According to the Rolling Stones*, Peter Wolf of the J. Geils Band related that he and Mick visited a nightclub (the Moulin Rouge) while in Vienna. When they walked in, the house band just happened to be performing "As Tears Go By" and Mick jumped up onstage and joined them for the song.

**Sunday, July 4, and Monday, July 5:** Müngersdorfer Stadion, Cologne, West Germany, with BAP and the J. Geils Band, Sunday at 1 p.m. and Monday at 4 p.m.

**Wednesday, July 7, and Friday, July 9:** Estadio Vicente Calderon, Madrid, Spain, with the J. Geils Band, Wednesday at 6 p.m. and Friday at 9:30 p.m.

The Stones had planned to play one show in Madrid and one in Barcelona but both gigs were almost canceled because Spain was in the midst of World Cup fever. The Madrid Football club ultimately allowed the band to use their stadium but the show in Barcelona did not take place, because Real Atletico was concerned that their football field would be ruined. Instead, the Stones played an extra concert in Madrid. The two shows attracted close to 140,000 people. Excellent soundboard recordings exist. The opening concert was marred by rain but the reporter from *Al Dia* gushed that it didn't matter because "Jagger, Richard and the others were there with a hundred thousand watts of sound and half a million watts of lightning at their disposal, pyrotechnics, and an intricate and spectacular set as the backdrop to the best of the contemporary bands. 'Under My Thumb,' 'When the Whip Comes Down,' 'Let's Spend the Night Together,' 'Black Limousine,' 'Brown Sugar,' 'Jumping Jack Flash' and the unforgettable 'I Can't Get No' and so many other songs, with the audience in an enraptured frenzy. Unforgettable music that thrilled the fans and that will be vividly remembered. The storm came with the Rolling Stones."

**Sunday, July 11, and Monday, July 12:** Stadio Comunale, Turin, Italy, with the J. Geils Band, Sunday at 3 p.m. and Monday at 6 p.m.

Over 120,000 fans turned out to see these shows. A third concert was scheduled for Tuesday but did not take place. In honor of Italy's victory in the World Cup, Mick ended the first show by putting on a blue Italian soccer team jersey. The fans had fun but Bill commented in his book, *Rolling with The Stones*, that the July 12 gig, which took place on the twentieth anniversary of their first gig at the Marquee, was "one of the worst shows of the tour. The tempos were all wrong and the sound was atrocious. I hated it."

**Thursday, July 15:** St. Jakob Fussball Stadion, Basel, Switzerland, with the J. Geils Band, 4 p.m.

The Stones sold all 50,000 seats to this show, the largest in Switzerland up to that time, in 48 hours. They took the stage for what was billed as "The High Mass of Rock." *Tribune Le Matin* reported, "There was the high priest Jagger—turquoise and red pants, vest and red leotard—skinny silhouette with an outsized voice, bouncing around, wide, jerky gestures, slightly out of sync with the sound. And there alongside were his buddies, and their hits. In the end, it was a great success ... a nice and memorable afternoon. But the wise investor would have consecrated his money toward tracking down a fine old

*Opposite:* **Poster for the Stones' concerts in Frankfurt, 1982 (collection of Ira Korman).**

Poster for the Stones' appearance in Turin in July 1982 (collection of Ira Korman).

copy of Beggars Banquet from back in the day. It's all a matter of choice. You can't have everything."

**Saturday, July 17:** Stadio San Paolo, Naples, Italy, with the J. Geils Band, 5 p.m.

Over 60,000 people descended on Naples for this massive concert. The Stones were welcomed to the city by Naples' communist mayor but were denounced by the Catholic cardinal because they stood for "a culture of violence and complete lack of moral values." The temperature rose to 99 degrees in the stadium and over fifty people had to be treated for heatstroke.

**Tuesday, July 20:** Parc Des Sports De L'Ouest, Nice, France, with the J. Geils Band, 7 p.m.

About 40,000 people attended this outdoor show. *Nice Matin* reported, "From where I was the Stones' heads were the size of peas but we could distinguish the musicians from their stage play. Keith Richards writhed with violence, Bill Wyman did not move a hair, Ron Wood was crazy and Charlie Watts beat his drums…. Jagger was not afraid to move, he jumped, ran, gesticulated, swayed, a real pleasure. As for the music, perfection was in order. There was a scholarly mix of new songs and the safe old ones."

**Saturday, July 24:** Slane Castle, Slane, County Meath, Ireland, with the J. Geils Band, the Chieftains and George Thorogood and the Destroyers, 1 p.m.

The Stones played their first Irish concert since 1965 at Slane Castle near Dublin. Mick told the *RTE News* that the outdoor show was "special for us. I love Ireland. I spent a lot of time here in my life. I used to live in Kilcullen for a little while. So it's special for me. We hope we have a good peaceful crowd and they don't get too out of hand." The show went off without a hitch. However, a letter from Keith came to light in 2016 that showed that the Stones had threatened to cancel the show at the very last minute because of the IRA's London bombing campaign.

**Sunday, July 25:** Roundhay Park, Leeds, England, UK, with Joe Jackson and George Thorogood and the Destroyers, 11 a.m.

The Stones, dressed in gaudy '80s fashion (Bill looked particularly ridiculous in a workout headband),

**Ticket for the Stones' concert in Leeds on July 25, 1982 (collection of Ira Korman).**

took the stage in late afternoon to play before a crowd of 80,000. The final show of the tour, and the band's last concert until 1989, was recorded and filmed. The concert was released as a double CD and DVD set in 2015 under the title *From the Vault-Live in Leeds*. The set consisted of: "Under My Thumb," "When the Whip Comes Down," "Let's Spend the Night Together," "Shattered," "Neighbors," "Black Limousine," "Just My Imagination," "Twenty Flight Rock," "Going to a Go Go," "Let Me Go," "Time Is on My Side," "Beast of Burden," "You Can't Always Get What You Want," "Little T&A," "Angie," "Tumbling Dice," "She's So Cold," "Hang Fire," "Miss You," "Honky Tonk Women," "Brown Sugar," "Start Me Up," "Jumping Jack Flash" and "Satisfaction."

To my ears, the first half of the concert was hit or miss. The first four songs were played much too fast. Mick shouted the songs rather then singing them and the guitars were sloppy. The band fared better on slower songs, such as "Black Limousine," "Just My Imagination," and "Beast of Burden" which were aided by the sparkling horns of Bobby Keys and Gene Barge. The second half of the show was more consistent. Mick sang a very nice version of "You Can't Always Get What You Want," with a tasty solo by Ronnie and Keith did a tight version of "Little T&A." "Hang Fire" and "Miss You" also were highlights. While superior live recordings exist, the Leeds show is a lot of fun and shows the band in an unpretentious setting, just playing good old rock 'n' roll without the over elaborate staging and theatrics we had grown accustomed to.

# Appendix 1:
# BBC Radio and Radio Luxembourg Appearances, 1963–1965

## 1963

**Tuesday, April 23:** BBC Studios, Maida Vale, London, UK

The Stones' first audition for BBC Radio took place without Bill or Charlie. Ricky Fenson and Carlos Little sat in for them. Brian was informed in a letter dated May 13 that the Stones did not pass the audition.

**Monday, September 23:** *Saturday Club*, BBC Radio, Playhouse Theatre, London, UK, aired October 26

The Stones first UK radio appearance was taped on this day. The band performed the Chuck Berry songs "Come On," "Talkin' Bout You," "Memphis" and "Roll Over Beethoven" as well as the Motown hit "Money." The performances of "Come On," "Memphis" and "Roll Over Beethoven" were officially released in 2017 on the CD *Rolling Stones on Air*.

While at the Playhouse Theatre, Bill, Charlie and Brian also backed Bo Diddley at his BBC session. Apparently the Stones' appearance on *Saturday Club* was an audition of sorts. The BBC wrote to Brian on November 13 to inform him that "your performance received favorable reports and your name has now been added to the list of artists available for broadcasting generally."

## 1964

**Friday, January 24:** *Go Man Go!,* BBC Studios, Maida Vale, London, UK

On this day the band taped versions of their second single, "I Wanna Be Your Man," as well as the Bo Diddley tune "Pretty Thing," which never appeared on a Stones LP, Chuck Berry's "Bye Bye Johnny," Arthur Alexander's ballad "You Better Move On," the B-side of their first single "I Want to Be Loved," and the Chuck Berry classic "Roll Over Beethoven."

**Monday, February 3:** *Saturday Club*, BBC Radio, Playhouse Theatre, London, UK, aired February 8

The Stones performed "Don't Lie to Me" and "Bye Bye Johnny" by Chuck Berry, as well as "You Better Move On," "I Wanna Be Your Man," the Bo Diddley classic "Mona," and Rufus Thomas' "Walking the Dog."

**Tuesday, February 18:** *Pop Inn*, BBC Radio, Paris Theatre, London, UK

The Stones were interviewed by Keith Fordyce and performed their new single "Not Fade Away."

**Wednesday, March 18:** *Nestle's Top Swinging Groups*, Radio Luxembourg, Regent Sound Studios, London, UK

The Stones taped fourteen songs for airing on Radio Luxembourg. The songs aired in fifteen-minute segments in April and May. The tracks were: "Bye Bye Johnny," the Bo Diddley song "Diddley Daddy," which was a mainstay of the Stones' act at this time but never appeared on an LP, "I Wanna Be Your Man," "Little by Little," "Look What You've Done," "Mona," "Not Fade Away," "Now I've Got a Witness," "Pretty Thing," "Reelin' and Rockin'," "Roll Over Beethoven," "Route 66, "Walking the Dog" and "You Better Move On."

**Thursday, March 19:** *Blues In Rhythm*, BBC Radio, Camden Theatre, London, UK, with Georgie Fame and the Blue Flames

The Stones played before a live audience. In addition to "Route 66," they performed "Cops And Robbers," another Bo Diddley classic that never made it on a Stones LP. They also played "You Better Move On" and "Mona." These tracks were released in 2012 as a bonus EP with "super deluxe" editions of *GRR* and also appeared on the 2017 compilation *Rolling Stones on Air*.

**Saturday, March 28:** *Saturday Club*, BBC Radio, UK

The BBC aired live recordings taped on unknown dates on the Stones' February-March tour. The songs aired were a rare version of "Beautiful Delilah," and "Roll Over Beethoven." The performance of "Beautiful Delilah" appeared on the 2017 compilation *Rolling Stones on Air*.

**Friday, April 10:** *The Joe Loss Pop Show*, BBC Radio, Playhouse Theatre, London, UK

The Stones performed "Not Fade Away," "Hi Heel Sneakers," "Little by Little," "I Just Want to Make Love to You," and "I'm Moving On" before a live audience. The performances of "Little by Little" and "I'm Moving On" were released on the 2017 compilation *Rolling Stones on Air*.

**Monday, April 13:** *Saturday Club*, BBC Radio, Playhouse Theatre, London, UK, aired April 18

The Stones played "I Just Want to Make Love to You," "Walking the Dog," "Not Fade Away," "Beautiful Delilah," the Tommy Tucker blues classic "Hi Heel Sneakers," and "Carol." All the songs, except "Not Fade Away," were released on the compilation *Rolling Stones on Air*.

**Monday, May 25:** *Saturday Club*, BBC Radio, Playhouse Theatre, London, UK

The Stones played the Howlin' Wolf classic "Down in the Bottom," which never appeared on a Stones LP, as well as "You Can Make It If You Try," "Route 66," "Confessing the Blues," and "Down the Road Apiece" on this edition of *Saturday Club* that aired on June 6.

**Thursday, July 16:** *The Teen and Twenty Disc Club*, Radio Luxembourg, Pye Studios, London, UK

The Stones performed their single "It's All Over Now."

**Friday, July 17:** *The Joe Loss Pop Show*, BBC Radio, Playhouse Theatre, London, UK, and *Top Gear*, BBC Radio, Playhouse Theatre, London, UK, with Cilla Black, P.J. Proby and the Animals, aired July 23

The Stones taped two radio shows. They first performed "It's All Over Now," "If You Need Me," "Confessing the Blues," "Carol" and "Mona" on the *Joe Loss Pop Show*. The first three songs were released on *Rolling Stones on Air*. They then performed "It's All Over Now," "Around and Around, "If You Need Me," "I Can't Be Satisfied," and a rare version of the Bo Diddley song "Crackin' Up" on the second edition of *Top Gear*, hosted by Brian Matthew. The performances of the latter two songs and "Around and Around" were released on *Rolling Stones on Air*.

**Thursday, October 8:** *Rhythm and Blues*, BBC Radio, Playhouse Theatre, London, UK, aired October 31

The Stones appeared on a program hosted by old friend Alexis Korner. They made their only known recording of the Keith/Brian instrumental "Dust My Pyramids," as well as "Around and Around," "If You Need Me," "Ain't That Loving You Baby," "Mona" and the instrumental "2120 South Michigan Avenue." The performances of the latter song and "Ain't That Loving You Baby" appeared on *Rolling Stones on Air*.

As Richard Havers discusses in the book of the same name, Eric Easton booked the Stones to tape episodes of *Saturday Club* and *Top Gear* on November 23. The Stones failed to show up. The BBC was incensed by their unprofessionalism. Easton apologized and noted, "The Stones had intimated some two or three weeks ago that they would rather not accept these engagements, but I was very keen … that they should appear on these programmes." The Stones compounded the BBC's anger by refusing to appear on December 4 to tape *The Joe Loss Pop Show*. The BBC considered suing them or blacklisting the Stones from future appearances, but cooler heads prevailed by late December.

# *1965*

**Monday, March 1:** *Top Gear*, BBC Radio, Studio 2, Broadcasting House, London, UK, aired March 6

The Stones made an increasingly rare radio appearance and played "Everybody Needs Somebody to Love," "Down the Road Apiece," "If You Need Me," and "The Last Time." All the performances, except "If You Need Me" were released on *Rolling Stones on Air*.

**Friday, August 20:** *Yeah! Yeah!*, BBC Radio, Broadcasting House, London, UK, aired August 30, and *Saturday Club*, BBC Radio, Broadcasting House, London, UK

The Stones performed "Mercy, Mercy," "Oh Baby," "(I Can't Get No) Satisfaction" and "The Spider and the Fly." The latter song and "Mercy Mercy" appeared on *Rolling Stones on Air*.

The Stones taped a second program on the same day. It turned out to be their last live radio performance for the BBC. They performed "(I Can't Get No) Satisfaction," "The Spider and the Fly," "Oh Baby," "Cry to Me," and their only recorded version of the Buster Brown blues "Fannie Mae." This program aired on September 18. The entire set, except "Spider and the Fly," was released on *Rolling Stones on Air*.

# Appendix 2: Television Appearances, 1963–1978

This list only includes television shows that featured performances by the Stones and does not include all of the many interviews they have given over the years on various programs or the many television shows that featured footage of Stones' concerts (these are usually referred to in the concert section). I have also omitted many TV programs that included promo films made by the Stones. The band began making these films in 1965. By the 1970s the band had virtually stopped performing on TV programs but continued to make such films in lieu of appearing.

## *1963*

**Sunday, July 7:** *Lucky Stars Summer Spin*, ABC TV, Alpha Studios, Birmingham UK, with Helen Shapiro, Mickie Most, Johnny Cymbal, Patsy Ann Noble, the Cadets and the Viscounts

The Stones, dressed in matching houndstooth stage outfits, mimed to their first single "Come On" on the summer edition of the popular *Thank Your Lucky Stars,* which ran from 1961 to 1966. Their TV debut aired on July 13 in the UK. Unfortunately, the film no longer exists. Indeed, the vast majority of footage of the Stones on British TV in the 1960s was erased. Television companies weren't far sighted enough to recognize the historical importance of programs they aired and most were not preserved.

**Friday, August 23:** *Ready Steady Go!*, Associated-Rediffusion TV, Television House, Kingsway, London, UK, with Jet Harris, Tony Meehan and Little Peggy March

The Stones, sans jackets but in matching vests, mimed to "Come On" on the third episode of the now legendary *Ready Steady Go!* Sadly the appearance is not in existence. Indeed, no TV footage of the Stones in 1963 survives.

**Thursday, August 29:** *Scene at 6:30*, Granada TV, Manchester, UK

This show was sometimes performed live and sometimes mimed. As the footage is lost, it is not clear whether the Stones played or mimed. In any case they performed "Come On."

**Sunday, September 8:** *Lucky Stars Summer Spin*, ABC TV, Alpha Studios, Birmingham, UK, with Craig Douglas, aired September 14

The Stones mimed to "Come On."

# READY, STEADY, GO!

CALLING ALL TEENAGERS! Associated-Rediffusion invites you to come along to your show in Studio 9, Television House, Kingsway, London W.C.2. Friday 23rd August 1963. 7.00—7.30 pm. Doors will be open at 6.15 pm. No admittance under 13 years of age.
**YOU CAN DANCE, COLLECT AUTOGRAPHS. OR JUST ENJOY THE SHOW**

# R!S!GO

Handbill seeking audience members for the taping of *Ready Steady Go* on August 23, 1963. The Stones made their second television appearance on this show (collection of Ira Korman).

**Sunday, November 17:** *Thank Your Lucky Stars*, ABC TV, Alpha Studios, Birmingham, UK, with Gene Pitney, Cliff Richard and the Shadows and Ronnie Carroll, aired November 23

The Stones mimed to their second single, "I Wanna Be Your Man."

**Friday, November 22:** *Ready Steady Go!*, Associated-Rediffusion TV, TV House, Kingsway, London, UK, with Gerry and the Pacemakers, Freddie and the Dreamers, Kathy Kirby and Kenny Lynch

The band again mimed to "I Wanna Be Your Man."

**Monday, December 9:** *Cops and Robbers*, BBC TV, St. Michael's Hall, Sydenham, London, UK

The Stones played the role of a band at a youth club for the pilot of this never aired show. They mimed to "Come On."

**Friday, December 27:** *Ready Steady Go!*, Associated-Rediffusion TV, TV House, Kingsway, London, UK, with Stevie Wonder

The Stones performed "I Wanna Be Your Man" and one other number.

# 1964

**Wednesday, January 1:** *Top of the Pops*, BBC TV, Studio A, Manchester UK, with Dusty Springfield, the Dave Clark Five, the Hollies

The Stones appeared on the first episode of this long running UK show and mimed to "I Wanna Be Your Man." The footage does not survive.

**Wednesday, January 29:** *Top of the Pops*, BBC TV, Studio A, Manchester, UK
The band mimed to "You Better Move On."

**Friday, February 7:** *The Arthur Haynes Show*, ATV, Elstree Studios, Borehamwood, Hertfordshire, UK
The earliest surviving TV footage of the Stones features them performing "I Wanna Be Your Man" and "You Better Move On."

**Friday, February 14:** *Ready Steady Go!*, Associated-Rediffusion TV, TV House, Kingsway, London, UK, with Dusty Springfield, the Crystals, Kenny Lynch, Heinz and the Woodpeckers and Laurie Jay and his Combo
The Stones performed their new single, "Not Fade Away," as well as "I Wanna Be Your Man" and "You Better Move On." This performance is lost.

**Saturday, February 22:** *Top of the Pops*, BBC TV, Weymouth, Dorset, UK, aired March 11
The Stones were filmed miming to "Not Fade Away" on a beach. Regrettably, this performance, like most *Tops of the Pops* footage from the 1960s, was erased.

**Sunday, February 23:** *Thank Your Lucky Stars*, ABC TV, Alpha Studios, Birmingham UK, with Dionne Warwick, Jackie Trent, Adam Faith, Mark Wynter, Kenny Ball, the Strangers and the Eagles
The Stones mimed to "Not Fade Away." The footage is lost.

**Wednesday, March 4:** *Top of the Pops*, BBC TV, Studio A, Manchester, UK, and *Scene at 6:30*, Granada TV, Manchester, UK
The Stones mimed to "Not Fade Away" on both programs.

**Friday, April 3:** *Ready Steady Go!*, Associated-Rediffusion TV, TV House, Kingsway, London, UK, with Billy J. Kramer and the Dakotas, Manfred Mann, Sounds Incorporated and Madeline Bell
Host Cathy McGowan interviewed the Stones, who performed "Not Fade Away" and "I Just Want to Make Love to You." The footage does not survive.

**Monday, April 20:** *Ready Steady Go!*, Associated-Rediffusion TV, Montreux, Switzerland, aired April 24
The Stones' appearance at the Golden Rose International TV Festival in Montreux was filmed by *RSG!* The Stones played "Mona," "Route 66," and "Not Fade Away," but the footage is lost.

**Wednesday, April 29:** *Top of the Pops*, BBC TV, Studio A, Manchester UK
The Stones mimed to "I Just Want to Make Love to You." The footage is lost.

**Monday, May 4:** *Scene at 6:30*, Granada TV, Manchester, UK
The Stones mimed to "Not Fade Away" but the footage is lost.

**Wednesday, May 6:** *Two Go Round*, ITV, Southampton, Hampshire, UK
The Stones mimed to "Not Fade Away."

**Saturday, May 9:** *Open House*, BBC TV, Riverside Studios, London, UK
The Stones performed "Hi Heel Sneakers."

**Sunday, May 24:** *Thank Your Lucky Stars*, ABC TV, Alpha Studios, Birmingham, UK, with the Barron Knights, the Overlanders, David John and the Mood, Julie Grant and the Caravelles, aired May 30

The Stones performed "Not Fade Away" and "I Just Want to Make Love to You." The footage is lost.

**Tuesday, June 2:** *The Les Crane Show*, WABC TV, New York

Les Crane interviewed the Stones on his New York only show (it became nationally syndicated in August). The Stones did not perform and the program is only listed because it was their first U.S. TV appearance. The footage is lost.

**Wednesday, June 3:** *The Hollywood Palace Show*, ABC TV, Los Angeles, CA

The band performed a highly charged version of "I Just Want to Make Love to You" that was shown on the June 13 episode hosted by Dean Martin. This was an important appearance by the Stones, as it marked the first time many Americans got a chance to see them. The second song the Stones performed, "Not Fade Away," wasn't aired until September 26.

**Saturday, June 13:** *Danceland*, local TV, Omaha, NE

**Circa June 15:** *Club 1270*, WXYZ TV, Detroit, MI

The Stones apparently played two songs. The footage is surely lost.

**Wednesday, June 17:** *Dance Party*, KDKA TV, Pittsburgh, PA, aired June 20

While in Pittsburgh, the band taped

Program for the *Hollywood Palace* taped on June 3, 1964. This was the Stones' first important U.S. television appearance (collection of Ira Korman).

an appearance on this local show, hosted by Clark Race, to perform "Route 66." Unfortunately, only stills exist.

**Thursday, June 18:** *The Mike Douglas Show*, KYW TV, Cleveland, OH
The Stones mimed to "Tell Me," and "I Just Want to Make Love to You" but performed "Not Fade Away" and "Carol" live.

**Saturday, June 20:** *The Clay Cole Show*, WPIX TV, New York
The Stones performed "Tell Me," "Carol" and "Not Fade Away" on this local show. The appearance is regrettably lost. In his fascinating book, *Rolling Stones on Air in the Sixties*, Richard Havers suggests that the appearance may actually have been taped at the beginning of the tour on June 2. Bill, however, says this day in his book, presumably based on his famous diaries.

**Friday, June 26:** *Ready Steady Go!*, Associated-Rediffusion TV, TV House, Kingsway, London, UK, with Millie Small, the Merseybeats, the McKinleys and the Jynx
The band mimed to "It's All Over Now" and "Good Times, Bad Times." The footage is lost.

**Saturday, June 27:** *Juke Box Jury*, BBC TV, Shepherd's Bush TV Studios, London, UK, and *Top of the Pops*, BBC TV, TV Centre, London, UK
The Stones appeared on the popular show *Juke Box Jury*, where guests rated records. It aired on July 4 and created controversy due to the Stones' negative opinions on almost every record played, including Elvis' latest. The Stones also mimed to "It's All Over Now" for *Top of the Pops*, which aired on July 1. Regrettably, both appearances are lost.

**Monday, July 6:** *Ready, Steady, Win*, ITV, London, UK
Brian took part in a panel, judging up and coming pop bands.

**Saturday, July 11:** *Day by Day*, Southern Television, UK

**Wednesday, July 15:** *Top of the Pops*, Studio A, Manchester, UK
The Stones again mimed to "It's All Over Now." The footage is lost.

**Thursday, July 23:** *Ready Steady Go!*, Associated-Rediffusion TV, TV House, Kingsway, London, UK, with the Animals, the Mojos, Sandie Shaw, the Fourmost, Kingsize Taylor and the Dominoes and the Paramounts
The Stones mimed to "It's All Over Now." The footage is lost.

**Tuesday, July 28:** *Lucky Stars Summer Spin*, ABC TV, Teddington, Middlesex, UK, aired August 8
The Stones performed "It's All Over Now."

**Wednesday, August 5:** *The Red Skelton Show*, CBS TV, Palladium, London, UK, aired September 22
The Stones appeared on the high-rated U.S. variety show hosted by comedian Red Skelton, broadcast from the famed London Palladium. However, they refused to stand on the prestigious stage (which they considered old fashioned) and mimed to "Tell Me," "Carol" and "It's All Over Now" on the steps.

**Friday, August 7:** *Ready Steady Go!*, Associated-Rediffusion TV, TV House, Kingsway, London, UK, with Cilla Black, Kenny Lynch, the Nashville Teens and Brian Poole and the Tremeloes

Brian and Bill acted as hosts (and acted in a short skit miming to the Beatles' "A Hard Days Night"). The Stones performed "Around and Around," "If You Need Me" and "It's All Over Now." This footage is lost.

**Monday, August 17:** *Ready, Steady, Win*, ITV, London, aired August 24
Mick took part in a panel, judging up and coming pop bands.

**Wednesday, September 2:** *Top of the Pops*, BBC TV, Studio A, Manchester UK
The Stones performed "If You Need Me." The footage is lost.

**Tuesday, September 15:** *Scene at 6.30*, Granada TV, Manchester, UK
The Stones mimed to "It's All Over Now." The footage is lost

**Sunday, October 18:** *Tienerklanken*, BRT TV, Amerikaans Theatre, Brussels, Belgium
The Stones played "Not Fade Away," "Walking the Dog," "If You Need Me," "I'm Alright," "Carol," "Time Is on My Side," "Tell Me," "It's All Over Now" and "Around and Around," which was almost halted due to stage invasions.

**Monday, October 19:** *Quoi De Neuf?*, ORTF 2 TV, Paris, France
The Stones appeared on French TV and mimed to "Carol," "Mona" and "It's All Over Now." Brian told *Disc*, "We had to borrow instruments for our first (French) TV show. And because it was Monday and most of the shops were closed, the only ones we could get made us look like old type rock 'n' rollers." This footage survives.

**Saturday, October 24:** *The Clay Cole Show*, WPIX TV, New York, aired October 31 and November 7
The Stones made their second appearance on this local show, miming to "If You Need Me," "Time Is on My Side," "Tell Me," "It's All Over Now," "Around and Around" and "Confessin' The Blues." The footage is lost.

**Sunday, October 25:,** *The Ed Sullivan Show*, CBS TV, Studio 50, New York, with Laurence Harvey, Stiller and Meara, Jack Jones and London Lee
The Stones performed "Around and Around" and "Time Is on My Side" on this highly influential show that also broadcast the first U.S. appearance of the Beatles. For many older Americans, it was their first glimpse of the Stones and some were upset by what they saw. Mick came in for criticism for his "unprofessional" attire: a sweatshirt. Columnist Jack O'Brien dismissed the group as "slobs" and "rubbishy musical riff-raff." Ed Sullivan swore he'd never have them on his show again. He rethought his strategy when he saw the ratings.

**Thursday, November 12:** *The Ann Colone Show*, WANE TV, Fort Wayne, IN
While in Fort Wayne, the Stones appeared on this local show. Mick recalled in *The Rolling Stones Monthly*, "We did a live interview type-program. Thousands of people all over the place and it was absolute chaos. It took the director five minutes to get the audience to keep quiet."

**Friday, November 20:** *Ready Steady Go!*, Associated-Rediffusion TV, TV House, Kingsway, London, UK, with Marvin Gaye and Them (featuring Van Morrison)
The Stones mimed to "Off the Hook," "Little Red Rooster," and "Around and Around." This is one of only a handful of appearances on the show that still exist. Portions of "Little Red Rooster" were used in the 1990 video *25x5*.

**Sunday, November 29:** *Lucky Stars Special*, ABC TV, Alpha Studios, Birmingham UK, with Petula Clark, Sandie Shaw, Herman's Hermits, Clinton Ford and Mark Wynter, aired December 5

The Stones mimed to "Around and Around," "Little Red Rooster," "Off the Hook" and "Empty Heart." The footage is lost.

**Tuesday, December 15:** *Shindig*, ABC TV, Halliford Studios, Shepperton, UK, aired January 20, 1965

The Stones taped promo films for "Oh Baby," "Down the Road Apiece, "Heart of Stone" and "Susie Q" to be aired on the U.S. show *Shindig*, hosted by Jimmy O'Neill.

**Thursday, December 31:** *Ready Steady Go!: The New Year Starts Here*, Associated-Rediffusion TV, TV House, Kingsway, London, UK, with the Dave Clark Five, the Animals and Dusty Springfield

The Stones appeared on a special episode of the show that also included clips of their November 20 appearance.

# 1965

**Wednesday, January 13:** *Thank Your Lucky Stars*, ABC TV, TV Studios, Teddington, Middlesex, UK, aired January 30

The Stones mimed to "Down Home Girl," "Under the Boardwalk," and "Susie Q." The footage is lost.

**Friday, January 15:** *Ready Steady Go!*, Associated-Rediffusion TV, TV House, Kingsway, London, UK, with the Kinks, the Righteous Brothers and Del Shannon

The Stones performed "What a Shame," "Time Is on My Side," "Down the Road Apiece," and ""Everybody Needs Somebody to Love." The footage is lost.

**Friday, January 29:** *Big Beat 65*, ATV-O TV, Melbourne, Australia, with Roy Orbison, aired February 12

The Stones appeared on this special program hosted by Roy Orbison. They mimed to "Walking the Dog," "Heart of Stone," "Little Red Rooster" and "Around and Around."

**Friday, February 26:** *Ready Steady Go!*, Associated-Rediffusion TV, TV House, Kingsway, London, UK, with the Who, the Dave Clark Five and the Animals

The Stones mimed to "Play with Fire," and "The Last Time," and performed a live version of "Everybody Needs Somebody to Love." During the latter song, Mick was pulled into the crowd.

**Saturday, February 27:** *The Eamonn Andrews Show*, ITV, TV Studios, Teddington, Middlesex, UK, with Keely Smith, Keith Mitchell and Jeremy Thorpe

The Stones performed "The Last Time" and Mick was interviewed.

**Thursday, March 4:** *Top of the Pops*, BBC TV, Studio A, Manchester UK, aired March 11

The Stones performed "The Last Time."

**Thursday, March 11:** *Scene at 6:30*, Granada TV, TV Centre, Manchester, UK

The Stones mimed to "The Last Time."

**Sunday, March 21:** *Thank Your Lucky Stars*, ABC TV, Alpha Studios, Birmingham UK
The Stones mimed to "The Last Time," "Play with Fire," "Off the Hook" and "Everybody Needs Somebody to Love." This footage is lost.

**Friday, April 2:** *Popside*, SVT 1, Cirkus Building, Stockholm, Sweden
While on tour in Sweden, the Stones appeared on this program. They performed "Everybody Needs Somebody to Love," "Tell Me," "Around and Around," "Little Red Rooster" and "The Last Time."

**Friday, April 9:** *Ready Steady Goes Live!*, Associated-Rediffusion TV, Studio Five, Wembley, UK, with the Animals, Goldie and the Gingerbreads, Dave Berry, Roger Miller and Madeline Bell
The Stones performed live versions of "Everybody Needs Somebody to Love," "Pain in My Heart," "I'm Alright" and "The Last Time." This footage is lost.

**Sunday, May 2:** *The Ed Sullivan Show*, CBS TV, Studio 50, New York, with Tom Jones, Dusty Springfield and Morecambe and Wise
The Stones made their second appearance on *Ed Sullivan* and performed "The Last Time," "Little Red Rooster," "Everybody Needs Somebody to Love," and the instrumental "2120 South Michigan Avenue."

**Monday, May 3:** *The Clay Cole Show*, WPIX TV, New York, aired May 29
The Stones performed "The Last Time," "Little Red Rooster" and "Down the Road Apiece." Unlike previous appearances on Cole's show, the Stones played live. Sadly, the footage is lost, though audio survives.

**Saturday, May 15:** *Hollywood a Go-Go*, ABC TV, KHJ Studios, Los Angeles, CA, with Chuck Berry, aired May 22
The Stones mimed to "Oh Baby," "Play with Fire" (with Brian on piano) and "The Last Time" on this short-lived show hosted by Sam Riddle.

**Sunday, May 16:** *Shivaree*, ABC TV, KABC Studios, Los Angeles, CA, aired June 5 and August 28
The Stones performed "Play with Fire," "The Last Time," "Down the Road Apiece" and "Little Red Rooster."

**Thursday, May 20:** *Shindig*, ABC TV, Television Center, Los Angeles, CA, with Sonny and Cher, Adam Wade, Bobby Sherman, Jackie DeShannon and Howlin' Wolf, aired May 26
The Stones taped new backing tracks in advance so that Mick could sing live vocals on "Little Red Rooster," "The Last Time" and "Play with Fire." The band also performed "Down the Road Apiece" and premiered "(I Can't Get No) Satisfaction," but mimed to the earlier Chess version featuring Brian on harmonica. In addition, they introduced special guest Howlin' Wolf, who sang "How Many More Years," while they sat on a riser and watched.

**Friday, June 4:** *Ready Steady Goes Live!*, Associated-Rediffusion TV, Studio Five, Wembley, UK, with Burt Bacharach, the Kinks and the Yardbirds
The Stones played live versions of "Oh Baby," "Good Times," "I'm Moving On," "I'm Alright" and "Play with Fire." The footage is lost.

**Sunday, June 6:** *Thank Your Lucky Stars*, ABC TV, Alpha Studios, Birmingham, UK, aired June 12

The Stones mimed to "I'm Alright," "I'm Moving On" and "Route 66" from their new EP. Again, the footage is lost.

**Thursday, June 10:** *Top of the Pops*, BBC TV, Studio A, Manchester UK

The Stones mimed to "I'm Alright." This footage is lost.

**Monday, July 26:** *Thank Your Lucky Stars*, ABC TV, Alpha Studios, Birmingham, UK, aired August 1

The Stones mimed to "(I Can't Get No) Satisfaction" but the footage is lost.

**Wednesday, July 28:** Shindig, ABC TV, Twickenham, Surrey, UK, aired September 16 and November 6

The Stones filmed performances of "(I Can't Get No) Satisfaction," "Mercy Mercy," "Hitch Hike," "That's How Strong My Love Is," "Good Times" and "Cry to Me" for inclusion on episodes of the American show *Shindig*. This footage appears to have disappeared.

**Thursday, August 19:** *Top of the Pops*, BBC TV, Studio 2, BBC TV Centre, Shepherd's Bush, London, UK, aired September 2

The Stones mimed to "(I Can't Get No) Satisfaction." The footage is lost.

**Monday, August 23:** *Scene at 6:30*, Granada TV, TV Centre, Manchester, UK, aired August 26

The Stones mimed to "(I Can't Get No) Satisfaction." The footage is lost.

**Friday, August 27:** *Ready Steady Goes Live!*, Associated-Rediffusion TV, Studio One, Wembley, UK, with Lulu, the Hollies and the Yardbirds

The Stones played live versions of "Mercy, Mercy," "Cry to Me" and "(I Can't Get No) Satisfaction." This footage is lost.

**Sunday, August 29:** *Lucky Stars Summer Spin*, ABC TV, Alpha Studios, Birmingham UK, aired September 4

The Stones mimed to "(I Can't Get No) Satisfaction." This footage is lost.

**Wednesday, September 2:** *Ready Steady Go! The Rolling Stones Special Show, Live*, Associated-Rediffusion TV, Studio One, Wembley, UK, with Manfred Mann, Chris Farlowe, Goldie and the Gingerbreads and the Preachers, aired September 10

This was a special Rolling Stones edition of *RSG!* As a joke, the Stones mimed to "I Got You Babe" with host Cathy McGowan and Brian playing Sonny and Cher and Keith pretending to blow into a tuba. Andrew Oldham and Mick also sang a verse to each other. The Stones also performed "Oh Baby," "That's How Strong My Love Is" and "(I Can't Get No) Satisfaction."

**Thursday, September 23:** *Top of the Pops*, BBC TV, TV Centre, London UK

The Stones mimed to "Spider and the Fly," "Cry to Me," and "(I Can't Get No) Satisfaction." The footage is lost.

**Tuesday, October 19:** *Top of the Pops*, BBC TV, TV Centre, Shepherd's Bush, London, UK

The Stones mimed to "Get Off of My Cloud."

**Friday, October 22:** *Ready Steady Goes Live!*, Associated-Rediffusion TV, Studio One, Wembley, UK, with the Animals, Chris Farlowe and the Searchers, aired October 26

The Stones performed "Cry to Me," "She Said Yeah," and "Get Off of My Cloud." The footage, sadly, is lost.

**Thursday, November 11:** *Hullabaloo*, NBC TV, RCA Building, New York, with Barry McGuire, Brenda Lee, the Kingsmen and Barbara McNair, aired November 15

Mick sang a live vocal over the taped backing track on "She Said Yeah" and "Get Off of My Cloud." This footage was released on a DVD compilation of *Hullabaloo* footage in 1998.

**Friday, December 31:** *Ready Steady Go! The New Year Starts Here,* Associated-Rediffusion TV, Studio One, Wembley, UK, with the Who, the Animals, Dusty Springfield, the Kinks, Lulu and Tom Jones

The Stones played "(I Can't Get No) Satisfaction" and "Get Off of My Cloud." This footage is lost.

# 1966

**Thursday, February 3:** *Top of the Pops*, BBC TV, TV Centre, London UK, aired February 3 and February 24

The Stones performed two versions of their new single, "19th Nervous Breakdown." A fragment of one version miraculously survived, but the second is lost.

**Sunday, February 6:** *The Eamonn Andrews Show*, ABC TV, Teddington Studios, Middlesex, UK, with Arthur Dooley, Moira Lister and Quintin Hogg

Mick engaged in a discussion with the host and his guests and sang a live vocal on "19th Nervous Breakdown" over a prepared backing track. This footage may exist, as audio has surfaced of the broadcast.

**Sunday, February 13:** *The Ed Sullivan Show*, CBS TV, Studio 50, New York, NY, with Ethel Merman, Hal Holbrook and Wayne Newton

The Stones performed "(I Can't Get No) Satisfaction," "As Tears Go By" and "19th Nervous Breakdown." This is one of the earliest color clips of the Stones that survives.

**Thursday, February 17:** *Bandstand*, Australian TV, TCN-9 Studios, Sydney, Australia, aired February 20

The Stones mimed to "I'm Moving On," "Get Off of My Cloud," "Play with Fire," "19th Nervous Breakdown," "As Tears Go By," and "(I Can't Get No) Satisfaction" on a confetti laced stage.

**Thursday, April 14:** *Top of the Pops*, BBC TV, TV Centre, Shepherd's Bush, London, UK, aired April 14, May 12 and 26

The Stones mimed to "Mother's Little Helper" and "Paint It Black." This footage is lost.

**Thursday, April 28:** *Top of the Pops*, BBC TV, TV Centre, London UK

The Stones mimed to "Lady Jane." This footage is lost.

**Sunday, May 8:** *Thank Your Lucky Stars*, ABC TV, Alpha Studios, Birmingham UK, aired May 14

The Stones performed "Lady Jane" and "Paint It Black." This footage is lost.

**Friday, May 27:** *Ready Steady Goes Live!*, Associated-Rediffusion TV, Studio 5, Wembley, UK, with Chris Andrews, the Animals and the Yardbirds

The Stones performed fantastic live versions of "Paint It Black," "I Am Waiting," and "Under My Thumb."

**Sunday, September 11:** *The Ed Sullivan Show*, CBS TV, Studio 50, New York, NY, with Louis Armstrong, Robert Goulet and Red Skelton

The Stones made their fourth appearance on the show. Mick sang live vocals over a pre-recorded backing track on "Paint It Black," "Lady Jane" and "Have You Seen Your Mother, Baby, Standing in the Shadow?"

**Tuesday, October 4:** *Ready Steady Goes Live!*, Associated-Rediffusion TV, Studio 5, Wembley, UK, aired October 7

The Stones performed "Paint It Black," "Lady Jane" and "Have You Seen Your Mother, Baby, Standing in the Shadow?" Mick sang live over prepared backing tracks. The footage is lost.

**Wednesday, October 5:** *Top of the Pops*, BBC TV, TV Centre, Shepherd's Bush, London UK

The Stones mimed to "Have You Seen Your Mother, Baby, Standing in the Shadow?" The footage is lost.

**Saturday, December 17:** *Top of the Pops*, BBC TV, TV Centre, Shepherd's Bush, London UK, aired December 22

The Stones again mimed to "Have You Seen Your Mother, Baby, Standing in the Shadow?" The footage is now lost.

**Tuesday, December 20:** *Ready Steady Go!*, Associated-Rediffusion TV, Studio 5, Wembley, UK, with the Who, Paul Jones, the Spencer Davis Group, Lulu, Donovan and Davy Dee, Dozy, Beaky, Mich and Tich, aired December 23

Mick appeared on the very last episode *of RSG!* to sing a duet with Chris Farlowe on "Out of Time" and "(I Can't Get No) Satisfaction."

# *1967*

**Sunday, January 15:** *The Ed Sullivan Show*, CBS TV, Studio 50, New York, NY, with Petula Clark, Allan Sherman and Alan King

The Stones made their fifth appearance on the show and performed "Ruby Tuesday" and "Let's Spend the Night Together," with live vocals over prepared tracks.

**Sunday, January 22:** *Sunday Night at the London Palladium*, ATV, London, UK

The Stones performed "Connection," "Ruby Tuesday," "It's All Over Now," and "Let's Spend the Night Together." Mick sang live vocals over prepared backing. The footage is sadly lost.

**Wednesday, January 25:** *Top of the Pops*, BBC TV, TV Centre, Shepherd's Bush, London UK

The Stones mimed to "Ruby Tuesday" and "Let's Spend the Night Together." The latter clip survives.

**Sunday, February 5:** *The Eamonn Andrews Show*, ABC TV, Teddington Studios, Middlesex, UK, with Terry Scott and Susan Maughan

Mick engaged in a discussion with the host and the band performed a rare live version of "She Smiled Sweetly" from *Between the Buttons*. The footage is probably lost. This was the Stones' last TV appearance for over a year, though individual members gave interviews to various shows.

# 1968

**Friday, November 29:** *Frost on Saturday*, ABC Film Studios, Wembley, UK

The Stones performed "Sympathy for the Devil" with Brian (seated at the piano) in his last TV performance with the group (other then the *Rock and Roll Circus*). Mick sang a live vocal over the prepared backing. This footage was released on a *Frost on Saturday* DVD in 2010.

**Wednesday, December 11:** *The Rolling Stones Rock 'n' Roll Circus*, Intertel Studios, London, with Taj Mahal, Jethro Tull, Marianne Faithfull, the Dirty Mac and The Who

See the entry under 1968 concerts.

# 1969

**Monday, June 16:** *The David Frost Show*, syndicated, Mayfair Theatre, London, UK, aired July 7 and August 21

The Stones performed "You Can't Always Get What You Want" and "Honky Tonk Women" with new member Mick Taylor. Jagger sang live over prepared backing. The songs aired on separate editions of the program.

**Thursday, July 3:** *Top of the Pops*, BBC TV, Lime Grove Studios, London UK

On the day Brian's death was reported, the Stones taped two different performances of "Honky Tonk Women" that aired on multiple occasions in July and August. Mick sang a live vocal over prepared backing. The footage is apparently lost.

**Tuesday, November 18:** *The Ed Sullivan Show*, CBS TV, Los Angeles, CA, aired November 23

Ed Sullivan was desperate to have the Stones on his show and agreed to come to California to tape a segment. Mick sang live vocals over prepared backing on "Gimme Shelter," "Love in Vain," and "Honky Tonk Women." It was the Stones' sixth and last appearance on the show. All of the Sullivan appearances were released on a special DVD in 2011.

**Friday, December 12:** *Top of the Pops*, BBC TV, TV Centre, London UK

The Stones performed "Honky Tonk Women" for the Christmas edition. Mick sang a live vocal over prepared backing. The footage survives.

**Friday, December 12:** *Ten Years of What?*, BBC TV, Studio E, TV Centre, London, UK, with the Bonzo Dog Band, aired December 28

Mick sang "Let It Bleed" over a prepared backing track. This footage is lost.

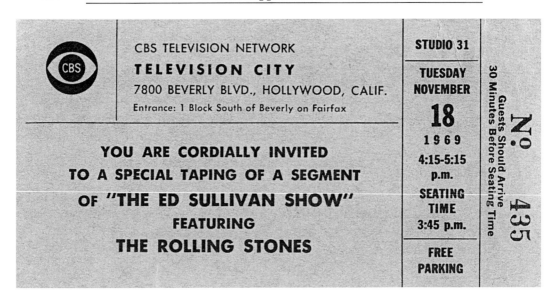

Ticket for the taping of the Stones' appearance on the *Ed Sullivan Show* on November 18, 1969 (collection of Ira Korman).

**Friday, December 12:** *Pop Go The 60s!*, BBC TV, TV Centre, London, UK, with the Who, the Kinks, the Hollies, Cliff Richard and the Shadows, Dusty Springfield and Sandie Shaw, aired December 31

The Stones performed a fantastic version of "Gimme Shelter," with Mick singing a live vocal.

# 1971

**Thursday, March 11:** *Top of the Pops*, BBC TV, TV Centre, London UK, aired April 15 and May 6

In the midst of their UK tour, the Stones taped an appearance for *Top of the Pops*. They performed "Brown Sugar," "Bitch" and "Wild Horses," with Mick singing live. The clip of "Brown Sugar," with Mick in a pink suit, appeared as a bonus on the 2015 release *The Marquee Club: Live in 1971*. The other two performances are apparently lost.

# 1978

**Saturday, October 7:** *Saturday Night Live*, NBC TV, New York

After a seven-year absence from network TV, the Stones chose to appear on the wildly popular *SNL*. They performed sloppy but fun versions of "Beast of Burden," "Respectable" and "Shattered" on a small stage. Mick's voice was shot but he still put on a great performance. Ron Wood told *Trouser Press*, "My voice was the first to go, and they all went, 'Ha, ha.' Then Keith's went. Then Mick's went the day of the recording… 'Cause we'd been up partying for three days straight. Trying to rehearse around that lot is impossible." Mick also took part in a comedy segment in which *SNL* regular Dan

Aykroyd, imitating Tom Snyder, interviewed him. Ron and Charlie appeared in the recurring "Cheeseburger, Cheeseburger" skit with Aykroyd, John Belushi and Bill Murray. The Stones' *SNL* performance and Mick's interview with Aykroyd were included on the 2011 DVD/Blu-ray of *Some Girls Live in Texas*.

**Saturday, December 16:** *Saturday Night Live*, NBC TV, New York
Mick performed "Don't Look Back" with Peter Tosh.

# Bibliography

## Books

Bockris, Victor. *Keith Richards: The Biography.* New York: Da Capo, 2003.
Booth, Stanley. *The True Adventures of the Rolling Stones.* New York: Vintage, 1985.
Carr, Roy. *The Rolling Stones: An Illustrated Record.* New York: Harmony, 1976.
Chapman, Rob. *New Barbarians: Outlaws, Gunslingers and Guitars.* Minneapolis: Voyageur, 2017.
Dalton, David. *The Rolling Stones: The First Twenty Years.* New York: Alfred A. Knopf, 1982.
Elliot, Martin. *The Rolling Stones Complete Recording Sessions, 1962–2012.* London: Cherry Red, 2012.
Flippo, Chet. *On the Road with the Rolling Stones.* Garden City, NY: Doubleday, 1985.
Fong-Torres, Ben (Ed.). *The Rolling Stone Rock 'n' Roll Reader.* New York: Bantam, 1974.
Fornatale, Pete. *The Rolling Stones: 50 Licks.* New York: Bloomsbury, 2013.
Greenfield, Robert. *A Journey Through America with the Rolling Stones.* St. Albans, England: Panther, 1975.
Havers, Richard. *The Rolling Stones on Air in the Sixties.* New York: Harper Design, 2017.
Houghton, Richard. *The Rolling Stones: I Was There.* London: Gotta Have, 2018.
Johns, Glyn. *Sound Man.* New York: Penguin, 2014.
Norman, Philip. *The Stones.* London: HarperCollins, 2012.
Oldham, Andrew Loog. *Rolling Stoned.* London: Because Entertainment, 2013.
Rej, Bent. *The Rolling Stones: In the Beginning.* Buffalo: Firefly, 2006.
Richards, Keith. *Life.* New York: Little, Brown, 2010.
Rolling Stones. *According to the Rolling Stones.* San Francisco: Chronicle, 2009.
Rolling Stones. *The Crazy World of England's Rolling Stones.* New York: Acme, 1964.
Trynka, Paul. *Brian Jones: The Making of the Rolling Stones.* New York: Plume, 2014.
Wyman, Bill, with Coleman, Ray. *Stone Alone.* London: Viking, 1990.
Wyman, Bill, with Havers, Richard. *Rolling with the Stones.* London: Dorling Kindersley, 2002.

## Articles

Note: In researching and writing this book I used articles that appeared throughout the years in the UK music publications *Beat Instrumental, Disc & Music Echo, Fabulous 208, Melody Maker, New Musical Express, Rave, Record Mirror, The Rolling Stones Monthly Book, Sounds,* and *Top Pops.* I also referred to articles that appeared in the American trade publications *Amusement Business, Billboard* and *Variety.* I also pored over copies of the American magazines *Crawdaddy, Datebook, GO Magazine, Hit Parader, KRLA Beat, Rolling Stone, Song Hits, Tiger Beat* and *Trouser Press.* In addition, I scoured countless newspapers and university publications looking for advertisements and reviews. I have referred to the authors and publications in the text. Information from the following sources was also used:

Alterman, Lorraine. "Stones Really Nice Guys." *Detroit Free Press,* July 1966.
Altham, Keith. "In Paris with the Stones." *New Musical Express,* April 1966.
Altham, Keith. "Our Fans Have Moved on with Us." *New Musical Express,* February 1967.
Altham, Keith. "Rolling Stones: France Votes for Les Stones," *Fabulous Magazine,* January 1964.
Altham, Keith. "The Stones Hit Back." *New Musical Express,* October 1965.
Boucher, Caroline. "The Stones Are Still the Bad Guys." *Disc Magazine,* August 18, 1973.
Carr, Patrick. "Rolling Stones on Tour." *Crawdaddy,* July 1972.
Chapman, Rob. "Brian Jones: The Bittersweet Symphony." *Mojo Magazine,* July 1999.
Charone, Barbara. "The Gospel According to the Glimmer Twins." *Sounds,* April 1976.

Charone, Barbara. "Keith Richards: The Pusher Behind the Stones." *Creem,* October 1976.
Cott, Jonathan. "The Mick Jagger Interview." *Rolling Stone,* 1968.
Criscione, Louise. "The Rolling Stones Saga." *KRLA Beat,* 1965.
Criscione, Louise. "The Stones Speak to the Press." *KRLA Beat,* January 8, 1966.
Eldridge, Royston. "Mick Taylor: A Year as a Stone." *Sounds,* October 1970.
Flippo, Chet. "Baptized in Baton Rouge, Castrated in San Antone." *Rolling Stone,* July 17, 1975.
Flippo, Chet. "The Road Ain't What It Used to Be." *Rolling Stone,* September 7, 1978.
Graff, Gary. "Mick Jagger: As Years Go By." *Creem,* February 1984.
Grant, Mike. "Mick Jagger." *Rave Magazine,* November 1967.
Greenfield, Robert. "Gotta Keep It Growing," *Rolling Stone,* August 1971.
Hancock, David. "Heil, Heil Rock 'N' Roll." *Record Mirror,* May 8, 1976.
Harry, Bill. "Four Days in Liverpool for the Stones." *Mersey Beat,* September 1964.
Ingham, John. "Say Good Night Keith, Good Night Keith." *Blast Magazine,* October 1976.
Kent, Nick. "It's Only Rock 'n' Roll but I Like It." *New Musical Express,* June 15, 1974.
Kent, Nick. "Mick Jagger Hits Out at Everything in Sight." *New Musical Express,* October 1977.
Kent, Nick. "The Rolling Stones: Stones-on-the Road Special." *New Musical Express,* September 22, 29 and October 27, 1973.
Lydon, Michael. "The Rolling Stones: A Play in the Apocalypse." *Ramparts,* March 1970.
Marinovich, Pete. "We Bloody Well Reach Them." *Arizona Days and Ways Magazine,* January 3, 1966.
Marsh, Dave. "Mick Jagger: I Can Get It Up, but I Can't Get It Down." *Creem,* August 1975.
Marsh, Dave. "The Rolling Stones: Just Another Rock Band?" *Rolling Stone,* August 10, 1978.
Schulps, Dave. "Ronnie Wood: New Stone Tries A Solo." *Trouser Press,* July 1979.
Simmons, Sylvie. "Rolling Stones: Shattered." *Mojo Magazine,* October 2002.
"The Standells Tell on the Rolling Stones." *Tiger Beat,* April 1967.
Stewart, Ian. "Girls and the Stones." *Datebook,* July 1967.
Trynka, Paul. "Little Boy Blue." *Mojo Magazine,* August 2012.
Welch, Chris. "An Outlaw at the Ritz." *Melody Maker,* January 13, 1979.
Welch, Chris. "Rolling Stones Rock and Roll Circus." *Melody Maker,* December 1968.
Wenner, Jann. "Mick Jagger Remembers." *Rolling Stone,* December 14, 1995.

## Websites and Radio

www.nzentgraf.de
www.therollingstonesmuseum.com
*The Rolling Stones Story.* 1973 BBC radio documentary
www.timeisonourside.com

# Index

Aarhus 181, 218
Aberdeen (Scotland) 65, 108, 295
Aberystwyth (Wales) 30
Adelaide 95, 129, 130, 211, 213
*Aftermath* 125, 126, 131, 133, 139, 151
"Ain't Too Proud to Beg" 223, 226, 228, 229, 232, 235, 236, 239, 240, 243, 244, 248
Akron 203, 271
Albany 102, 103
Albuquerque 200
"All Down the Line" 194, 197, 200, 201, 205, 208, 210, 211, 212, 214, 215, 219, 220, 228, 229, 232, 235, 236, 239, 240, 253, 256, 257, 258, 260, 262, 263, 280, 281, 283, 285, 286, 287
Altamont 2, 167, 176-77, 183, 194, 196, 197, 199, 286
Altham, Keith 47, 54, 88, 101, 110, 111, 126, 131, 136, 145
Altrincham 42
"Am I Grooving You" 224, 268, 269, 270, 274
Amsterdam 187, 220
Anaheim 263, 264
"Angie" 149, 207, 214, 216, 219, 220, 228, 231, 232, 244, 304
The Animals 41, 87, 101, 107, 307, 312, 314, 315, 317, 318
Ann Arbor 268
Antwerp 220
"Apartment No. Nine" 251, 267, 269, 270, 272
April Wine 252, 260
Arden, Don 16, 34
Ardwick 145
Arizona State University 291
Arnold, Shirley 20
"Around And Around" 5, 111, 253, 313
"As Tears Go By" 188, 300, 317
Asbury Park 137, 138
Ashby, Hal 280, 287, 291, 294
Athens 157
Atlanta 104, 235, 247, 257, 271, 285
Atlanta Rhythm Section 235, 260
Atlantic City 136
Auburn University 172
Auckland 94, 131, 209
Aylesbury 54

"Backstreet Girl" 144, 147
Baez, Joan 115
Baldock 45
Baldry, "Long" John 3, 6, 8, 28, 75, 87, 110
Ballymena 72
Baltimore 120, 134, 175
Banbury (Oxfordshire) 29
The Banshees 91
Barcelona 245, 300
Barge, Gene 295, 304
The Barron Knights 29, 54, 66, 67, 71, 72, 74, 75, 311
Basel 300
Bath 41
The Batmen 151-152
Baton Rouge 226-227
The Beach Boys 68, 82, 104, 105, 126
"Beast of Burden" 254, 256-258, 260, 262, 263, 268, 281, 283, 285-289, 291, 293, 304, 320
The Beatles 14, 15, 17, 21, 22, 25, 30, 32, 36, 37, 39, 41, 47, 49, 51, 62, 67, 95, 101, 108, 111, 125, 126, 129, 131, 133, 135, 138, 141, 144, 166, 183, 214, 232, 313
Beck, Jeff 144, 224, 225, 267
Bedford (UK) 53
"Before They Make Me Run" 254, 268-270, 274
*Beggar's Banquet* 158, 160, 188
Belfast 72, 91, 111
Belushi, John 268, 321
Bergman, Jo 150, 166, 194
Berlin 113, 114, 180, 183, 220, 240, 297
Bern 216
Bern Elliot and the Fenmen 51-54, 58
Berry, Chuck 4, 47, 50-51, 63, 82, 103, 170, 172, 197, 294, 315
Berry, Mike 55-58, 62, 65, 77-80
*Between the Buttons* 128, 144, 146, 147, 150, 151, 319
The Big Three 37, 41
Billy J Kramer & the Dakotas 60, 62, 82, 310
Birkenhead 62
Birmingham (AL) 104
Birmingham (UK) 25, 28, 30, 32, 38, 41, 57, 59, 66, 80, 87, 108, 116, 145, 216, 308-311, 314-316, 318
"Bitch" 189, 193, 200, 201, 211, 320
Black, Cilla 60, 101, 307, 312
*Black and Blue* 224, 225, 231, 238, 278
"Black Limousine" 281-283, 285-288, 291, 293, 300, 304
Blackburn 58
Blackpool 58, 72, 74
Bletchley 59
Bloomington 201, 235
Blues By Six 6, 19-21
*Blues in Rhythm* 58, 306
Bologna 152
Bonis, Bob 67, 101, 104, 105, 117, 131
Booth, Stanley 16, 17, 40, 73, 166, 170, 172
Boston 118, 119, 175, 176, 204, 229, 281
Boulder 261, 282, 285
Bournemouth 14, 38, 56, 63, 74, 75
Bowie, David 42
Boyle, Billy 55-58
Brabanthal 131
Bradford 37, 43, 58, 63, 65, 79, 115
"Breathe on Me" 268-270, 274
Bremen 151-152, 240
Brian Poole and the Tremeloes 54, 62, 312
Bridlington 63, 71
Brisbane 93, 129, 211
Bristol 45, 80, 114, 145, 191, 299
Brooks, Elkie 110
Brown, James 82, 85, 87, 99, 103
Brown, Joe 62
Brown, Ollie 226, 229, 239, 242, 252
"Brown Sugar" 167, 177, 180, 183-185, 188-190, 193, 197, 200-205, 208, 209, 211, 212, 214, 216, 218, 220, 226, 228, 229, 231, 232, 236, 239, 240, 242-245, 249, 253, 256-260, 262, 263, 281, 283-288, 291, 293, 300, 304, 320
Brussels 81, 220, 240, 313
*The Brussels Affair* 220
Buffalo 135, 226, 229, 236
Buffalo Springfield 142

325

# Index

Bundgaard, Erling 218
Burdon, Eric 41, 87, 107
"Buried Alive" 269, 270
"Bye Bye Johnny" 23, 28, 47, 58, 59, 81, 197, 200, 201, 205, 211, 305, 306
The Byrds 105, 106, 122, 176

Cambridge, UK 34, 116
"Can I Get a Witness" 27, 49, 55, 78, 88
Cannock (Staffordshire) 66
Cannon Brothers 108
Capote, Truman 196
The Caravelles 66, 311
Cardiff (Wales) 36, 57, 78, 115, 146, 215
Carlisle 78, 115
Carnegie Hall 70
"Carol" 51, 73, 81, 101, 169, 170, 172, 176–178, 185, 306, 307, 312, 313
Carr, Roy 14, 51, 221
Catford (London) 63
Cavern Club 37, 39
Cavett, Dick 205
Champaign (IL) 172
[qm]Chantilly Lace" 295
Chapman, Tony 7–9, 12, 17, 18
Charles Dickens and the Habits 114–116
*Charlie Is My Darling* 88, 96, 111
Charlotte 121, 203
Chatham 58
Checkerboard Lounge 289
The Checkmates 43, 54, 91, 96–98, 108, 114–116
Cheltenham 3, 4, 36, 55, 77, 115
Chen, Phil 272
Chess, Marshall 188, 190, 194, 204
Chester 61, 78, 115
The Cheynes 51–54
Chicago 50, 68, 85, 87, 88, 90, 101, 105, 123, 139, 172, 201, 233, 246, 260, 269, 289
Chris Barber Band 3, 6
Christchurch 93–94
Cincinnati 122, 246, 270
Clapton, Eric 45, 160, 168, 184, 205, 223, 224, 231, 238, 242, 248, 249
Clark, Petula 61, 314, 318
Clarke, Stanley 266, 268–272
*Clay Cole Show* 70, 82, 312, 313, 315
Clearwater 104
Cleveland 70, 84, 134, 229, 259, 270, 312
Cliff Bennett & the Rebel Rousers 63, 87
*Cocksucker Blues* 180, 195, 197, 205
Colchester 56, 77
Coleman, Ray 47, 51, 55, 58
Cologne 152, 184, 214, 244, 300
"Come On" 15, 16, 18, 22–25, 27, 29, 32, 34, 38, 39, 52, 53, 55, 108
"Come to Realize" 268–270, 274
The Commodores 231
Comstock, Bobby 70

"Confessin' the Blues" 8, 81, 313
Copenhagen 98, 110, 132, 180, 181, 219
*Cops and Robbers* 309
Cornell University 117
Cott, Jonathan 128, 147
"Country Honk" 248, 249
Coventry 41, 54, 61, 66, 190
"Crackin' Up" 251, 253, 307
Crawdaddy Club 13, 18–31, 33
Crewe 41
Croft, Brian 209, 227
Croydon 43, 61, 72, 87
The Crusaders 229, 233–235
"Cry to Me" 114, 117, 118, 307, 316, 317
Curtis, Lee 29
Cutler, Sam 166, 170
The Cyclones 66, 67

Dallas 122, 172, 195, 201, 226, 232, 262, 286
Dalston 42
"Dance Little Sister" 228
"Dancing with Mr. D" 209, 214, 220
Daniels, Charlie 232, 233
Dave Berry & the Cruisers 33, 51–54, 65, 66, 96–98, 315
Dave Clark Five 62, 309, 314
David John and the Mood 61, 66, 67, 311
Davies, Cyril 3, 4, 8, 17–19, 28
Davies, Ray 11
Davis, Billie 32, 55–58, 62, 65
Dayton 85, 122
"Dead Flowers" 180, 184, 185, 189, 190, 193, 201, 208, 249
*December's Children* 125
Dee, Dave 61, 133, 162
The Defenders 74, 98, 99, 132
Denver 123, 201, 233, 271
Derby 36
The Detours *see* The Who
Detroit 68–70, 122, 138, 174, 204, 235, 260, 269, 278, 311
Diddley, Bo 4, 5, 16–18, 21, 33–39, 103, 122, 305
Didi and the ABC Boys 111–114, 151
Dodd, Dick 136, 139, 141
Doncaster 36, 43, 79, 116
Donovan 101, 116, 318
"Don't Lie to Me" 29, 58, 63, 305
"Don't Look Back" 255, 258, 261, 265, 321
"Doo, Doo, Doo (Heartbreaker)" 207, 209, 214, 219, 220, 232
The Doobie Brothers 261
Dorothy Norwood Singers 201, 202
Dorsey, Mike 75, 81, 91, 96, 98, 101, 104
Dortmund 152, 244
"Down the Road Apiece" 5, 8, 23, 96, 110, 281, 287, 306, 307, 314, 315
Downliners Sect 71
Dublin 91, 111, 303

Duke D'Mond and the Barron Knights 66, 67, 71, 74, 75
Dundee 65, 108
Dunedin (NZ) 94
Dunstable 27, 28, 32, 54
Dylan, Bob 119, 126, 134, 204, 205, 238, 249, 266, 283

The Eagles 228, 229, 232, 253
Ealing Club 8–11, 17–20
*Eamonn Andrews Show* 96, 128, 314, 317, 319
East Grinstead 59
East Ham 66
Easton, Eric 14, 15, 22, 23, 37, 49, 51, 67, 75, 81, 87, 90, 307
The Easybeats 151, 152
*Ed Rudy Show* 81
*Ed Sullivan Show* 51, 81, 82, 102, 104, 128, 144, 147, 174, 257, 313, 315, 317–320
Edinburgh 66, 79, 108, 296
Edmonton (North London) 34, 55, 65, 80, 96
Eel Pie Island 22–33
El Mocambo Club 251, 252, 268
*Emotional Rescue* 266, 267, 275, 276, 278, 281
Epsom 43, 52
The Esquires 101
Essen 112, 131, 180, 187, 219
Everly Brothers 16, 34–39
"Everybody Needs Somebody to Love" 84, 96, 99, 101, 105, 106, 109, 111, 113, 117, 118, 120, 121, 124, 125, 280, 307, 314, 315
Exeter 75, 80, 110
*Exile on Main Street* 189, 194, 243

Fabulous Thunderbirds 286
The Faces 221, 224, 225, 227, 229, 237, 238, 251
Faith, Adam 67, 310
Faithfull, Marian 80, 91, 128, 132, 160, 162, 168, 319
Fame, Georgie 13, 44, 101, 132, 306
"Far Away Eyes" 254–263
Farlowe, Chris 59, 316–318
Fenson, Ricky 9–11, 18, 19, 22
"Fingerprint File" 223, 228, 231, 232, 236
*First Barbarians: Live from Kilburn* 224
*Fitzcarraldo* 277
The Five Embers 65, 66, 71, 74, 75
The Flintstones 34–39
Flippo, Chet 228, 252, 253, 255, 257, 268, 275
*Flowers* 150
Flying Burrito Brothers 166, 167, 176, 177
Folkestone (Kent) 59, 65
"Fool to Cry" 225, 238–240, 243, 244, 246, 248, 253
Fort Collins 169, 233
Fort Wayne 85, 313
Fort Worth 122, 201, 255, 262, 271
"Fortune Teller" 25, 34, 53, 128
The Four Fours 128, 129, 131

The Fourmost 60, 110, 312
Foxx, Charlie 77–81
Foxx, Inez 77–81
Frank, Robert 195, 197, 201
Frankfurt 185, 218, 238, 239, 300
Fraser, Robert 149
Freddy and the Dreamers 54
Frederiksberg (Denmark) 109
Fresno 106
*From the Vault-Live in Leeds* 304
*Frost on Saturday Show* 163, 319
"F.U.C. Her" 268–270, 274

Gaye, Marvin 82, 90, 313
Genoa 153
Gerry & the Pacemakers 43, 44, 62, 82, 309
"Get Off of My Cloud" 91, 111, 117–125, 128, 129, 131, 132, 134, 136–141, 144, 145, 151, 153, 154, 226, 228, 229, 232, 235, 236, 239, 240, 243, 244, 248, 316, 317
*Get Yer Ya Ya's Out* 170, 175, 176, 179, 251
"Gimme Shelter" 165, 169, 177, 178, 197, 200–203, 205, 208, 210–212, 214, 215, 218, 220, 228, 229, 232, 236, 319, 320
*Gimme Shelter* (film) 2, 167, 176
*Gimme Some Neck* 266–268
Glad Rag Ball 87
Glasgow 37, 52, 108, 115, 145, 190, 216, 240, 242, 295
Gleason, Ralph 105, 166, 167
The Go-Go's 282
*Goat's Head Soup* 196, 207, 209, 214, 223, 278
Godard, Jean-Luc 158, 160
"Goin' Home" 126, 151, 153, 154, 157
"Going to a Go-Go" 287, 288, 291, 294
Golden Rose International TV Festival 61, 310
Goldie and the Gingerbreads 96–98, 315, 316
Golding, Colin 10, 11, 17, 18
Goldsboro, Bobby 70
Gomelsky, Giorgio 10, 13, 14, 19, 21–23, 28
The Gonks 91, 110
Gore, Leslie 82
*Got Live If You Want It* (EP) 96
*Got Live If You Want It* (LP) 105, 128, 145, 146, 180, 251
Gothenburg 99, 180, 181, 218, 299
Graham, Bill 170, 197, 208, 209, 279, 283, 289, 294
Graham Bond Quartet 19, 44
Grant, Julie 34–39, 63, 65, 66, 71, 74, 91, 110, 311
Grant, Peter 34
Great Pop Prom 32
Great Yarmouth 110
Greenfield, Robert 17, 67, 72, 126, 154, 169, 190, 191, 195, 199, 203
Greenford (UK) 56, 97
Greensboro 119, 120, 235, 258
The Groundhogs 189–191, 193

Gruber, Mike 117, 131, 133, 139
Guernsey 74
Guildford (Surrey) 21–24, 27, 35, 44, 55, 59, 97
Guy, Buddy 179–185, 187, 289

The Hague 156, 180, 243, 267
Hamburg 112, 151, 152, 180, 182–183, 218, 240
Hamilton (Scotland) 65
Hammersmith (London) 39, 91
Hammond, John, Jr. 85, 134, 137
Hampstead 55
Hampton (VA) 236, 258, 291, 294
"Hand of Fate" 225, 238–240, 243, 244, 248, 253
"Hang Fire" 278, 281, 283, 285–288, 291, 293, 299, 304
Hanley 37, 56, 79, 115
Hannover 268, 297
Hansen, Patti 275
"Happy" 194, 197, 200, 201, 205, 208, 210–212, 214, 215, 218, 220, 228–229, 231–233, 235, 236, 240, 243, 244, 249, 253, 256–258, 260, 262, 263, 279
Hardy, Francoise 132
Harris, Jet 55–58, 62, 65, 308
Harrisburg 70
Harrison, George 21, 22, 39, 149
Harrow (London) 32, 51
Hartford 135, 287
Hassinger, Dave 84, 105
Hastings 25, 54, 61, 72
Hathaway, Bruce 140
"Have You Seen Your Mother Baby, Standing in the Shadows" 128, 144, 146, 318
Hayes (Middlesex) 27
Heart (band) 282
"Heart of Stone" 84, 90, 94, 314
Hefner, Hugh 201
Heinz 37, 54, 62, 310
Hell's Angels 167, 168, 176
Helsingborg 150
Helsinki 181
Hendrix, Jimi 137, 175, 184
Hereford 43
Herman's Hermits 42, 101, 103–104, 133, 314
Herzog, Werner 277
"Hey Crawdaddy" 20, 21, 101
"Hey Negrita" 238–240, 243, 244, 248
"Hi-Heel Sneakers" 27, 60, 62, 71, 73, 306, 310
High Wycombe 29, 41, 45
"Hitch Hike" 84, 90, 316
The Hollies 17, 25, 47, 58, 62, 67, 96–98, 108, 309, 316, 320
*Hollywood A Go-Go* 105, 315
*Hollywood Palace* 50, 67, 311
"Honest I Do" 21, 52
Hong Kong 96, 206, 209
"Honky-Tonk Women" 164, 165, 169–172, 174, 176–178, 180, 183–187, 190, 193, 200, 211–216, 220, 228, 229, 232, 233, 235, 236, 239, 240, 242–245, 249, 253, 256–

260, 262, 263, 267, 269–270, 274, 280, 281, 283, 285–289, 291, 293, 304, 319
Honolulu 142, 209
Hooker, John Lee 71
Hopkins, Nicky 150, 160, 190, 194, 197, 199, 200, 202, 209, 211, 214, 277
Horsham 27
*Hot Rocks* 194
"Hot Stuff" 225, 238–240, 243, 244, 248, 253
"Hound Dog" 258
Houston 139, 140, 201, 263, 271, 286
Hove (Sussex) 63
Howlin' Wolf 51, 234, 315
Huddersfield 97
Hull 37, 79
Hunter, Meredith 177, 183
Hyde Park 165, 168

"I Can Feel the Fire" 224, 268–270, 274
"I Can't Be Satisfied" 88, 307
"I Just Want to Make Love to You" 49, 50, 62, 77, 280, 306, 310–312
"I Wanna Be Your Man" 17, 36, 37, 39, 41, 42, 45, 52, 53, 55, 58, 63, 66, 69, 102, 305, 306, 309, 310
"I Want to Be Loved" 13, 16, 21, 305
"If You Need Me" 77, 81, 307, 313
"I'm a King Bee" 21, 49, 52
"I'm Alright" 21, 60, 62, 69, 77, 81, 82, 96, 101, 105, 109, 111–113, 117, 128, 132, 146, 313, 315, 316
"I'm Free" 90, 111, 169, 170, 176
"I'm Moving On" 27, 96, 109, 113, 114, 132, 306, 315–317
Indiana State University 235
Indianapolis 139, 204, 235
"Infekshun" 268–270
Innsbruck 216
Invercargill 94
Ipswich 39, 59, 80, 145
Isle of Man 74, 111
Isle of Wight 59
Ithaca (NY) 117
"It's All Over Now" 50, 51, 73, 75, 77, 81, 82, 84, 88, 93, 94, 99, 101, 108, 145, 208, 306, 307, 312, 313, 318
"It's Only Rock 'N' Roll" 221, 226, 228, 231, 232, 236, 240, 242–245, 249, 253
*It's Only Rock 'N' Roll* (LP) 223
"I've Got the Blues" 193

J. Geils Band 229, 232, 235, 283–285, 296, 297, 299, 300, 303
Jacksonville 104, 105, 235
Jagger, Bianca 189, 190, 196, 205, 208, 227, 232
"Jaguar and the Thunderbird" 27, 29, 58
James, Etta 257, 258, 260, 263, 277, 287, 294
James, Sonny 104, 105

## Index

*Jammin' with Edward* 194
Jan and Dean 82
Jay and the Americans 70
Jaymes, John 166
JB & the Playboys 102
Jefferson Airplane 142, 167, 176, 177
Jersey (Channel Islands) 74
Jethro Tull 160, 162, 163, 246, 319
*Joe Loss Pop Show* (radio) 61, 71, 306, 307
John, Elton 227, 233
Johnny Carr and the Cadillacs 41, 53, 63
Johnny Kidd and the Pirates 37, 52, 54
Johns, Glyn 7, 8, 13, 15, 87, 91, 96, 163, 169, 175, 176, 185, 191, 193
Jones, George 68
Jones, Newman E. 213
Jones, Tom 71, 101, 315, 317
Joplin, Janis 175, 176
Journey 260, 281
*Juke Box Jury* 71, 312
"Jumping Jack Flash" 158, 162, 163, 169, 172, 174, 176–178, 180, 181, 184, 185, 190, 193, 197, 199–205, 208, 210–214, 216, 219, 220, 226, 228, 229, 231, 232, 235, 236, 239, 240, 242–245, 249, 253, 256–260, 263, 267–270, 274, 280 281, 283–288, 291, 293, 300, 304
"Just My Imagination" 257–260, 262, 263, 268, 281, 282, 285–288, 291, 293, 304

Kane, Eden 58, 67
Kansas (band) 259, 261
Kansas City 201, 228, 291
Kaufman, Murry "The K" 51, 62, 67, 70, 82
Keith Powell & the Valets 55, 63
Ken Colyer Jazz Club (Studio 51) 9–11, 20–33, 42, 45
Kent, Nick 49, 57, 196, 197, 207, 220, 223, 243, 250
Kettering 52
Keylock, Tom 114, 150, 155, 157, 165
Keys, Bobby 180, 190, 197, 199–202, 208–209, 213, 216, 220, 233, 263, 266, 268–270, 276, 277, 284, 293, 295, 304
Kidderminster 59
Kiel (Germany) 240
Kilburn (London) 41, 224
Kimsey, Chris 254, 278
King, B.B. 169, 170, 172, 174–176
*King Biscuit Flower Hour* 258–260, 263
Kings of Rhythm Orchestra 144–146
Kingston-upon-Thames 32, 56
The Kinks 93, 101, 147, 314, 315, 317, 320
Klein, Allen 90, 117, 166, 179, 196, 225
Knebworth Festival 248, 267, 272
Knoxville 120, 121, 203

The Konrads 96–98
Korner, Alexis 3–6, 8, 9, 71, 80, 149, 168, 267, 307
Kracker 207, 213–220

*LA Friday* 233
La Belle, Patti 117–125
*Ladies and Gentlemen the Rolling Stones* 194, 195, 221
"Lady Jane" 126, 131, 134–142, 144, 146, 152–156, 226, 231, 232, 317, 318
Lakeland 255, 256, 285
Largo (MD) 231, 270, 291
"The Last Time" 88, 91, 96, 99, 101, 102, 105, 106, 108, 109, 111, 113, 114, 116–120, 123, 124, 129, 131–134, 136–138, 140, 142, 145, 149, 153, 156, 158, 200, 307, 314, 315
*Last Waltz* 249
Lawrence, Trevor 214, 233
Leavell, Chuck 279, 286, 295
Led Zeppelin 34, 36, 267, 272
Leeds 40, 71, 116, 144, 189, 191, 294, 303, 304
Leek 45
Leicester 29, 54, 55, 66, 72, 77, 97, 110, 116, 242
Lennon, John 17, 21, 129, 150, 160, 175, 277
The Le Roys 55–57, 62, 77–81
*Les Crane Show* 67, 311
"Let It Bleed" 178, 280, 281, 283, 285–288, 291, 293, 319
*Let It Bleed* (LP) 164, 165
"Let It Rock" 180, 185, 189, 190, 193, 200, 255–260, 262, 263, 268
"Let Me Go" 281, 283, 285–288, 291, 293, 299, 304
"Let's Go Steady Again" 269, 270
"Let's Spend the Night Together" 144, 146, 147, 150, 152–154, 157, 200, 248, 253, 281, 282, 285, 286, 287, 288, 291, 293, 297, 300, 304, 318, 319
*Let's Spend the Night Together* (film) 280, 287, 294
Lexington (KY) 258–259, 291
Lewis, Furry 232
Lewisham 39, 80
Leyton 42, 61
Leyton, John 55–57
"Lies" 254, 257, 258, 260, 263
Lincoln (UK) 46, 79
Lindsey-Hogg, Michael 158, 163, 240, 248, 278
Little, Carlos 7, 18, 19, 22
"Little By Little" 49, 55, 306
"Little Queenie" 169, 170, 172, 176–178, 180, 184, 185, 190, 193, 211, 212
"Little Red Rooster" 51, 77, 87, 88, 91, 93, 94, 96, 99, 101, 104–106, 108, 109, 248, 253, 313–315
Little Richard 16, 34–39, 214
"Little T&A" 278, 281, 283, 285–287, 304
The Live Five 141

"Live with Me" 164, 170, 172, 176–178, 180, 184, 185, 187, 190, 193, 208
*Live'r Than You'll Ever Be* 170
Liverpool 37, 39, 43, 57, 78, 96, 116, 144, 191
Loewenstein, Prince Rupert 188, 292
London 4–11, 13, 17–34, 37, 39, 41–43, 45, 51–56, 58, 59, 61–63, 65, 66, 71–74, 77, 80, 87, 91, 94, 96, 97, 101, 110, 111, 114, 116, 144, 149, 157, 162, 168, 178, 187, 193, 207, 214, 239, 242, 248, 253, 268, 276, 278, 296, 299, 305–320
London (Ontario) 102
Long Beach 84, 90, 106, 199
Los Angeles 67, 84, 91, 105, 125, 142, 169, 174, 194, 197, 199, 200, 208, 232, 246, 271, 277, 283, 294, 311, 315, 319
"Lost and Lonely" 268–270
Louisiana State University 227
Louisville 87, 235, 286
"Love in Vain" 169, 170, 172, 175–178, 180, 184, 185, 187, 190, 193, 197, 200–205, 210–212, 256–263, 269, 270, 319
*Love You Live* 243, 244, 250, 251
"Loving Cup" 169, 197
Lowestoft (Suffolk) 30, 54, 60
Lulu and the Luvers 71
Lundstrom, Astrid 166, 190
Luton 42, 62, 77
"Luxury" 223, 228, 231, 253
Lydon, Michael 166, 169, 172, 174
Lynch, Kenny 32, 60, 71, 309, 310, 312
Lynn (MA) 133, 134, 139
Lyon (France) 132, 185, 244, 297

Madaio, Steve 214, 233
*Made in the Shade* 225, 277
Madrid 300
Magdalen College (Oxford) 71
Maidstone (Kent) 52
Malmo (Sweden) 110, 150, 180
Malo, Ron 51, 85
Manchester 30, 37, 42, 51, 54, 58, 61–63, 66, 73, 74, 78, 96, 97, 108, 115, 145, 190, 215, 308–310, 312–314, 316
Mandel, Harvey 225
Manfred Mann 60, 62, 93, 310, 316
Mankowitz, Gered 117
Mannheim 214
"Mannish Boy" 253, 289
Mansfield (Nottinghamshire) 52
Margate (Kent) 29
Mark Peters and the Silhouettes 65
Marquee Club 4, 6, 8, 17–19, 163, 193, 320
Marseille 132, 137
Marsh, Dave 229, 238, 255
Max Merrit and the Meteors 128, 129
Mayall, John 23, 71, 110, 164
Maysles, Albert 167, 175, 176, 180

Maysles, David 167, 175, 176, 180
McCartney, Paul 17, 150, 168, 248
The McCoys 133–142
McLagan, Ian 224, 256, 266, 268, 276–280
Melbourne 93, 129, 211, 314
"Memo from Turner" 180
Memphis 121, 226, 232, 258
Mercado, Gay 245
"Mercy, Mercy" 90, 120, 124, 131, 307, 316
The Merseybeats 33, 60, 62, 67, 312
*Metamorphosis* (album) 49, 225
The Meters 227, 228, 232, 233, 235, 239, 240, 242–246, 266, 289, 291
Miami 121
Middlesbrough 25
"Midnight Rambler" 165, 169, 170, 172, 175–178, 180, 181, 184, 185, 187, 190, 193, 196, 197, 200–203, 205, 208, 210–214, 218–220, 228, 229, 231, 232, 235, 236, 239, 240, 242–246, 249, 254
Mighty Avengers 61, 63
Mighty Clouds of Joy 231
Mike and the Shades 108
Mike Tobin and the Magnettes 63
Milan 152, 153, 185
Miles, John 244, 245
*Milestones* 194
Miller, Jimmy 158, 196, 207
Millie Small and the No Names 63
Milwaukee 85, 122, 228, 267, 269, 276
The Miracles 82
"Miss You" 254, 256–263, 268, 277, 281, 283, 285–288, 291, 293, 304
Mitchell, Mitch 160
Mobile (AL) 202
Modeliste, Joseph 266, 268
The Mojos 77–80
"Mona" 49, 51, 52, 84, 280, 281, 296, 306, 307, 310, 313
Monck, Chip 166, 190, 195, 209
"Money" 28, 29, 34, 41, 47
Money, Eddie 258, 259, 261, 263
*Monkey Grip* 221
Montreal 101, 117, 118, 136, 204, 247
Montreux 61, 194, 196, 310
The Moody Blues 101, 110, 115, 229
Moon, Keith 232
"Moonlight Mile" 189, 223
*More Hot Rocks* 207
Morecambe 33, 58
Most, Mickie 34–39
"Mother's Little Helper" 134, 138, 141, 142, 144, 317
Munich 112, 157, 180, 207, 216, 218, 221, 224, 225, 245, 248, 297
Münster 61, 112, 240
Myrtle Beach 258
"Mystifies Me" 224, 269, 270

Naples 303
Nashville 121, 202

*Ned Kelly* 165, 277
"Neighbors" 278, 281, 282, 285–287, 299, 304
Nelson (UK) 62, 72
Neville Brothers 286, 289
New Barbarians 268–273
New Brighton 30, 74
New Haven 70, 118
New York 49, 62, 67, 68, 70, 71, 81, 85, 87, 88, 90, 101–103, 107, 117, 119, 128, 133, 134, 144, 147, 166, 175, 205, 225, 226, 229, 253, 254, 255, 258, 263, 270, 275–279, 287, 294, 311–313, 315, 317, 318, 320, 321
Newark 119
The Newbeats 92–95
Newcastle 37, 41, 63, 79, 87, 116, 145, 189, 215, 216, 299
Nice (France) 245, 303
"19th Nervous Breakdown" 126, 128, 129, 131, 132, 134, 136–138, 140–145, 153, 154, 156, 207, 317
Nitzsche, Jack 84, 147
NME Poll-Winner's Concert 62, 101, 133, 158, 162
"No Expectations" 160, 163, 169, 208
Norfolk (VA) 203, 236
Northampton 116
Northwich (Cheshire) 29, 42
Norwich (Norfolk) 62
"Not Fade Away" 47, 52, 54, 57, 60, 62, 63, 66, 71, 77, 81, 84, 92, 94, 102, 108, 124, 125, 129, 131, 132, 137, 142, 146, 306, 310–313
Nottingham 38, 52, 57
"Now I've Got a Witness" 49, 55
Nuneaton 41

Oakland 166, 170, 199, 263, 271, 274
Odense (Denmark) 98
"Off the Hook" 77, 82, 87, 88, 101, 102, 105, 106, 108 313–315
"Oh Baby" 84, 114, 307, 314–316
*Old Grey Whistle Test* 215, 216, 218, 244
Oldham, Andrew Loog 14, 15, 17, 22, 23, 25, 29, 34, 41, 47, 49, 51, 81, 96, 104, 132, 147, 193, 316
Omaha 68, 140, 311
"100 Years Ago" 214, 215
*1234* (LP) 277
Orbison, Roy 92–95, 133, 314
Orchard Park (NY) 236, 260, 281
Orebro 151
Original Checkmates 43, 54
Orlando 285
Oshawa 266, 268
Oslo 108
Ottawa 101, 102
*Out of Our Heads* 90, 105, 114
"Outa Space" 226, 228, 231, 232, 236, 240, 243, 244, 249
The Overlanders 43, 61, 63, 66, 67, 74, 75, 133, 311
Oxford 51, 71

Page, Jimmy 144, 193, 225, 253, 267

"Pain in My Heart" 84, 88, 96, 101, 105, 108, 109, 111, 113, 315
"Paint It Black" 126, 131, 133–137, 140–142, 153, 154, 156, 188, 317, 318
Pallenberg, Anita 112, 162, 190, 275
Palmer, John "Spike" 34
"Parachute Woman" 160, 163
The Paramounts 30, 57–58, 74, 110, 312
Paris 81, 87, 101, 131, 132, 149, 154, 184, 239, 244, 250, 252, 254, 278, 295, 297, 313
Parsons, Gram 166, 190, 191, 196, 216
Passaic 255, 257
Paul Revere and the Raiders 105, 106, 122, 124
*Performance* 160
Perkins, Wayne 225, 238
Perrin, Les 154, 209
Perth 95, 211, 212
Pete McClaine and the Clan 43
Peter and Gordon 65, 66
Peter Jay and the Jaywalkers 43, 63
Peterborough 33
Philadelphia 103, 119, 174, 205, 231, 247, 251, 255, 257, 279, 281
Philippines 144
Phoenix 123, 170
Pitney, Gene 47, 55, 309
Pittsburgh 70, 122, 134, 205, 247, 270, 311
Plant, Robert 36
"Play with Fire" 91, 106, 108, 122, 125, 129, 131–133, 314, 315, 317
Plymouth (UK) 75
"Poison Ivy" 17, 21, 25, 29, 34, 41, 47, 53
Pontiac (MI) 289
Pop, Iggy 289
The Pop Hit Parade 67
*Pop Inn* 306
Portland, OR 141
Portsmouth 56, 110
Powell, Jimmy 45, 71
Prestatyn (Wales) 30
Preston (UK) 39, 54
Preston, Billy 213–216, 218–220, 226, 228, 229, 239, 242, 244, 246, 252, 256, 271
"Pretty Thing" 21, 23, 29, 32, 33, 53, 58, 305, 306
Price, Jim 180, 190, 197, 199, 200, 209, 214
Prince 283
"Prodigal Son" 160, 169, 170, 172, 176, 178, 180, 185, 190
Providence 84, 118, 281
Putney 45

Quickly, Tommy 110
Quiet Five 52, 54, 87, 91, 110

The Rackets 111–114
Radziwell, Lee 196, 205
Raleigh 119
Ramsgate (Kent) 59

# Index

The Rattles 35–39
Ray Columbus and the Invaders 92–95
Reading 43, 45, 51, 59
*Ready Steady Go* 42, 45, 56, 59–61, 71–73, 87, 91, 96, 101, 107, 111, 117, 125, 132, 133, 145, 146, 308–310, 312–318
Ready Steady Go Mod Ball 60
*Red Skelton Show* 110, 312
Redlands 149
Reichel, Achim 151, 152
Reid, Terry 169, 170, 172, 174–176
Remo 4 110
"Respectable" 254, 256–258, 260–263, 266, 268, 320
Rhone, Marty 128, 129
*Rhythm and Blues* (radio show) 80, 307
Richard, Cliff 62, 133, 162, 309, 320
Richmond (UK) 11, 13, 18–33, 41, 73
Richmond Jazz Festival 28
The Righteous Brothers 82, 104, 105, 314
"Rip This Joint" 197, 201, 205, 208, 210, 212, 214, 219, 220, 228, 231, 232, 236, 249, 253
The Rivets 111–114
"Road Runner" 33, 53, 55
Robbins, Marty 104
Robinson, Lisa 227, 257, 271
Rochdale 61
Rochester (NY) 118
Rochester (UK) 39, 56, 97
Rocket 88 267, 276, 277
Rockford 282
Rockin' Ramrods 117–125
"Rocks Off" 197, 200, 203, 205, 208, 211, 212, 228
The Roemans 104
"Roll Over Beethoven" 29, 52, 53, 55, 58, 180, 184, 185, 305, 306
*Rolling Stones* (first LP) 49
*Rolling Stones No. 2* 88
*Rolling Stones Rock 'N' Roll Circus* 160, 162, 163, 168, 278, 319
Rome 153, 168, 185
Romford 43, 57, 80, 98
The Ronettes 47, 51–54, 140
Ronstadt, Linda 263
Ross, Scott 88
Rotterdam 180, 213, 219, 220, 225, 296
"Route 66" 20, 21, 23, 29, 51, 53, 58, 67, 84, 96, 99, 101, 105, 108, 109, 163, 208, 249, 253, 306, 310, 312, 316
"Ruby Tuesday" 146, 147, 152–154, 157, 318, 319
Rudge, Peter 194, 195, 209, 211, 213, 227, 232, 239
Rufus (with Chaka Khan) 228, 229, 233, 306
Rugby (UK) 55, 97
"Run Rudolph Run" 255
Rundgren, Todd 248, 268, 272
Russell, Ethan 166

Sacramento 82, 106, 107, 124, 141
"Sad Day" 207
St. Albans 39
St. Kilda (Australia) 93, 95, 129
St. Louis 140, 203, 261, 288
St. Paul 229, 260, 288
Salisbury 38, 53, 58
Salt Lake City 141, 271
"Salt of the Earth" 163
San Antonio 68, 101, 140, 228
San Bernardino 67, 83, 84, 105, 106, 142
San Diego 84, 106, 125, 170, 200, 272, 283
San Francisco 105, 124, 142, 166, 170, 197, 199, 233, 249, 279, 281, 285
San Jose 106, 124
Santa Monica 82, 283
Santana 167, 176, 208, 231, 263, 289
Sarne, Mike 55–58
"Satisfaction" 90, 91, 105, 110–114, 117–125, 128, 129, 131–145, 151, 153, 154, 157, 162, 169, 170, 172, 175–178, 180, 185, 190, 193, 195, 200, 205, 239, 248, 258, 260, 262, 263, 280–283, 285–288, 291, 293, 297, 304, 307, 315–318
*Saturday Club* 33, 55, 61, 66, 111, 305–307
*Saturday Night Live* 263, 265, 268, 320, 321
Scarborough 97, 111
*Scene at 6:30* 30, 58, 111
Schaarbeek 131
Scheveningen 73
Schneider, Ronnie 117, 134, 141, 166
Scott, Simon 77–81
Screaming Jay Hawkins 287
The Searchers 43, 60, 62, 101, 128, 129, 131, 317
Seattle 124, 141, 197, 233, 246, 272, 284
The Seekers 54, 101, 133
Sessler, Freddie 208, 226, 232, 278
"Seven Days" 266, 268–270, 274
"Shattered" 254, 256–263, 268, 278, 281, 282, 285–288, 291, 293, 304, 317, 320
Sheffield 38, 41, 57, 67, 97, 116
"She's So Cold" 276, 280, 281, 283, 285–288, 291, 293, 299, 304
*Shindig* 60, 87, 106, 110, 111, 314–316
*Shivaree* 106, 315
Shreveport 121
Shrewsbury 54, 115
Shrimpton, Chrissie 24, 107
"(Si Si) Je Suis un Rock Star" 277, 294
"Silver Train" 214, 215
Singapore 95
Sir Douglas Quintet 105
Slough 52, 62, 67
Small Faces 133
Smith, Patti 257
SMU University 172

*Some Girls* 254, 258, 263, 268, 276, 278
*Some Girls Live in Texas* 256, 321
Sounds Incorporated 60, 62, 101, 133, 310
South Oxhey 9–11
Southampton 38, 59, 63, 80, 114, 146, 310
Southend (Essex) 35, 57, 80, 98
Southport 43
Southsea (Hampshire) 32, 63
Southside Johnny and the Asbury Jukes 260, 272
Spector, Phil 47, 55, 77, 82, 144
Spencer Davis Group 114–116, 133, 318
"Spider and the Fly" 105, 129, 131, 132, 134, 136, 137, 307, 316
Springfield, Dusty 45, 54, 101, 133, 162, 309, 310, 314, 315, 317, 320
Stafford 239, 242
The Standells 133–142
"Star, Star" 207, 209, 226, 232, 235, 283, 285
Starr, Ringo 35, 232, 268, 277
Statesboro 104
Steampacket 110
Stevenage 59, 248, 272
Stewart, Ian "Stu" 6–8, 10, 12, 13, 15, 25, 27, 35, 62, 65, 67, 73, 74, 75, 77, 80, 81, 91, 96–99, 101, 103, 111, 115, 117, 131, 150, 164, 166, 180, 207, 209, 226, 239, 251, 256, 267, 279, 280, 283, 289, 295
Stewart, Rod 24, 45, 110, 193, 224, 225, 227
*Sticky Fingers* 188, 189, 193
Stigwood, Robert 77
*Still Life* 280, 287, 289, 291, 293, 294
Stills, Stephen 142, 176, 187, 289
Stockholm 99, 132, 180, 181, 315
Stockport 66
Stockton-on-Tees 56, 79, 116, 145
Stoke-on-Trent 42, 65
*Stone Age* 188
"Stray Cat Blues" 169, 172, 176–178, 180, 184, 185, 190, 193, 208, 248
The Stray Cats 285, 288
Streatham (South London) 34
"Street Fighting Man" 160, 169, 170, 172, 174, 176–178, 180, 184, 185, 187, 190, 193, 197, 199–202, 205, 208, 210–214, 216, 218–220, 228, 231, 232, 236, 239–245, 249, 256, 257, 261, 281, 283
"Stupid Girl" 134, 136–138, 140, 141
Stuttgart 184, 245
*Sucking in the Seventies* 277
*Sunday Night at the London Palladium* 147, 318
Sunderland 56, 97
The Supremes 82
"Sure the One You Need" 224, 228, 269, 270
Sutton (South London) 7, 10, 11, 13, 17–21
"Sweet Little Rock and Roller" 267–270, 274

# Index

"Sweet Little Sixteen" 257, 258, 260, 262, 263
"Sweet Virginia" 194, 197, 200, 201, 203, 205, 208, 210–212, 214
Swindon 41, 53, 60
Swinging Blue Jeans 51–57, 62, 67
Sydenham 45, 309
Sydney 92, 93, 128, 129, 209, 213, 317
"Sympathy for the Devil" 158, 163, 168, 169, 172, 176–178, 180, 184, 185, 190, 194, 231, 233, 242, 243, 280, 319
Syndicate of Sound 138
Syracuse University 289

Taj Mahal 160, 162, 319
"Talkin' 'Bout You" 29, 32, 41, 53, 55, 58
Tamworth 43
*Tattoo You* 266, 276, 278, 281, 282
Taunton 38, 75
Taylor, Dick 5–7, 9, 11, 74
Taylor, Vince 81, 101
Teen Age Music International (TAMI) Awards 82
"Tell Me" 49, 62, 81, 99, 312, 313, 315
Terry Judge and the Barristers 54, 59
*Thank Your Lucky Stars* 16, 21, 25, 30, 41, 57, 66, 87, 98, 108, 110, 133, 308–311, 314–316, 318
"That's How Strong My Love Is" 90, 105, 114, 117, 118, 121, 124, 125, 129, 131, 132, 136, 316
"That's Life" 226, 228, 231, 232, 236
*Their Satanic Majesties Request* 147, 150
Them (with Van Morrison) 101, 313
Thorogood, Frank 165
Thorogood, George 269, 281–283, 285, 289, 291, 296, 297, 299, 303
"Time Is on My Side" 51, 62, 81, 82, 88, 94, 96, 99, 101, 105, 106, 109, 111, 113, 132, 146, 281, 283, 285–288, 291, 293, 297, 304, 313, 314
Tokyo 96, 206, 209
Tooting (London) 52, 116
Top Beat Pop Prom 62
*Top Gear* 71, 96, 307
*Top of the Pops* 51, 54, 57, 58, 62, 71, 77, 96, 108, 111, 114, 117, 128, 129, 133, 144–146, 165, 178, 189, 191, 193, 309, 310, 312–314, 316–320
"Tops" 281, 283
Toronto 88, 102, 117, 136, 204, 229, 247, 250–252, 255, 267, 268, 281
Torquay 75
The Torquays 92, 105
Tosh, Peter 255, 257–263, 265, 321
Tottenham (London) 45, 55, 59
Townshend, Pete 45, 204

The Tradewinds 133–142
Trower, Robin 243, 245
Troy, Doris 108
Trudeau, Margaret 251
Tucson 200, 263
Tulsa 122
"Tumbling Dice" 194, 197, 201, 202, 205, 208, 210–214, 220, 228, 231, 232, 236, 239–244, 249, 253, 256–260, 262, 263, 281, 283, 285–288, 291, 293, 304
Tunbridge Wells 58
Turin 300
Turner, Ike 128, 144–146, 170, 175
Turner, Tina 128, 144–146, 170, 175, 287
Tuscaloosa 202
TV21 295, 296
"Twenty Flight Rock" 281, 285–288, 291, 293, 294, 304
Twinkle 87, 91, 101, 110

"Under My Thumb" 126, 145, 149, 154, 167, 169, 170, 172, 176–178, 280–282, 285–288, 291, 293, 297, 300, 304, 318
"Under the Boardwalk" 77, 92, 94, 314
*Undercover of the Night* 266
The Undertakers 67
Unit Four + 2 114–116
University of Alabama 202
University of Illinois 172
University of Leeds 191
University of Michigan 268
University of New Mexico 200
"Uptight" 195, 205
Urmston 42

Van Halen 261, 285
Vancouver 123, 140, 141, 197
Vee, Bobby 68, 103
The Vibrants 84, 106
The Vibrations 117–125
Vienna 114, 152, 180, 185, 213, 214, 238, 246, 300
Vincent, Gene 63
Virginia Beach 138

"Waiting on a Friend" 278, 281, 283, 285–288, 291, 293
The Walker Brothers 110, 133
"Walking the Dog" 21, 27, 49, 51, 55, 58–60, 73, 77, 81, 93, 94, 306, 313, 314
Wallington (Surrey) 62
Walmer (Kent) 30
Walthamstow (East London) 34, 52
Warrington 42
Warsaw 154
Washington D.C. 120, 134, 203, 247, 257
Waters, Muddy 3, 4, 51, 70, 205, 253, 260, 289
Watford 32, 35, 43, 56, 80
Wayne Fontana and the Mindbenders 41, 67, 101, 131

"We Love You" 150
Welch, Bob 272
Welch, Chris 42, 168, 169, 178
Wellington 94, 129
Wells, Junior 179–187, 260, 269, 289
Wembley (London) 60, 62, 67, 87, 101, 107, 125, 133, 145, 162, 214, 299, 315–319
Wenner, Jann 7, 189
West Palm Beach 176
Weston-super-Mare 75
Weymouth 74, 310
"When the Whip Comes Down" 254, 256–258, 260, 262, 263, 268, 278, 280–282, 285–288, 291, 293, 299, 300, 304
Whitcomb, Ian 124, 131, 132
Whitehead, Peter 88, 111, 128, 144, 150
Whitley Bay 41
The Who 45, 51, 133, 149, 160, 162, 180, 191, 195, 299, 314, 317–320
Wigan 42, 78, 115
"Wild Horses" 167, 176, 189, 190, 201, 228, 231, 232, 236, 249, 320
Wilde, Marty 51–54
Willenhall 55
Wimbledon 54, 59, 74
Winchester 45
Windsor 11, 17–25, 27–31, 33, 59
Winnipeg 140
Wisbech 26
Woking 29
Wolverhampton 36, 58, 80
Womack, Bobby 236, 277, 291, 294
Wonder, Stevie 195–205, 309
Woolwich 54
Worcester (MA) 102, 280
Worcester (UK) 36, 43
"Worried Life Blues" 253, 270, 274
The Worryin' Kind 61

The Yardbirds 44, 59, 128, 133, 144–146, 315, 316, 318
"Yesterday's Papers" 151, 153, 154, 157
York 57
"You Better Move On" 21, 27, 28, 47, 52, 55, 58, 305, 306, 310
"You Can't Always Get What You Want" 163, 165, 196, 197, 200–203, 205, 208, 210–214, 219, 220, 228, 231–233, 235, 236, 239, 240, 243, 244, 251, 254, 281, 283, 285–288, 291, 293, 304, 319
"You Can't Catch Me" 88
"You Gotta Move" 167, 170, 172, 176, 178, 226, 228, 229, 232, 235, 236, 239, 240, 243, 244, 248
Yteri Beach (Finland) 109

Zagreb 246
Zürich 154, 180, 245
ZZ Top 209, 286